Your Lie in April

I met the girl
under full-bloomed cherry blossoms,
and my fate has begun to change.

7

Naoshi Arakawa

STORY & CHARACTERS

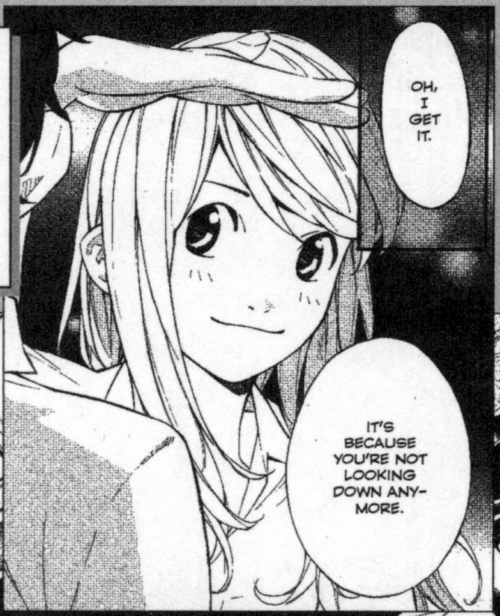
OH, I GET IT.
IT'S BECAUSE YOU'RE NOT LOOKING DOWN ANY-MORE.

Kaori Miyazono

A violinist who is overwhelmingly unique. She was invited to play in the Tōwa Hall gala concert at the recommendation of the sponsor, but never appeared for her performance.

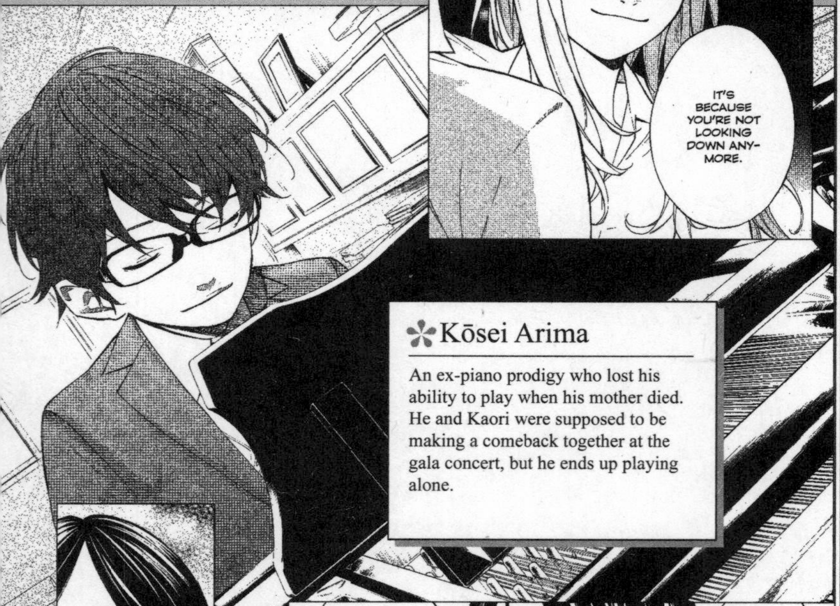

Kōsei Arima

An ex-piano prodigy who lost his ability to play when his mother died. He and Kaori were supposed to be making a comeback together at the gala concert, but he ends up playing alone.

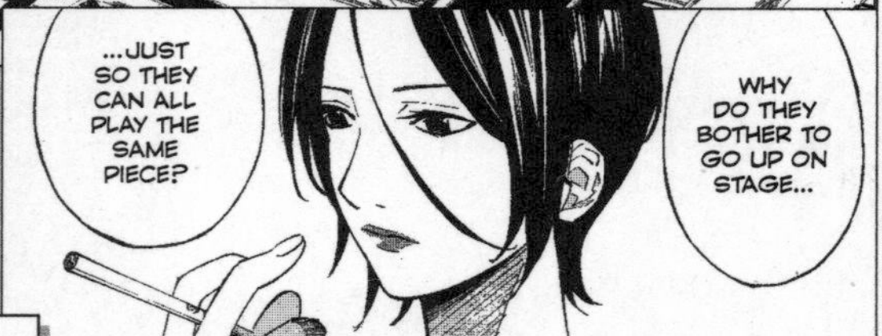
WHY DO THEY BOTHER TO GO UP ON STAGE...
...JUST SO THEY CAN ALL PLAY THE SAME PIECE?

Hiroko Seto

Japan's leading pianist. She agrees to be Kōsei's piano instructor. She went to music school with Kōsei's mother, Saki Arima.

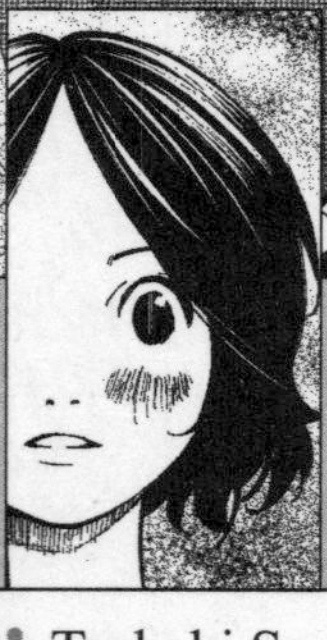

Tsubaki Sawabe

A longtime friend of Kōsei's. An athlete good enough to be the school softball team's power hitter. Seems to have trouble in all academic endeavors.

When his mother died in the autumn of his 12th year, piano prodigy Kōsei Arima lost his ability to play. Without a purpose, his days lost all color and continued on in a drab monotone. But the spring he was 14, he met the exceptionally quirky violinist Kaori Miyazono.

As he accompanied Kaori and even played solo in a piano competition, Kōsei's days gradually filled with color. Then, Kaori was invited to play at the Tōwa Hall gala concert. Watari and the others rejoiced at the prospect of seeing Kōsei & Kaori, the invincible duo that had been showered in the audience's applause, back in action. But the day of the concert, Kaori was nowhere to be seen!!

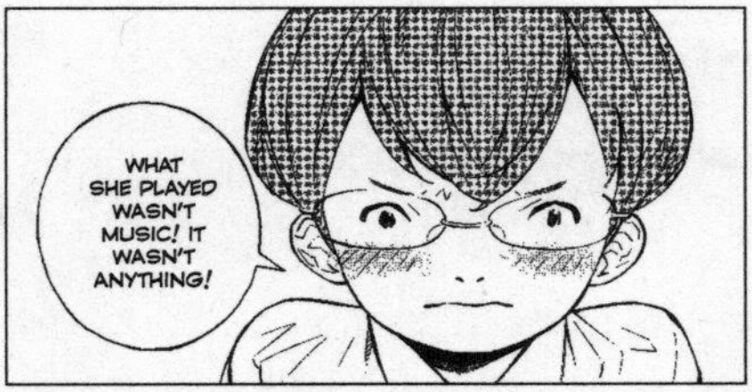
WHAT SHE PLAYED WASN'T MUSIC! IT WASN'T ANYTHING!

Kōsei tried to buy some time by switching the performance order. However, when Miike, the competition's winner, belittled Kaori's playing, Kōsei resolved to take the stage alone. A murmur ran through the audience when the accompanist began to play solo. Kōsei had given in to his rage, and the music he played was anything but pleasant.

Concentrating on his performance, Kōsei is plunged into a world devoid of music, where he realized how violently he had been playing. "This piece was my mother's favorite. Did she play it like this?" The boy's performance made a drastic change, and the listeners were enveloped in sparkling sounds. Through memories of his mother and the things she used to say, the boy's performance built up to its climax...

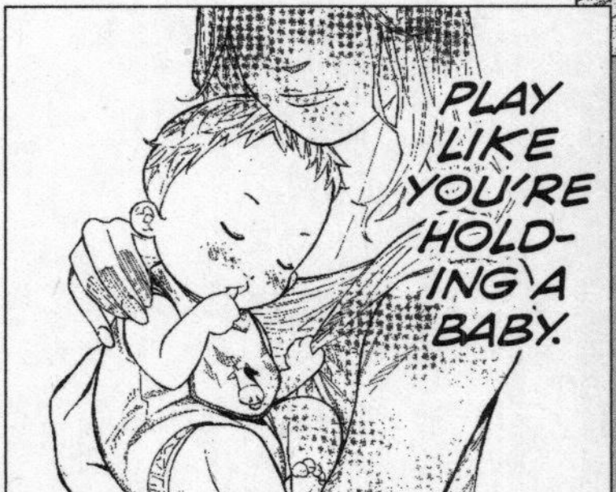
PLAY LIKE YOU'RE HOLDING A BABY.

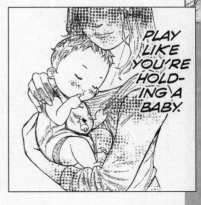

contents

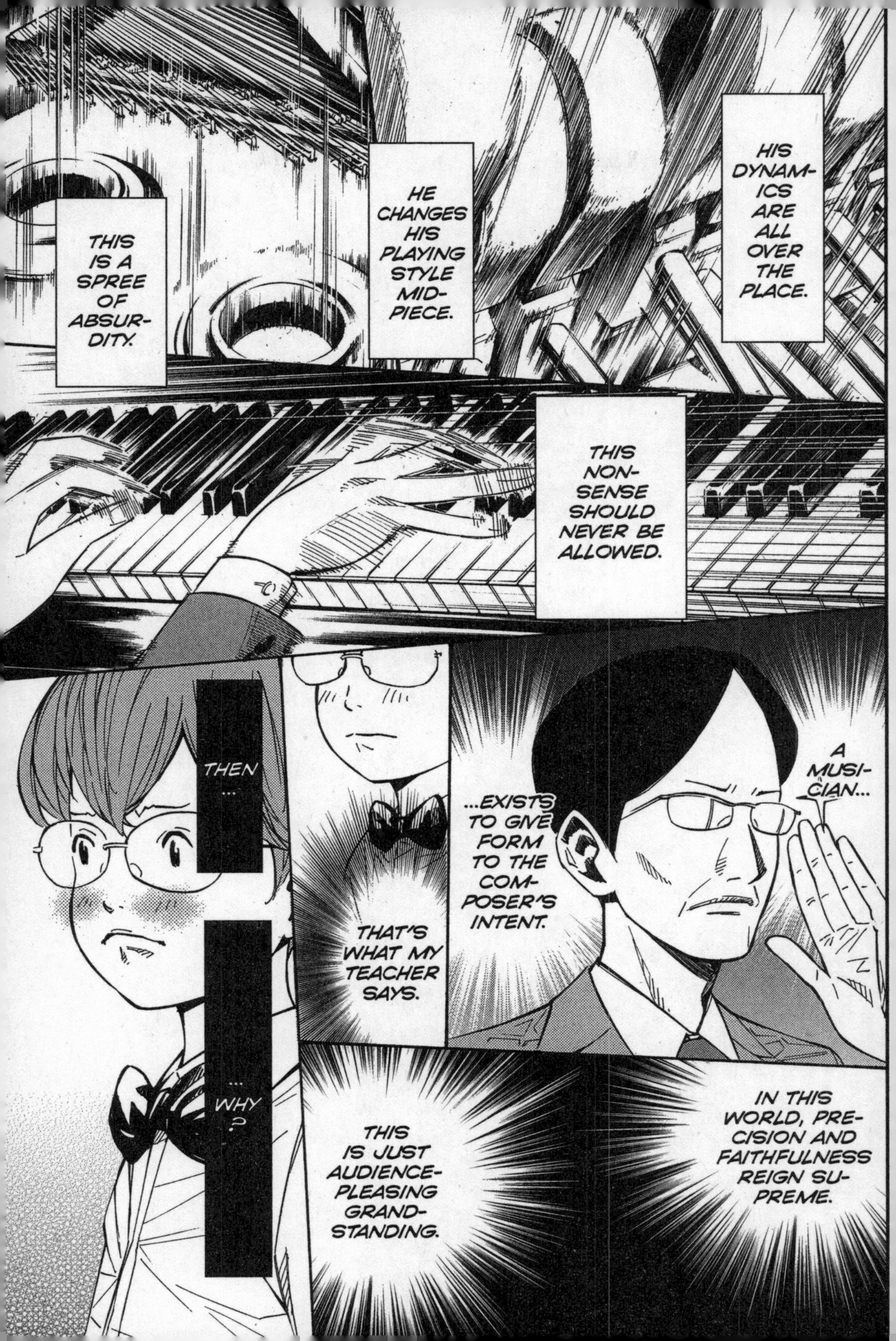
HIS DYNAMICS ARE ALL OVER THE PLACE.
HE CHANGES HIS PLAYING STYLE MIDPIECE.
THIS IS A SPREE OF ABSURDITY.
THIS NONSENSE SHOULD NEVER BE ALLOWED.
A MUSICIAN...
...EXISTS TO GIVE FORM TO THE COMPOSER'S INTENT.
THAT'S WHAT MY TEACHER SAYS.
IN THIS WORLD, PRECISION AND FAITHFULNESS REIGN SUPREME.
THIS IS JUST AUDIENCE-PLEASING GRANDSTANDING.
THEN ...
... WHY ?

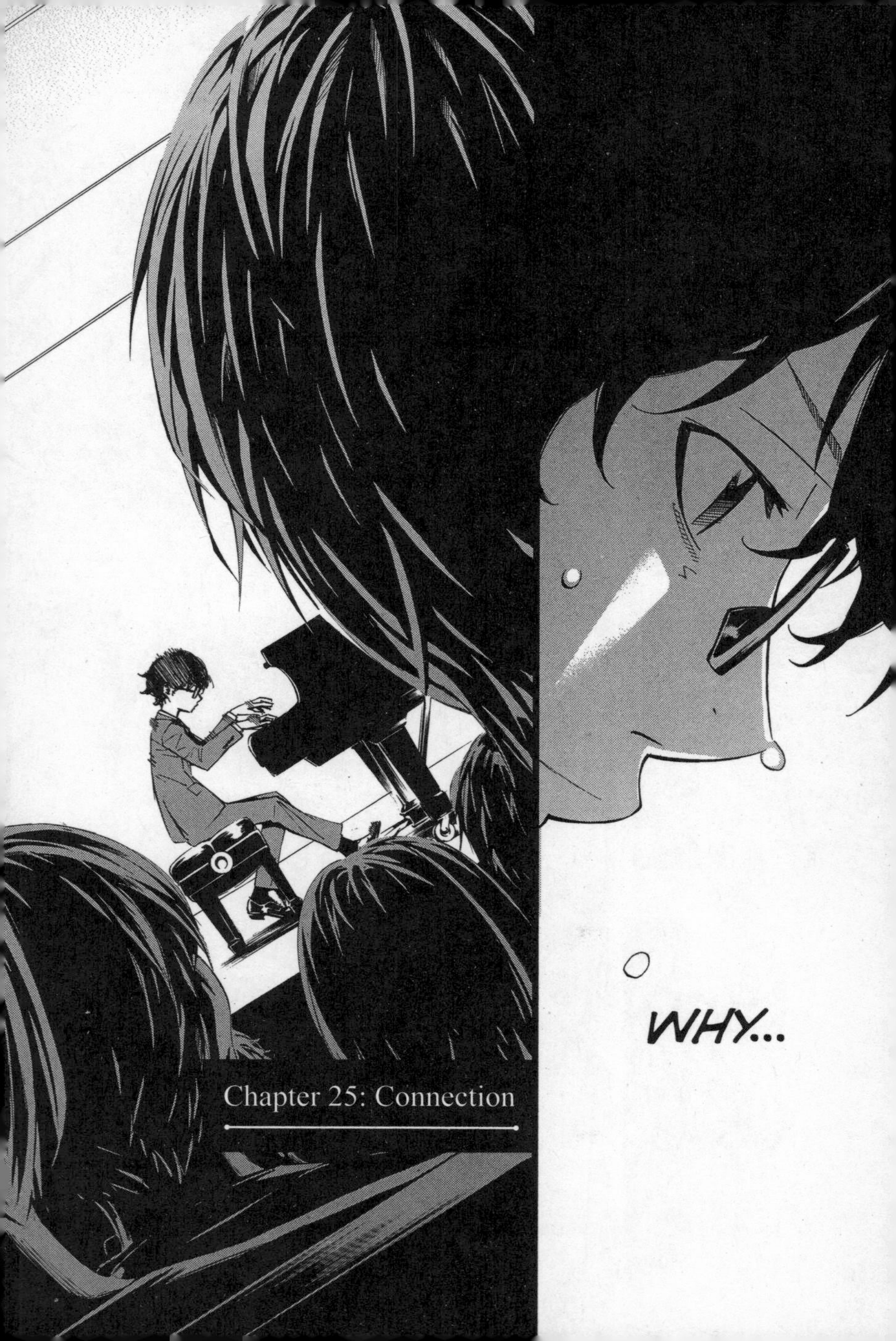
WHY...
Chapter 25: Connection

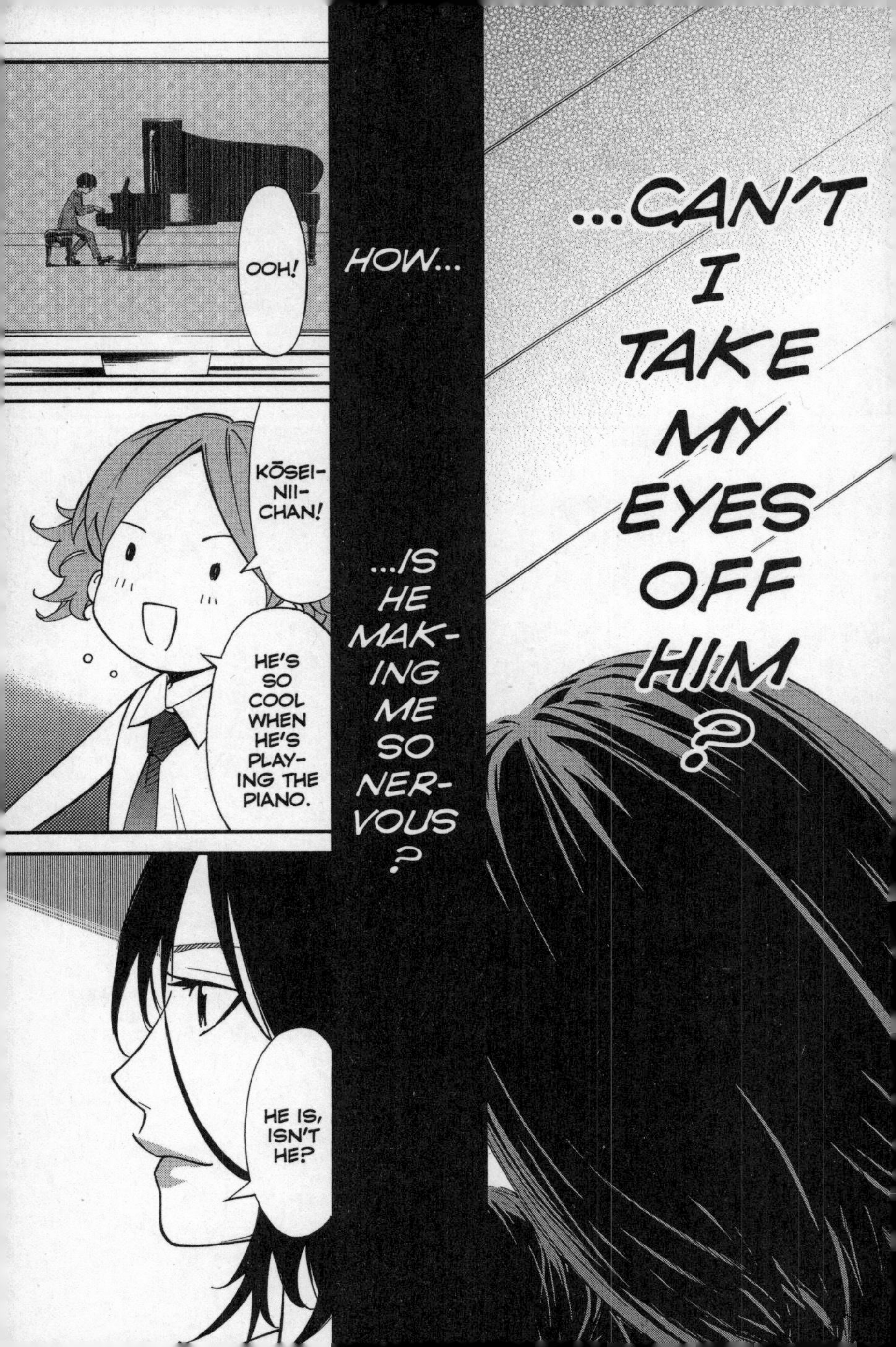
...CAN'T I TAKE MY EYES OFF HIM?
HOW...
...IS HE MAKING ME SO NERVOUS?
OOH!
KŌSEI-NII-CHAN!
HE'S SO COOL WHEN HE'S PLAYING THE PIANO.
HE IS, ISN'T HE?

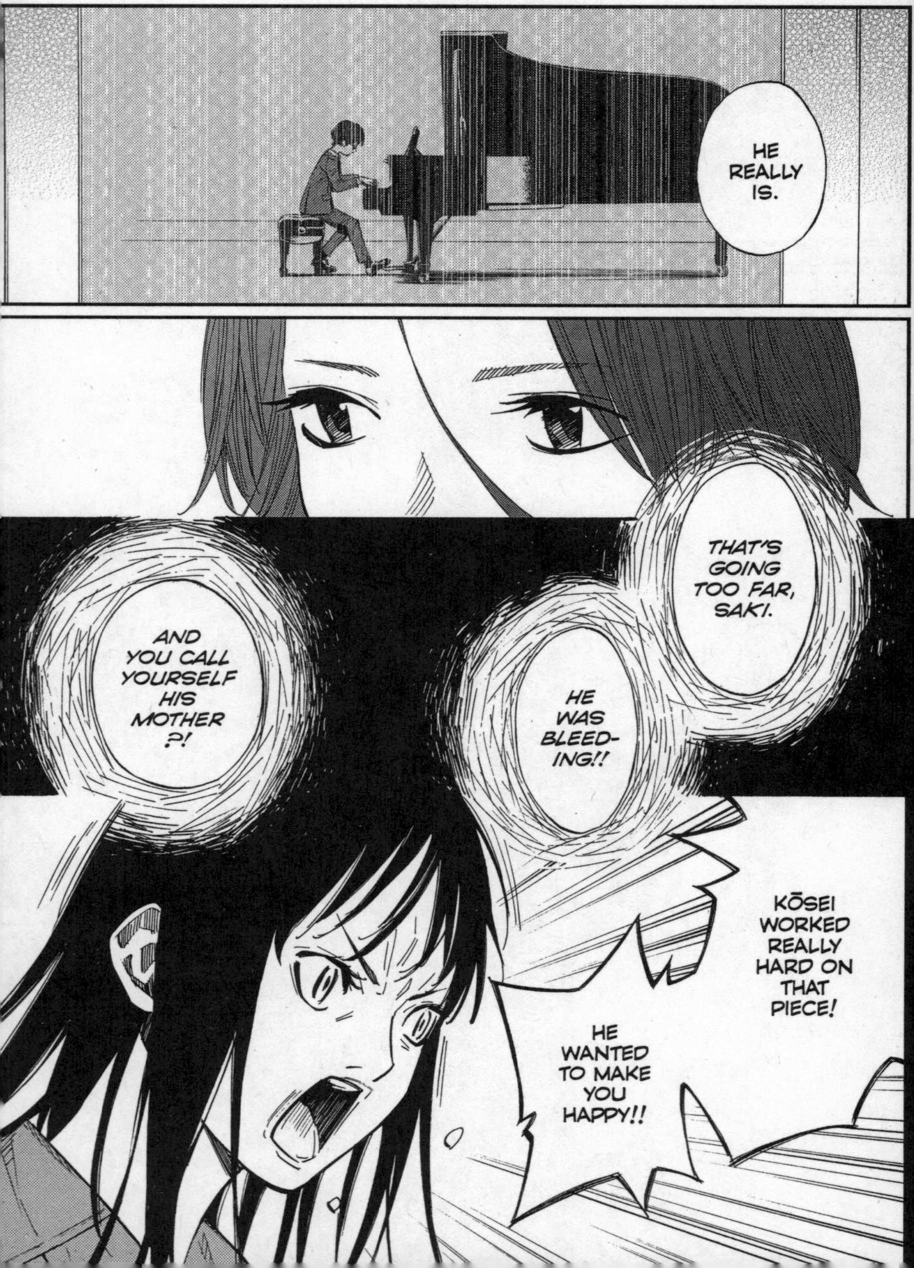
HE REALLY IS.
THAT'S GOING TOO FAR, SAKI.
HE WAS BLEEDING!!
AND YOU CALL YOURSELF HIS MOTHER?!
KŌSEI WORKED REALLY HARD ON THAT PIECE!
HE WANTED TO MAKE YOU HAPPY!!

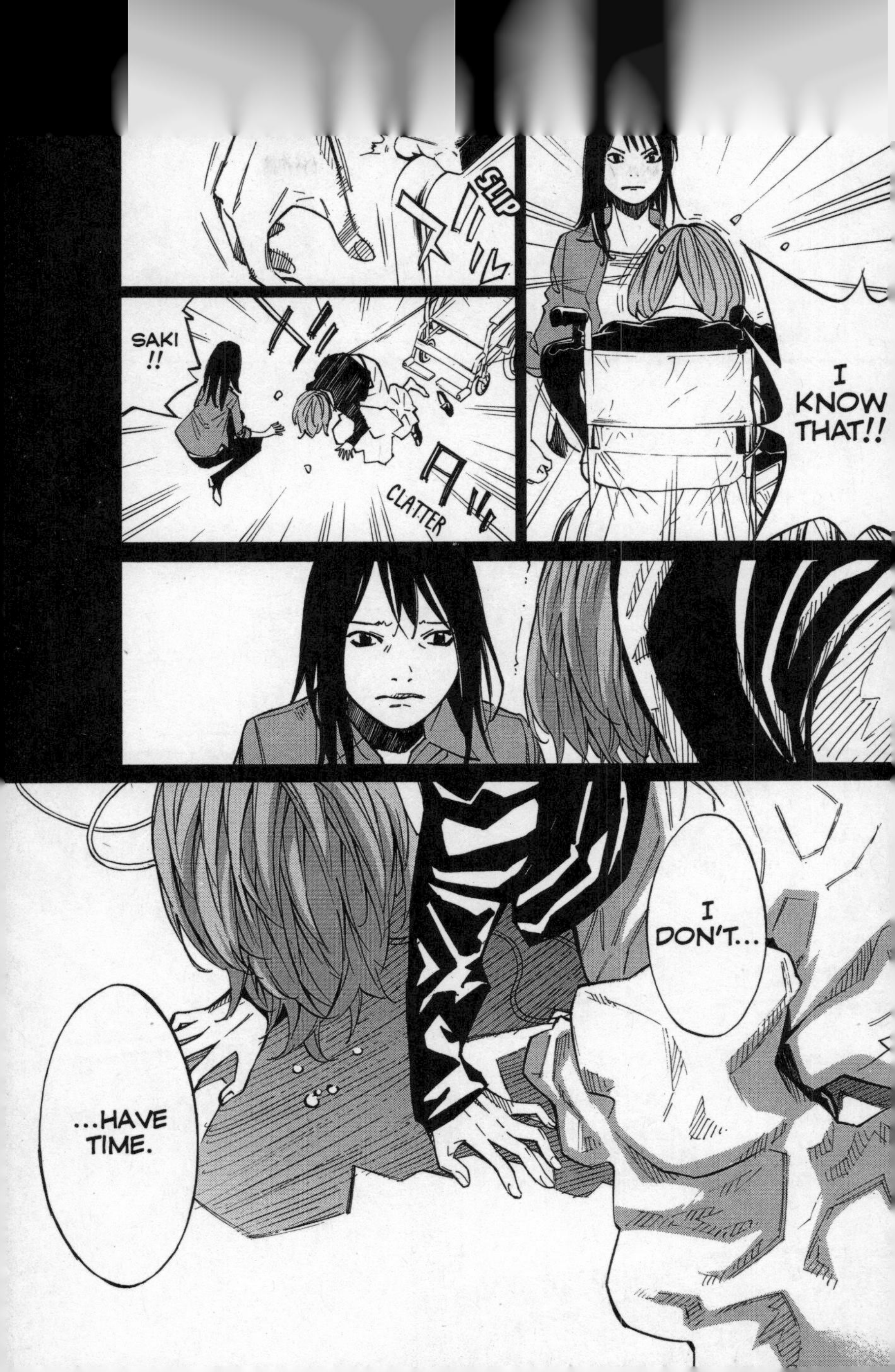
I KNOW THAT!!
SLIP
SAKI!!
CLATTER
I DON'T...
...HAVE TIME.

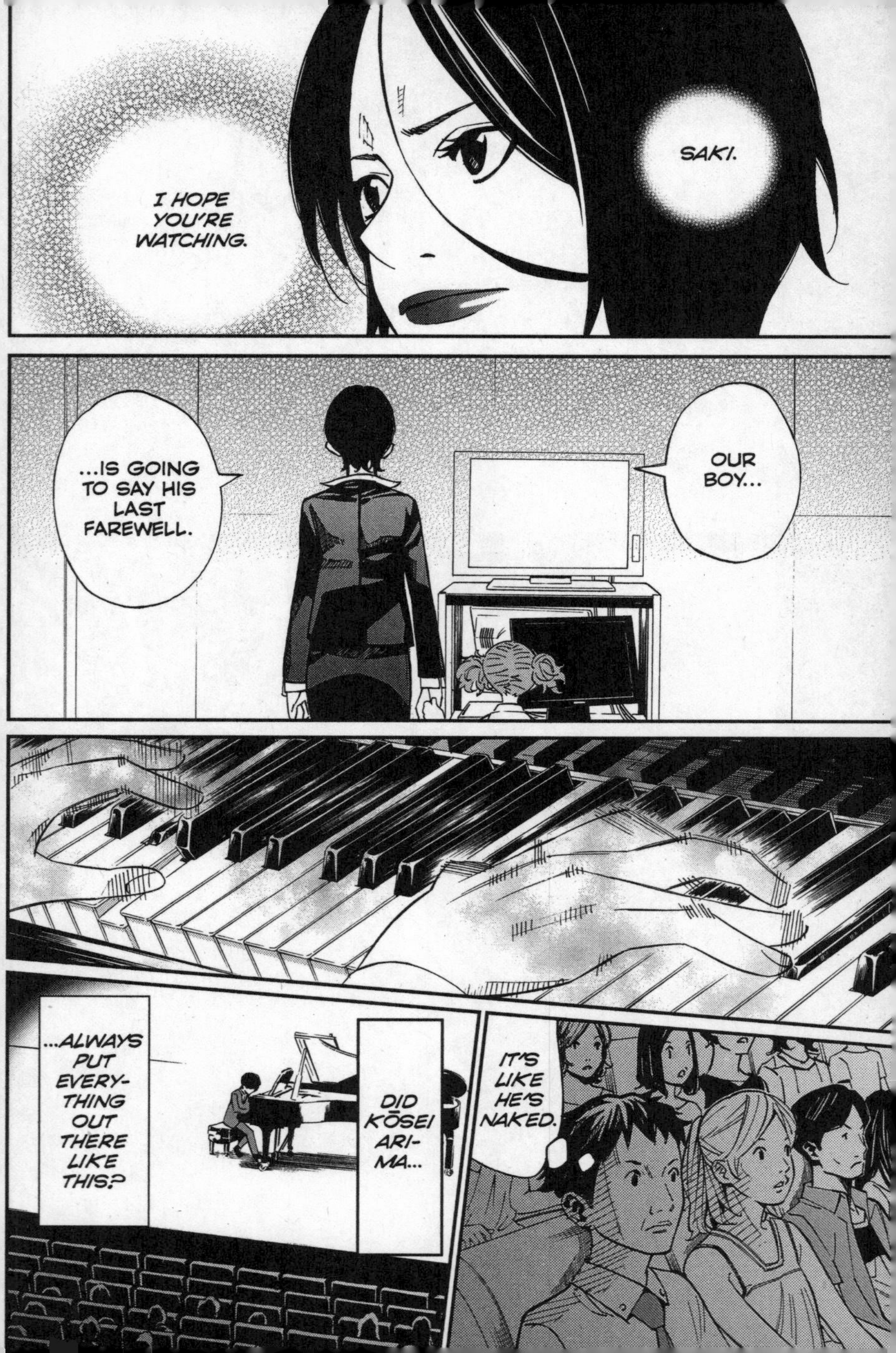
SAKI.
I HOPE YOU'RE WATCHING.
OUR BOY...
...IS GOING TO SAY HIS LAST FAREWELL.
IT'S LIKE HE'S NAKED.
DID KŌSEI ARIMA...
...ALWAYS PUT EVERYTHING OUT THERE LIKE THIS?

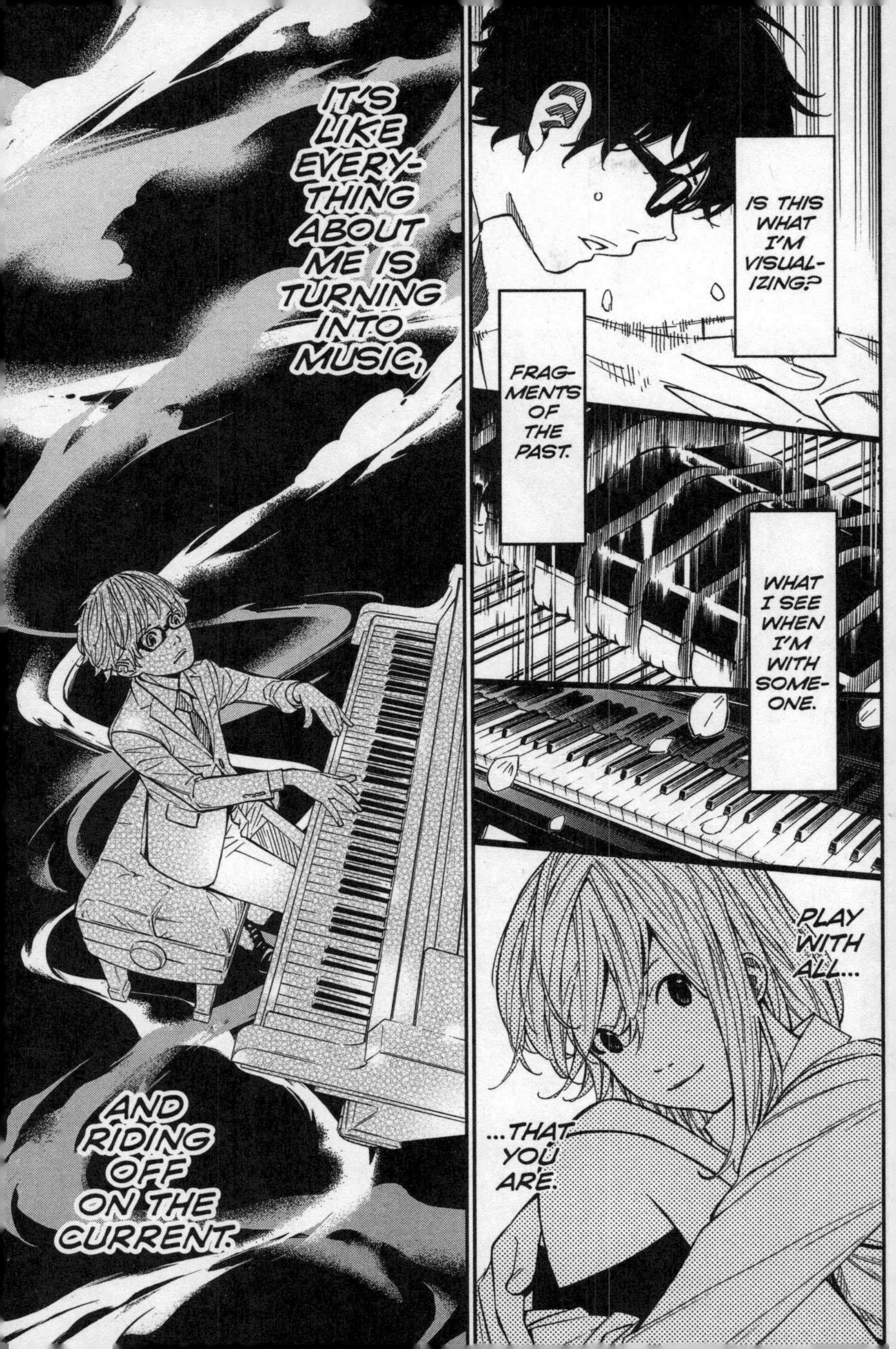
IS THIS WHAT I'M VISUAL-IZING?
FRAG-MENTS OF THE PAST.
WHAT I SEE WHEN I'M WITH SOME-ONE.
PLAY WITH ALL...
...THAT YOU ARE.
IT'S LIKE EVERY-THING ABOUT ME IS TURNING INTO MUSIC,
AND RIDING OFF ON THE CURRENT.

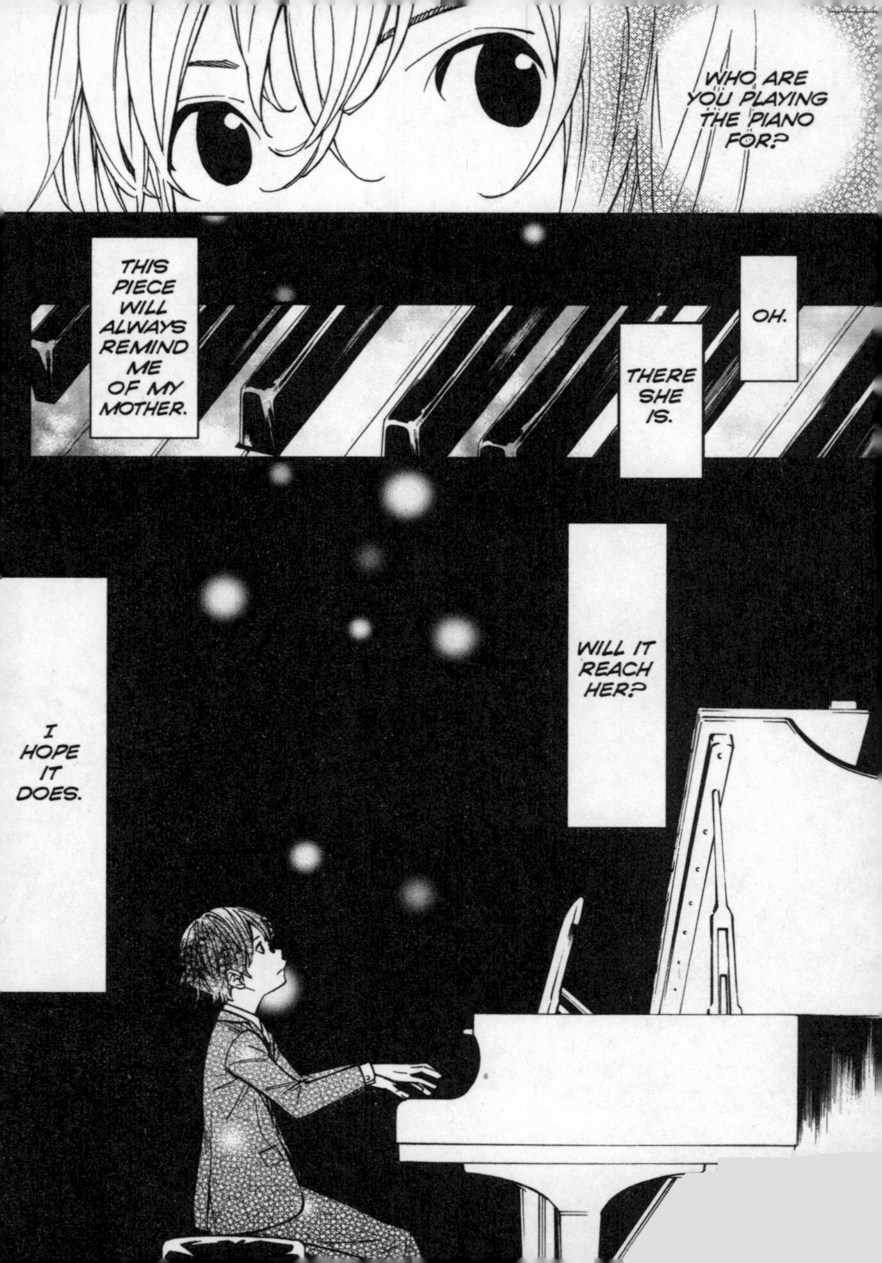
WHO ARE YOU PLAYING THE PIANO FOR?
OH.
THERE SHE IS.
THIS PIECE WILL ALWAYS REMIND ME OF MY MOTHER.
WILL IT REACH HER?
I HOPE IT DOES.

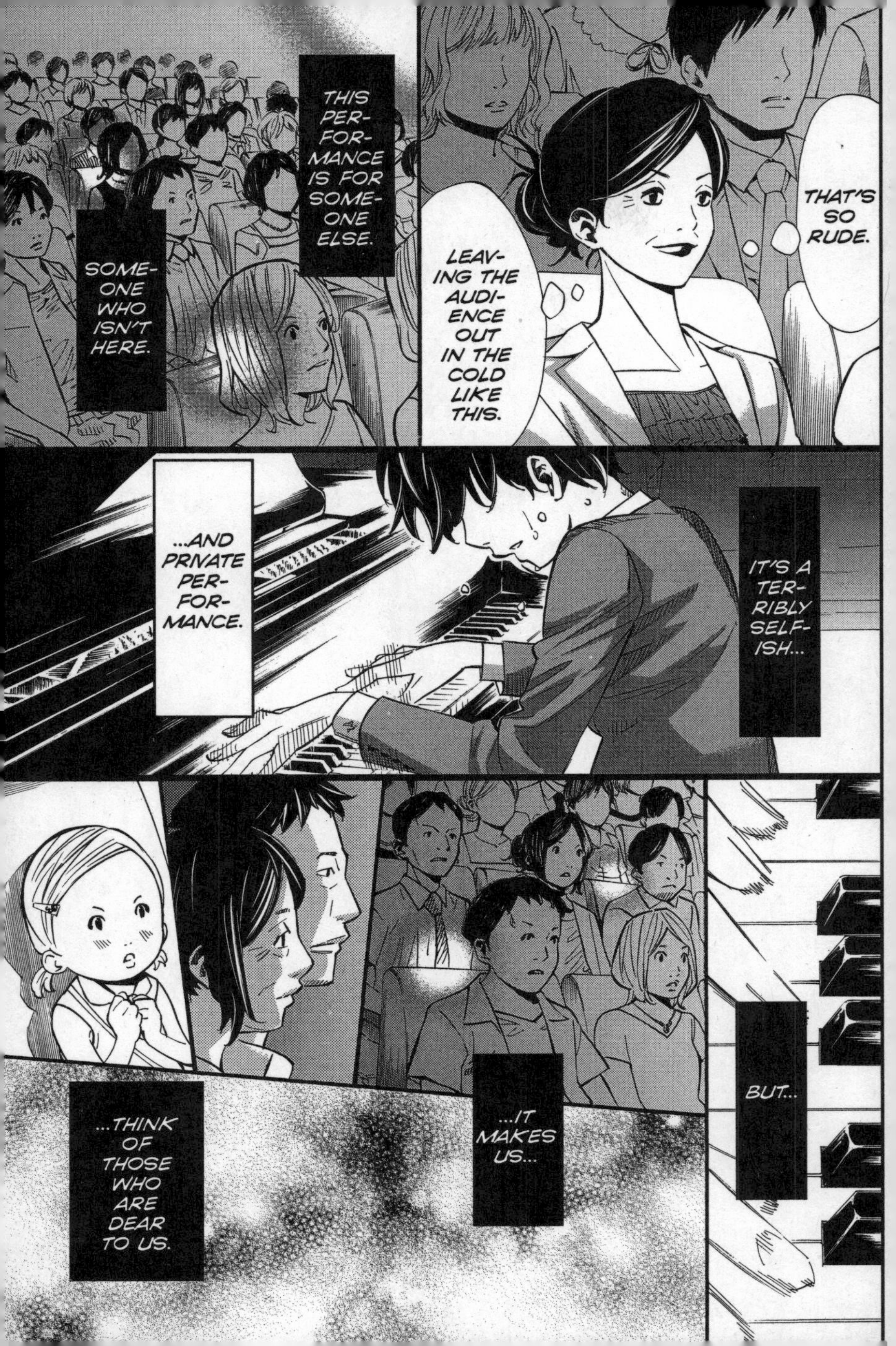
THAT'S SO RUDE.
LEAVING THE AUDIENCE OUT IN THE COLD LIKE THIS.
THIS PERFORMANCE IS FOR SOMEONE ELSE.
SOMEONE WHO ISN'T HERE.
IT'S A TERRIBLY SELFISH...
...AND PRIVATE PERFORMANCE.
BUT...
...IT MAKES US...
...THINK OF THOSE WHO ARE DEAR TO US.

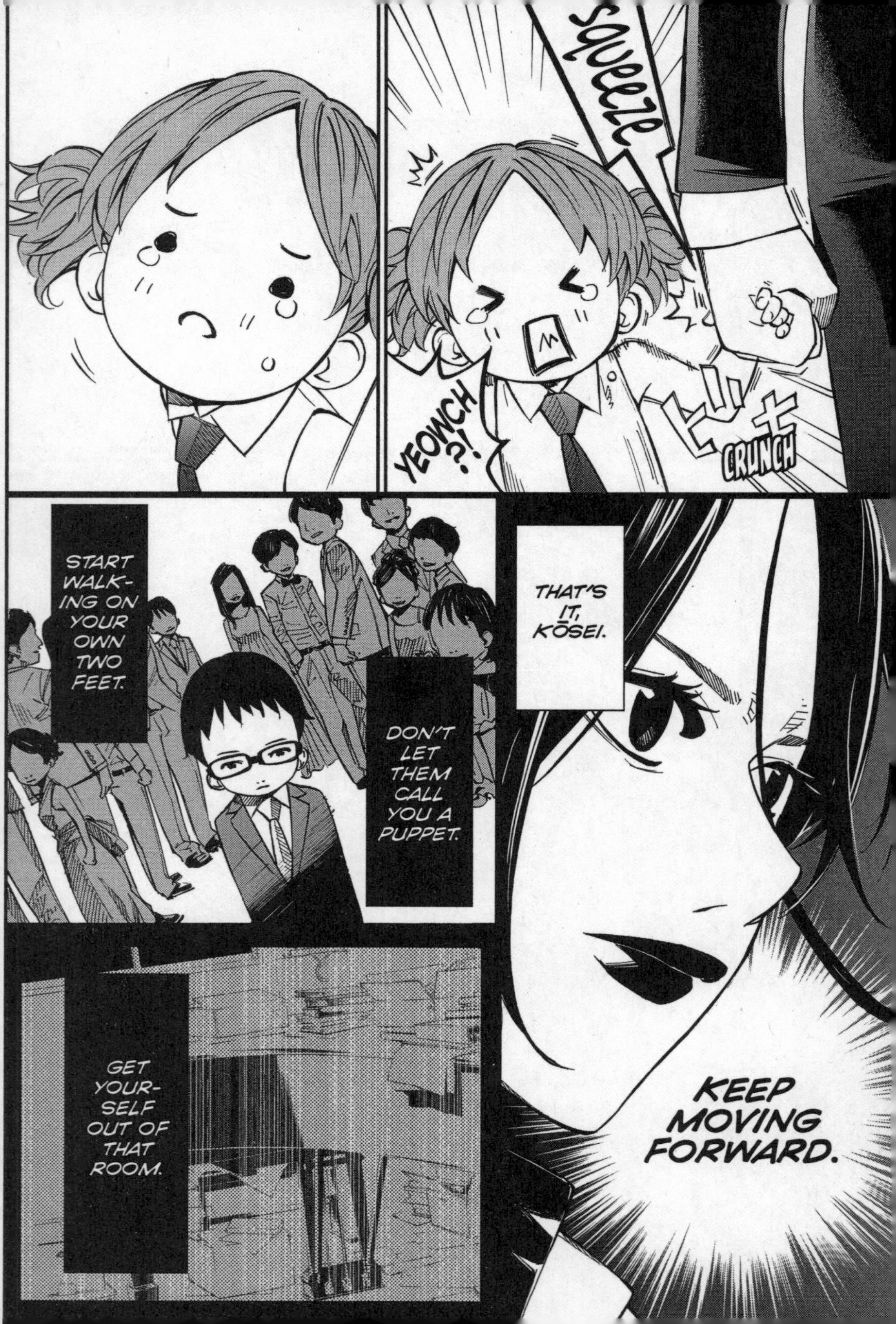
SQUEEZE
CRUNCH
YEOWCH?!
THAT'S IT, KŌSEI.
KEEP MOVING FORWARD.
START WALKING ON YOUR OWN TWO FEET.
DON'T LET THEM CALL YOU A PUPPET.
GET YOURSELF OUT OF THAT ROOM.

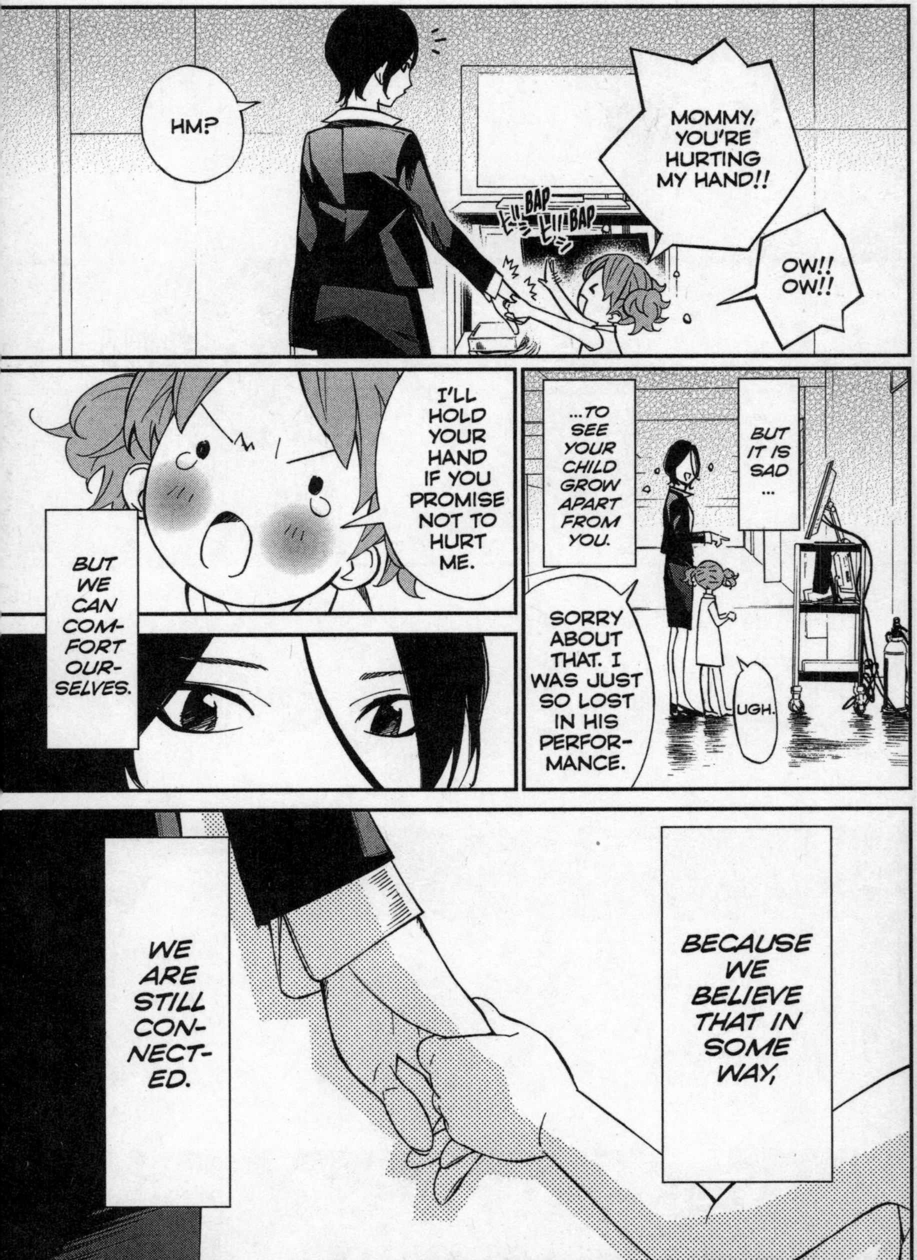
MOMMY, YOU'RE HURTING MY HAND!!
OW!! OW!!
BAP BAP
HM?
BUT IT IS SAD ...
...TO SEE YOUR CHILD GROW APART FROM YOU.
SORRY ABOUT THAT. I WAS JUST SO LOST IN HIS PERFORMANCE.
UGH.
I'LL HOLD YOUR HAND IF YOU PROMISE NOT TO HURT ME.
BUT WE CAN COMFORT OURSELVES.
BECAUSE WE BELIEVE THAT IN SOME WAY,
WE ARE STILL CONNECTED.

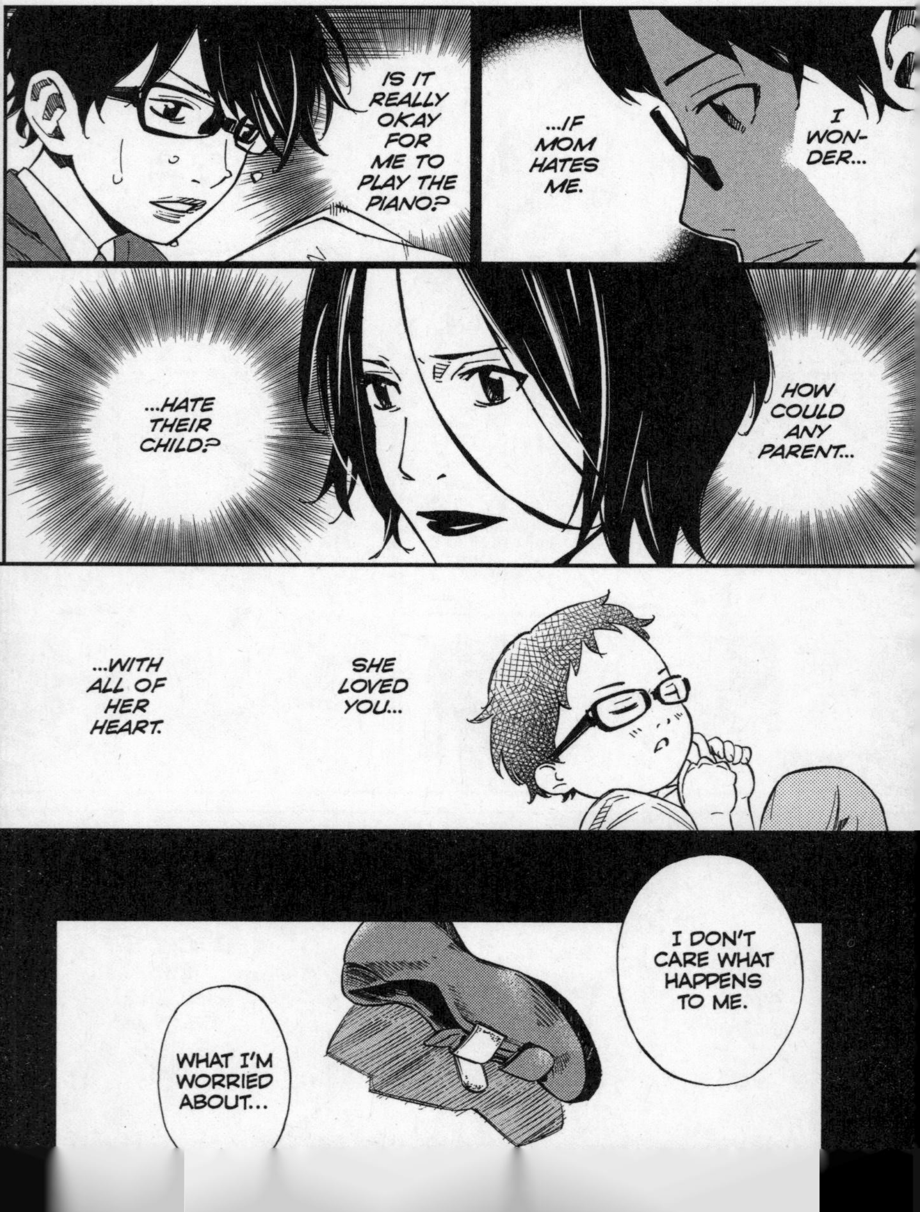
I WONDER...
...IF MOM HATES ME.
IS IT REALLY OKAY FOR ME TO PLAY THE PIANO?
HOW COULD ANY PARENT...
...HATE THEIR CHILD?
SHE LOVED YOU...
...WITH ALL OF HER HEART.
I DON'T CARE WHAT HAPPENS TO ME.
WHAT I'M WORRIED ABOUT...

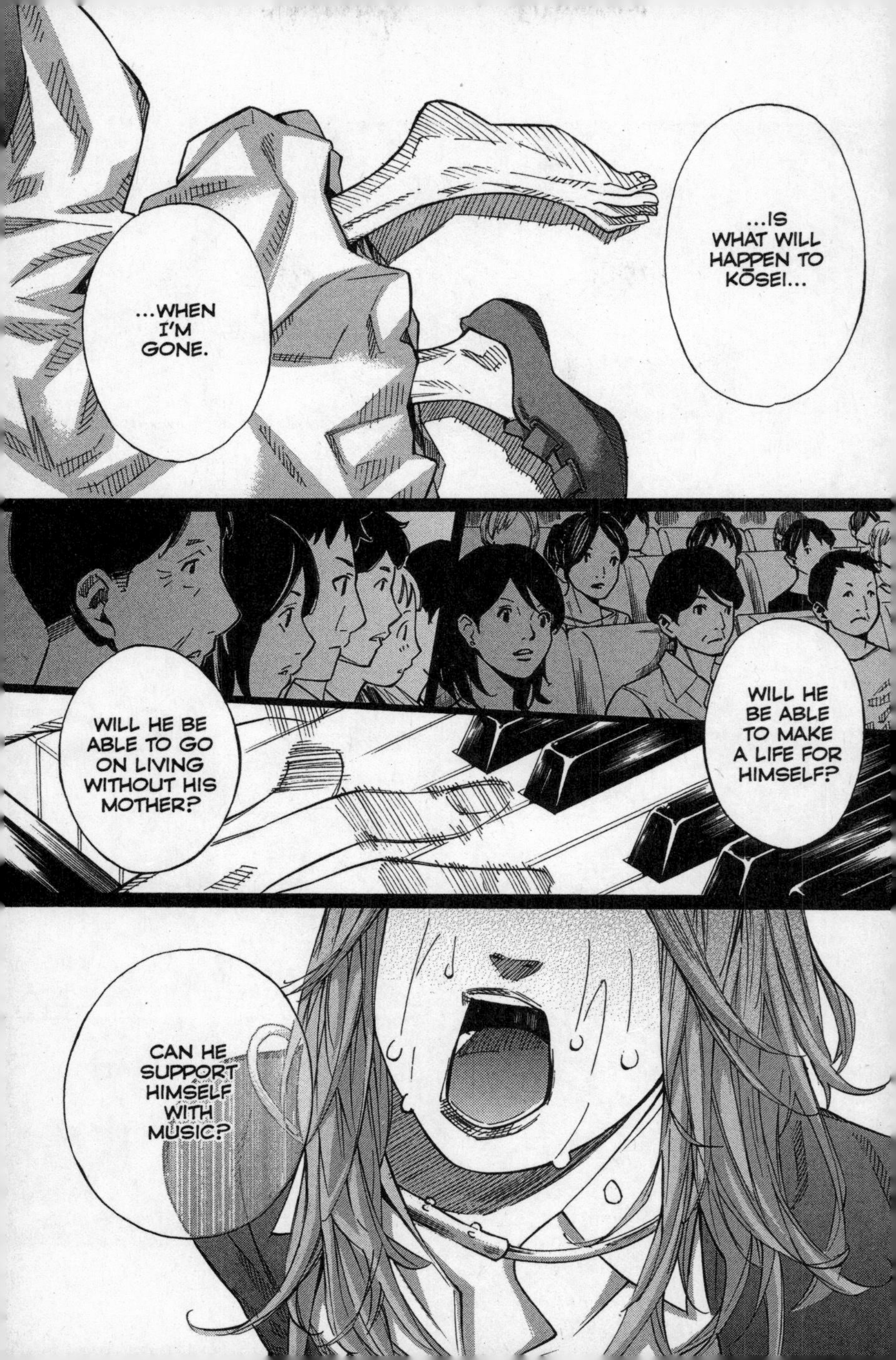
...IS WHAT WILL HAPPEN TO KŌSEI...
...WHEN I'M GONE.
WILL HE BE ABLE TO MAKE A LIFE FOR HIMSELF?
WILL HE BE ABLE TO GO ON LIVING WITHOUT HIS MOTHER?
CAN HE SUPPORT HIMSELF WITH MUSIC?

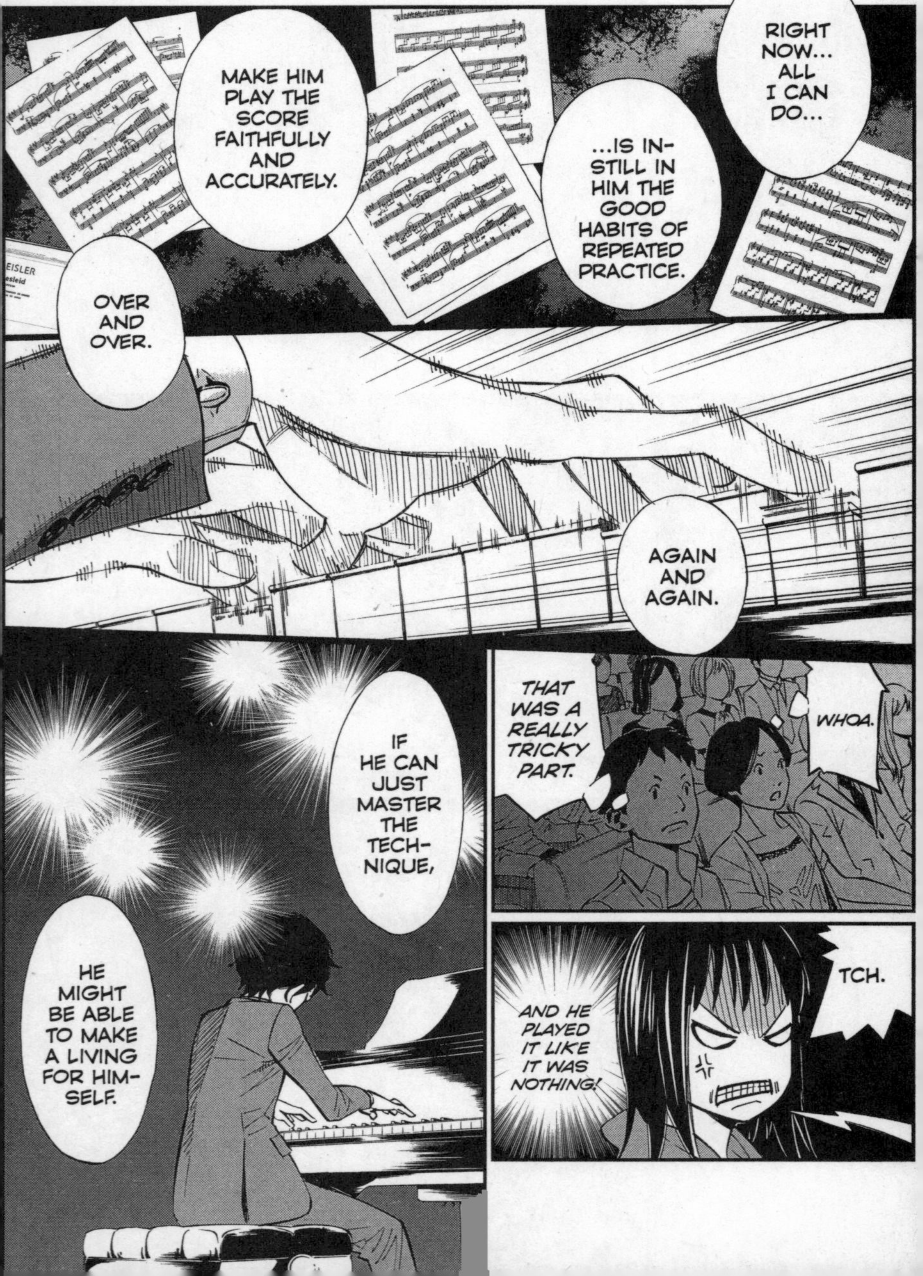
RIGHT NOW... ALL I CAN DO...
...IS IN-STILL IN HIM THE GOOD HABITS OF REPEATED PRACTICE.
MAKE HIM PLAY THE SCORE FAITHFULLY AND ACCURATELY.
OVER AND OVER.
AGAIN AND AGAIN.
WHOA.
THAT WAS A REALLY TRICKY PART.
TCH.
AND HE PLAYED IT LIKE IT WAS NOTHING!
IF HE CAN JUST MASTER THE TECH-NIQUE,
HE MIGHT BE ABLE TO MAKE A LIVING FOR HIM-SELF.

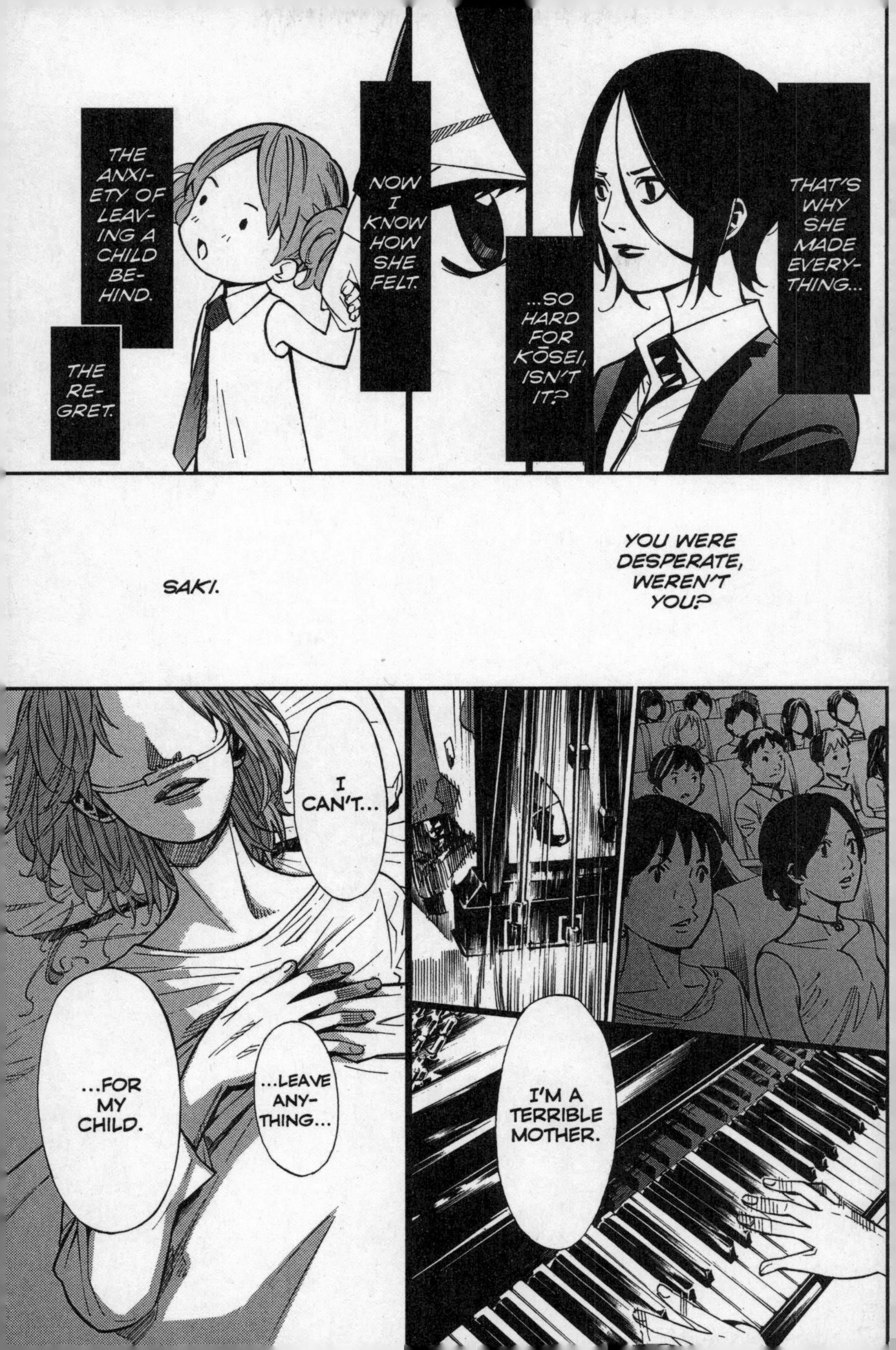
THAT'S WHY SHE MADE EVERYTHING...
...SO HARD FOR KŌSEI, ISN'T IT?
NOW I KNOW HOW SHE FELT.
THE ANXIETY OF LEAVING A CHILD BEHIND.
THE REGRET.
YOU WERE DESPERATE, WEREN'T YOU?
SAKI.
I'M A TERRIBLE MOTHER.
I CAN'T...
...LEAVE ANYTHING...
...FOR MY CHILD.

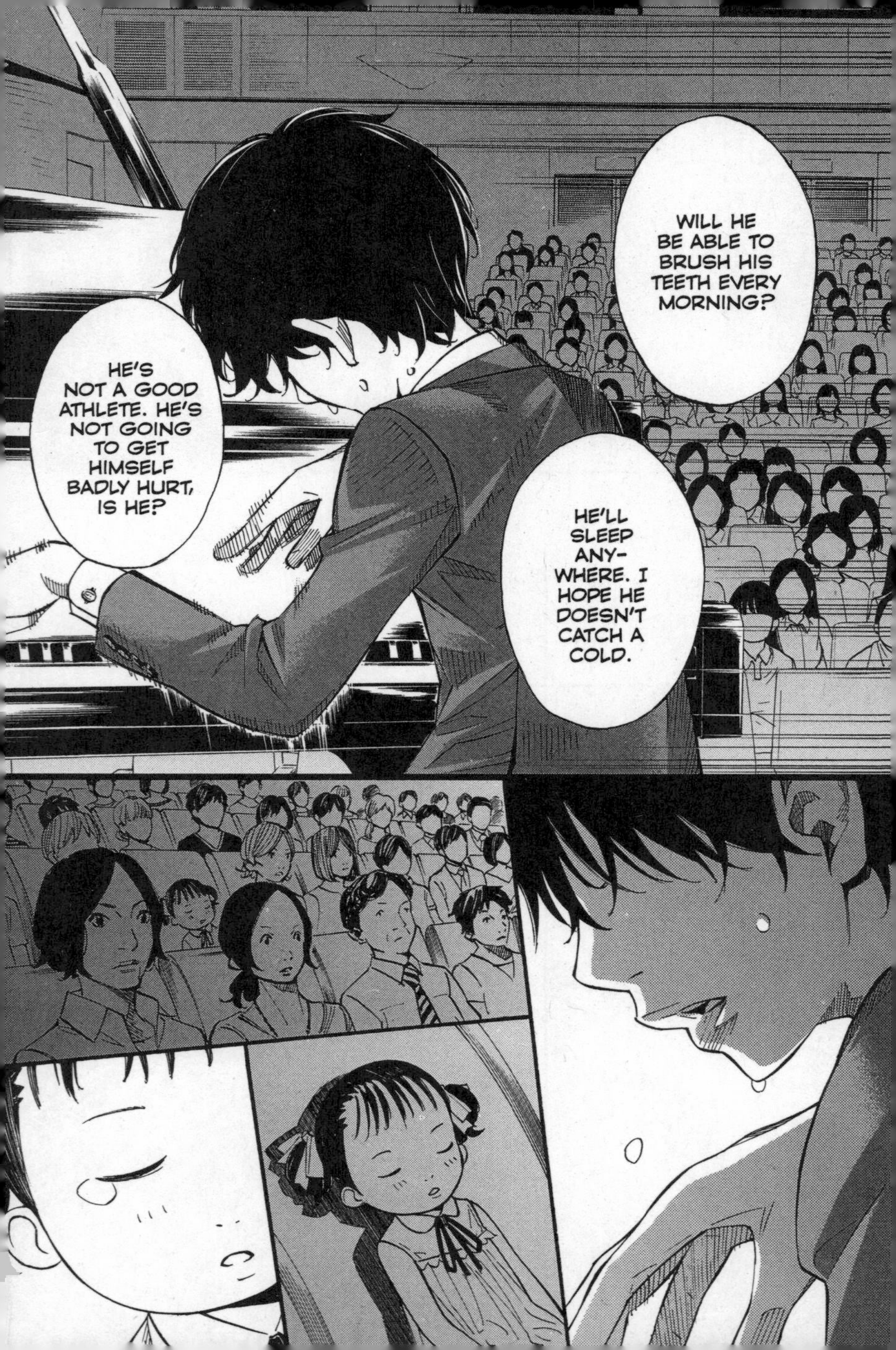
WILL HE BE ABLE TO BRUSH HIS TEETH EVERY MORNING?
HE'LL SLEEP ANY-WHERE. I HOPE HE DOESN'T CATCH A COLD.
HE'S NOT A GOOD ATHLETE. HE'S NOT GOING TO GET HIMSELF BADLY HURT, IS HE?

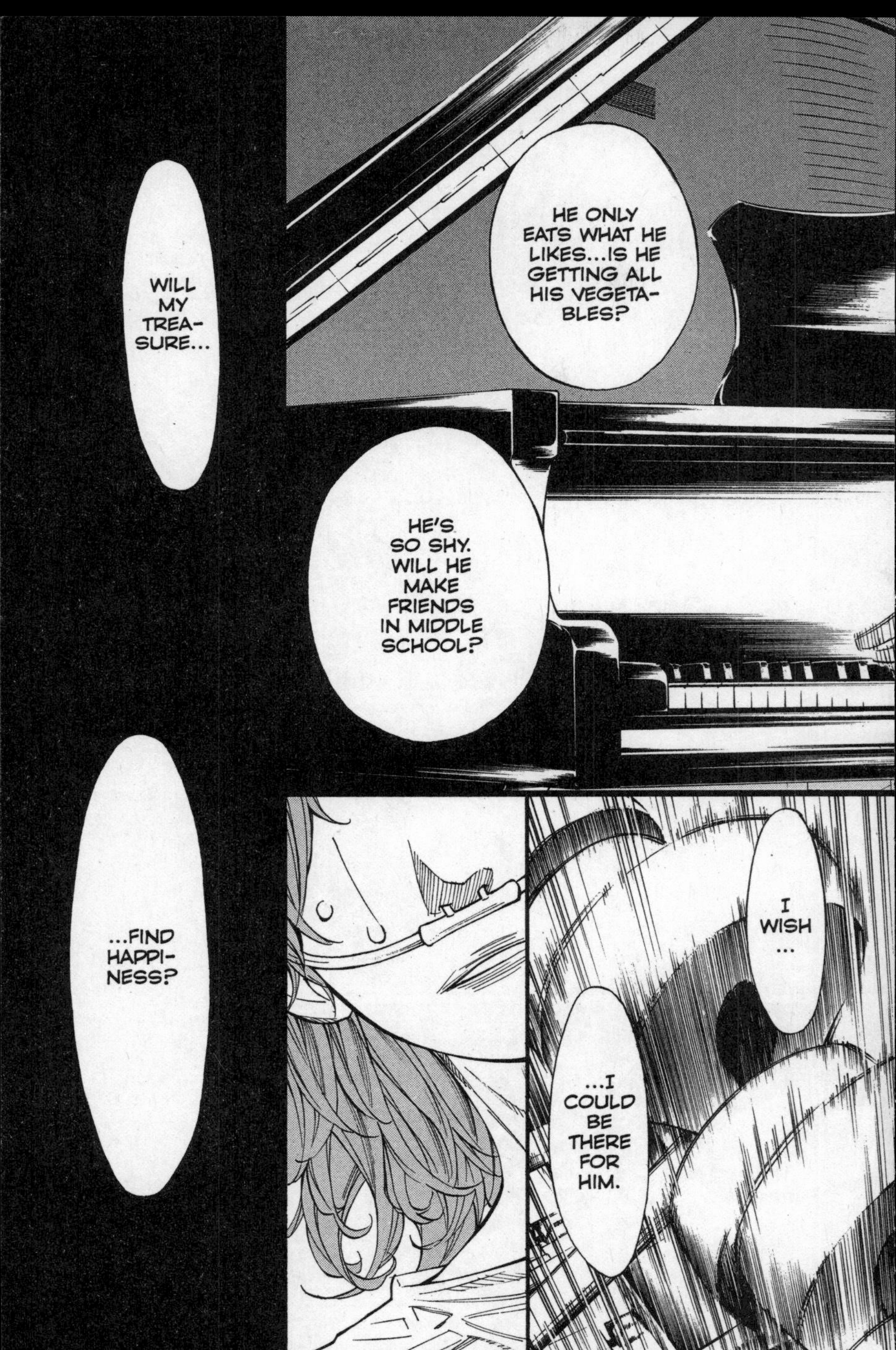
HE ONLY EATS WHAT HE LIKES...IS HE GETTING ALL HIS VEGETA-BLES?
HE'S SO SHY. WILL HE MAKE FRIENDS IN MIDDLE SCHOOL?
I WISH ...
...I COULD BE THERE FOR HIM.
WILL MY TREA-SURE...
...FIND HAPPI-NESS?

I ALWAYS KNEW.

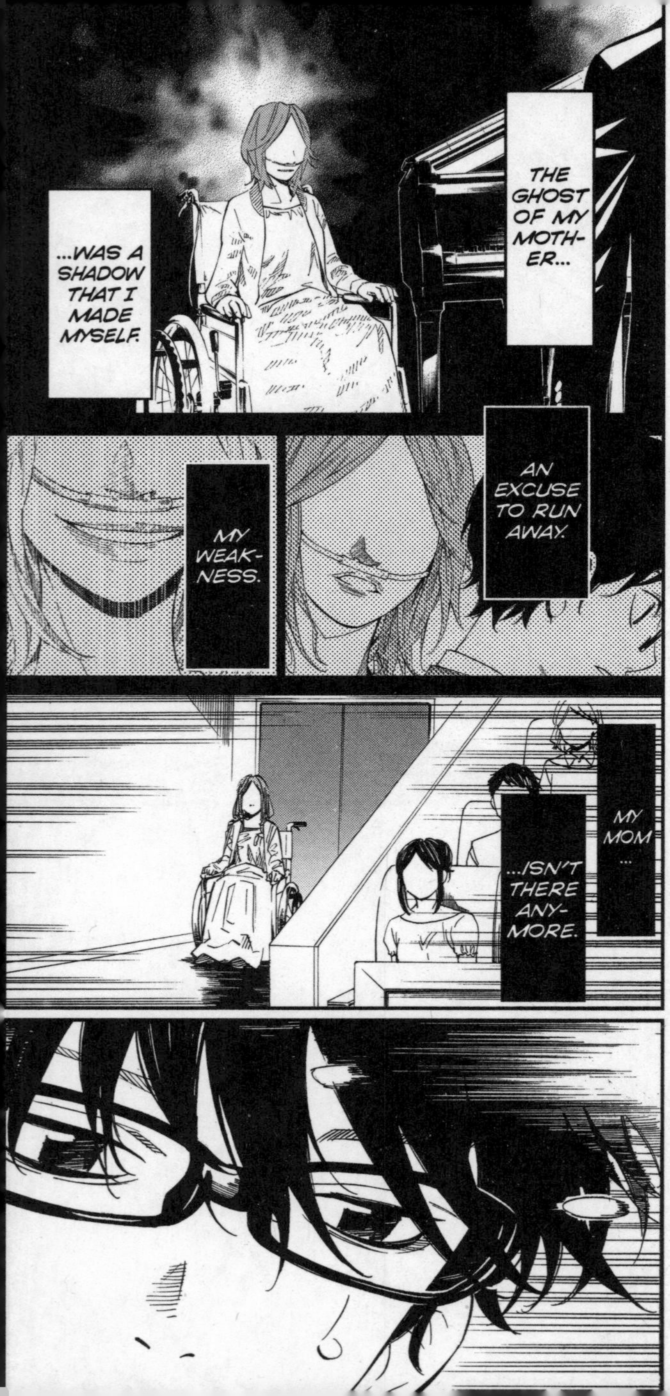
THE GHOST OF MY MOTHER...
...WAS A SHADOW THAT I MADE MYSELF.
AN EXCUSE TO RUN AWAY.
MY WEAKNESS.
MY MOM...
...ISN'T THERE ANYMORE.

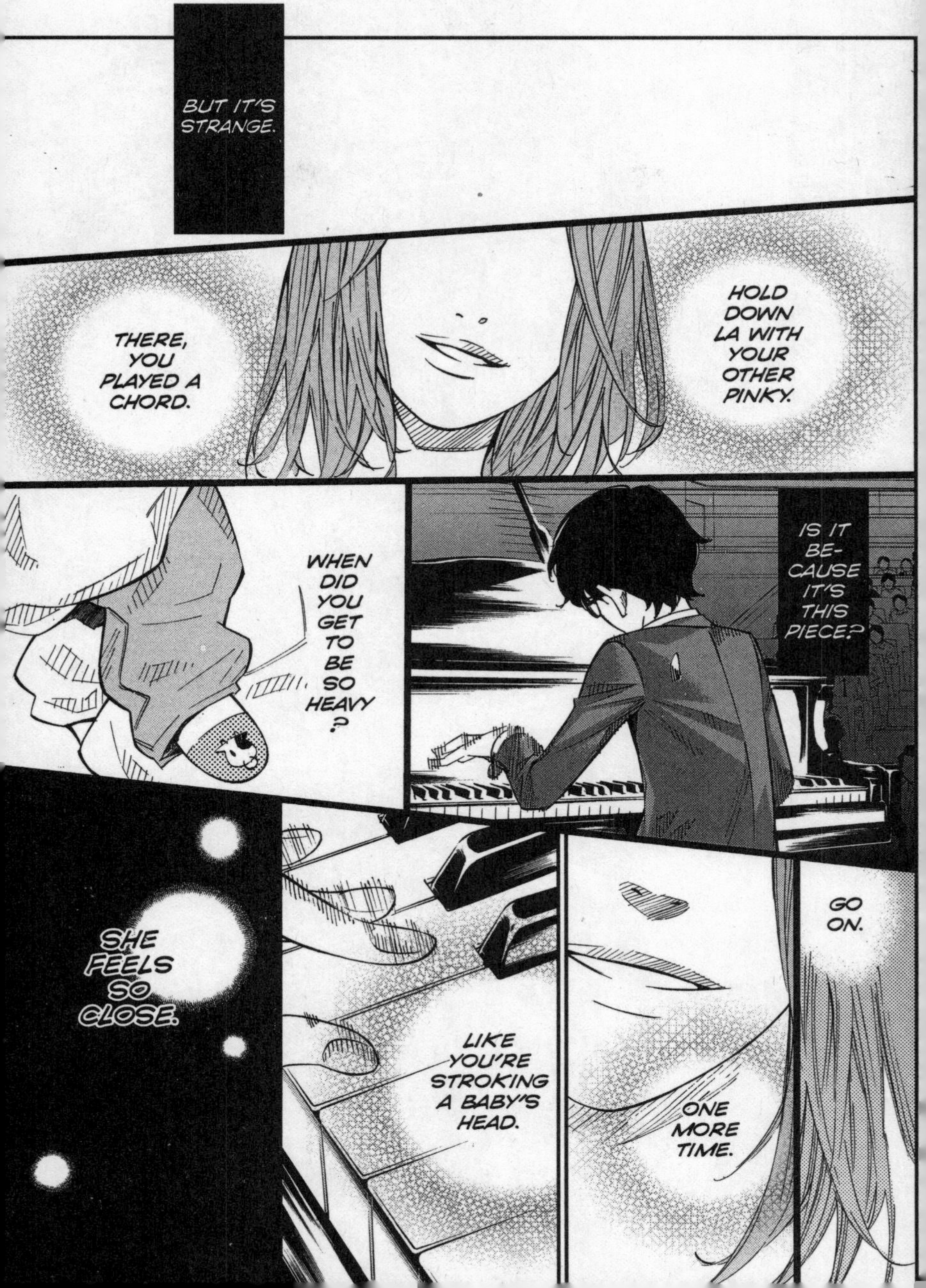
BUT IT'S STRANGE.
HOLD DOWN LA WITH YOUR OTHER PINKY.
THERE, YOU PLAYED A CHORD.
IS IT BE-CAUSE IT'S THIS PIECE?
WHEN DID YOU GET TO BE SO HEAVY?
GO ON.
ONE MORE TIME.
LIKE YOU'RE STROKING A BABY'S HEAD.
SHE FEELS SO CLOSE.

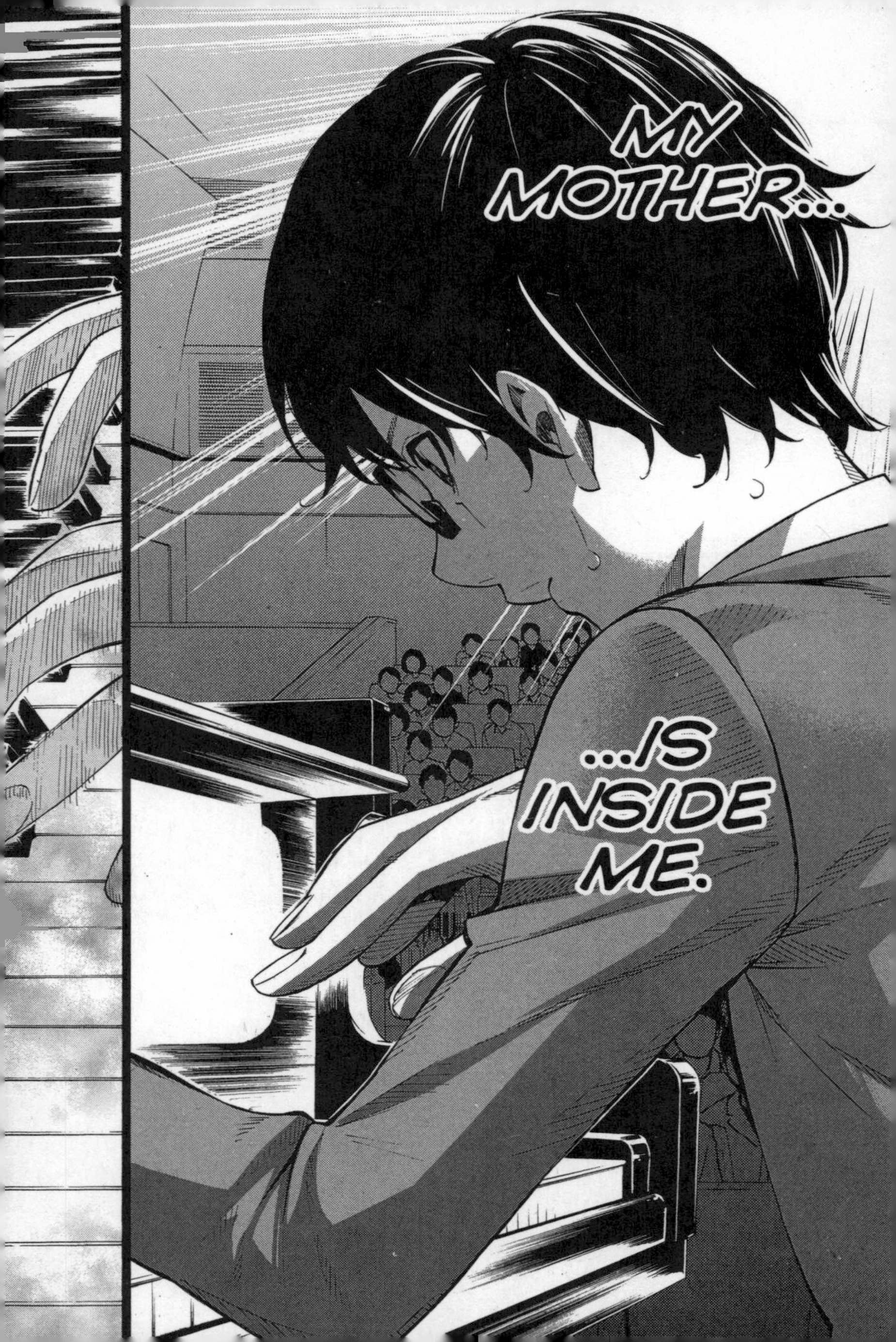
MY MOTHER...
...IS INSIDE ME.

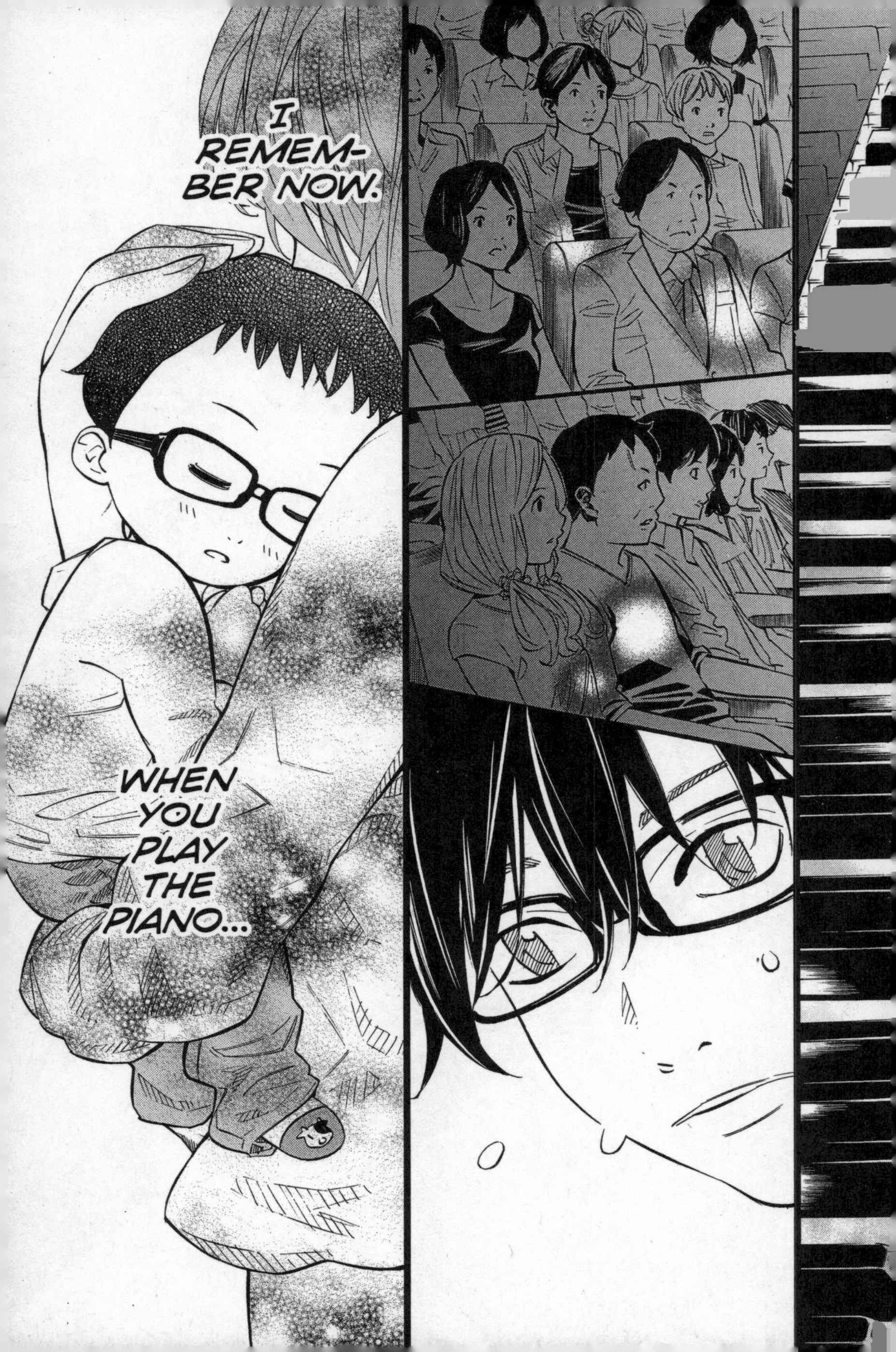
I REMEM-
BER NOW.
WHEN YOU PLAY THE PIANO...

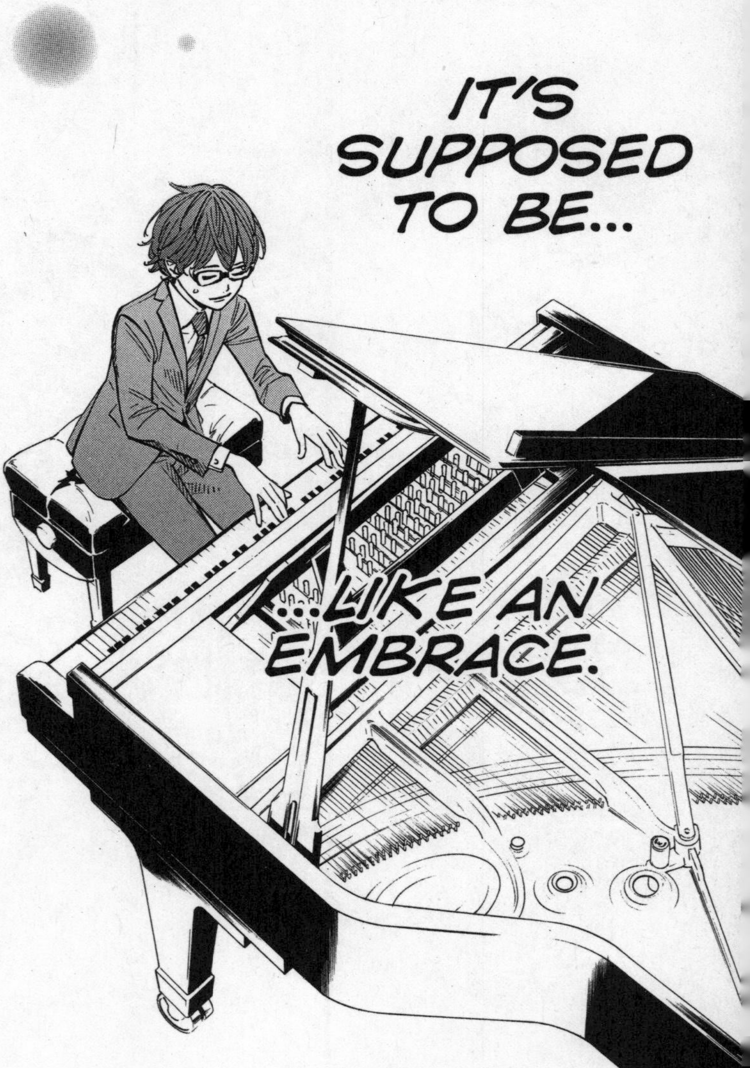
IT'S SUPPOSED TO BE...
...LIKE AN EMBRACE.

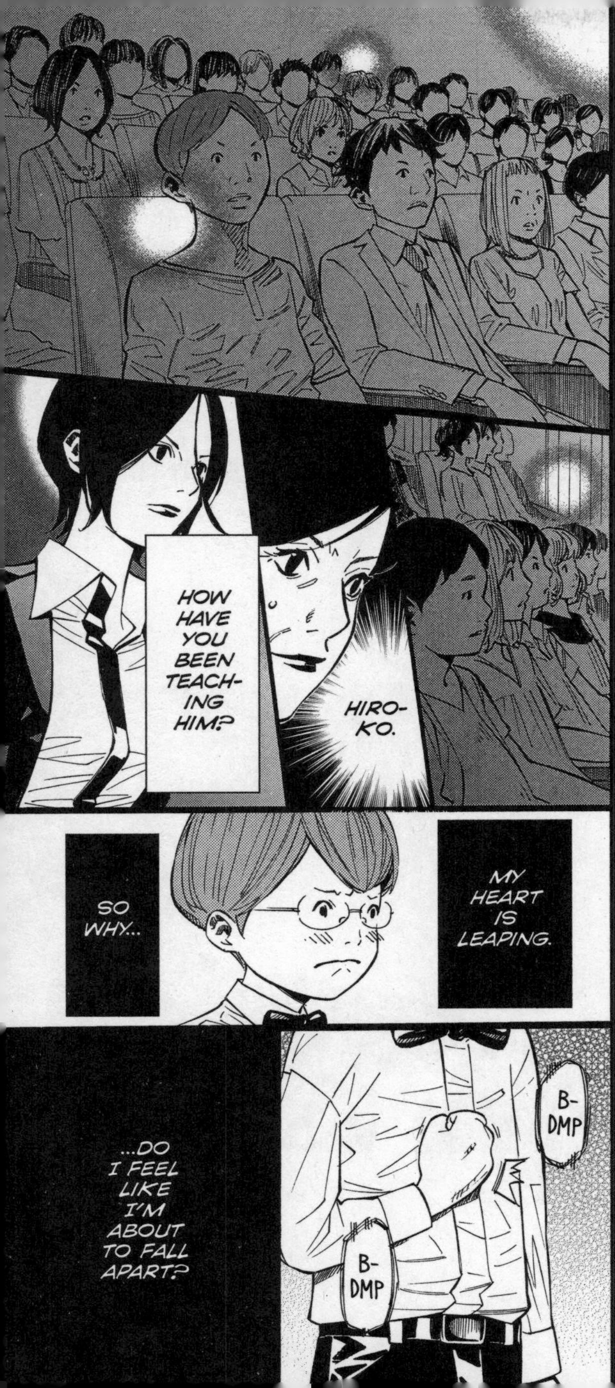
HIRO-KO.
HOW HAVE YOU BEEN TEACH-ING HIM?
MY HEART IS LEAPING.
SO WHY...
B-DMP
...DO I FEEL LIKE I'M ABOUT TO FALL APART?
B-DMP

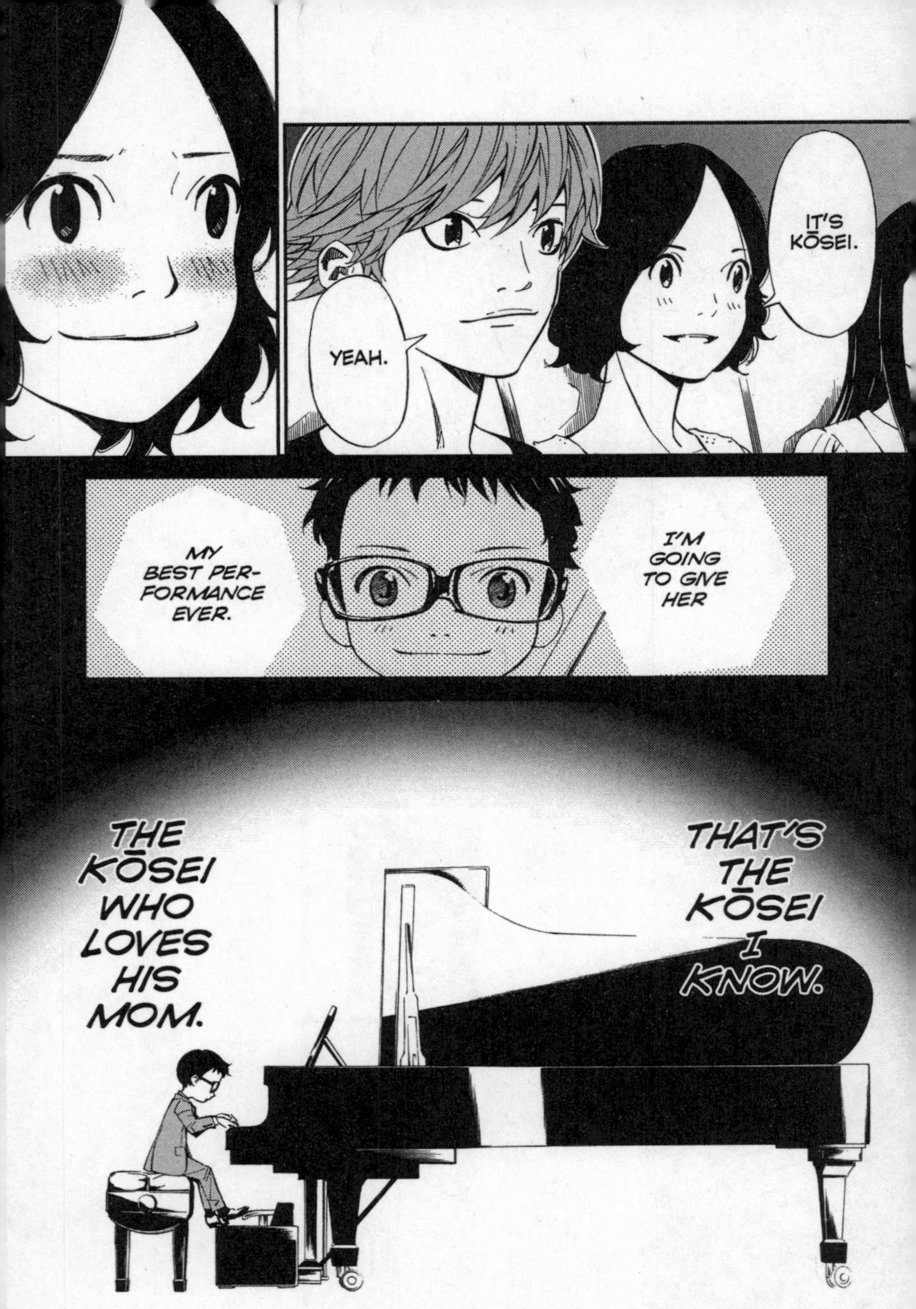
IT'S KŌSEI.
YEAH.
I'M GOING TO GIVE HER
MY BEST PER-FORMANCE EVER.
THAT'S THE KŌSEI I KNOW.
THE KŌSEI WHO LOVES HIS MOM.

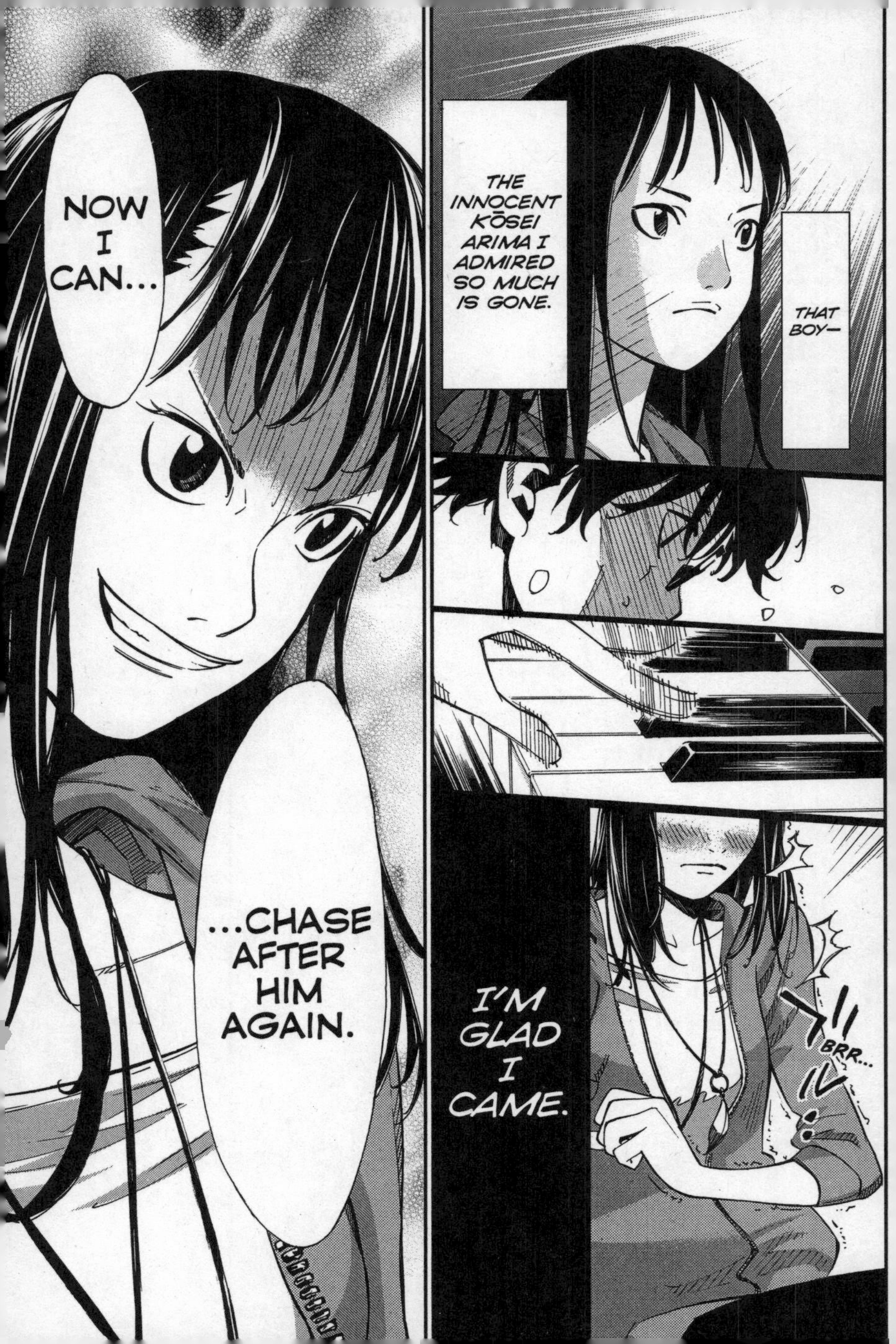
THAT BOY—
THE INNOCENT KŌSEI ARIMA I ADMIRED SO MUCH IS GONE.
BRR...
I'M GLAD I CAME.
NOW I CAN...
...CHASE AFTER HIM AGAIN.

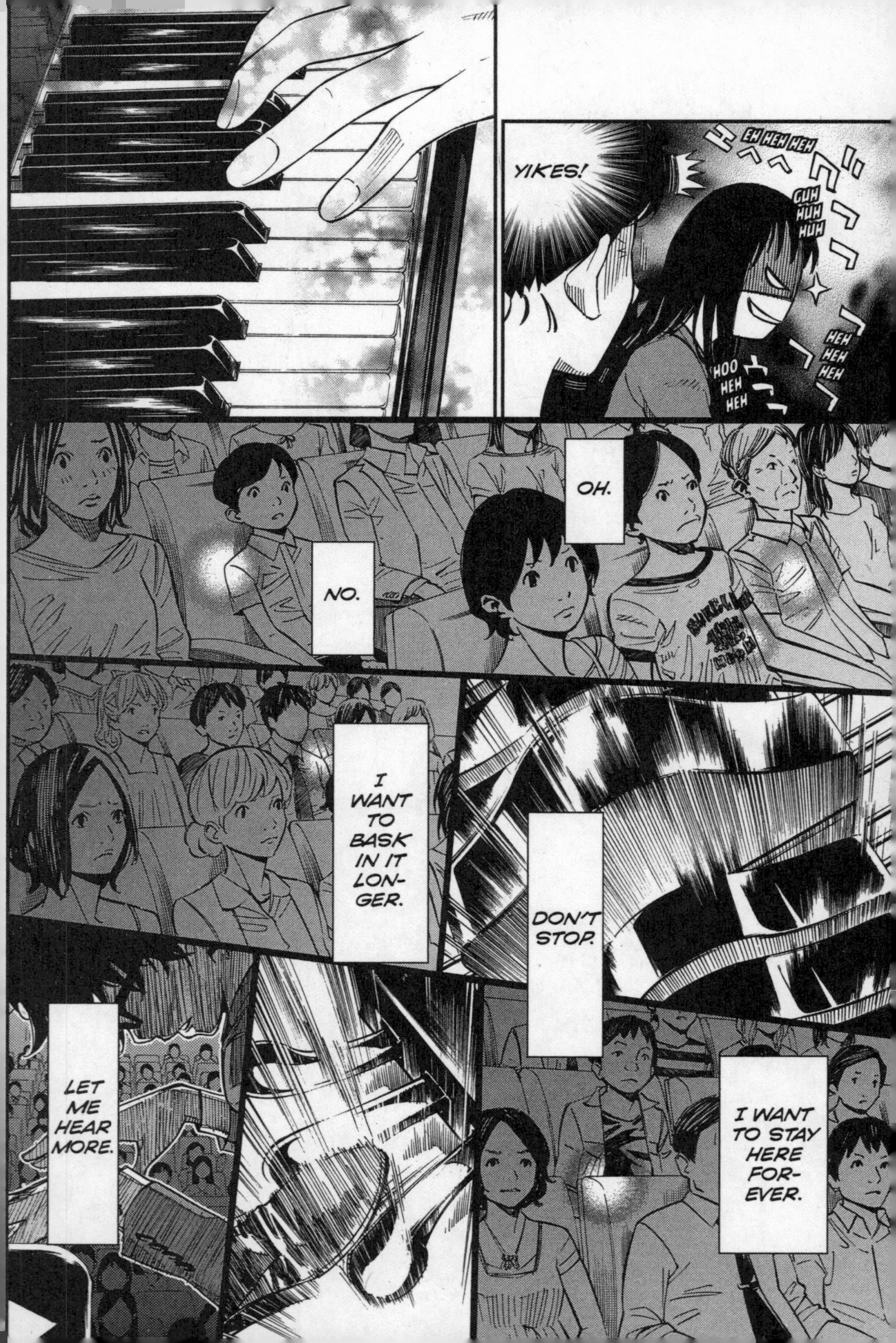

EH HEH HEH
GUH HUH HUH
YIKES!
HEH HEH HEH
HOO HEH HEH
OH.
NO.
DON'T STOP.
I WANT TO BASK IN IT LONGER.
I WANT TO STAY HERE FOREVER.
LET ME HEAR MORE.

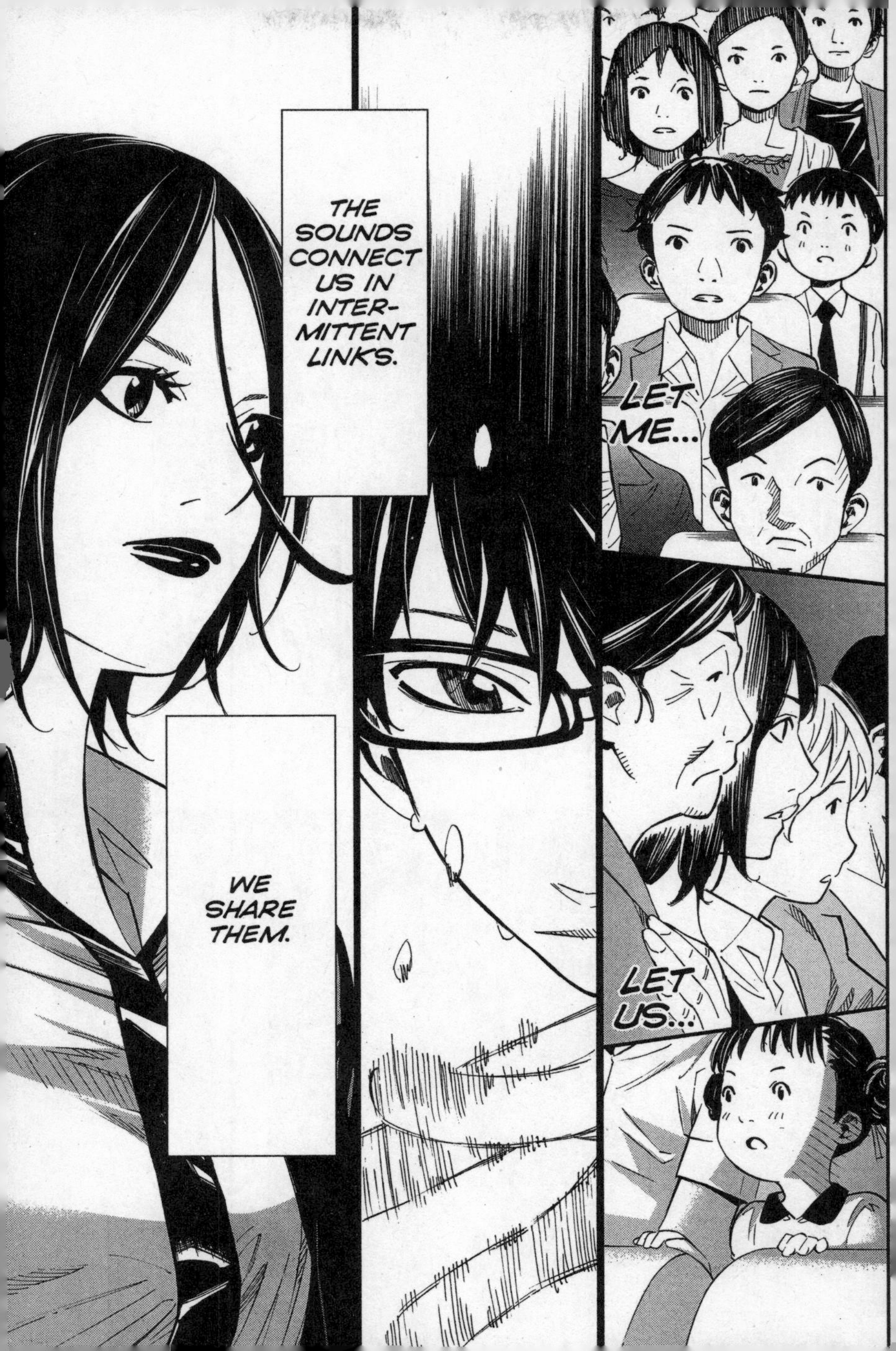
LET ME...
LET US...
THE SOUNDS CONNECT US IN INTER-MITTENT LINKS.
WE SHARE THEM.

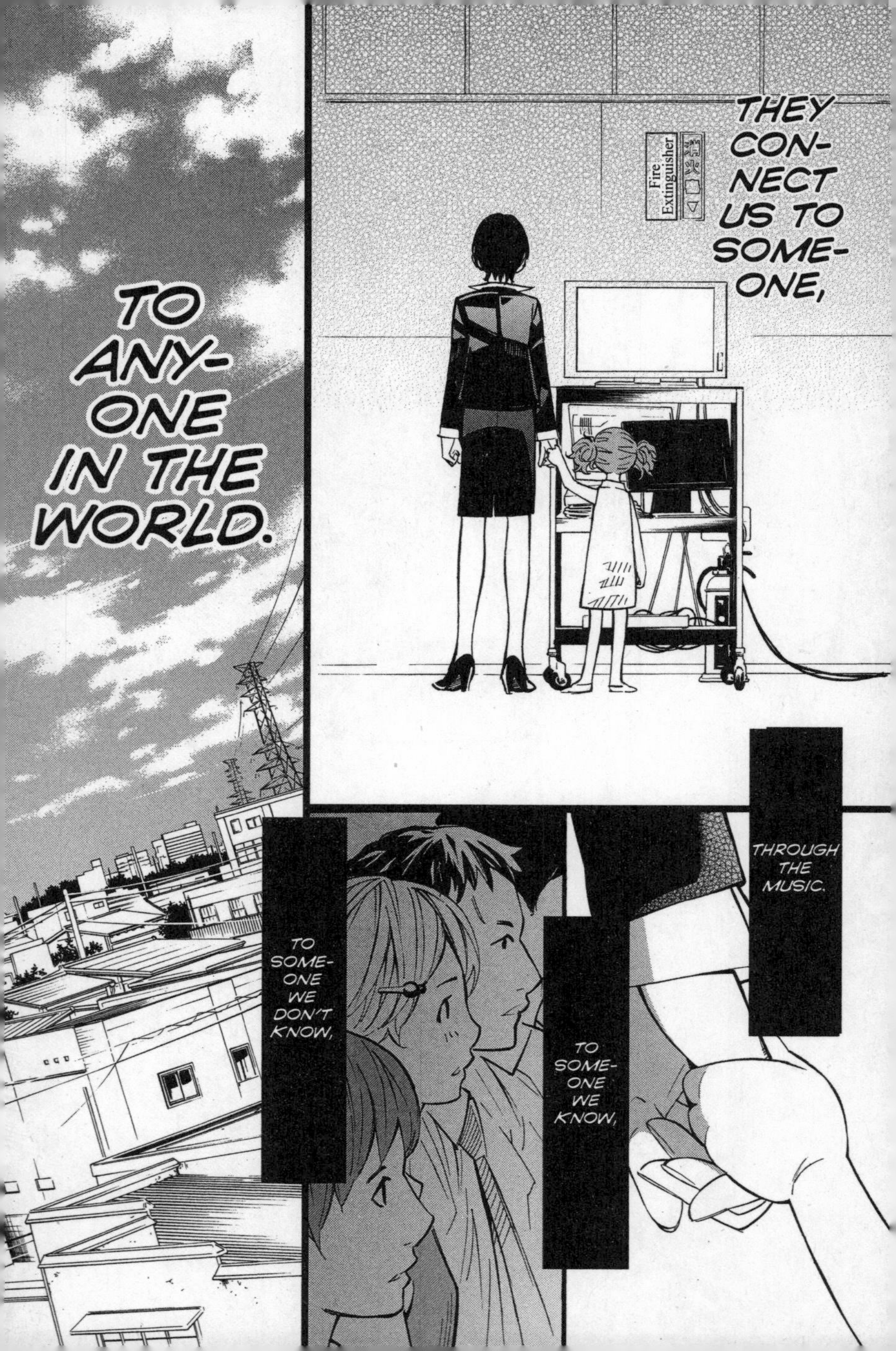
Fire Extinguisher
THEY CONNECT US TO SOMEONE,
THROUGH THE MUSIC.
TO SOMEONE WE KNOW,
TO SOMEONE WE DON'T KNOW,
TO ANYONE IN THE WORLD.

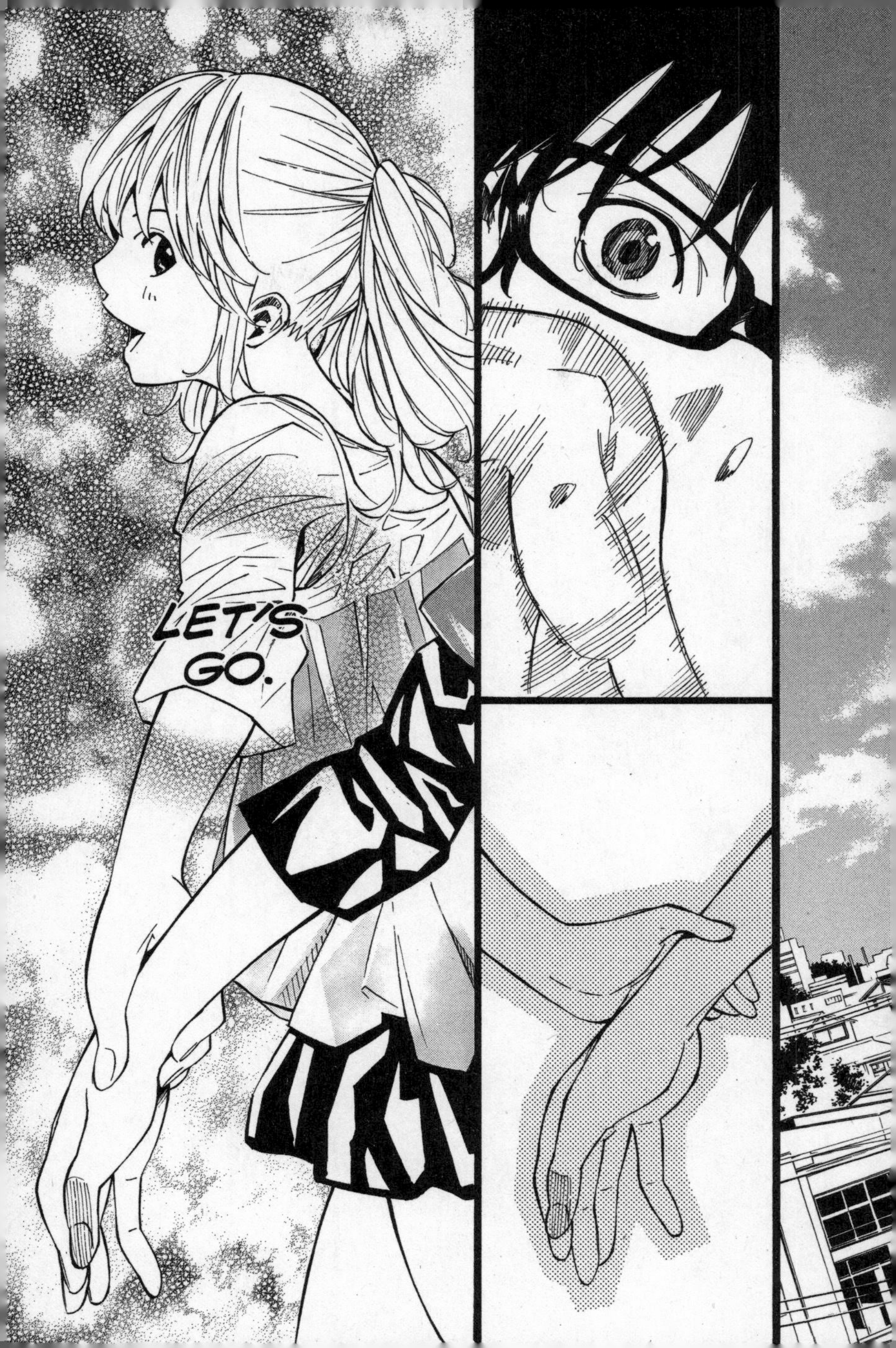
LET'S GO.

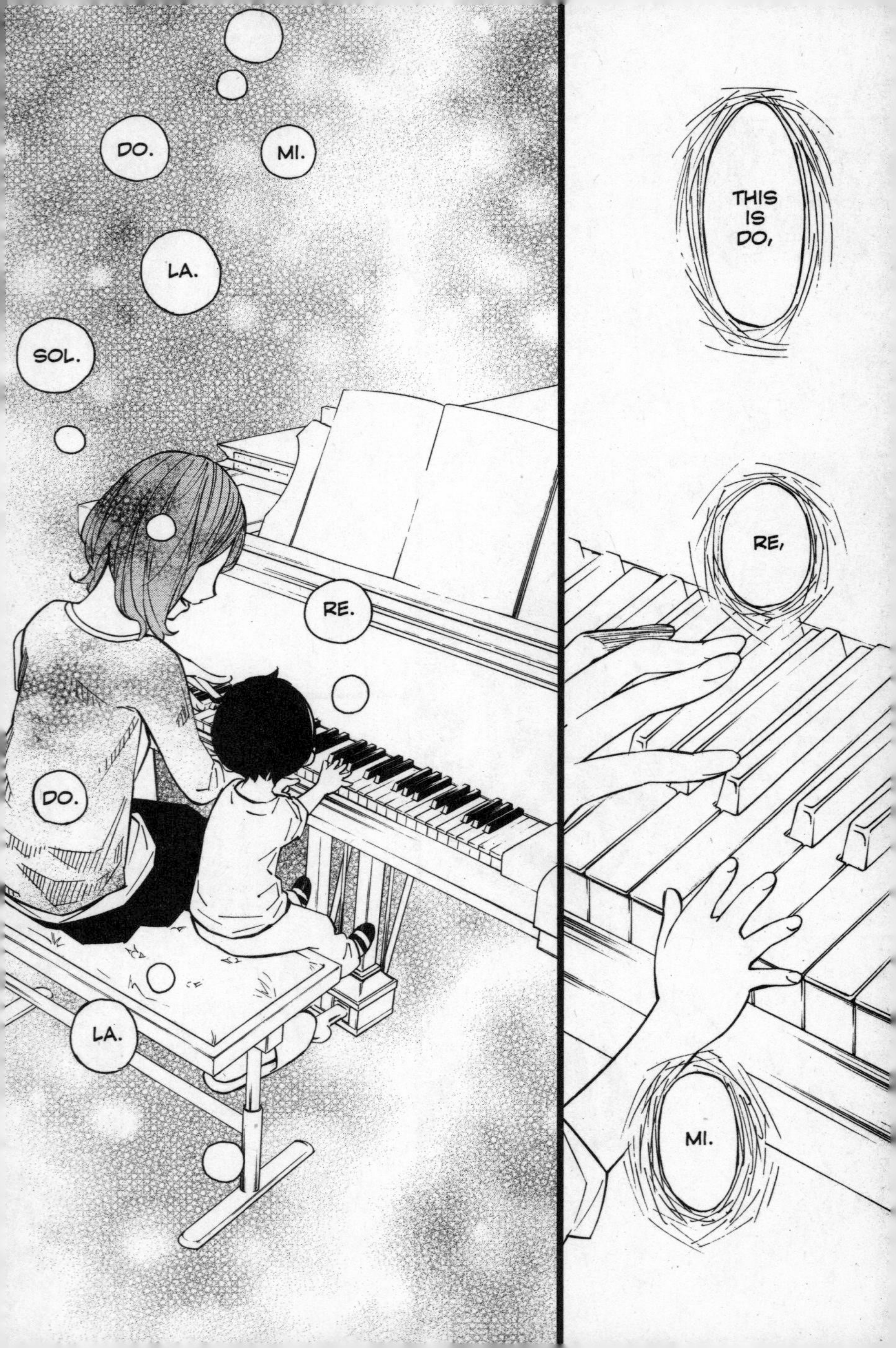
THIS IS DO,
RE,
MI.
MI.
DO.
LA.
SOL.
RE.
DO.
LA.

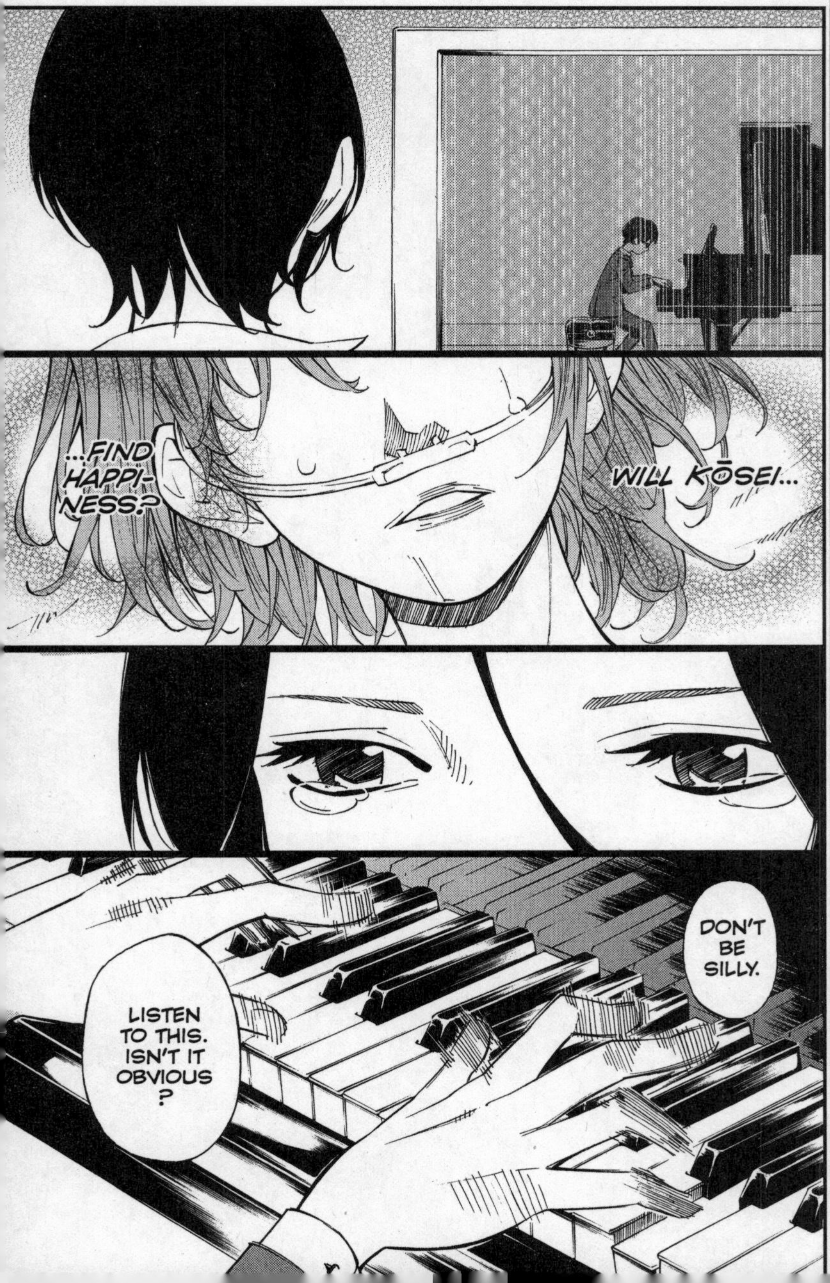

WILL KŌSEI...
...FIND HAPPI-NESS?
DON'T BE SILLY.
LISTEN TO THIS. ISN'T IT OBVIOUS?

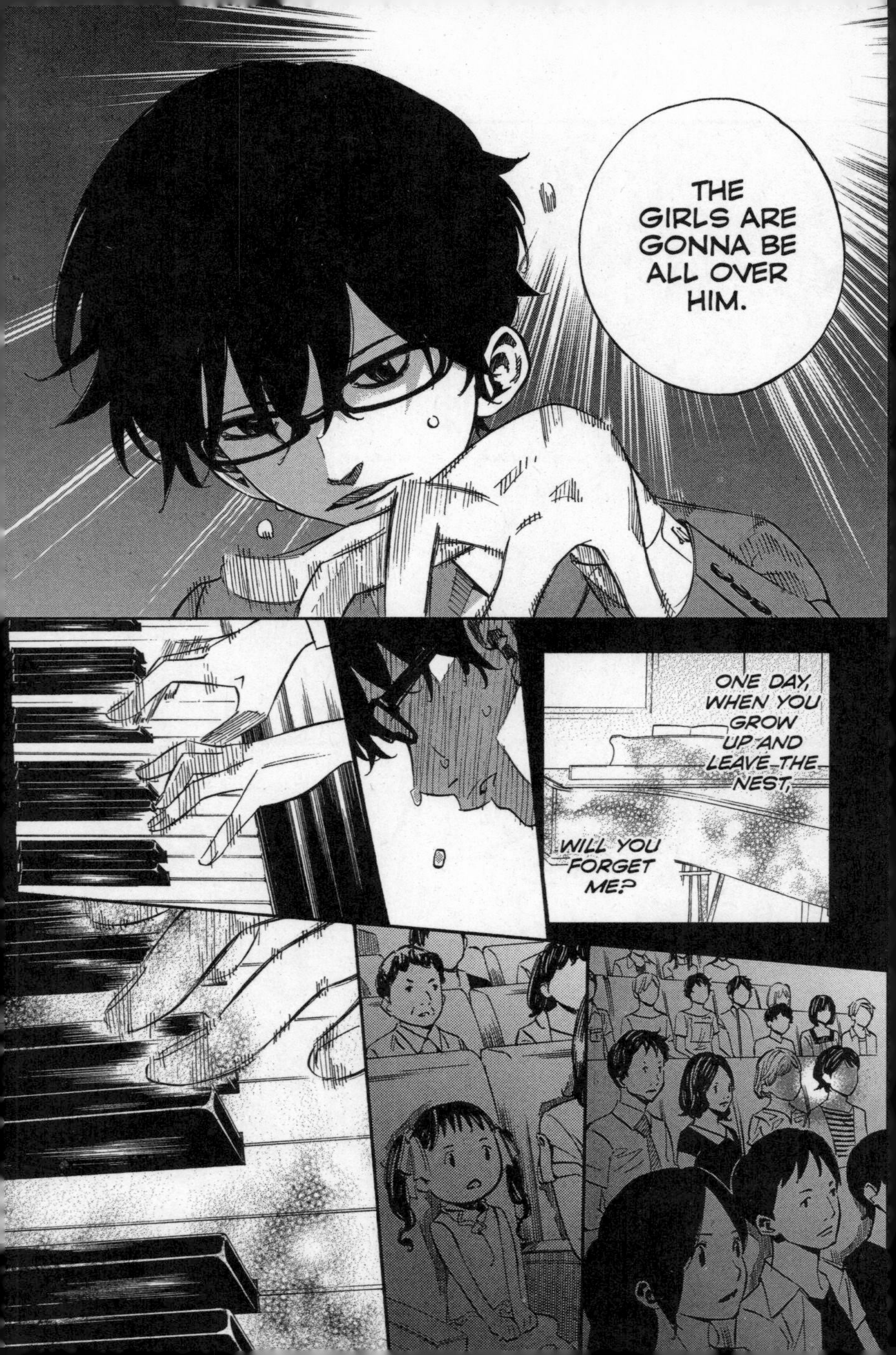
THE GIRLS ARE GONNA BE ALL OVER HIM.
ONE DAY, WHEN YOU GROW UP AND LEAVE THE NEST,
WILL YOU FORGET ME?

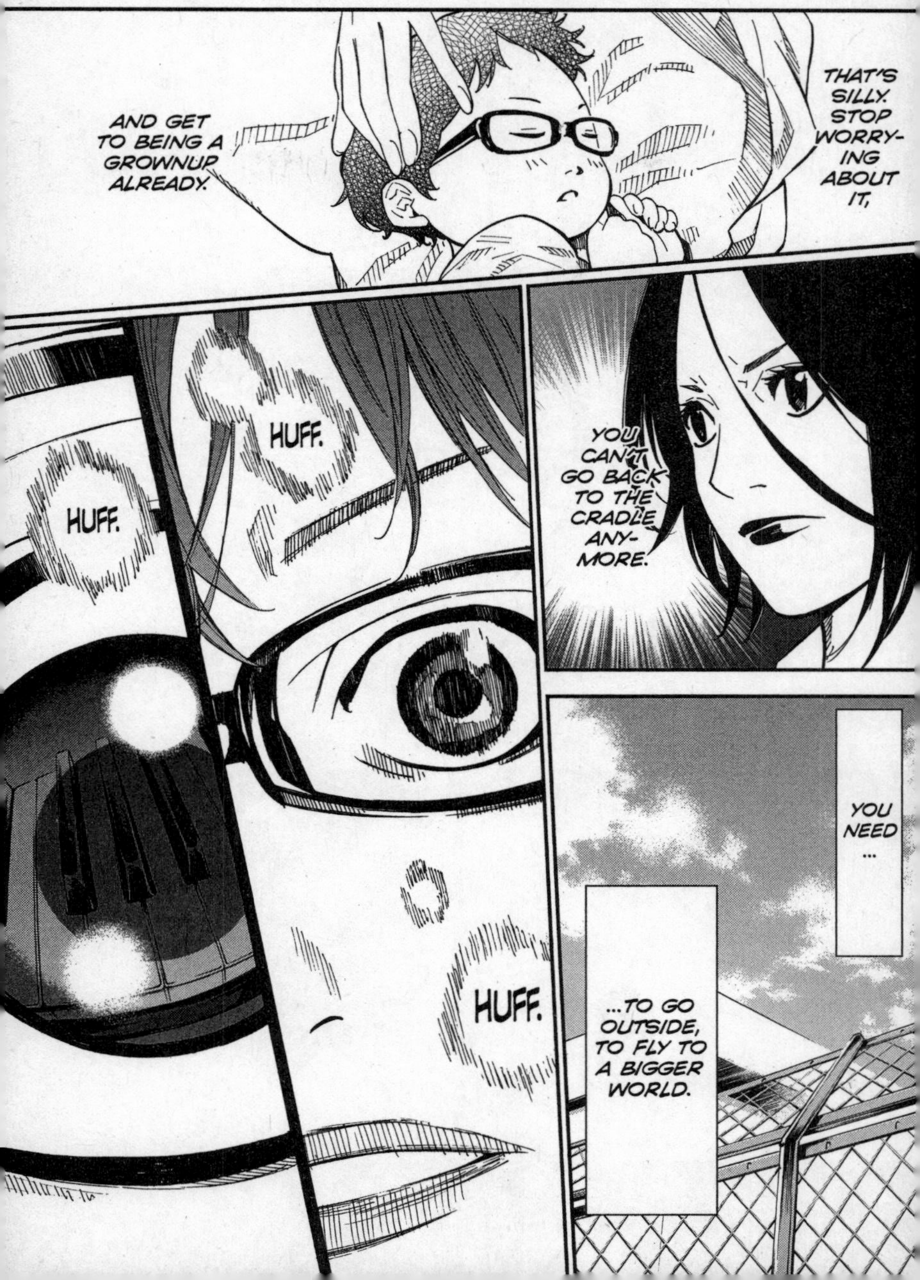
THAT'S SILLY. STOP WORRYING ABOUT IT,
AND GET TO BEING A GROWNUP ALREADY.
YOU CAN'T GO BACK TO THE CRADLE ANYMORE.
YOU NEED ...
...TO GO OUTSIDE, TO FLY TO A BIGGER WORLD.
HUFF.
HUFF.
HUFF.

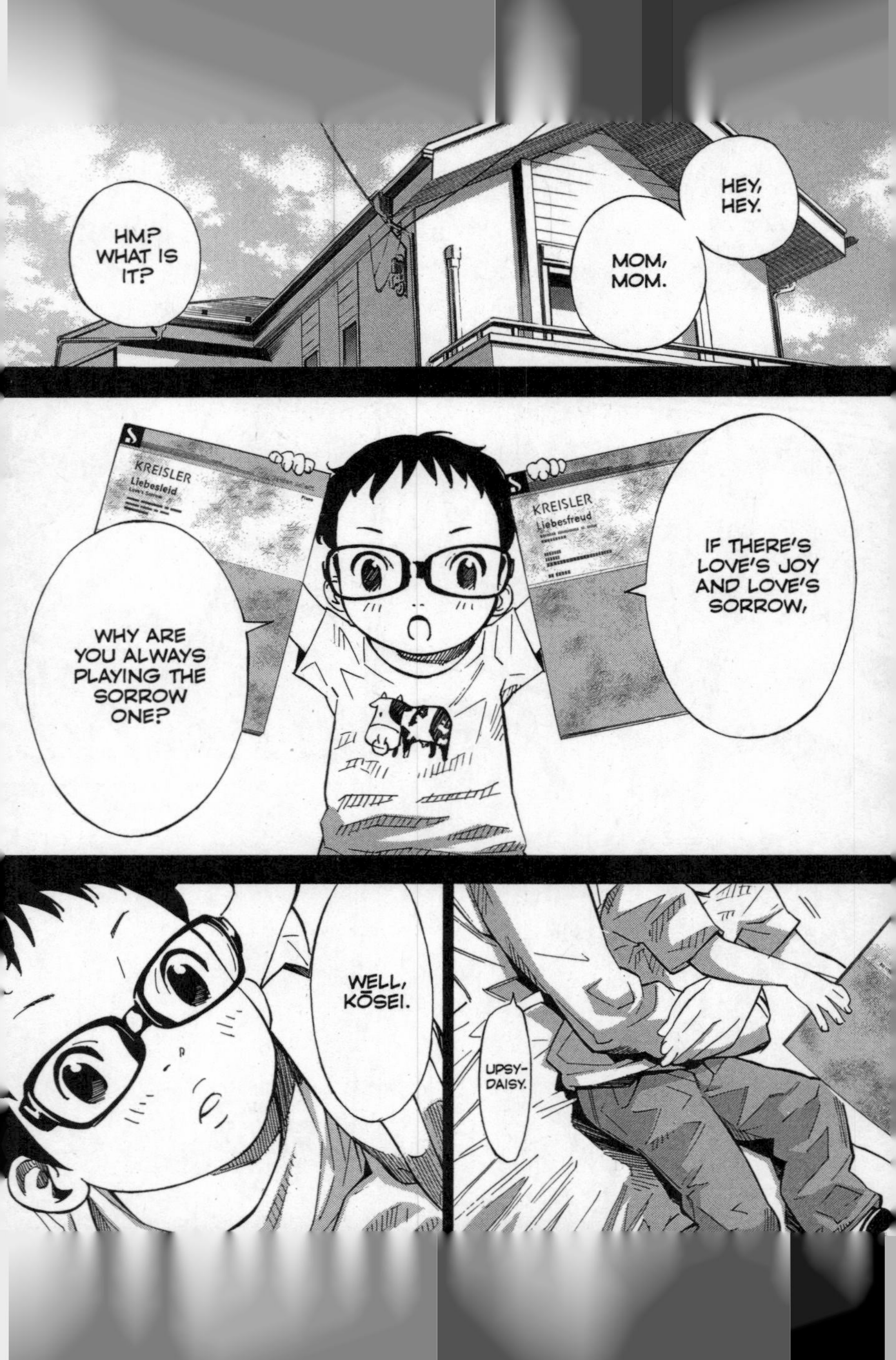
HEY, HEY.
MOM, MOM.
HM? WHAT IS IT?
KREISLER
Liebesfreud
IF THERE'S LOVE'S JOY AND LOVE'S SORROW,
KREISLER
Liebesleid
Love's Sorrow
WHY ARE YOU ALWAYS PLAYING THE SORROW ONE?
UPSY-DAISY.
WELL, KŌSEI.

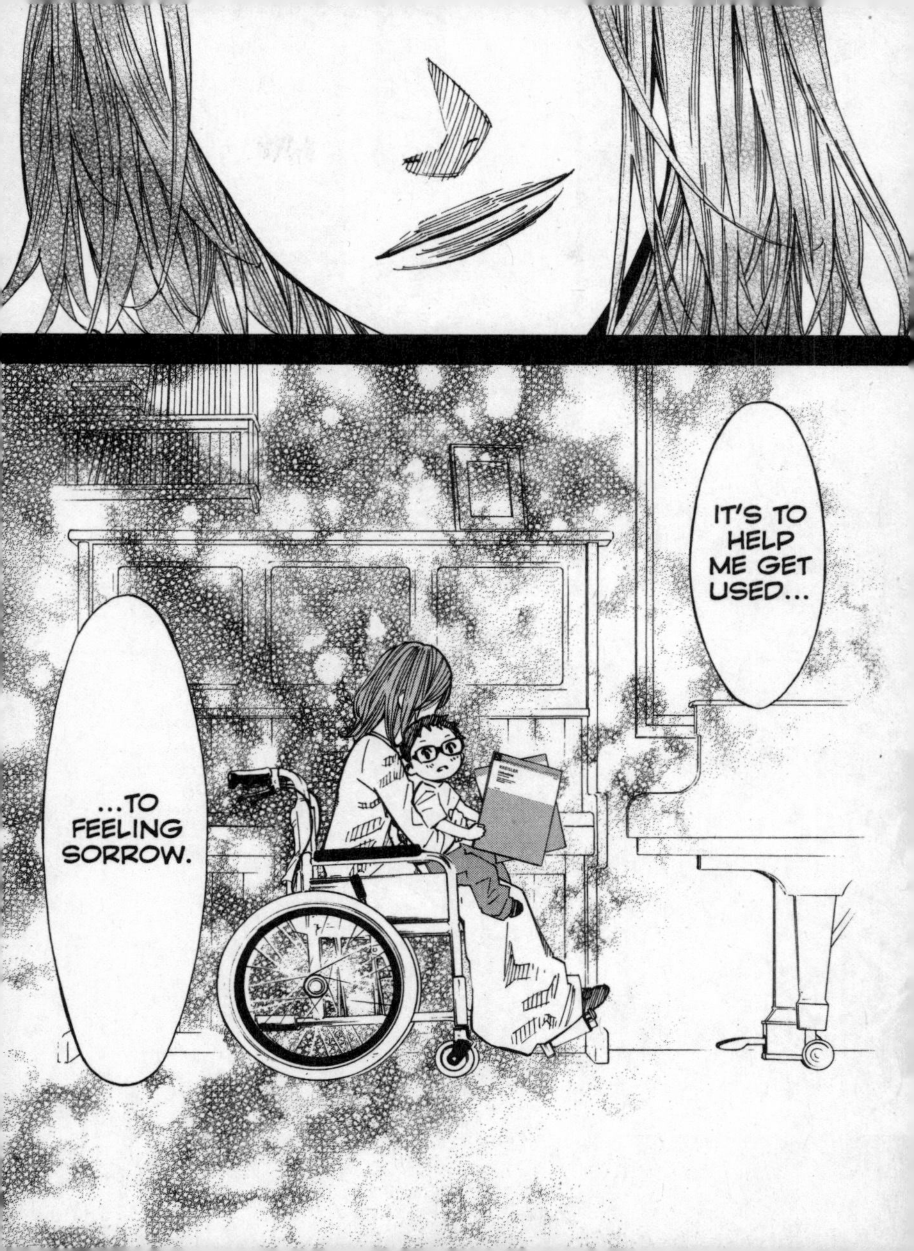
IT'S TO HELP ME GET USED...
...TO FEELING SORROW.

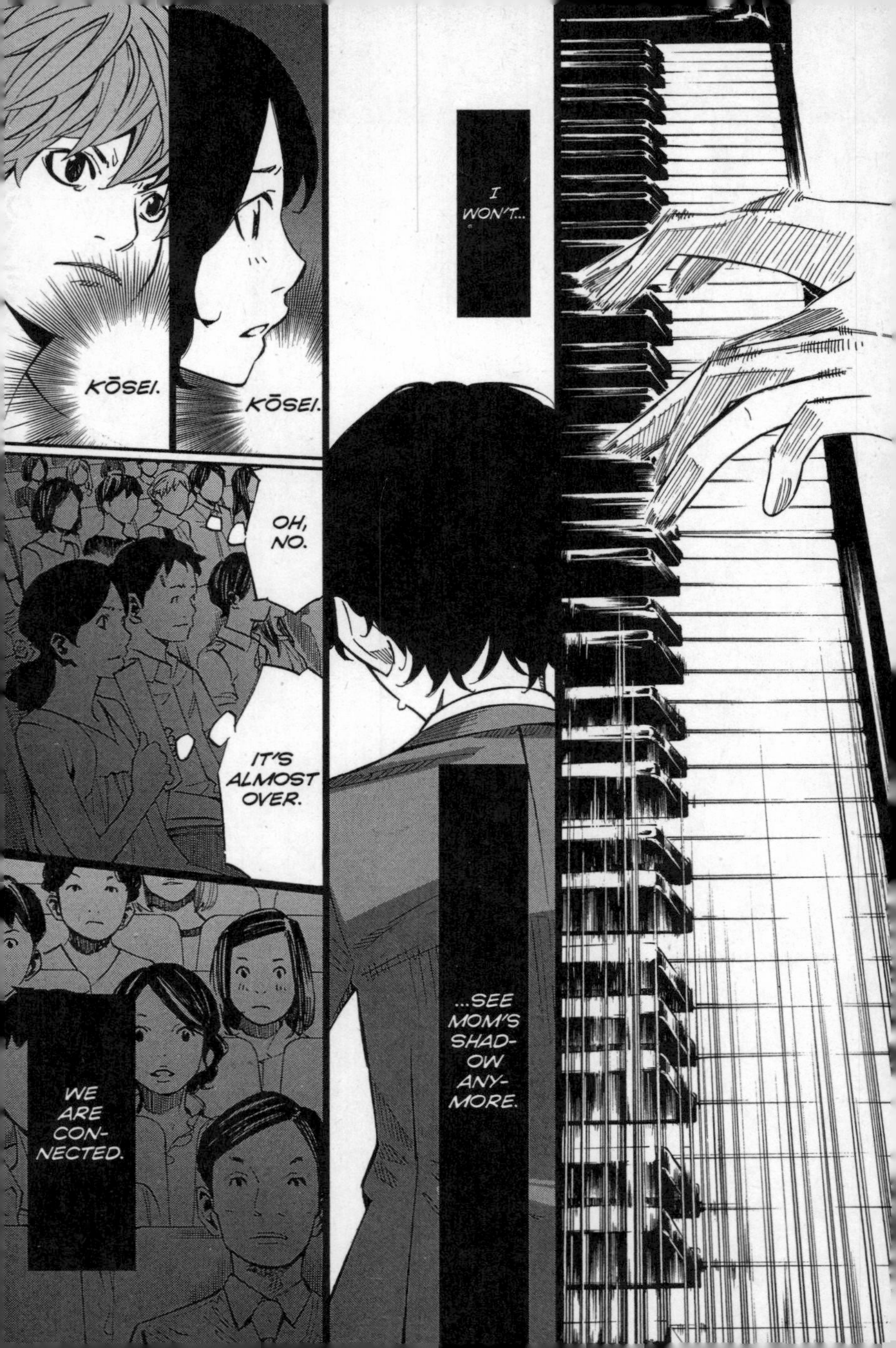
I WON'T...
...SEE MOM'S SHADOW ANYMORE.
KŌSEI.
KŌSEI.
OH, NO.
IT'S ALMOST OVER.
WE ARE CONNECTED.

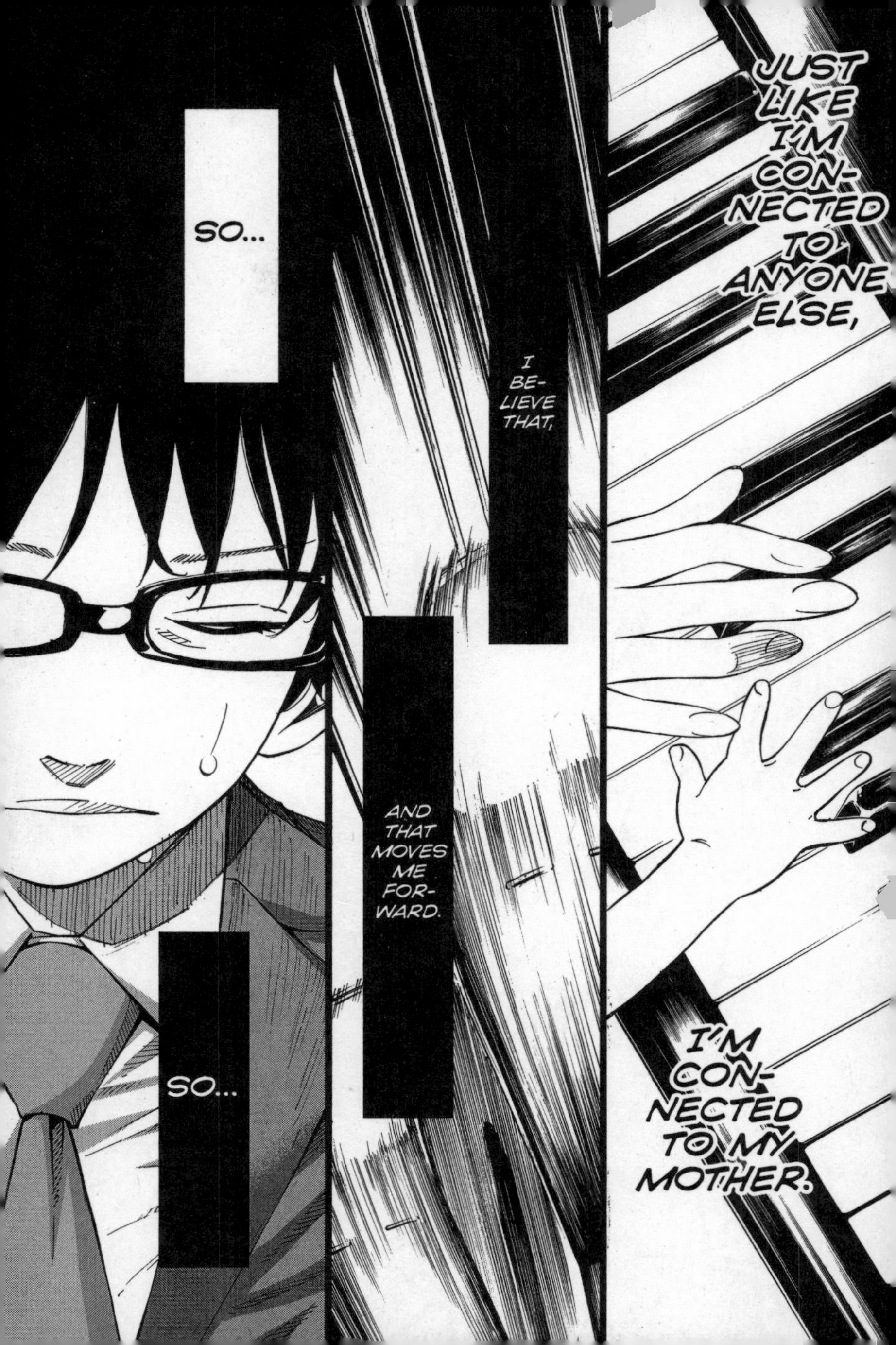
JUST LIKE I'M CONNECTED TO ANYONE ELSE,
I'M CONNECTED TO MY MOTHER.
I BELIEVE THAT,
AND THAT MOVES ME FORWARD.
SO...
SO...

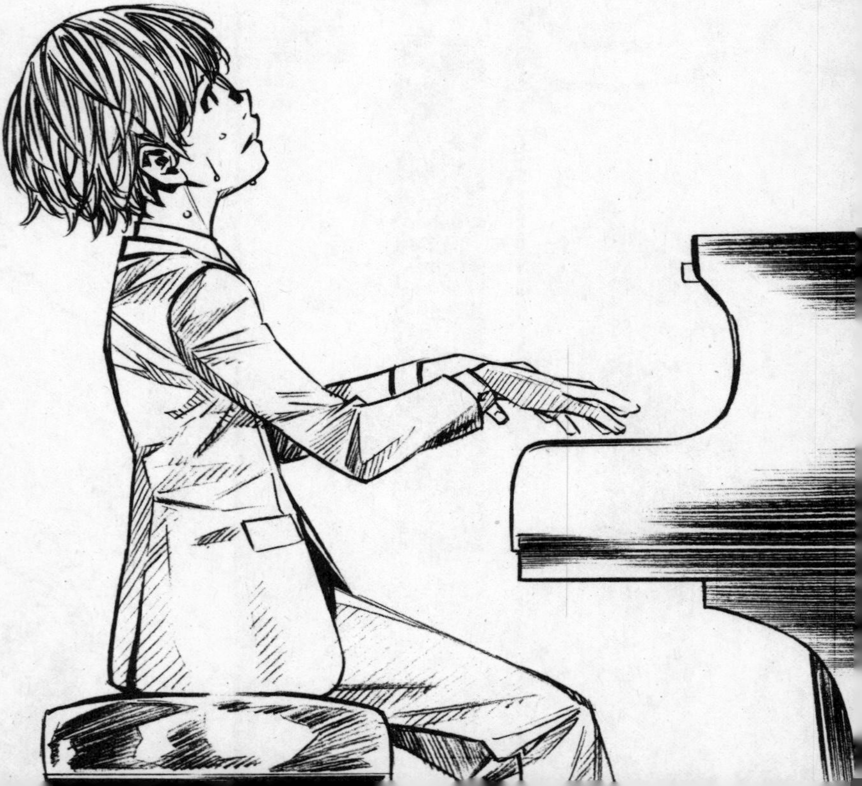

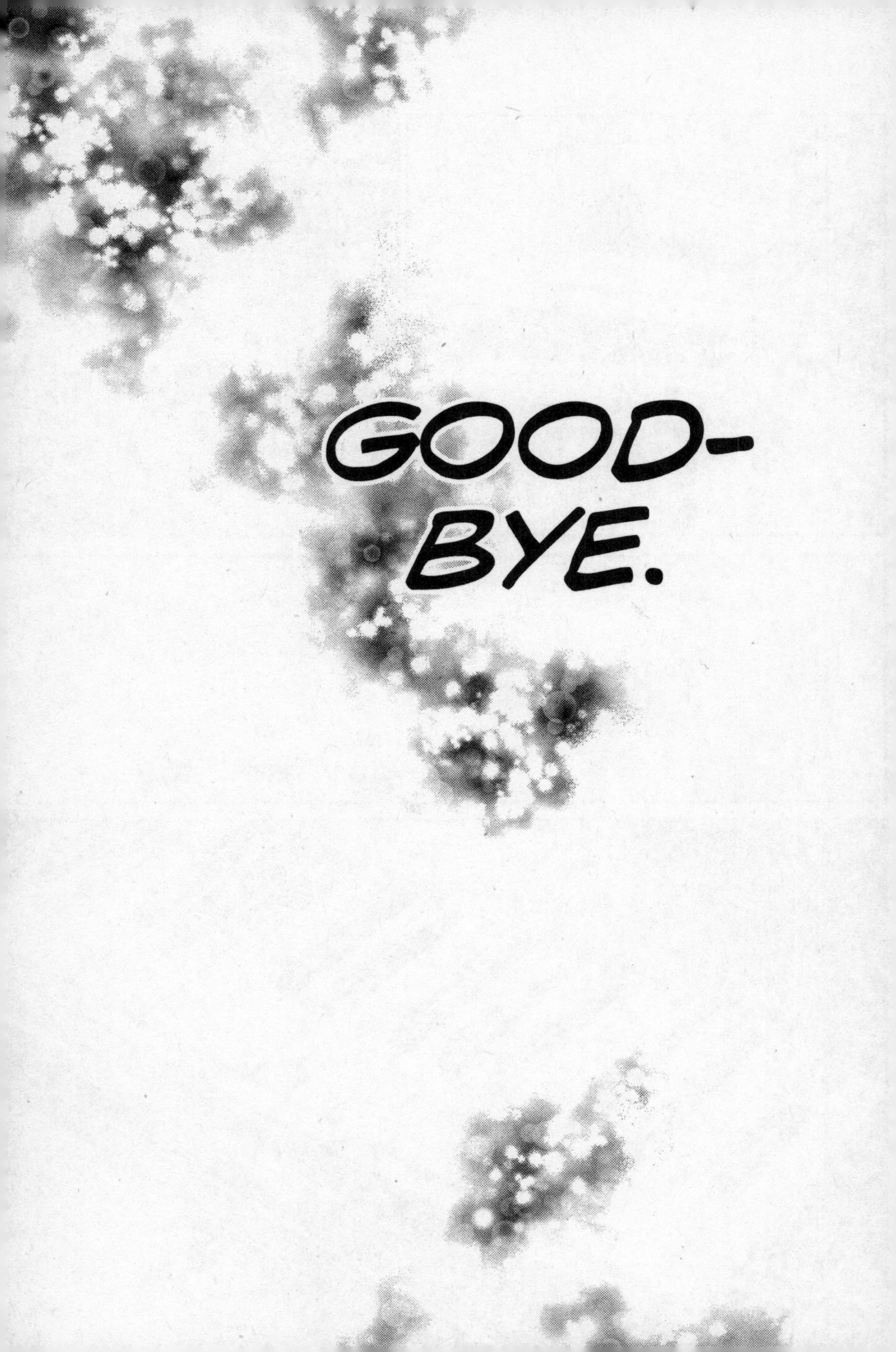
GOOD-BYE.

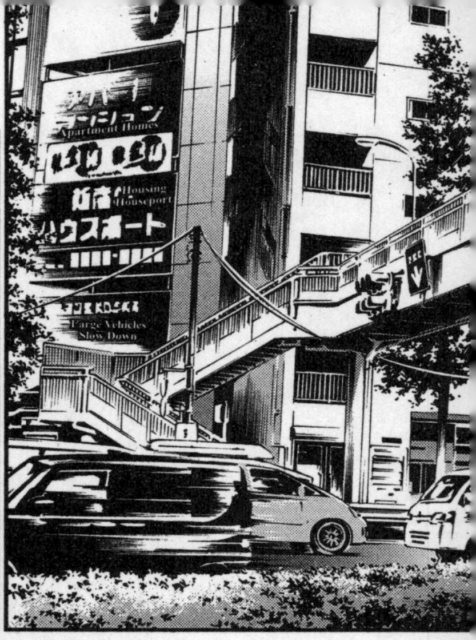
Apartment Homes
Housing
Houseport
ハウスオート
Large Vehicles
Slow Down
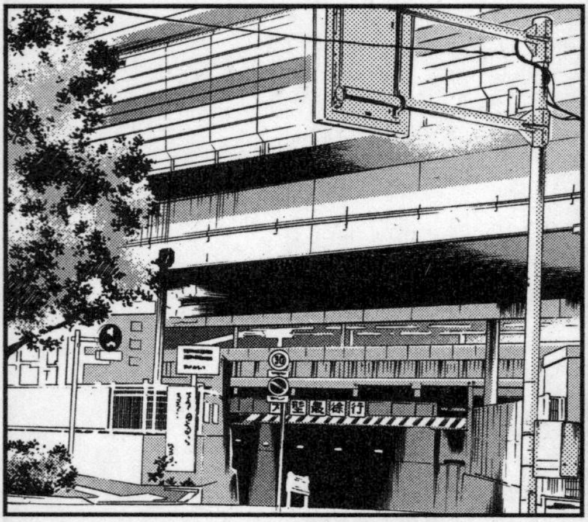
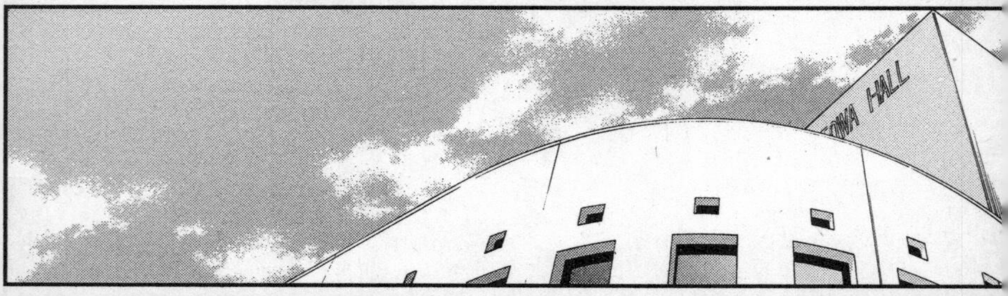
HALL
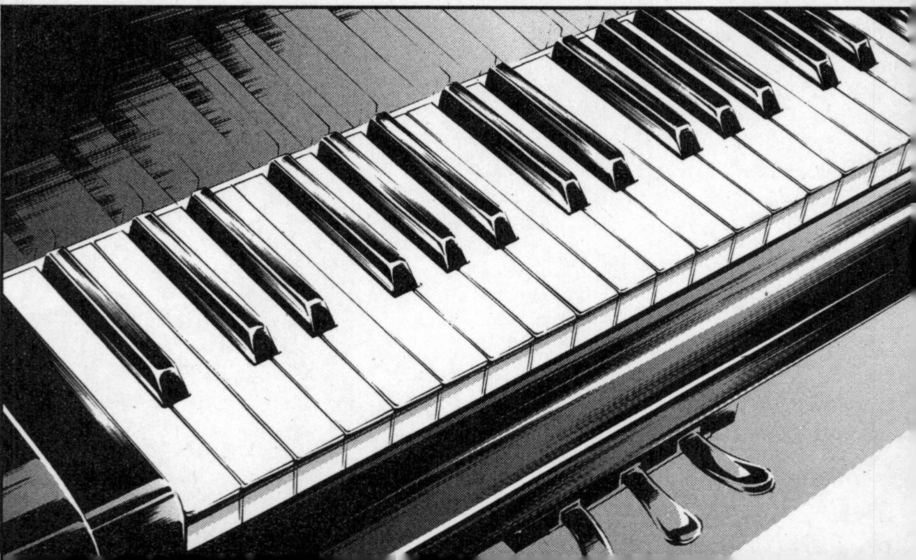

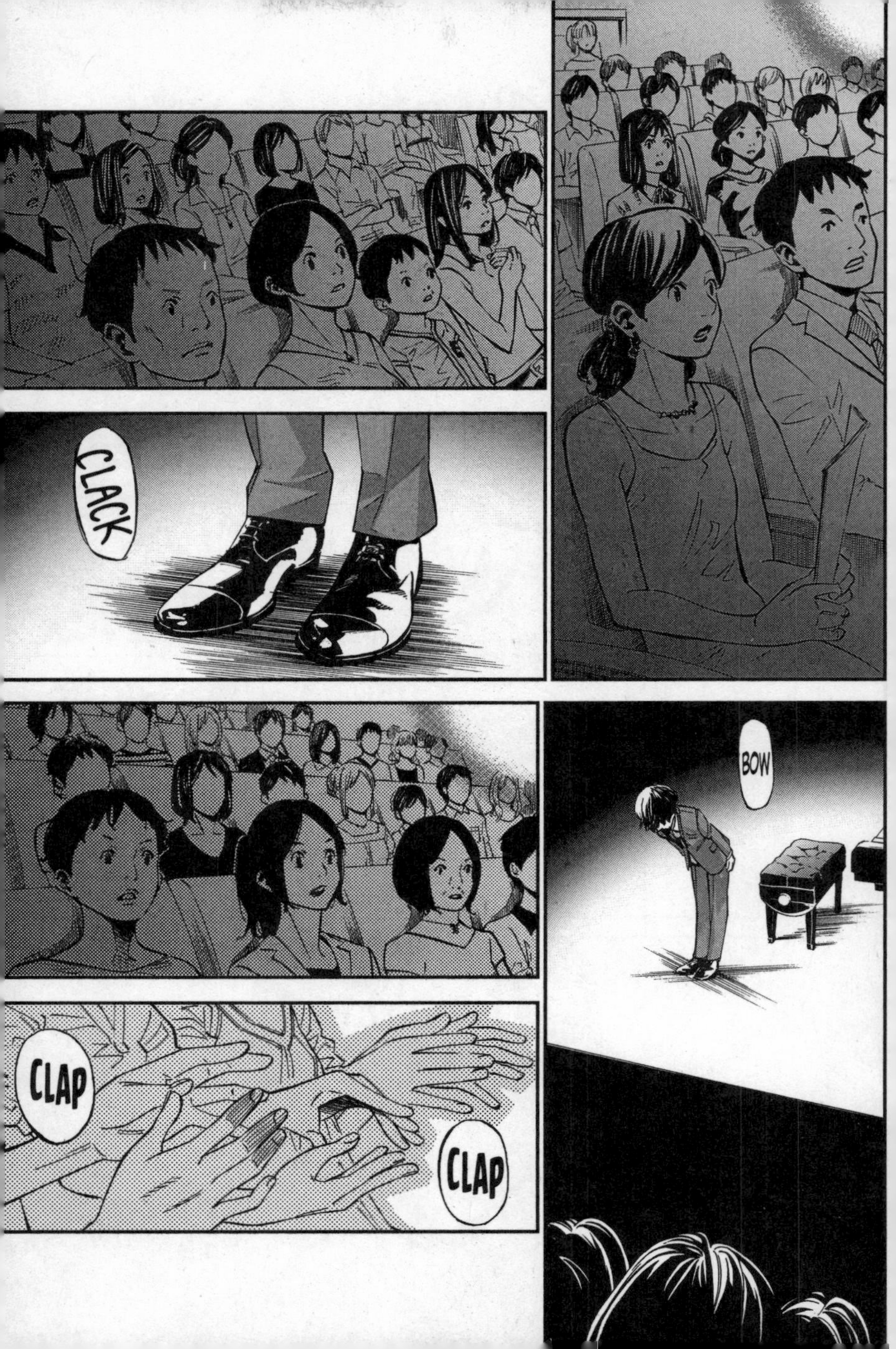
CLACK
BOW
CLAP
CLAP

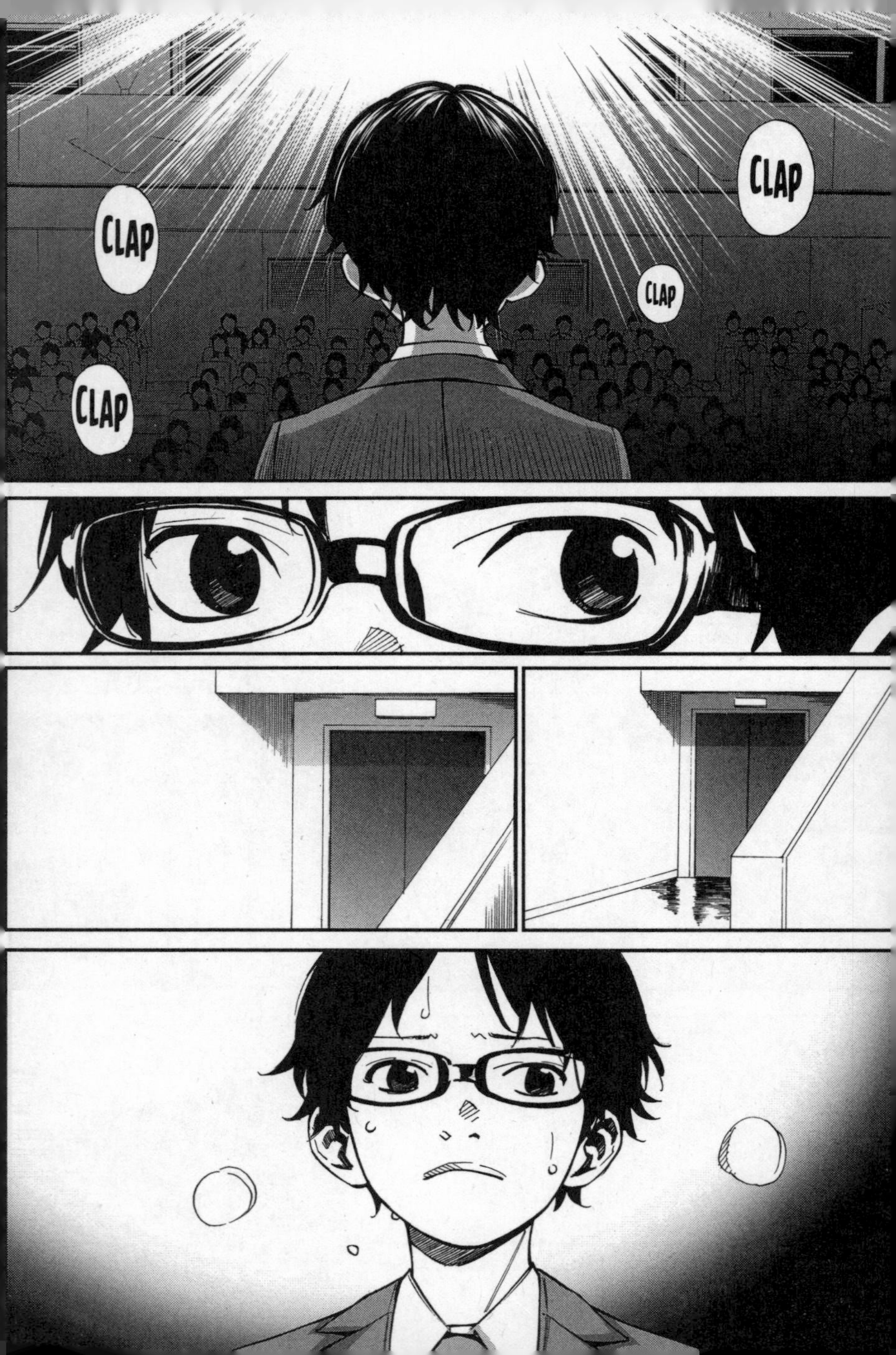
CLAP
CLAP
CLAP
CLAP

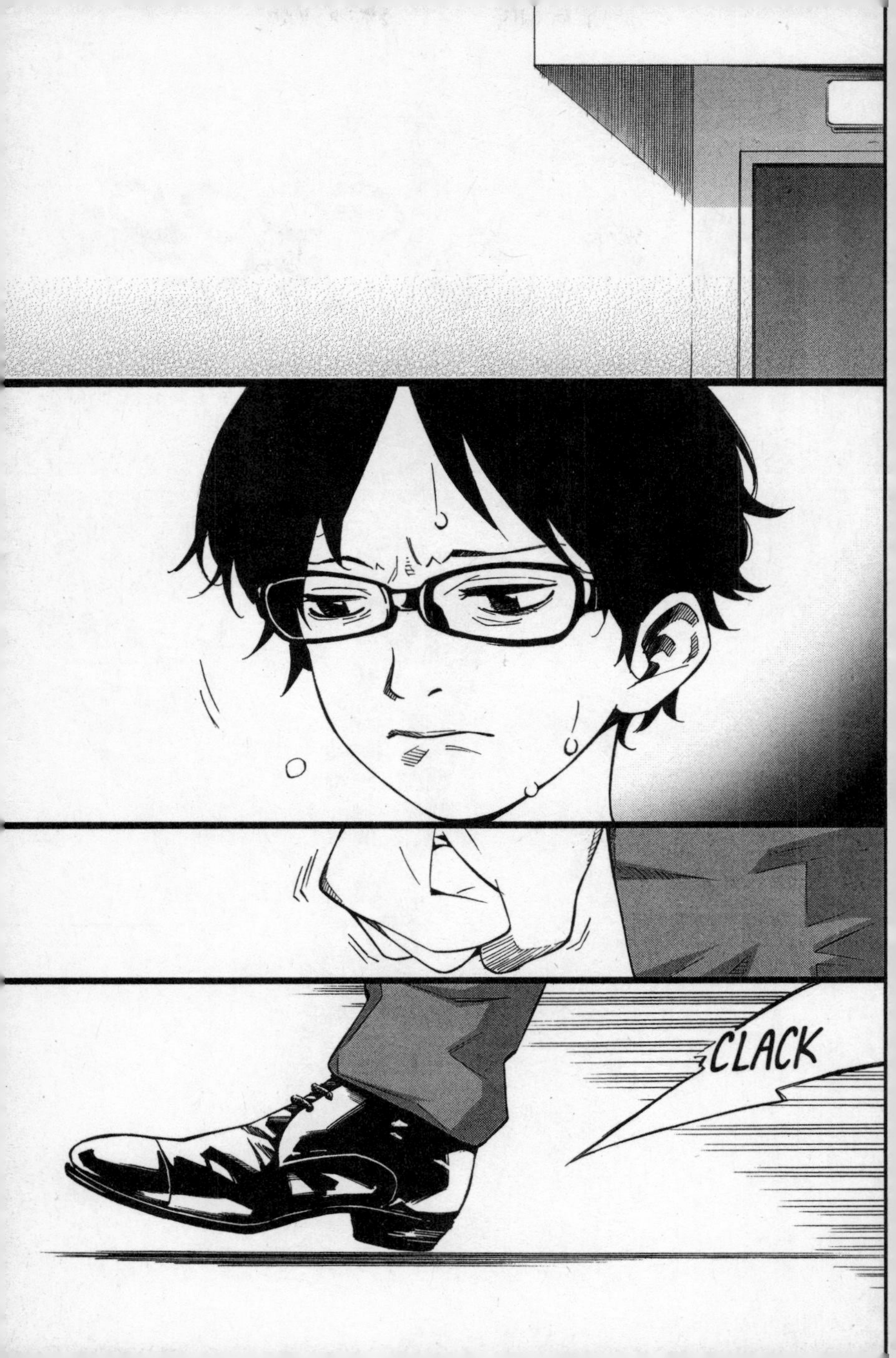
CLACK

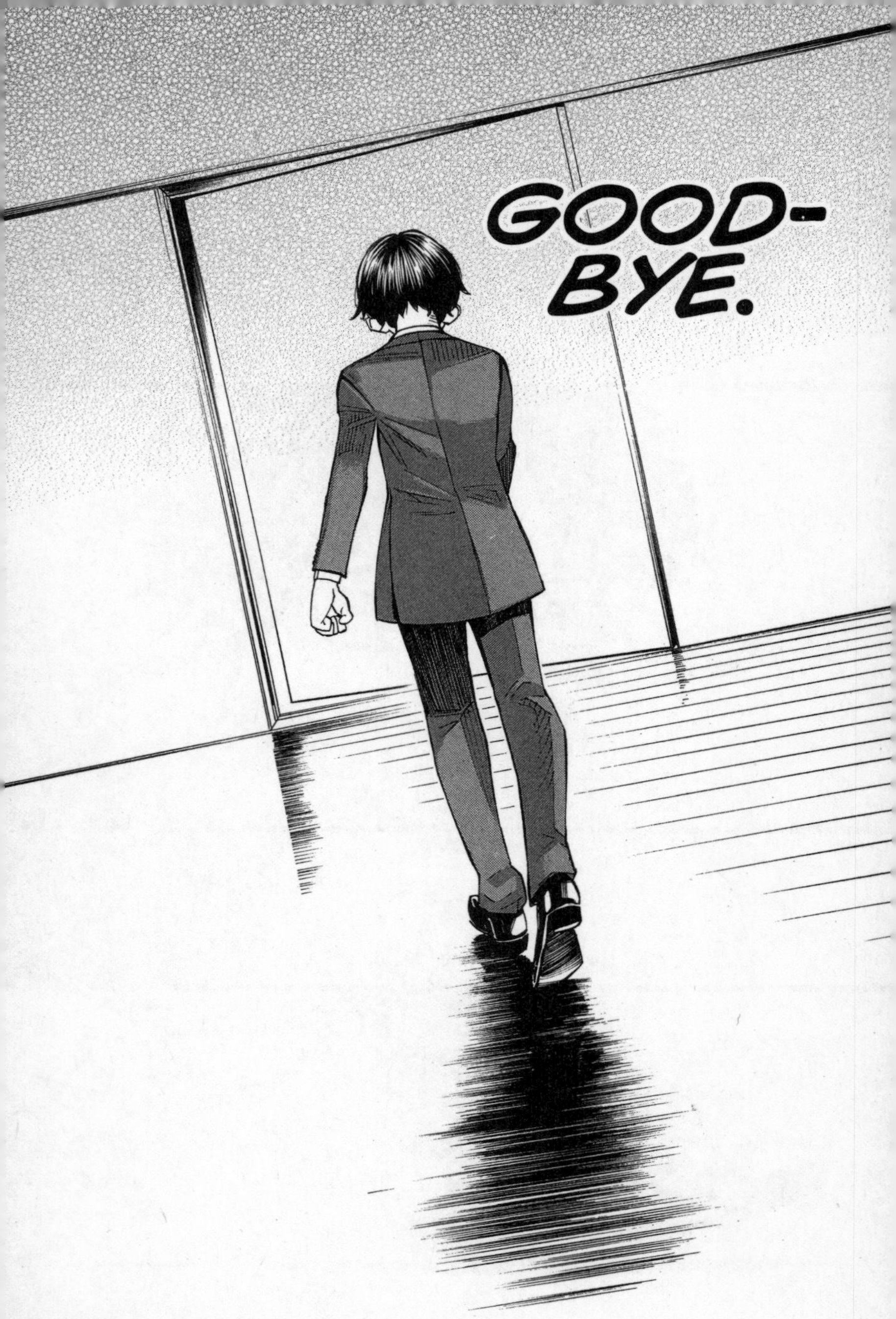
GOOD-BYE.

CONNECTION / END

Your Lie in April

I met the girl under full-bloomed cherry blossoms, and my fate has begun to change.

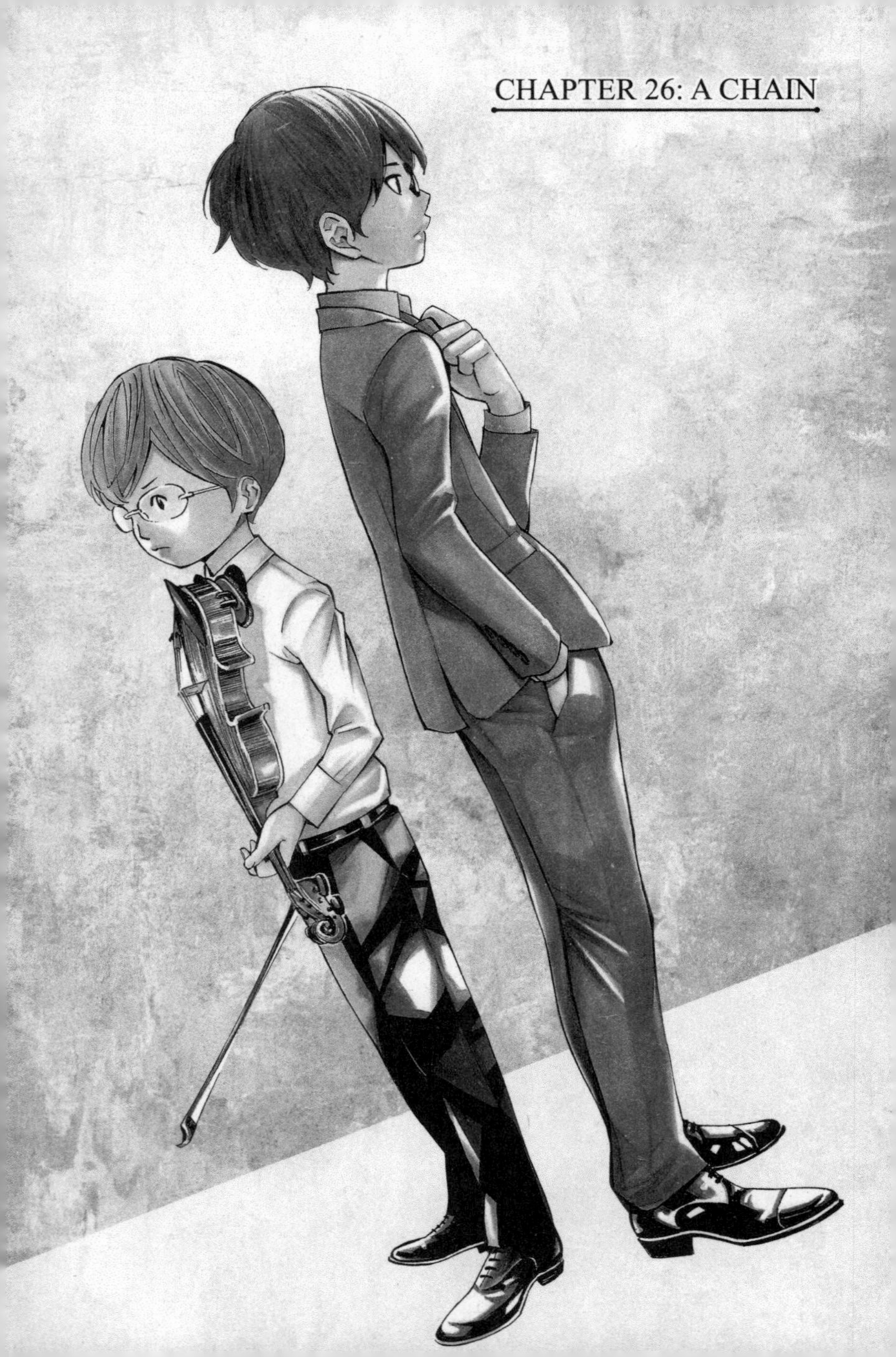
CHAPTER 26: A CHAIN

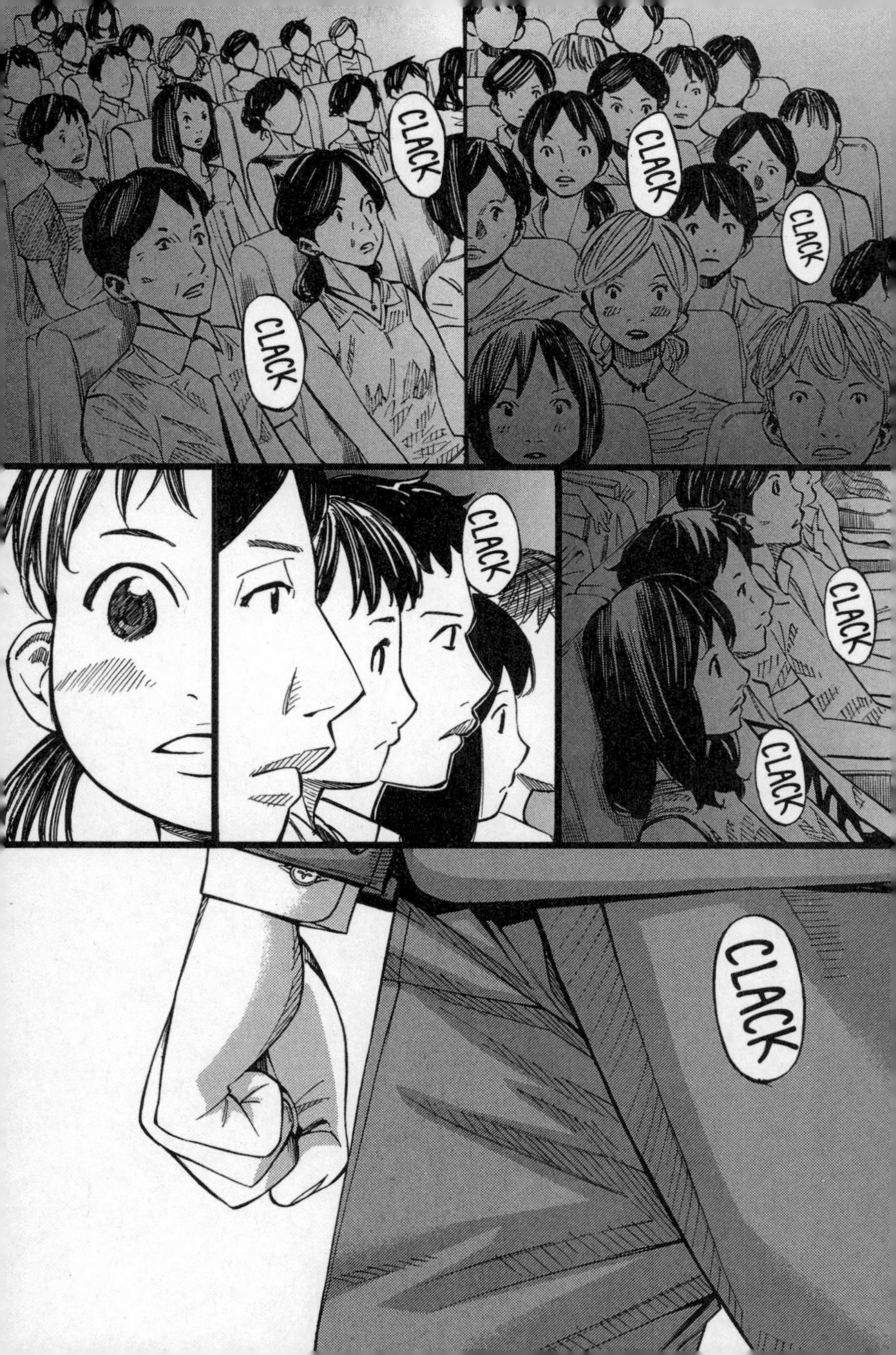
CLACK
CLACK
CLACK
CLACK
CLACK
CLACK
CLACK
CLACK

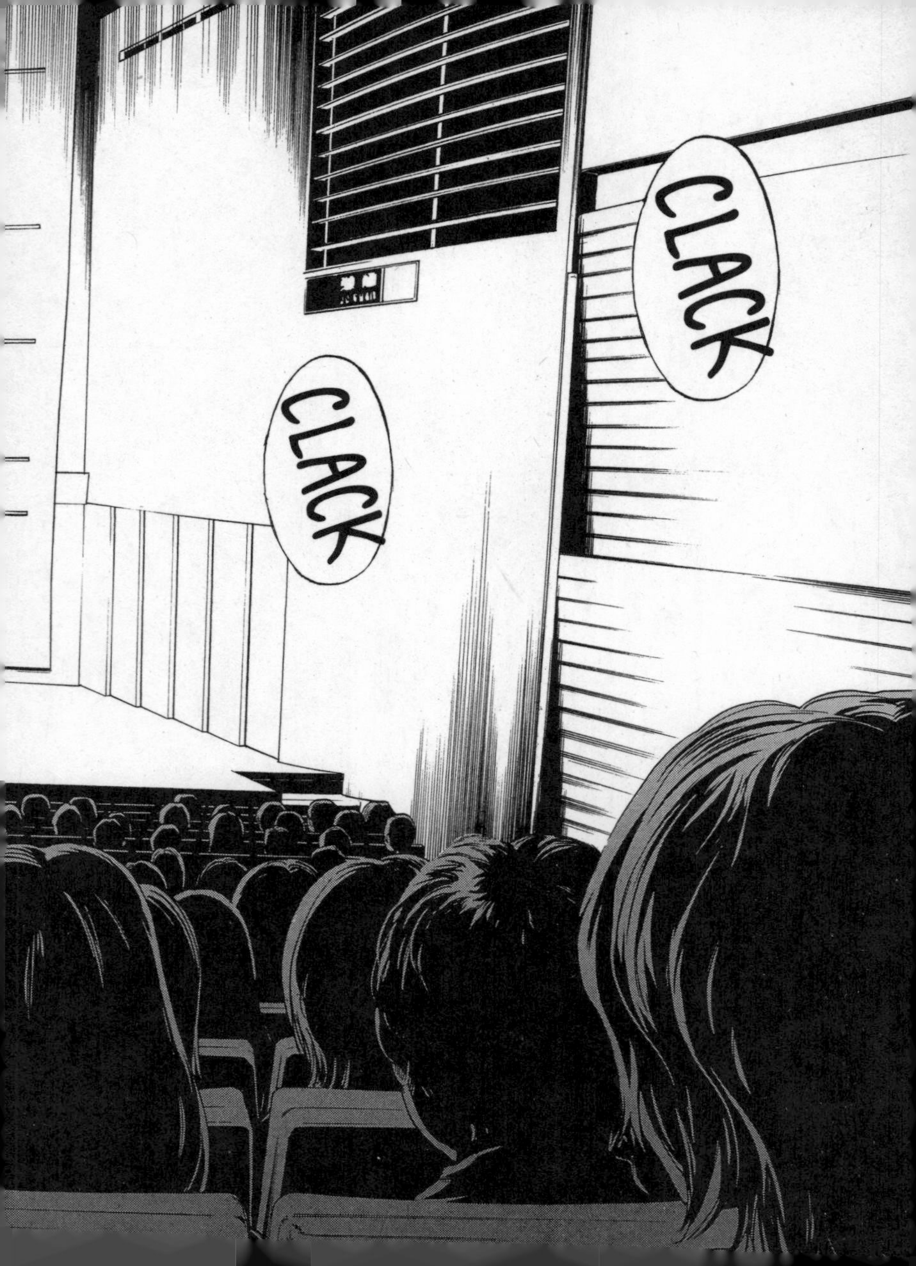
CLACK
CLACK

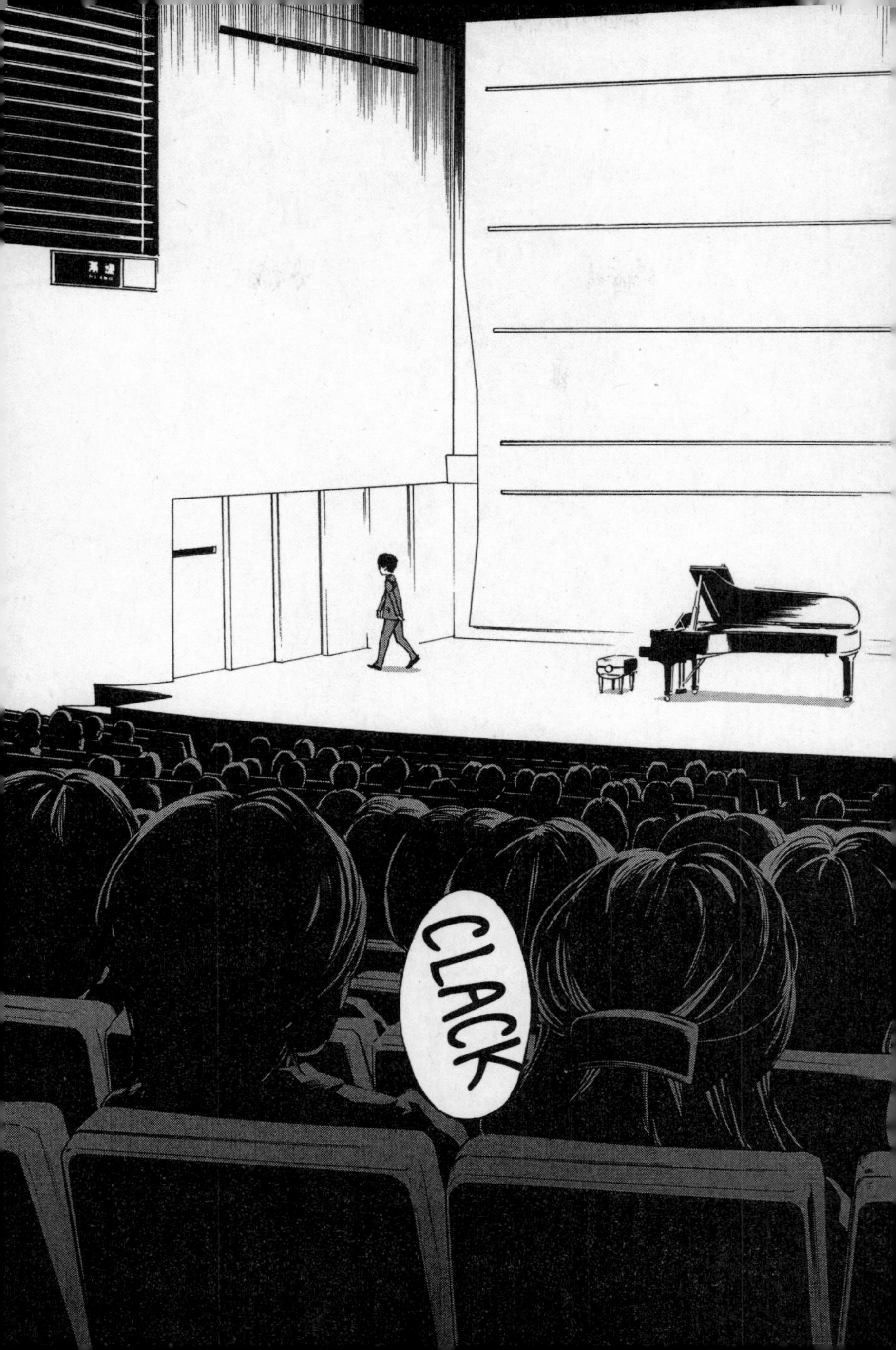
CLACK

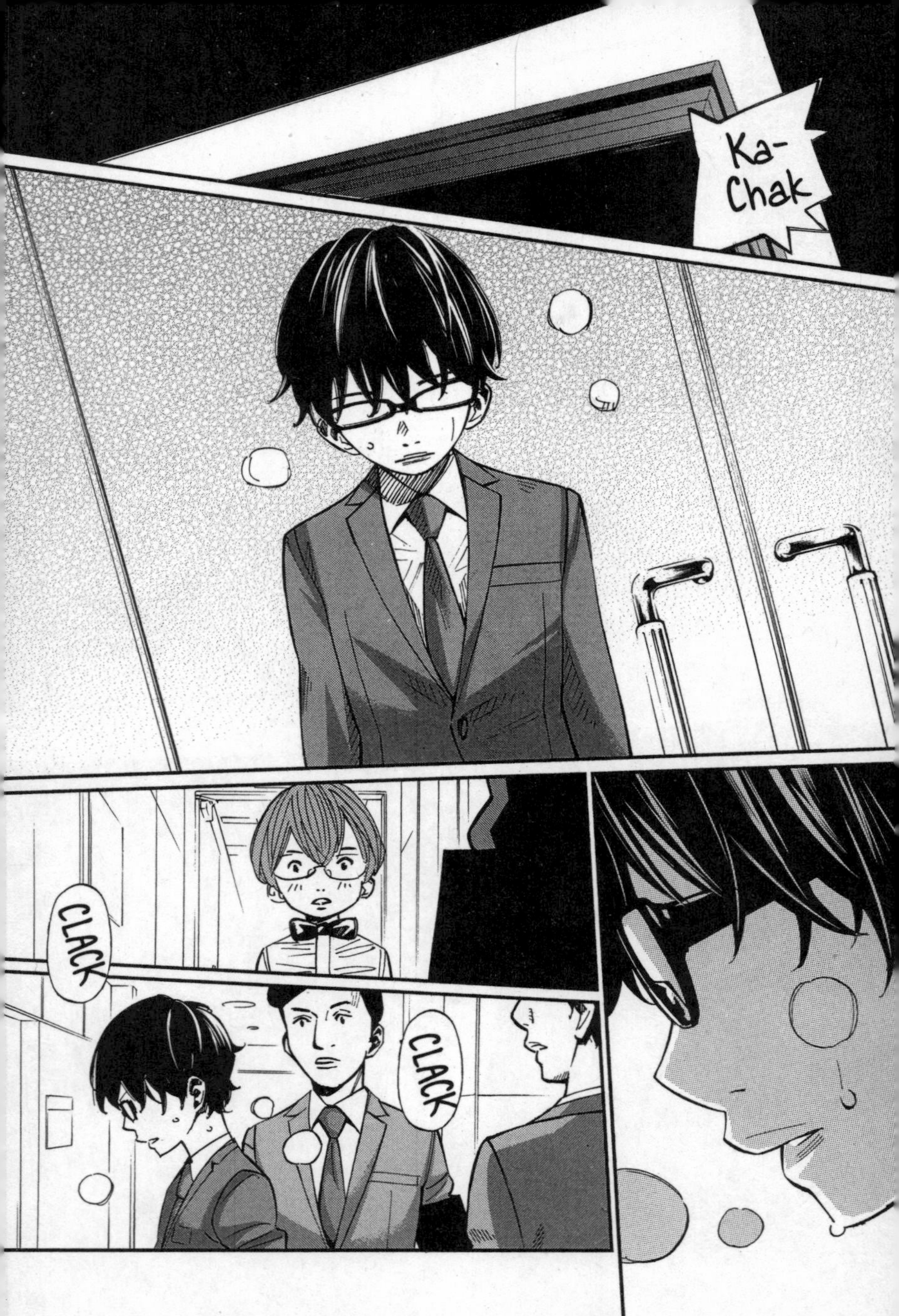
Ka-Chak
CLACK
CLACK

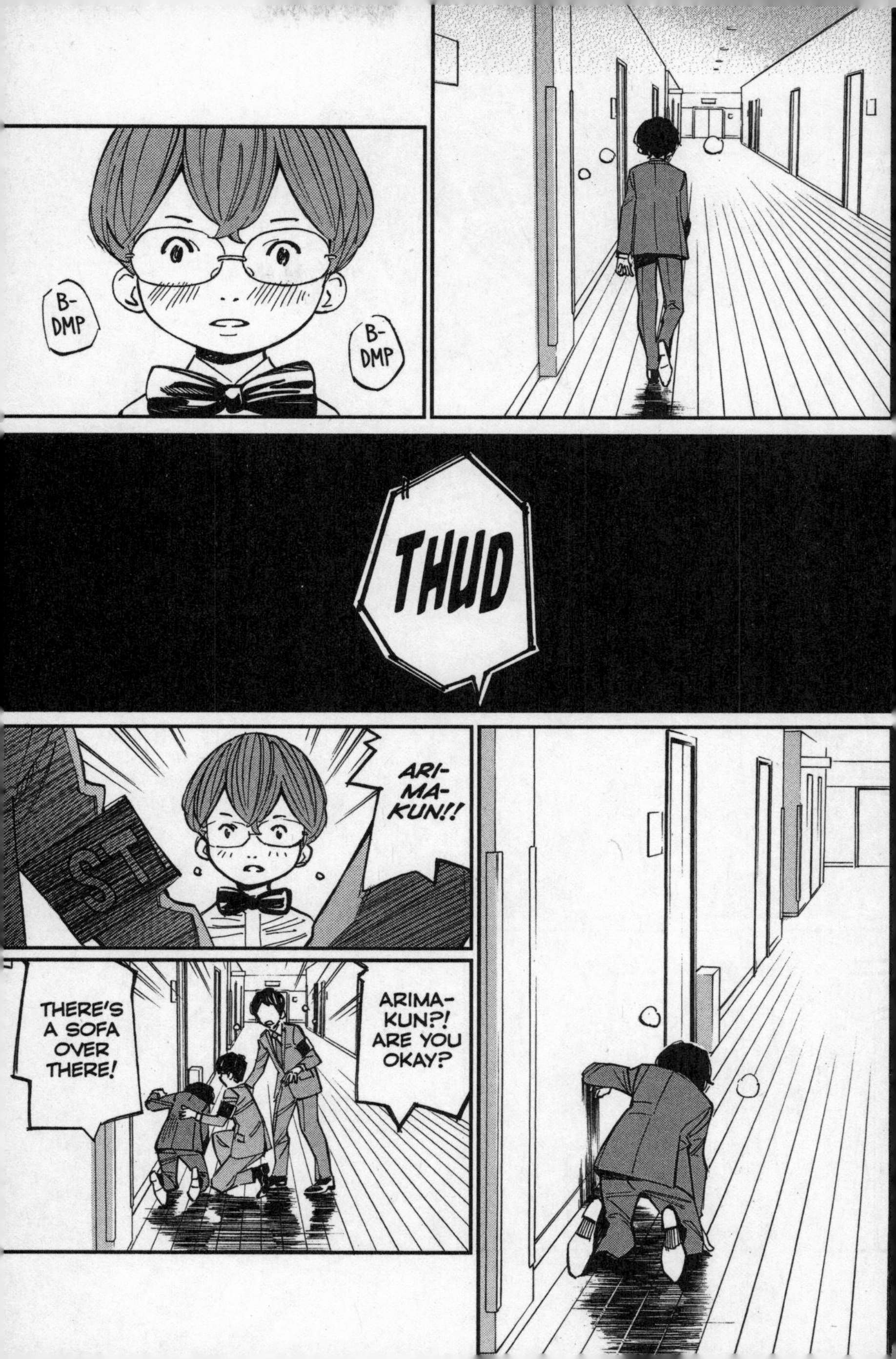
B-DMP
B-DMP
THUD
ARI-MA-KUN!!
ST
ARIMA-KUN?! ARE YOU OKAY?
THERE'S A SOFA OVER THERE!

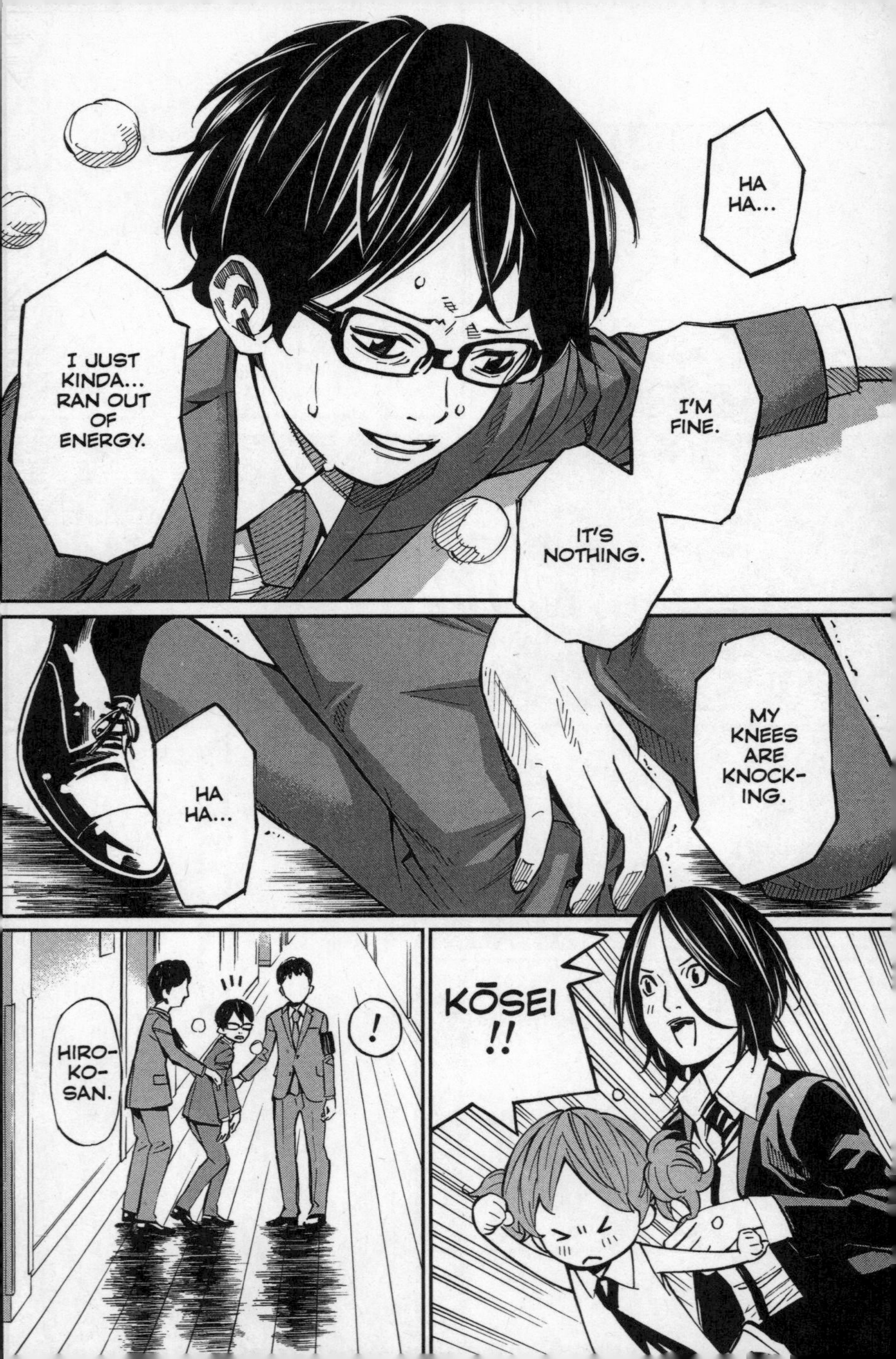
HA HA...
I'M FINE.
IT'S NOTHING.
I JUST KINDA... RAN OUT OF ENERGY.
MY KNEES ARE KNOCK-ING.
HA HA...
KŌSEI!!
!
HIRO-KO-SAN.

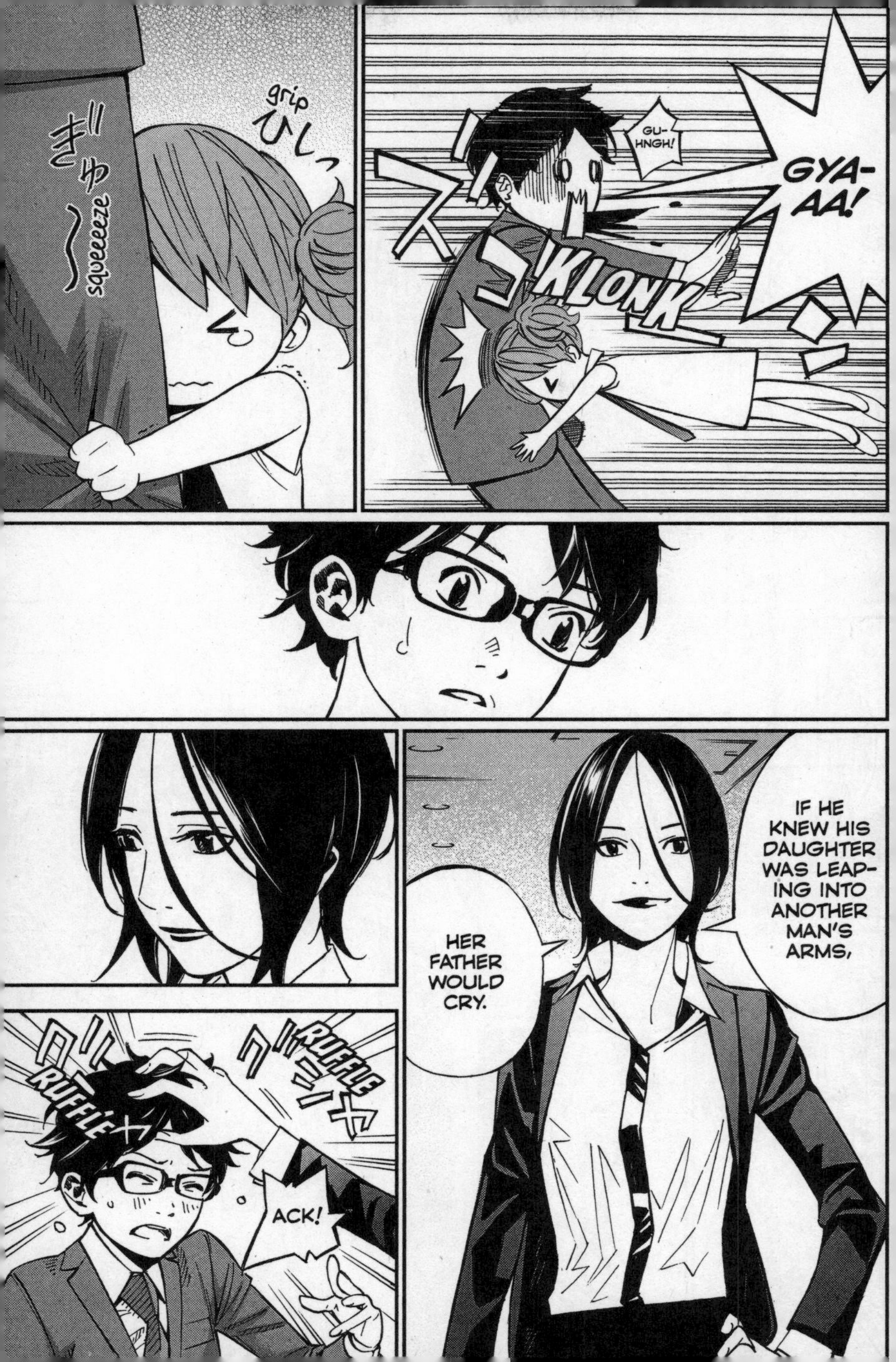
GU-HNGH!
GYAA-AA!
KLONK
grip
ひしっ
ぎゅ〜
squeeeeze
IF HE KNEW HIS DAUGHTER WAS LEAP-ING INTO ANOTHER MAN'S ARMS,
HER FATHER WOULD CRY.
RUFFLE
RUFFLE
ACK!

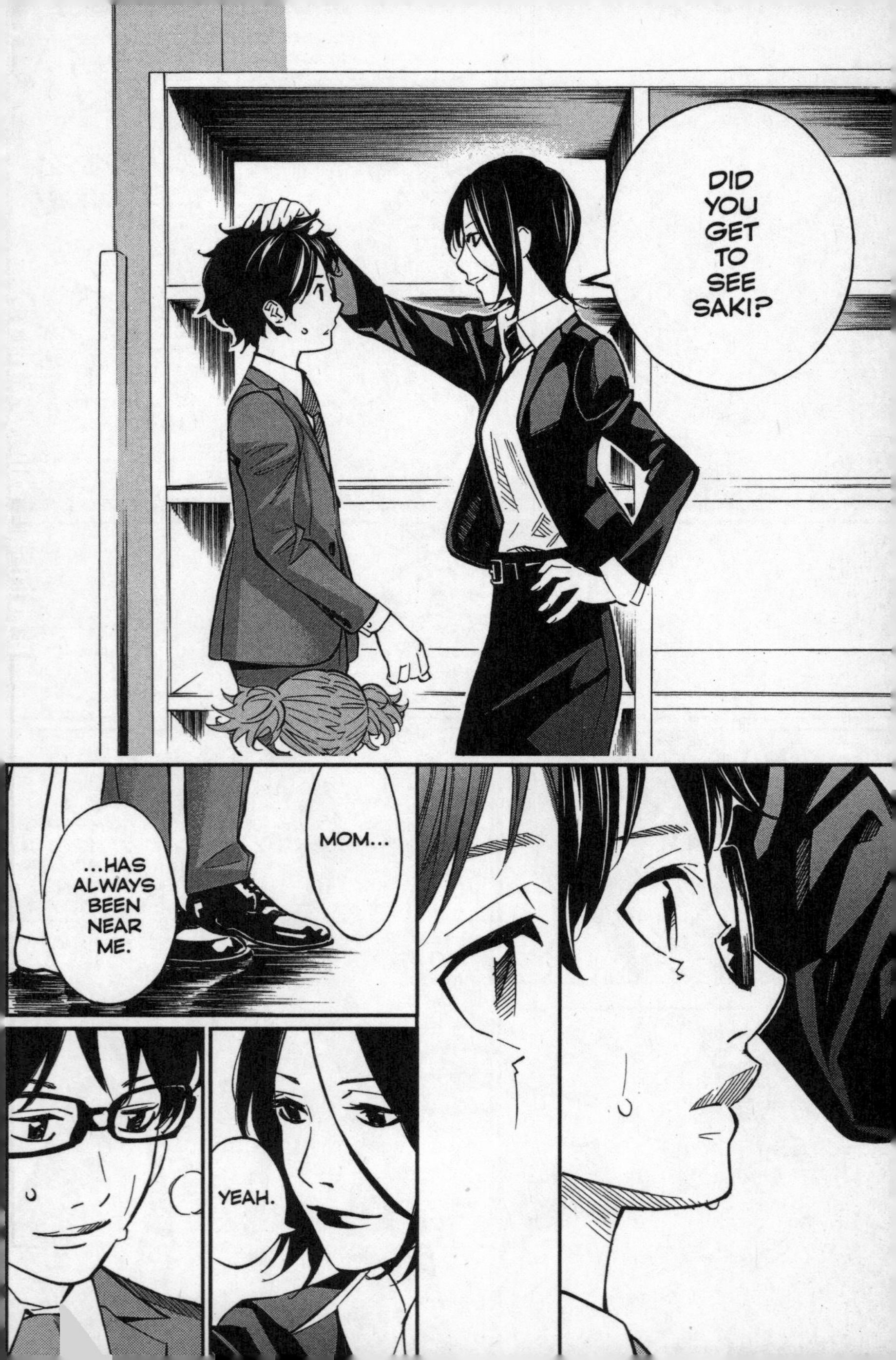
DID YOU GET TO SEE SAKI?
MOM...
...HAS ALWAYS BEEN NEAR ME.
YEAH.

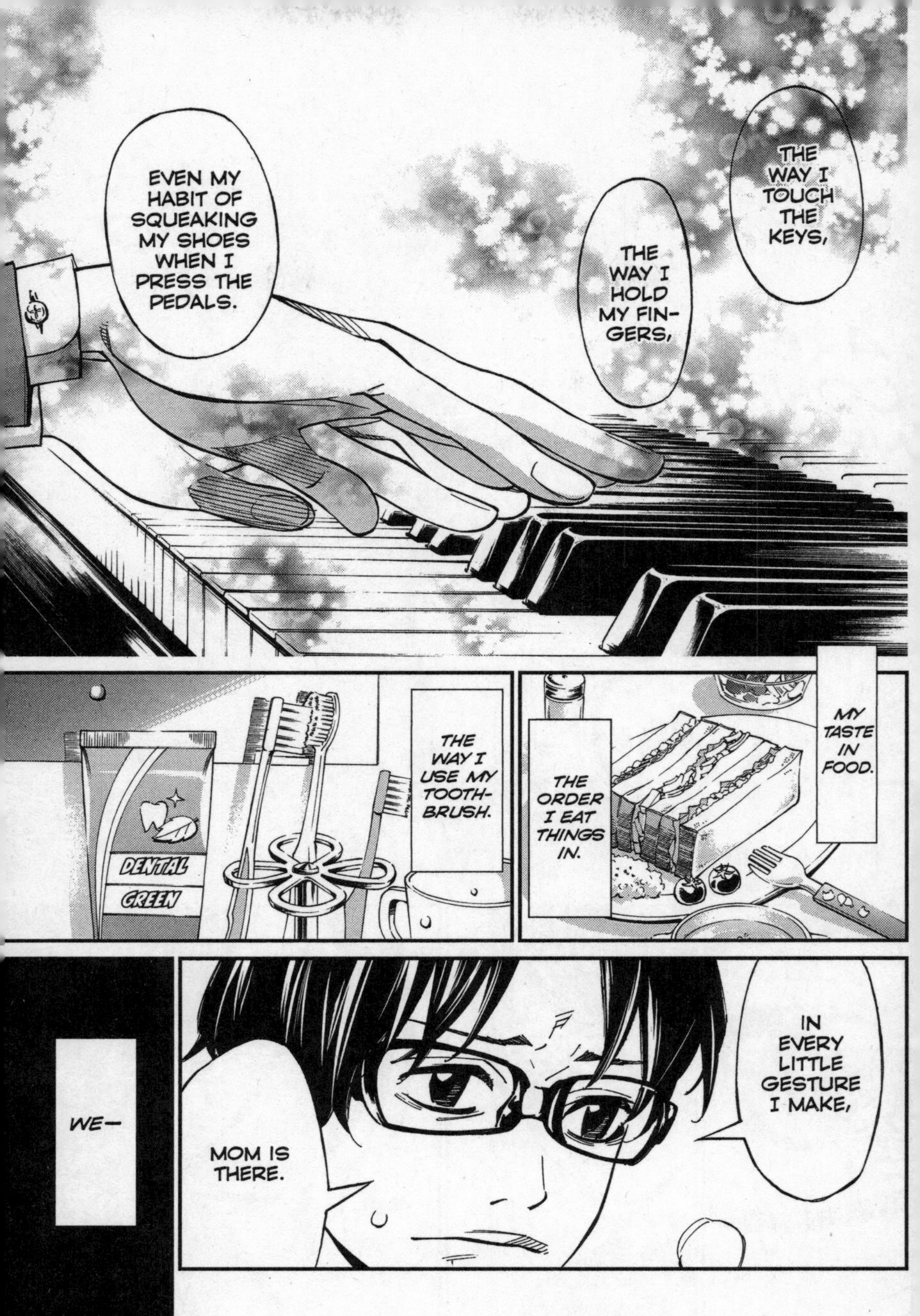
THE WAY I TOUCH THE KEYS,
THE WAY I HOLD MY FIN-GERS,
EVEN MY HABIT OF SQUEAKING MY SHOES WHEN I PRESS THE PEDALS.
MY TASTE IN FOOD.
THE ORDER I EAT THINGS IN.
THE WAY I USE MY TOOTH-BRUSH.
DENTAL GREEN
IN EVERY LITTLE GESTURE I MAKE,
MOM IS THERE.
WE—

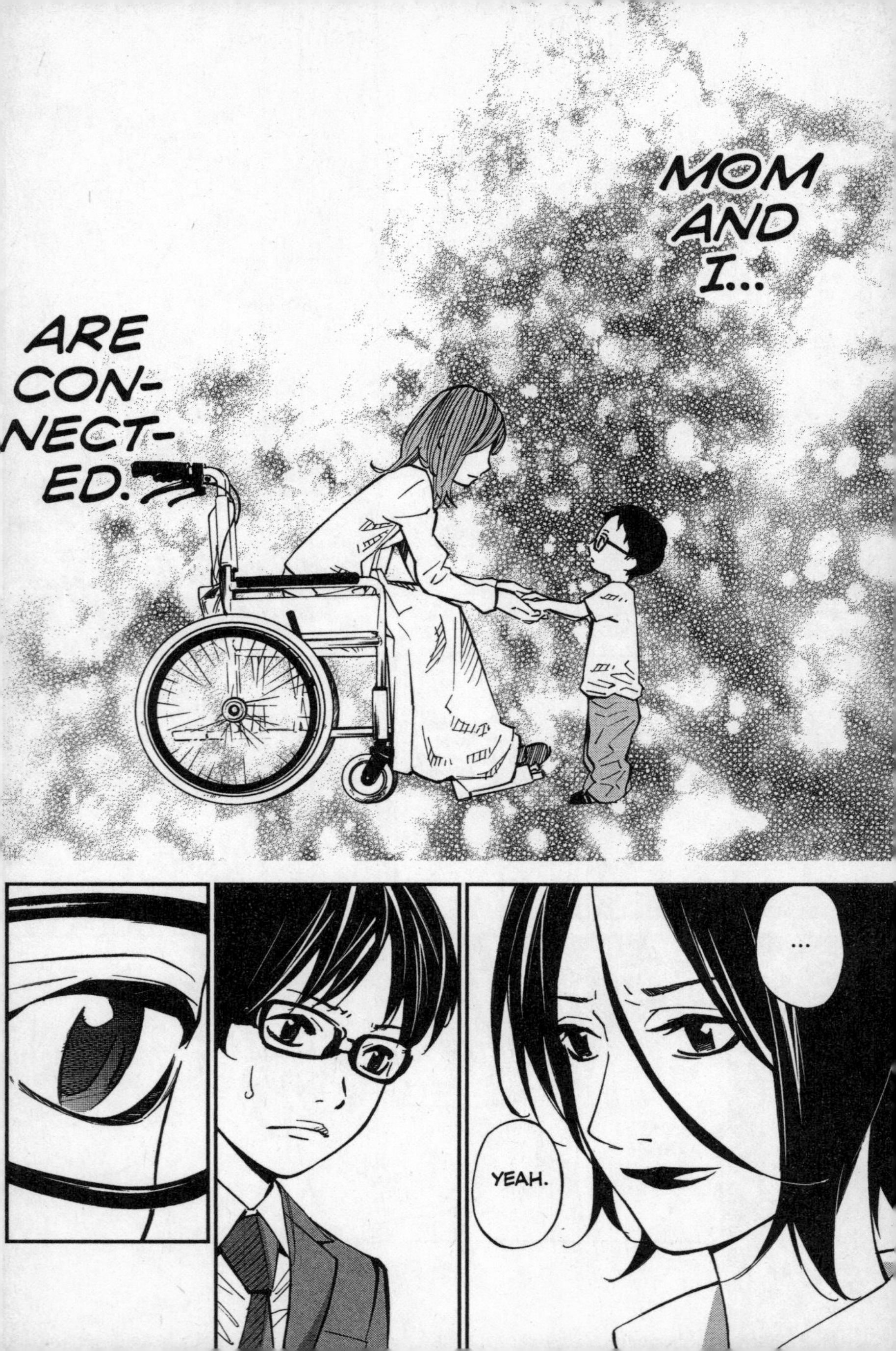
MOM AND I...
ARE CON-NECT-ED.
...
YEAH.

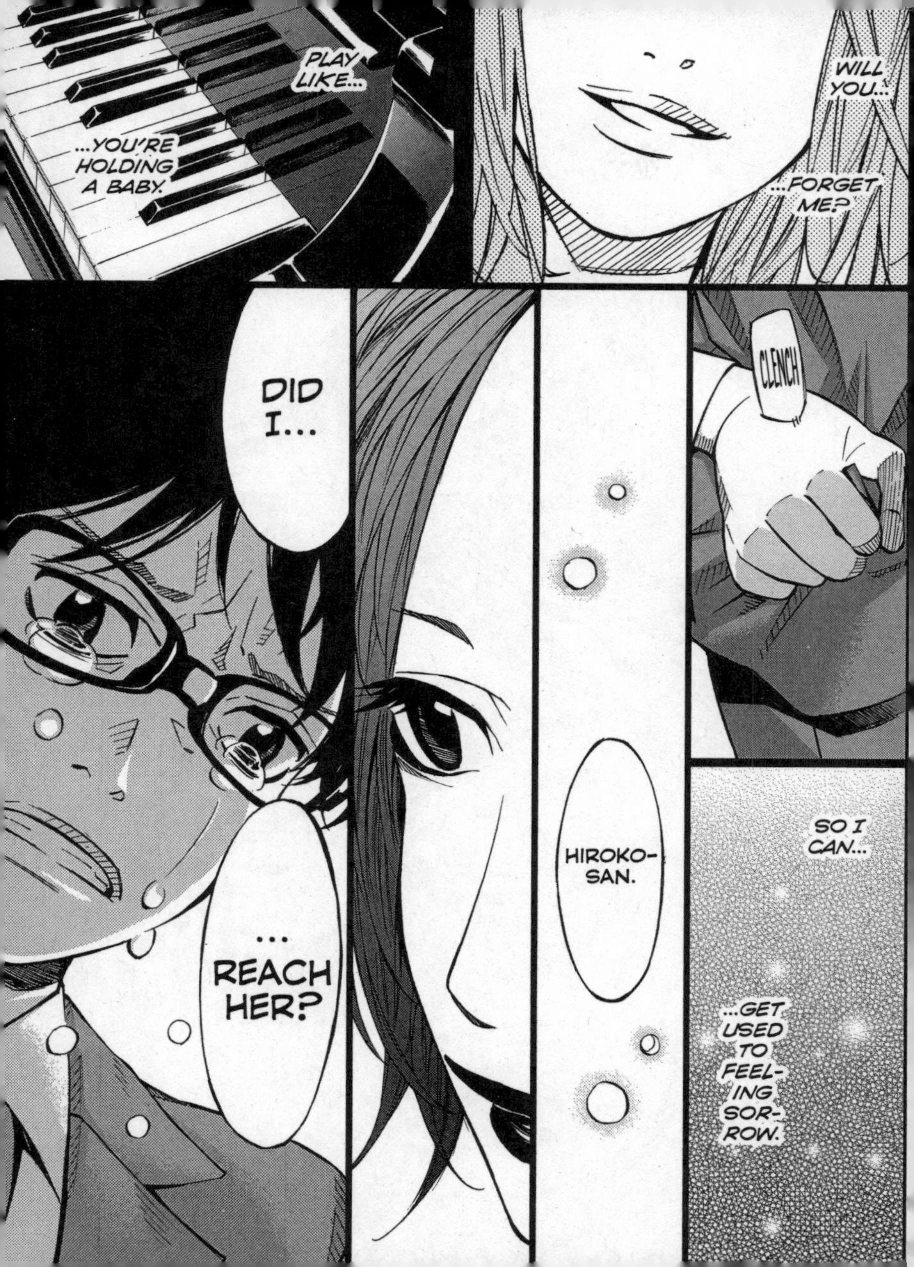
WILL YOU...
...FORGET ME?
PLAY LIKE...
...YOU'RE HOLDING A BABY.
CLENCH
SO I CAN...
...GET USED TO FEEL-ING SOR-ROW.
HIROKO-SAN.
DID I...
... REACH HER?

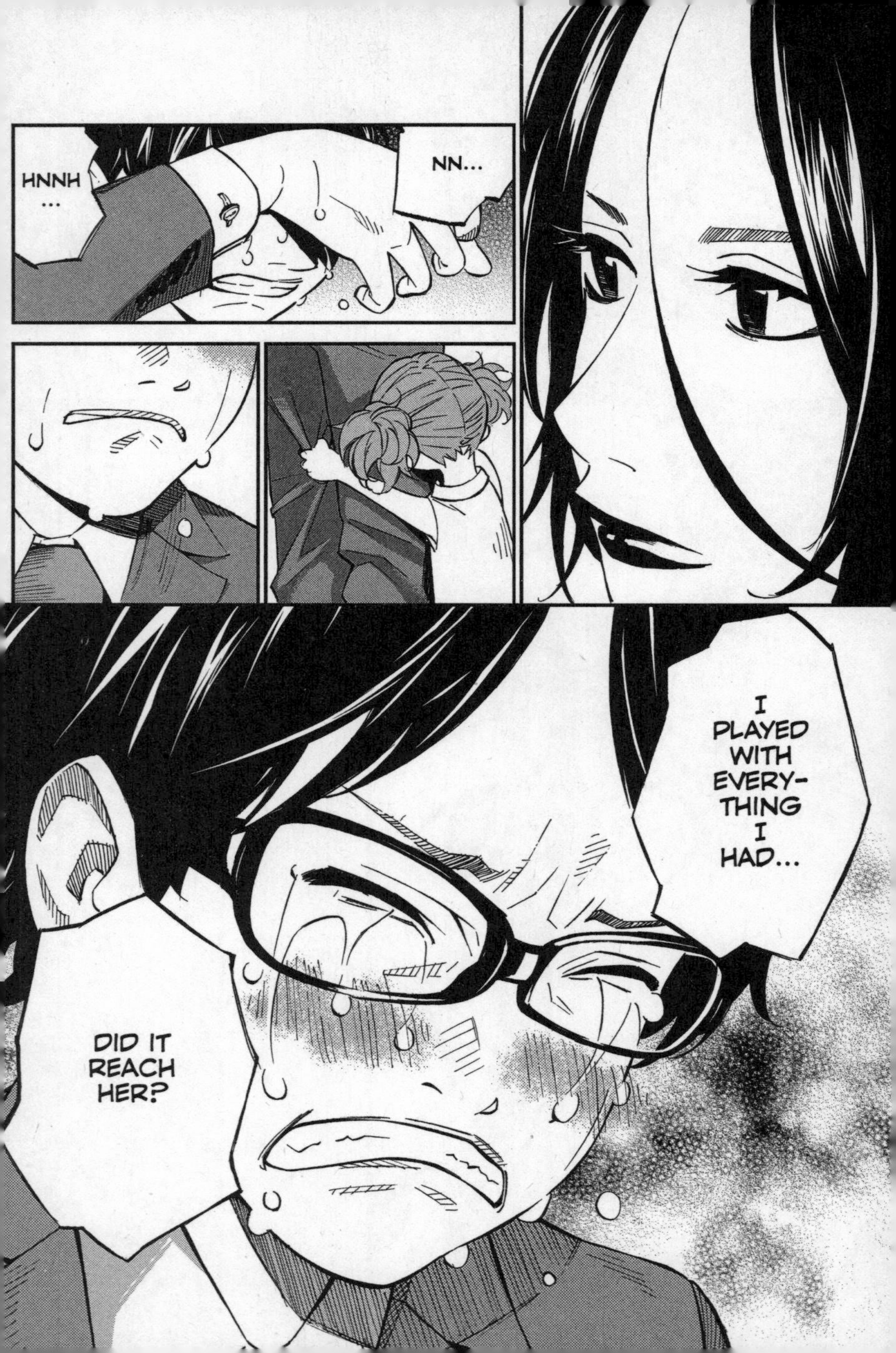
NN...
HNNH ...
I PLAYED WITH EVERY-THING I HAD...
DID IT REACH HER?

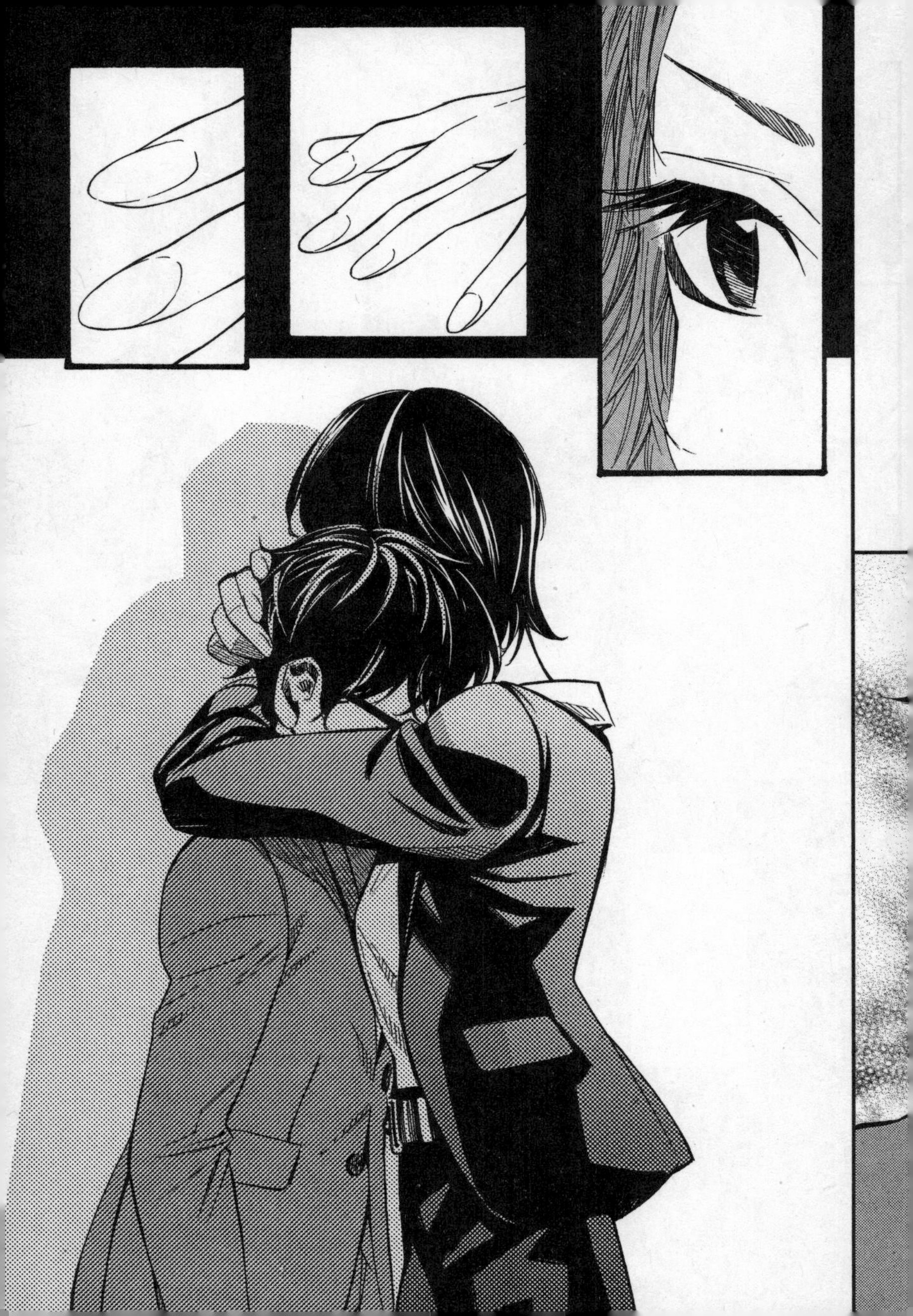

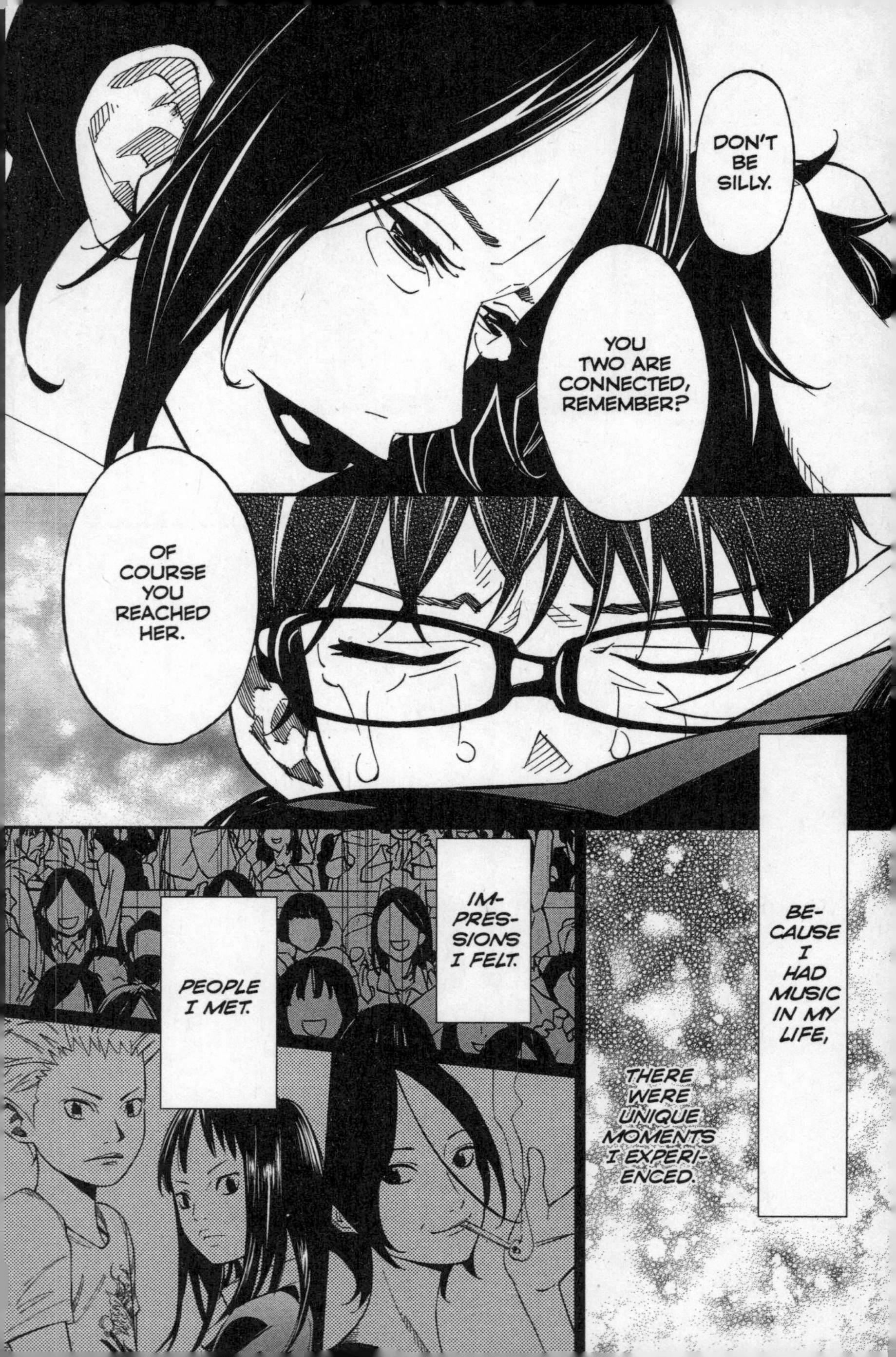
DON'T BE SILLY.
YOU TWO ARE CONNECTED, REMEMBER?
OF COURSE YOU REACHED HER.
BE-CAUSE I HAD MUSIC IN MY LIFE,
THERE WERE UNIQUE MOMENTS I EXPERI-ENCED.
IM-PRES-SIONS I FELT.
PEOPLE I MET.

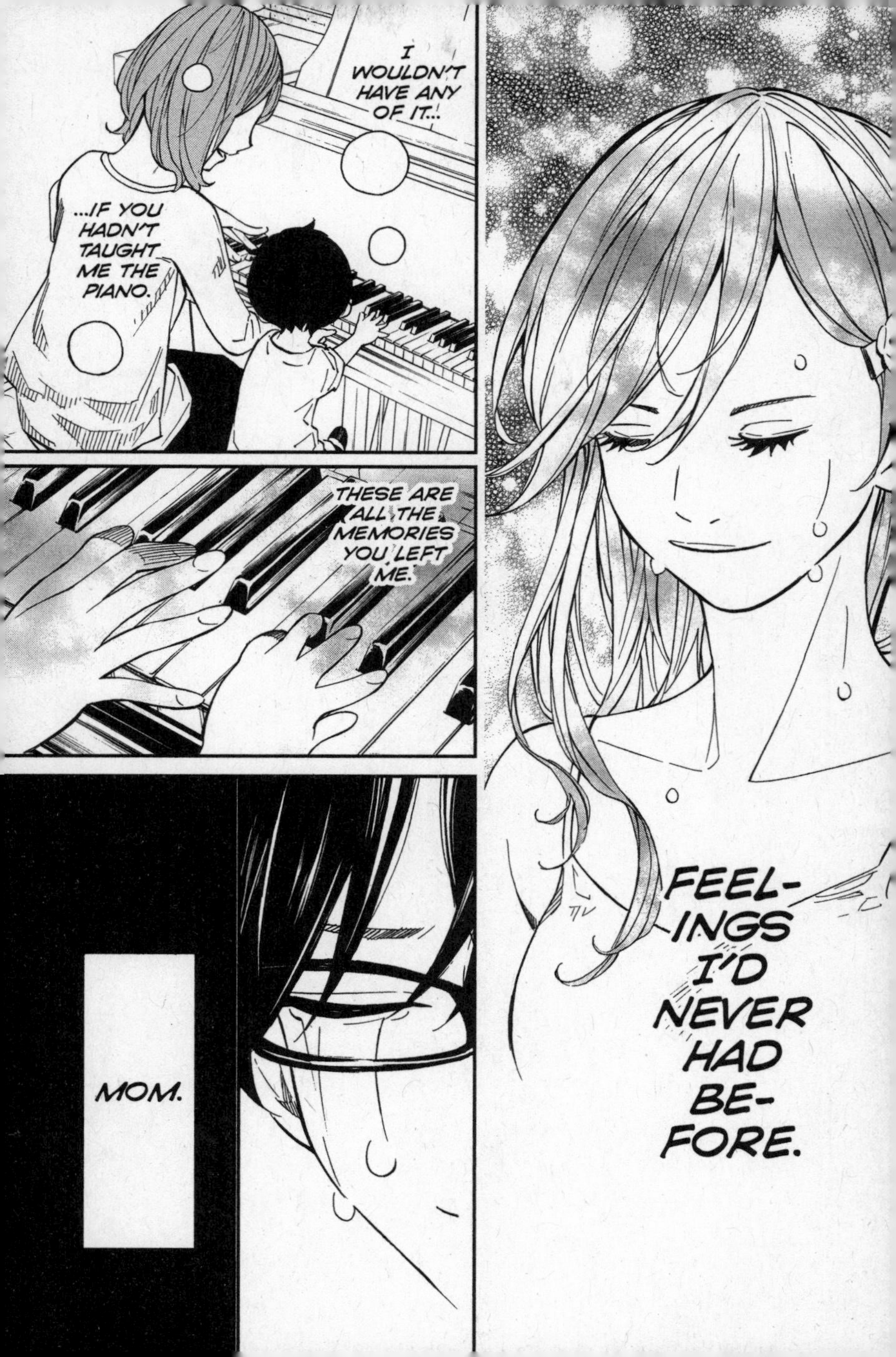
FEEL-INGS I'D NEVER HAD BE-FORE.
I WOULDN'T HAVE ANY OF IT...
...IF YOU HADN'T TAUGHT ME THE PIANO.
THESE ARE ALL THE MEMORIES YOU LEFT ME.
MOM.

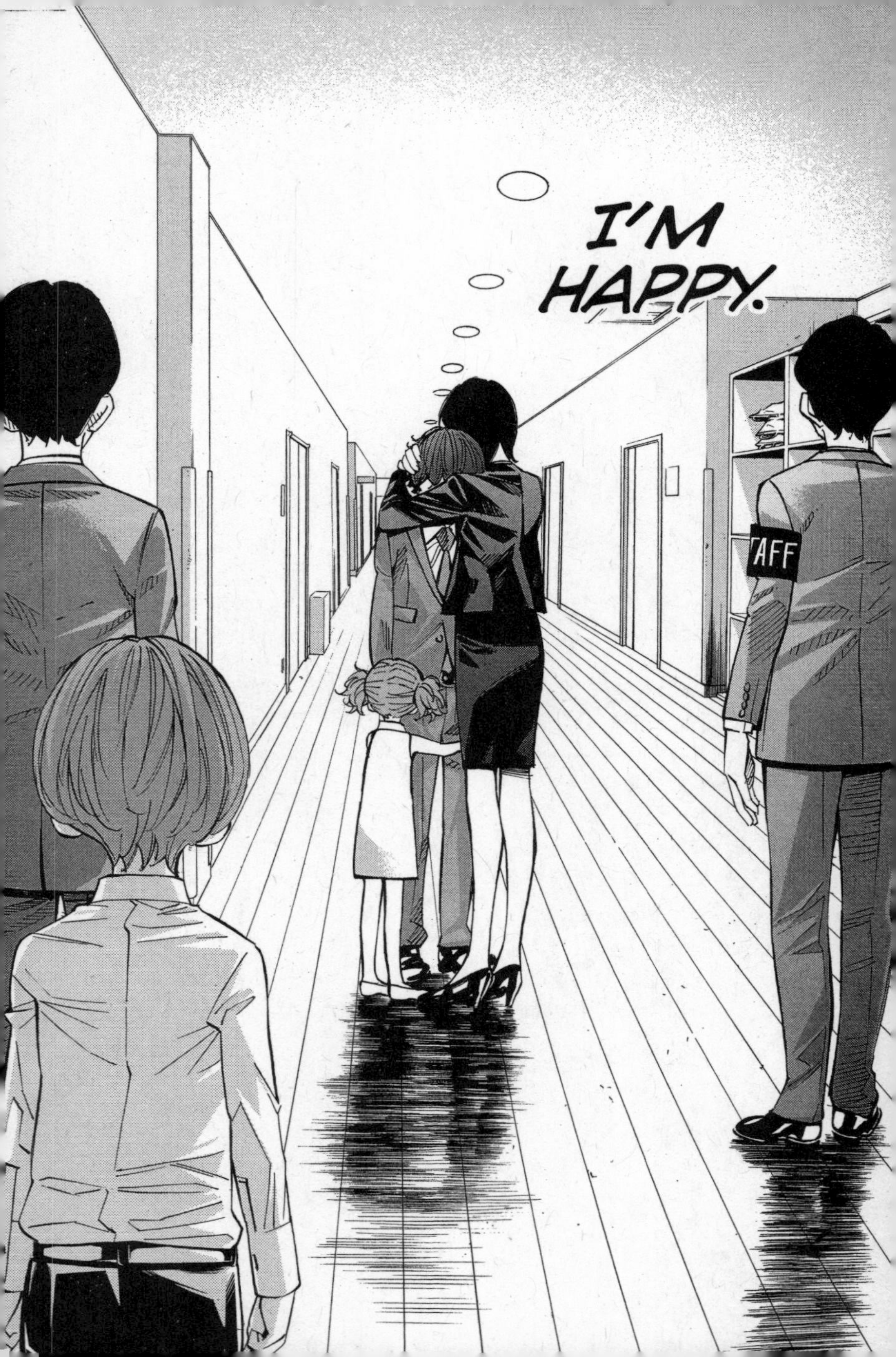
I'M HAPPY.
STAFF

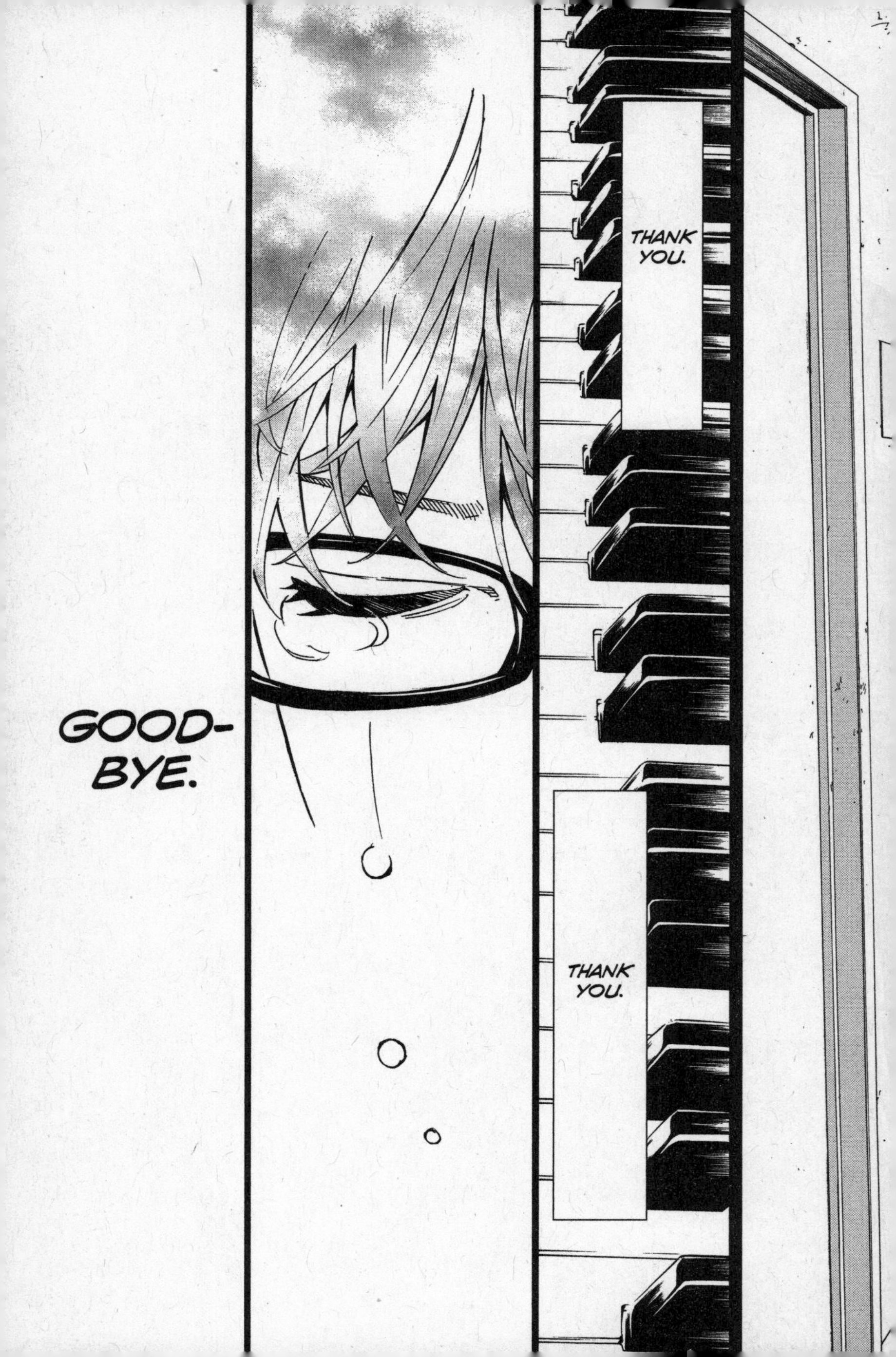
THANK YOU.
THANK YOU.
GOOD-BYE.

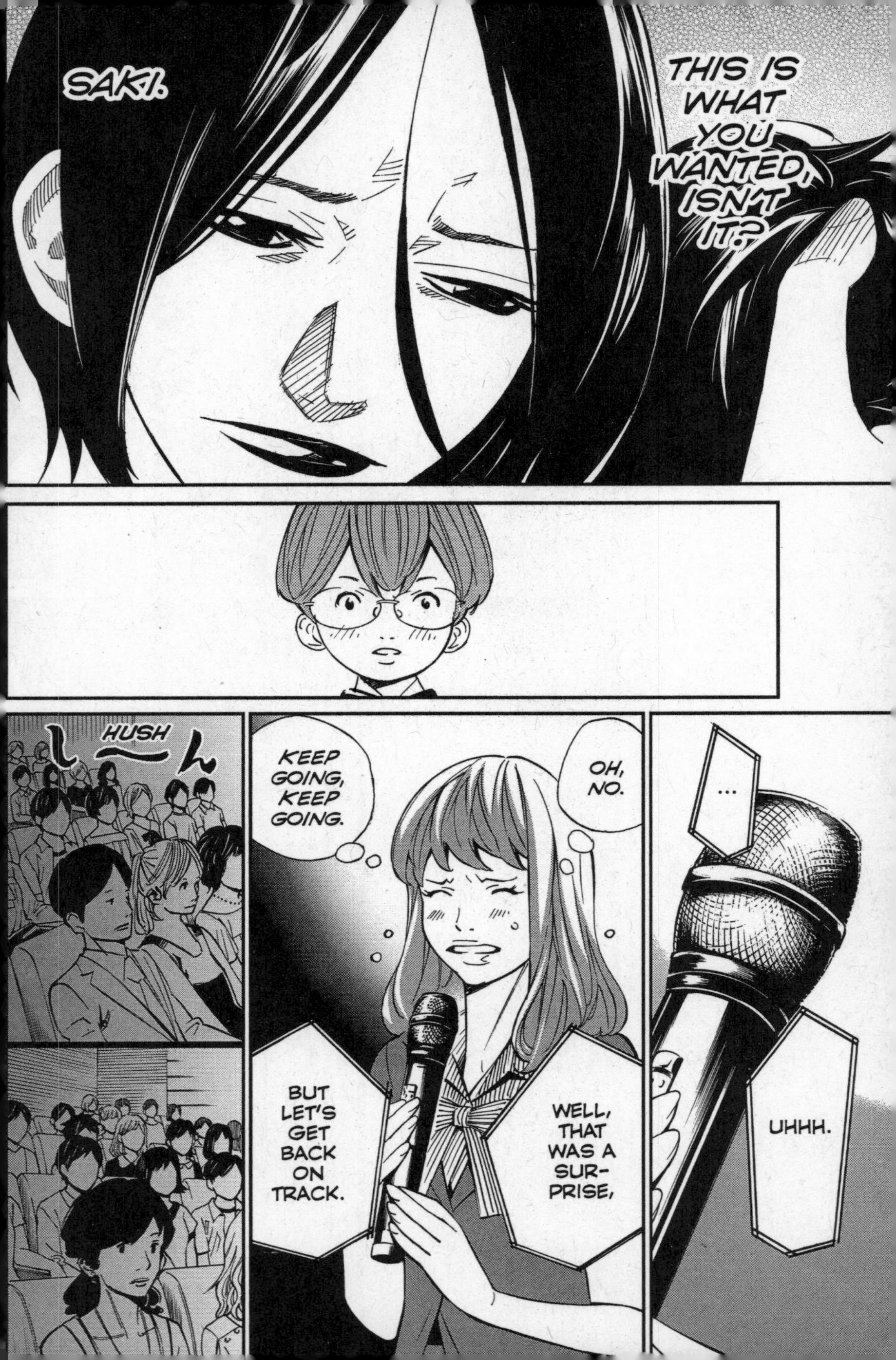
THIS IS WHAT YOU WANTED, ISN'T IT?
SAKI.
...
UHHH.
OH, NO.
KEEP GOING, KEEP GOING.
WELL, THAT WAS A SUR-PRISE,
BUT LET'S GET BACK ON TRACK.
しーん HUSH

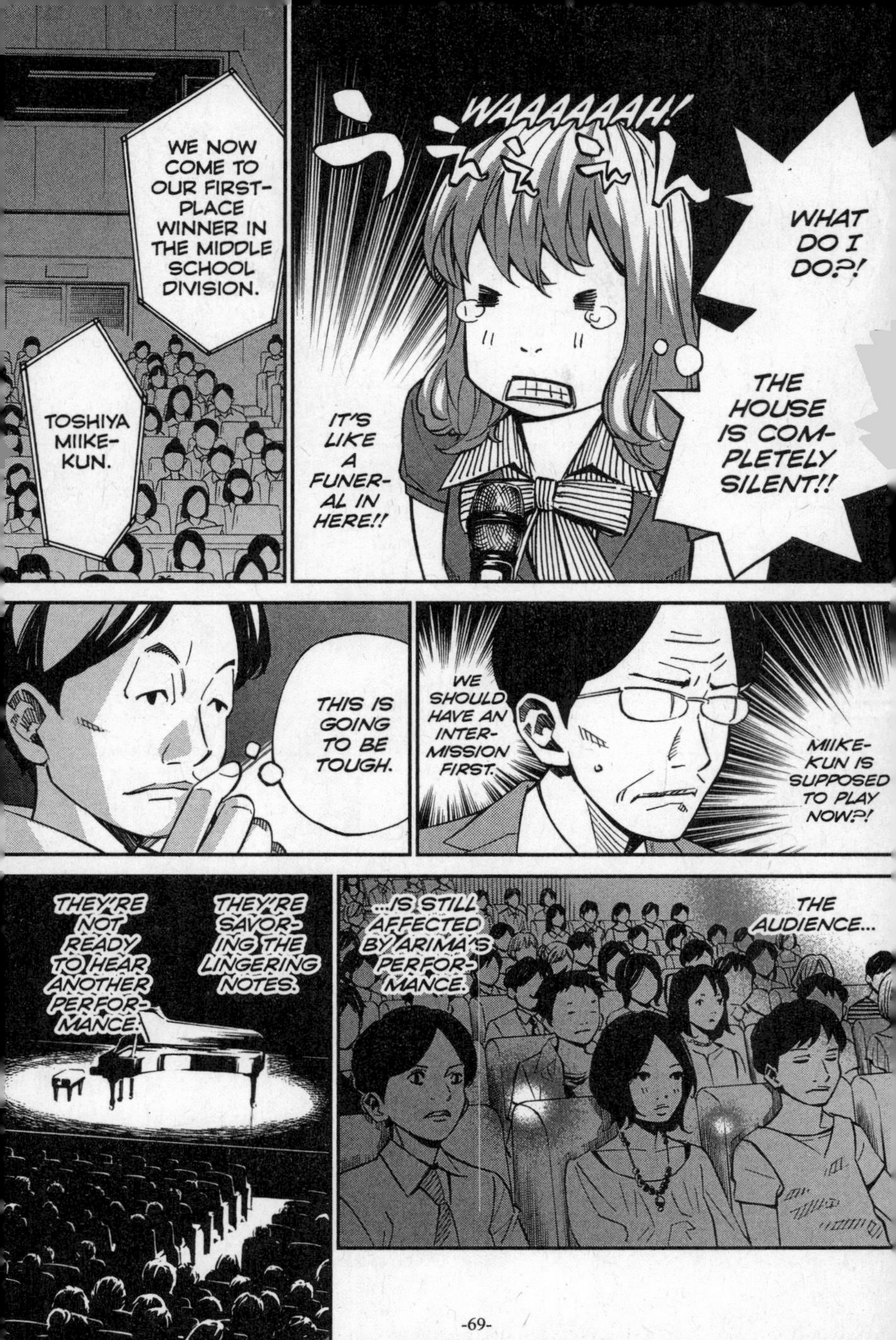
WAAAAAAH!
WHAT DO I DO?!
THE HOUSE IS COMPLETELY SILENT!!
IT'S LIKE A FUNERAL IN HERE!!
WE NOW COME TO OUR FIRST-PLACE WINNER IN THE MIDDLE SCHOOL DIVISION.
TOSHIYA MIIKE-KUN.
MIIKE-KUN IS SUPPOSED TO PLAY NOW?!
WE SHOULD HAVE AN INTERMISSION FIRST.
THIS IS GOING TO BE TOUGH.
THE AUDIENCE...
...IS STILL AFFECTED BY ARIMA'S PERFORMANCE.
THEY'RE SAVORING THE LINGERING NOTES.
THEY'RE NOT READY TO HEAR ANOTHER PERFORMANCE.

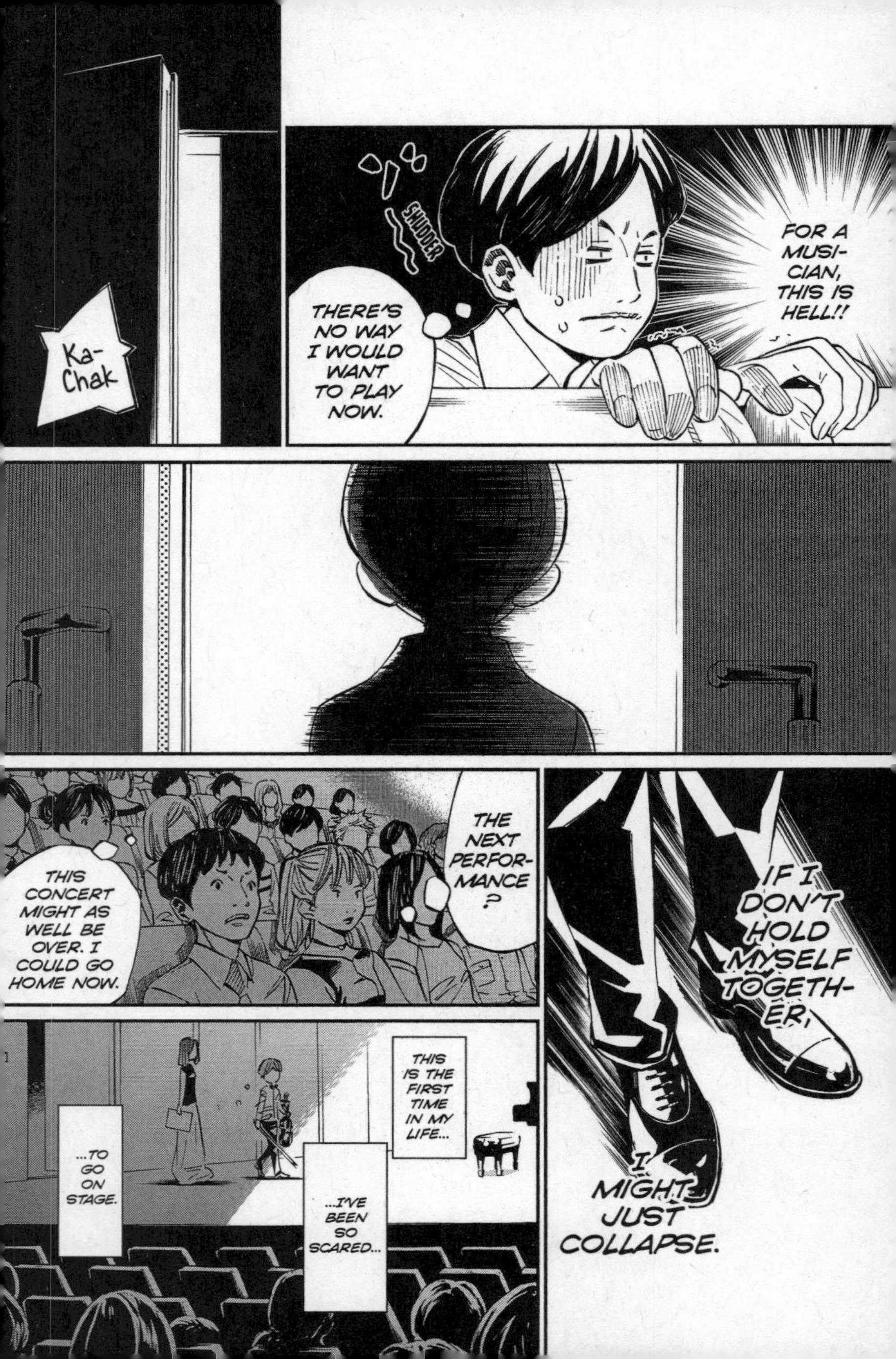
FOR A MUSI-CIAN, THIS IS HELL!!
SHUDDER
THERE'S NO WAY I WOULD WANT TO PLAY NOW.
Ka-Chak
IF I DON'T HOLD MYSELF TOGETH-ER,
I MIGHT JUST COLLAPSE.
THE NEXT PERFORM-ANCE?
THIS CONCERT MIGHT AS WELL BE OVER. I COULD GO HOME NOW.
THIS IS THE FIRST TIME IN MY LIFE...
...I'VE BEEN SO SCARED...
...TO GO ON STAGE.

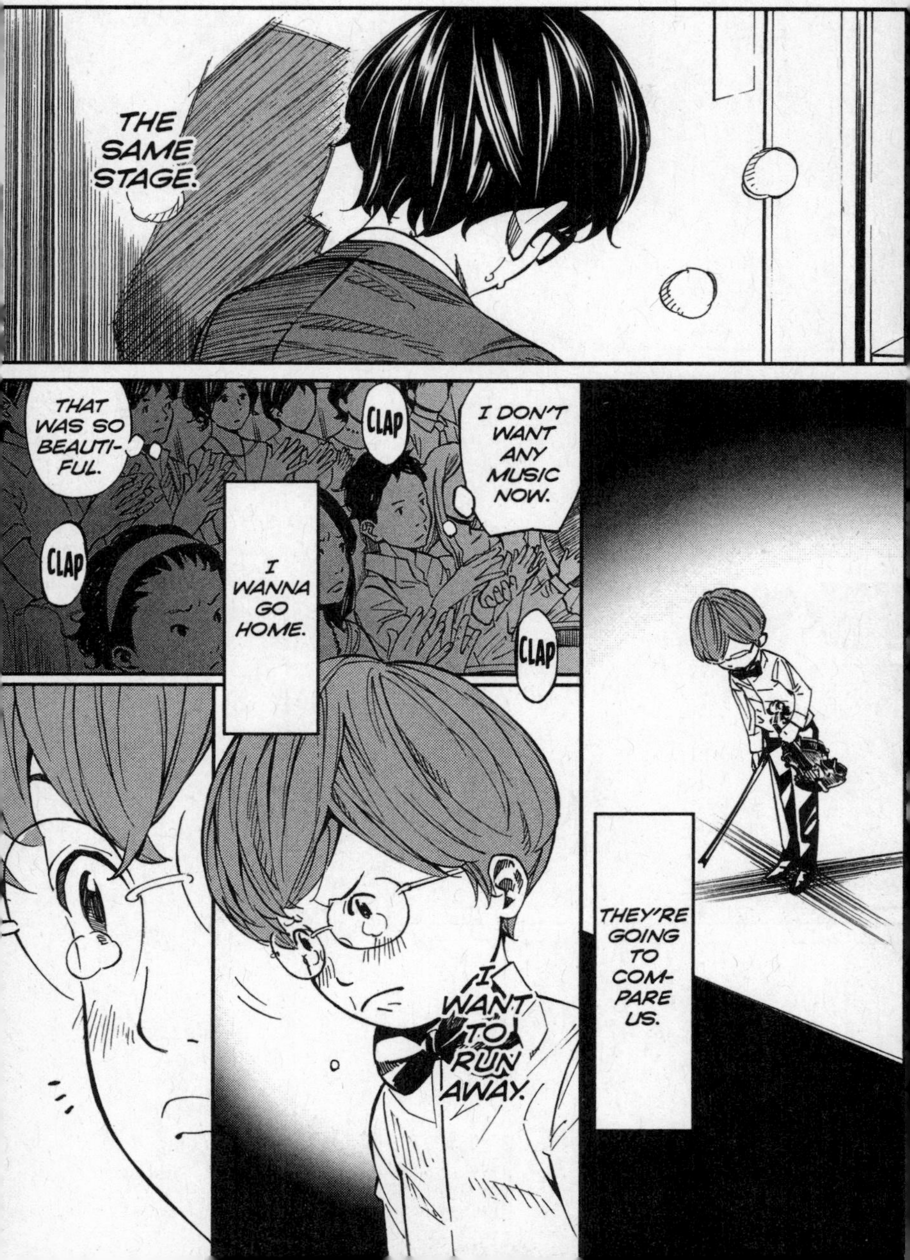
THE SAME STAGE.
THEY'RE GOING TO COM-PARE US.
I DON'T WANT ANY MUSIC NOW.
CLAP
THAT WAS SO BEAUTI-FUL.
CLAP
I WANNA GO HOME.
CLAP
I WANT TO RUN AWAY.

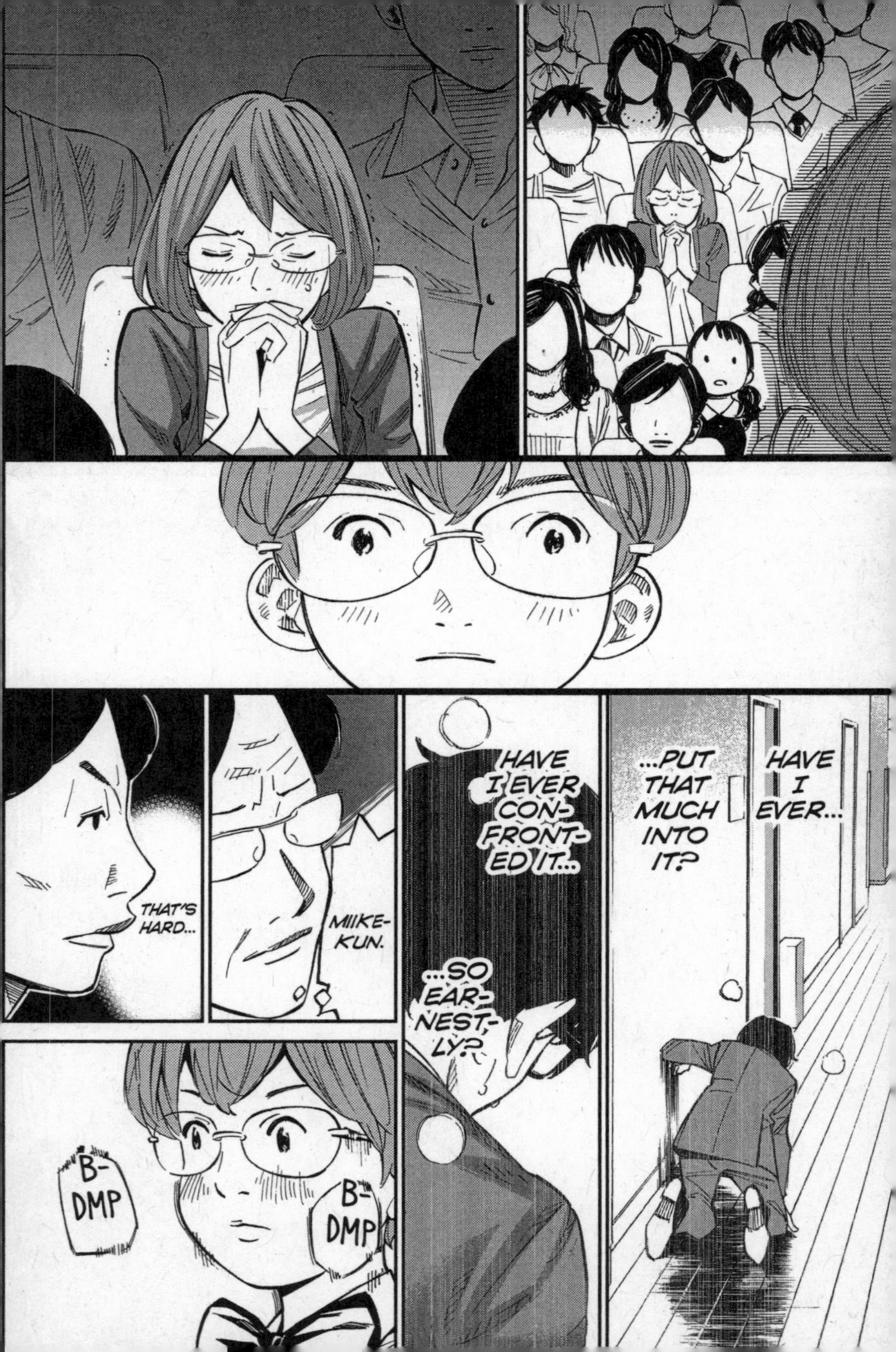
HAVE I EVER...
...PUT THAT MUCH INTO IT?
HAVE I EVER CON-FRONT-ED IT...
...SO EAR-NEST-LY?
MIIKE-KUN.
THAT'S HARD...
B-DMP
B-DMP

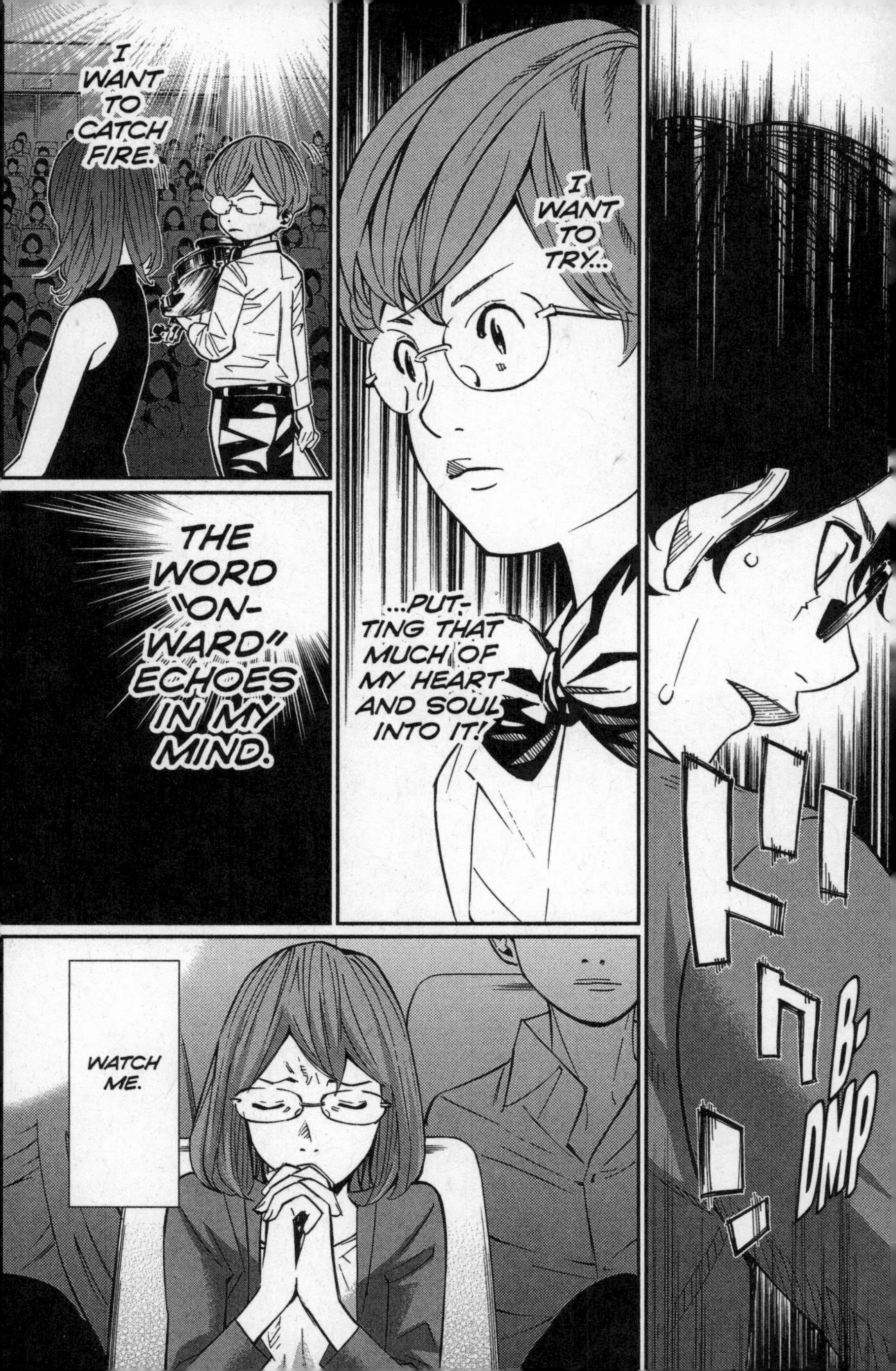
B-DMP
I WANT TO TRY...
...PUTTING THAT MUCH OF MY HEART AND SOUL INTO IT!
I WANT TO CATCH FIRE.
THE WORD "ONWARD" ECHOES IN MY MIND.
WATCH ME.

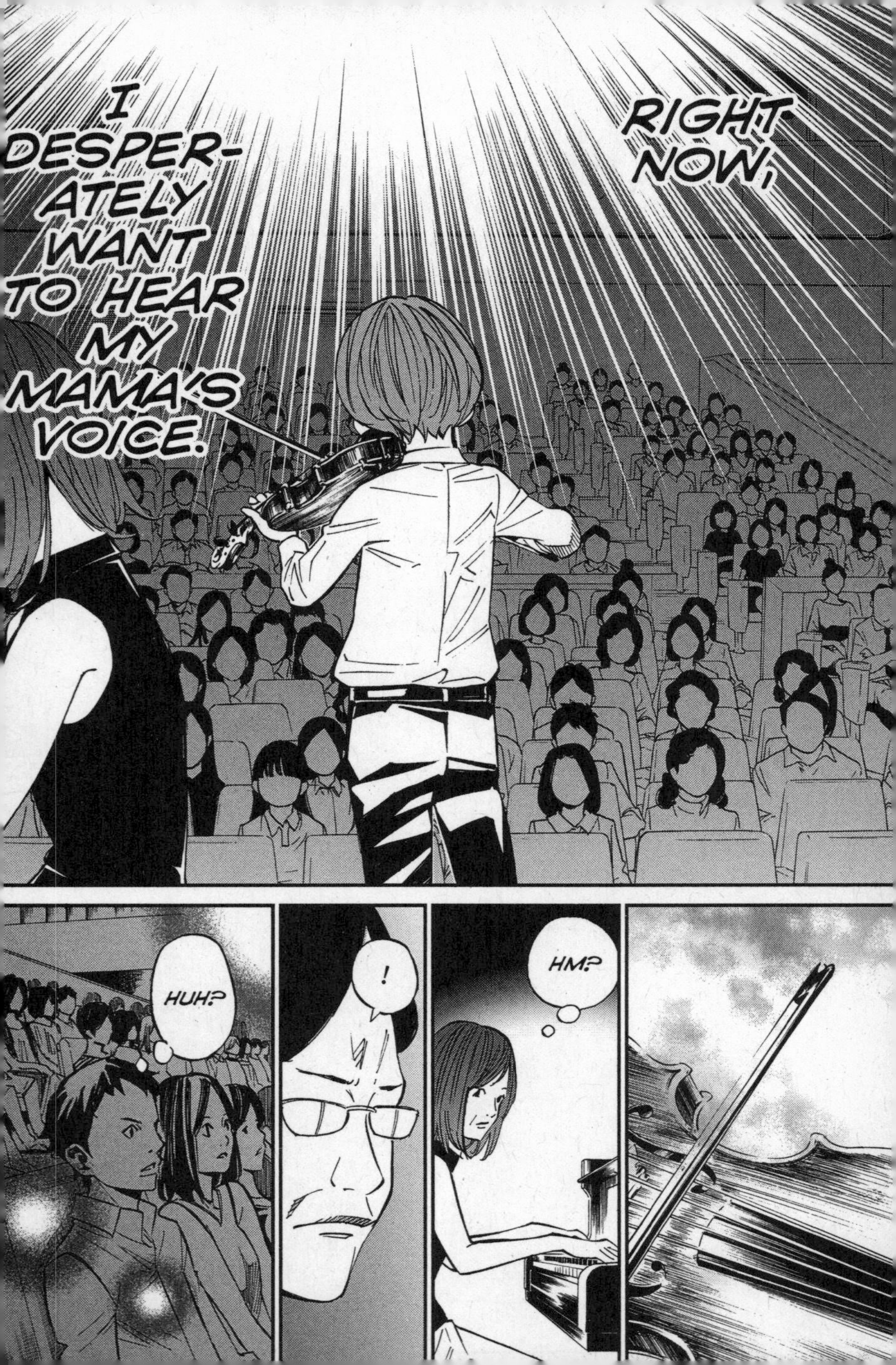
RIGHT NOW,
I DESPER-ATELY WANT TO HEAR MY MAMA'S VOICE.
HM?
!
HUH?

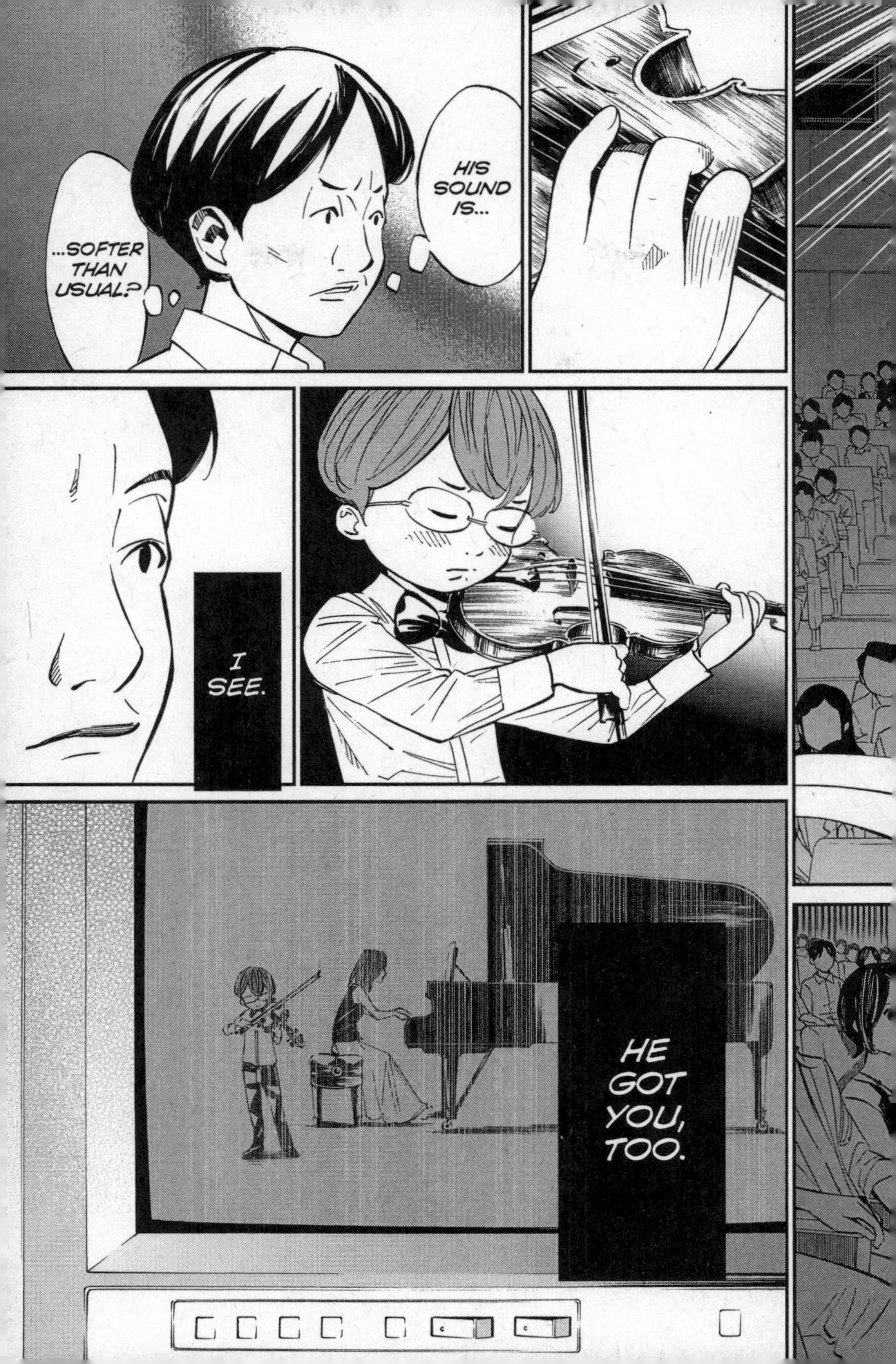

HIS SOUND IS...
...SOFTER THAN USUAL?
I SEE.
HE GOT YOU, TOO.

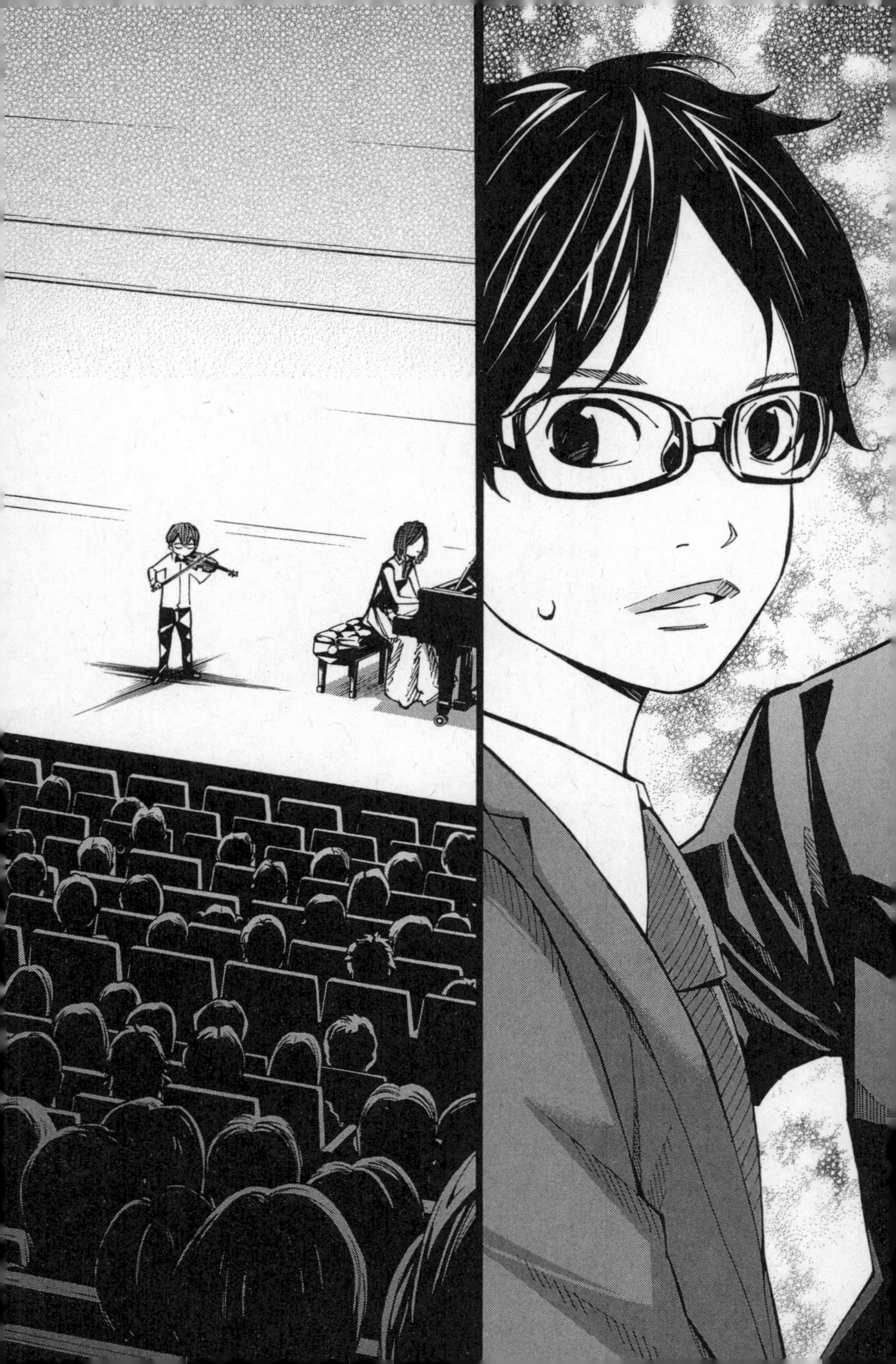

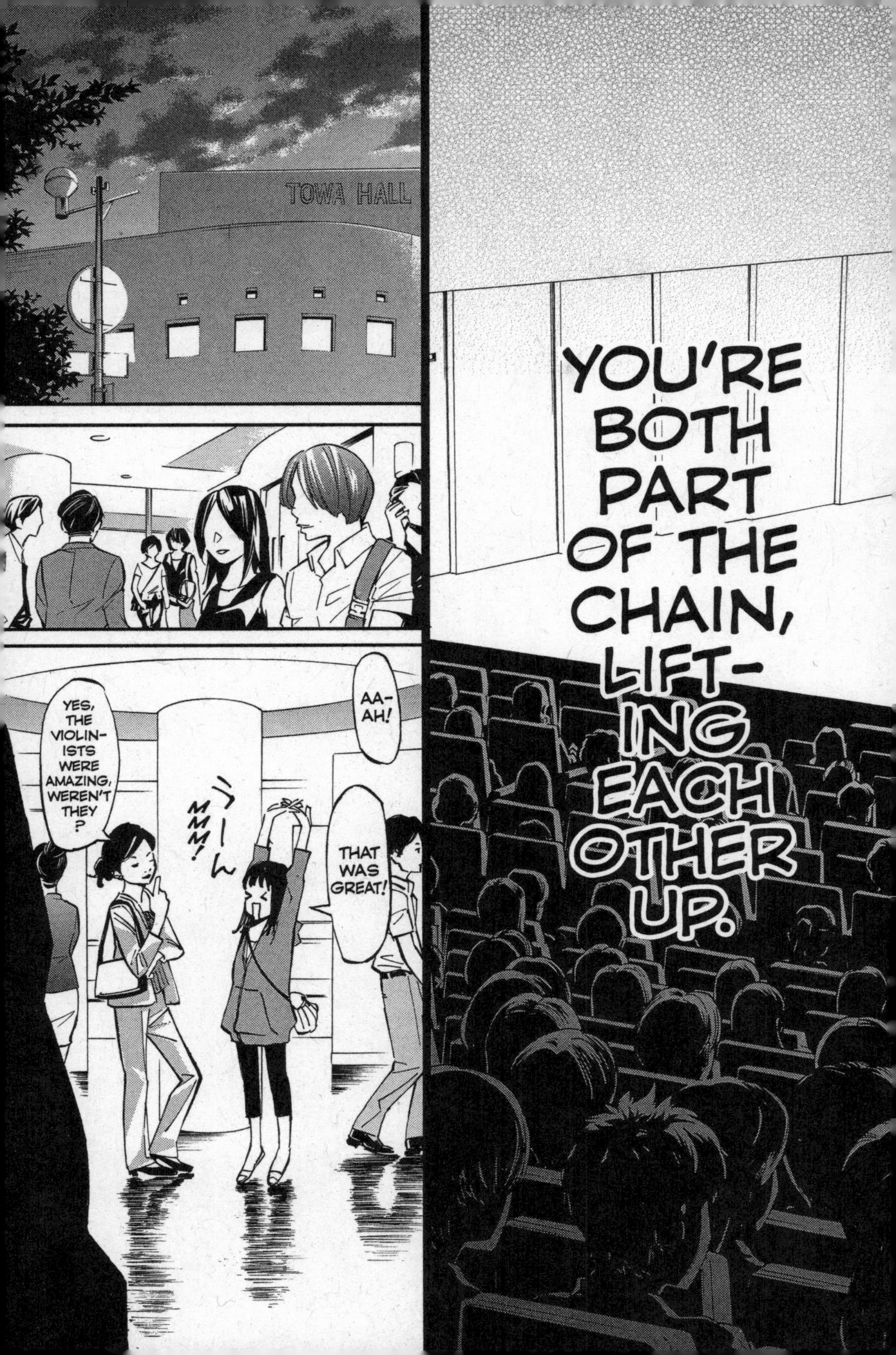
YOU'RE BOTH PART OF THE CHAIN, LIFT-ING EACH OTHER UP.
TOWA HALL
AA-AH!
THAT WAS GREAT!
うーん
MMM!
YES, THE VIOLIN-ISTS WERE AMAZING, WEREN'T THEY?

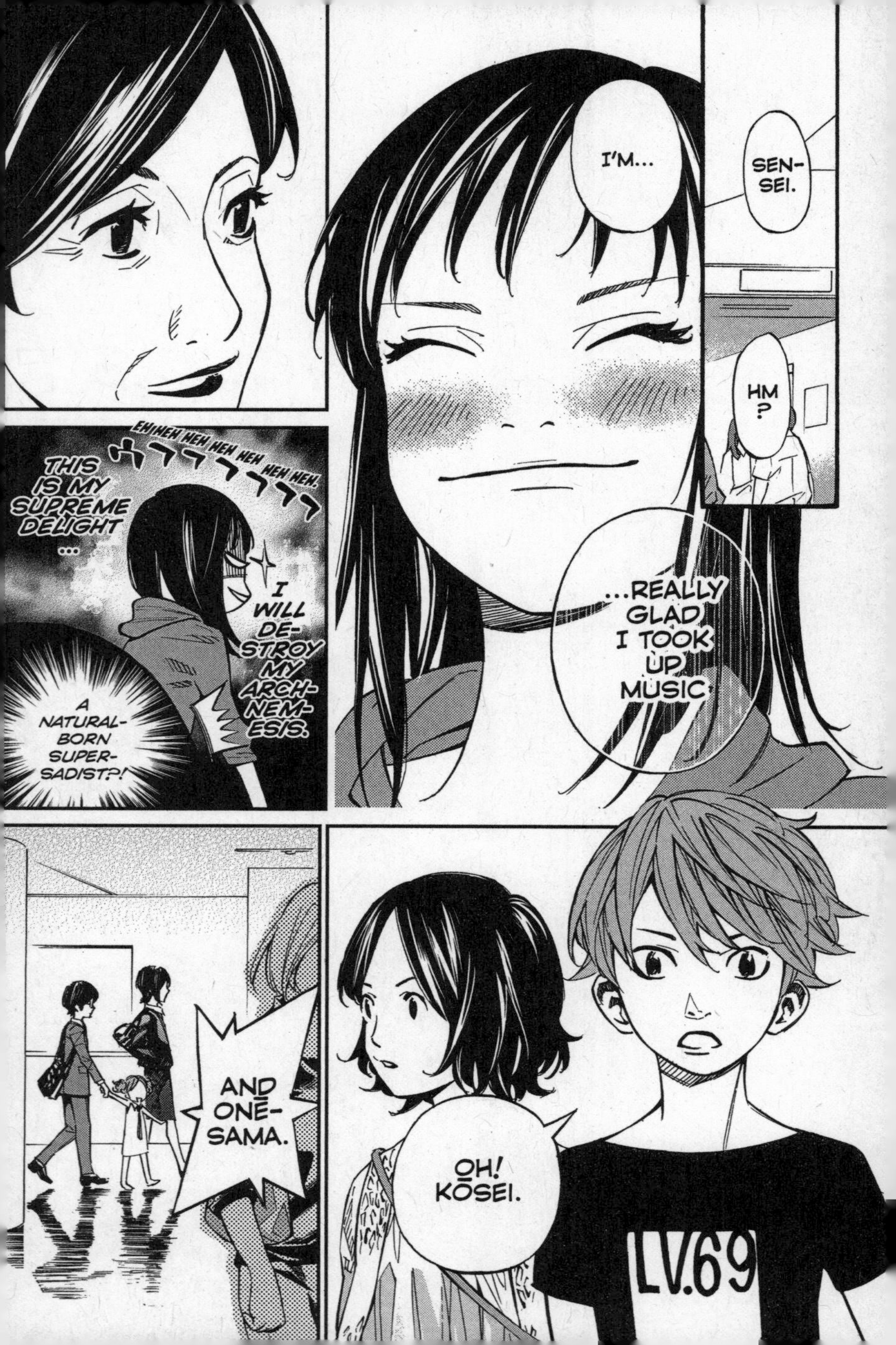

SENSEI.
HM?
I'M...
...REALLY GLAD I TOOK UP MUSIC
EHHEH HEH HEH HEH HEH HEH.
THIS IS MY SUPREME DELIGHT...
I WILL DESTROY MY ARCHNEMESIS.
A NATURAL-BORN SUPER-SADIST?!
OH! KŌSEI.
LV.69
AND ONĒ-SAMA.

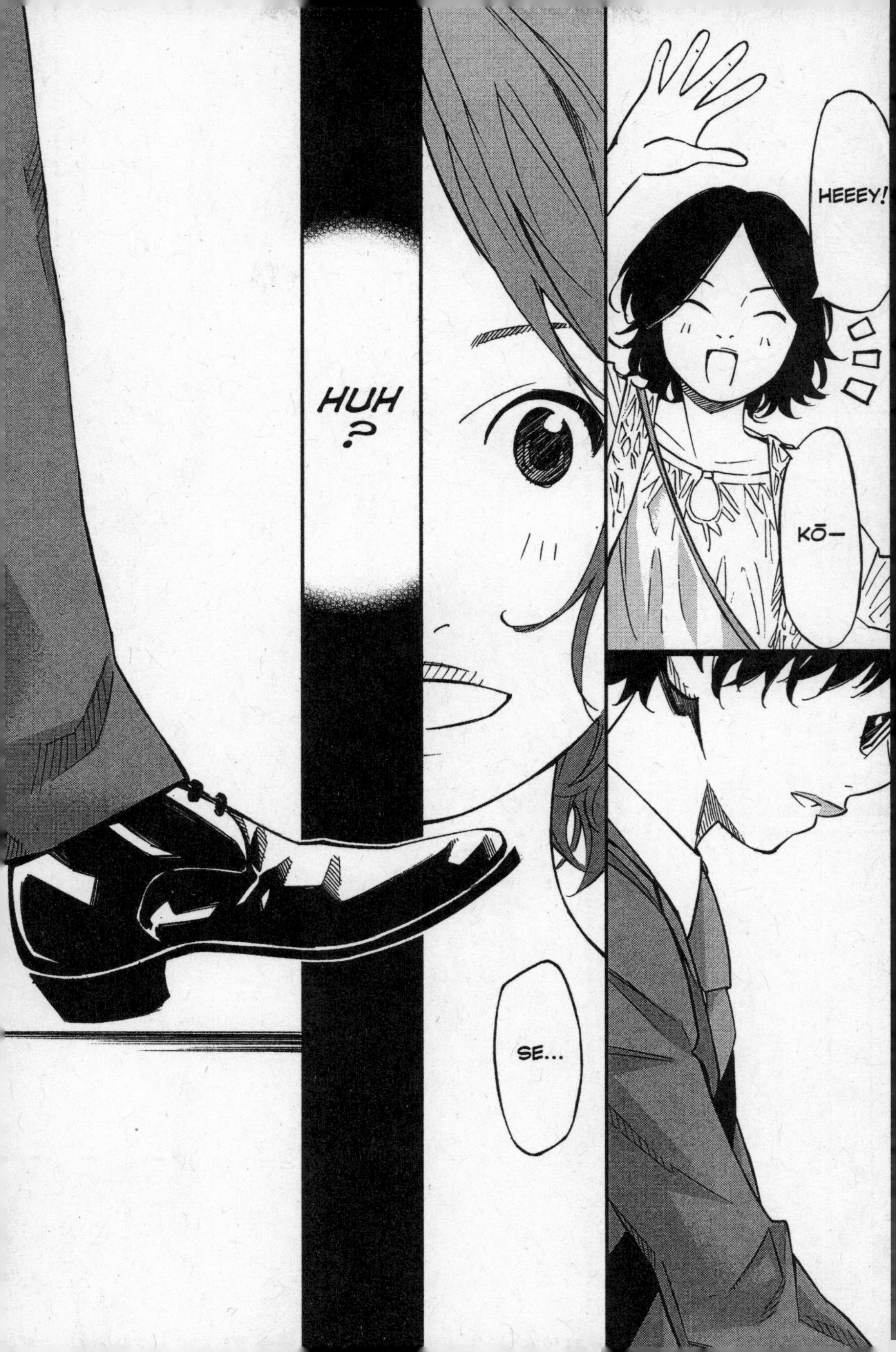
HEEEY!
KŌ—
SE...
HUH?

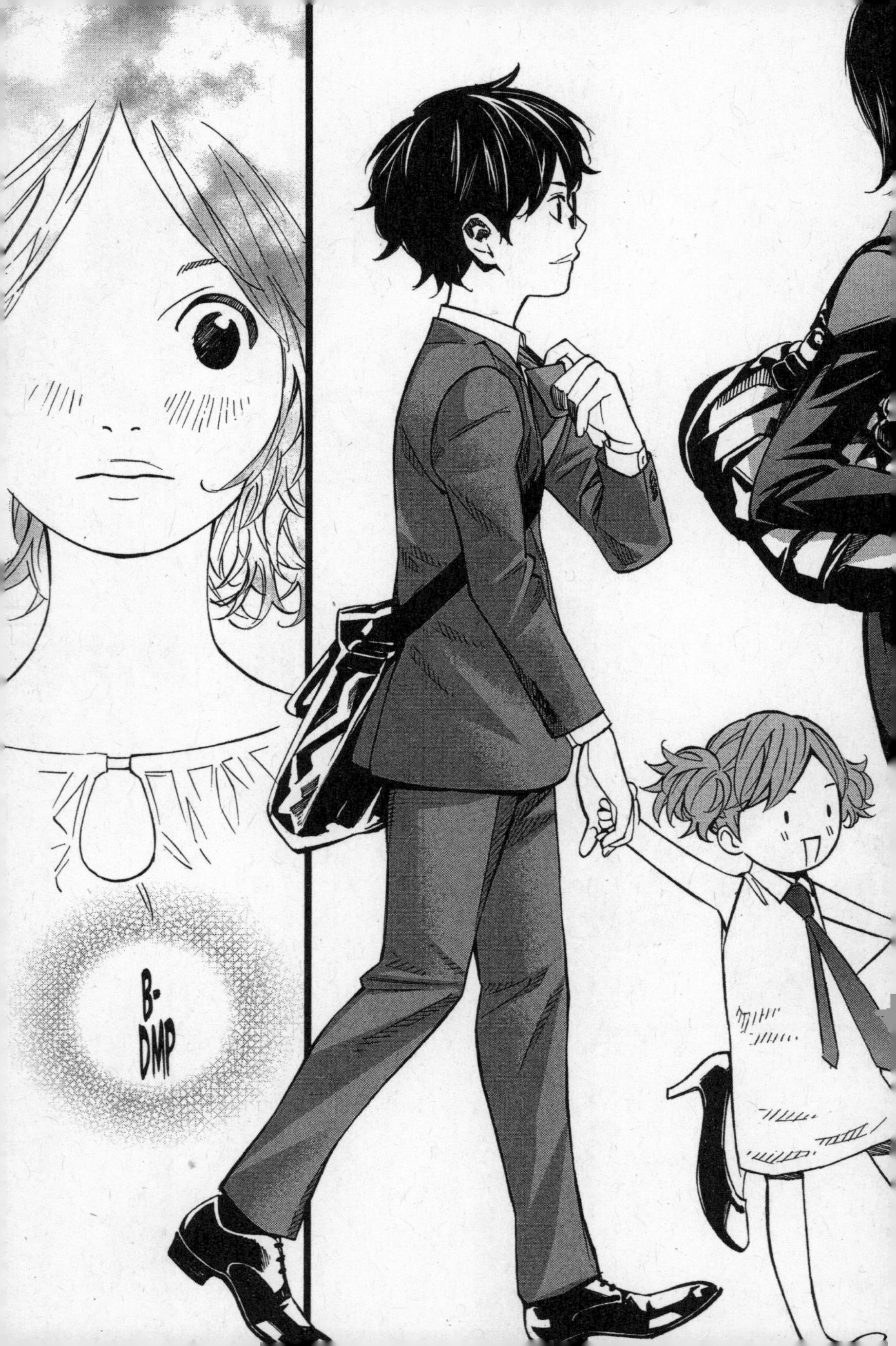
B-DMP

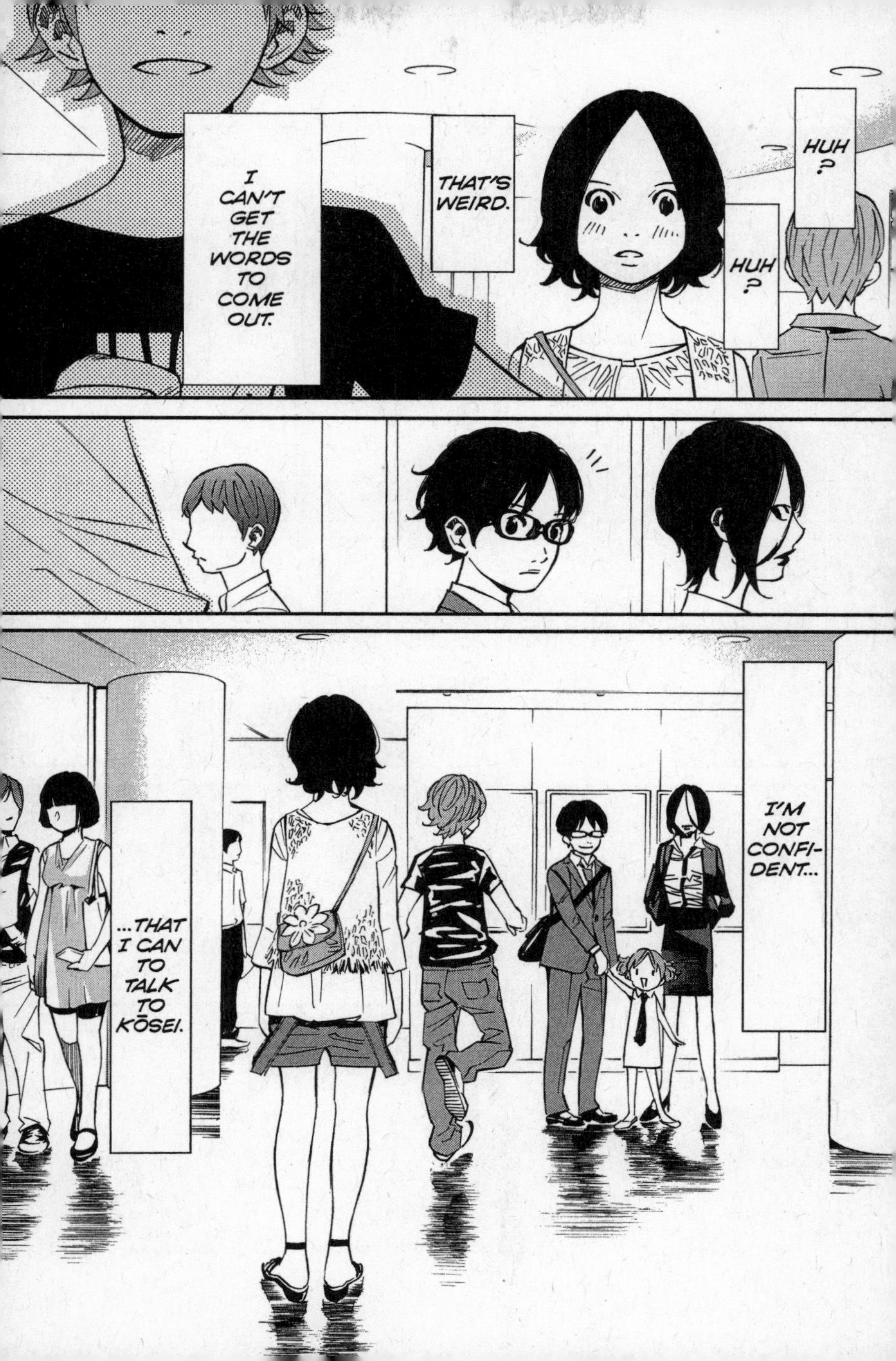
HUH?
HUH?
THAT'S WEIRD.
I CAN'T GET THE WORDS TO COME OUT.
I'M NOT CONFIDENT...
...THAT I CAN TO TALK TO KŌSEI.

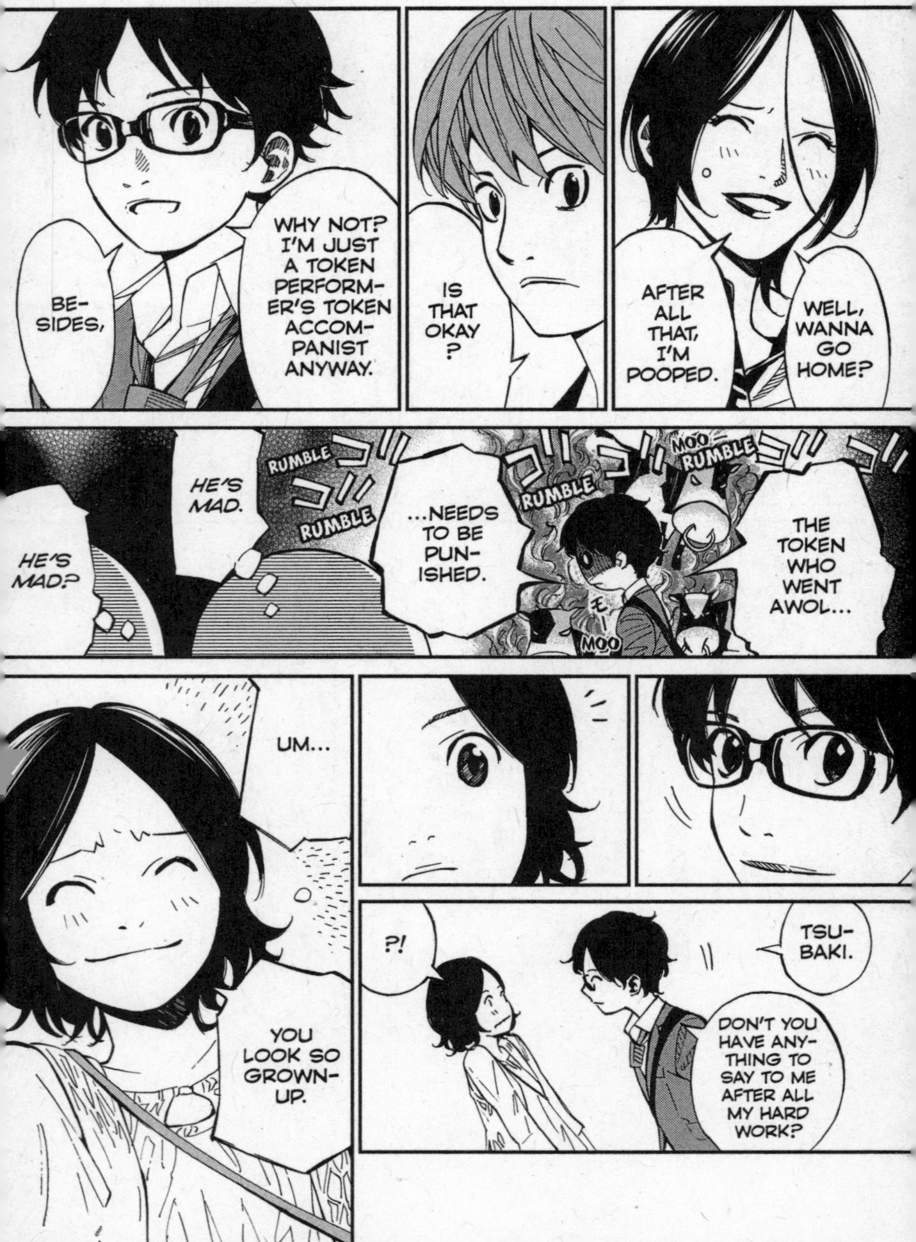
WELL, WANNA GO HOME?
AFTER ALL THAT, I'M POOPED.
IS THAT OKAY?
WHY NOT? I'M JUST A TOKEN PERFORMER-ER'S TOKEN ACCOMPANIST ANYWAY.
BE-SIDES,
THE TOKEN WHO WENT AWOL...
MOO
RUMBLE
RUMBLE
MOO
...NEEDS TO BE PUN-ISHED.
RUMBLE
RUMBLE
HE'S MAD.
HE'S MAD?
TSU-BAKI.
DON'T YOU HAVE ANY-THING TO SAY TO ME AFTER ALL MY HARD WORK?
?!
UM...
YOU LOOK SO GROWN-UP.

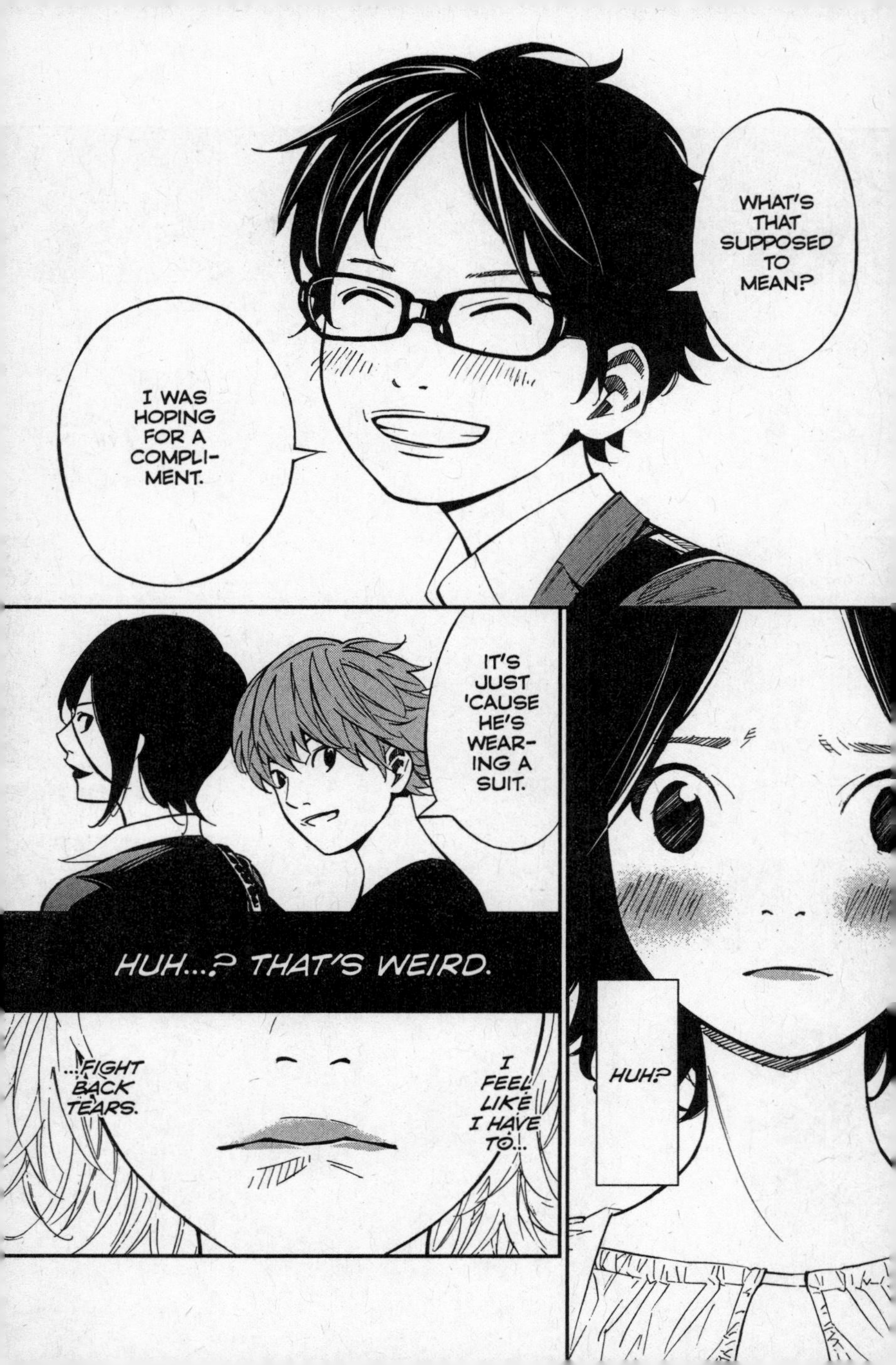
WHAT'S THAT SUPPOSED TO MEAN?
I WAS HOPING FOR A COMPLI- MENT.
HUH?
IT'S JUST 'CAUSE HE'S WEAR- ING A SUIT.
HUH...? THAT'S WEIRD.
I FEEL LIKE I HAVE TO...
...FIGHT BACK TEARS.

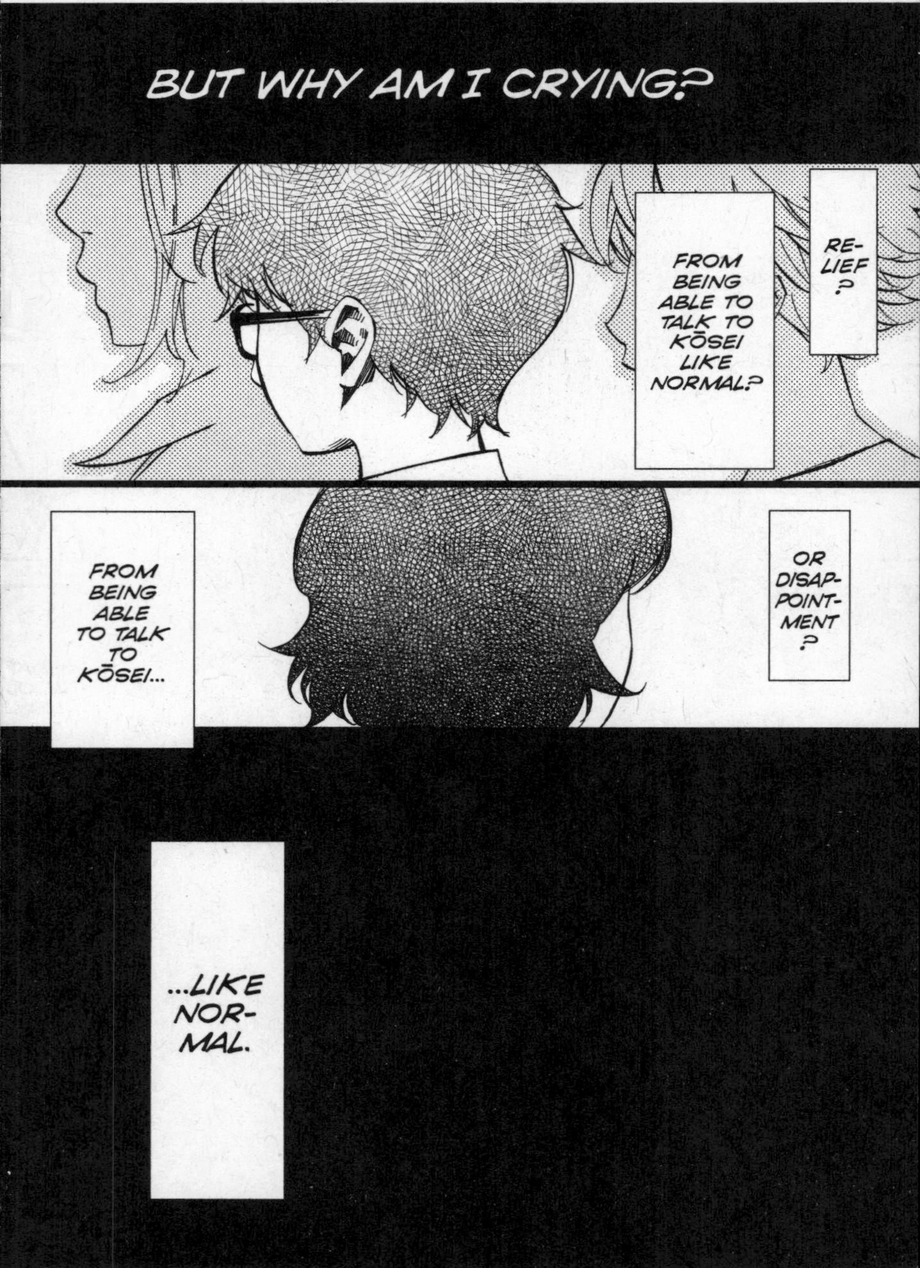
BUT WHY AM I CRYING?
RE-LIEF?
FROM BEING ABLE TO TALK TO KŌSEI LIKE NORMAL?
OR DISAP-POINT-MENT?
FROM BEING ABLE TO TALK TO KŌSEI...
...LIKE NOR-MAL.

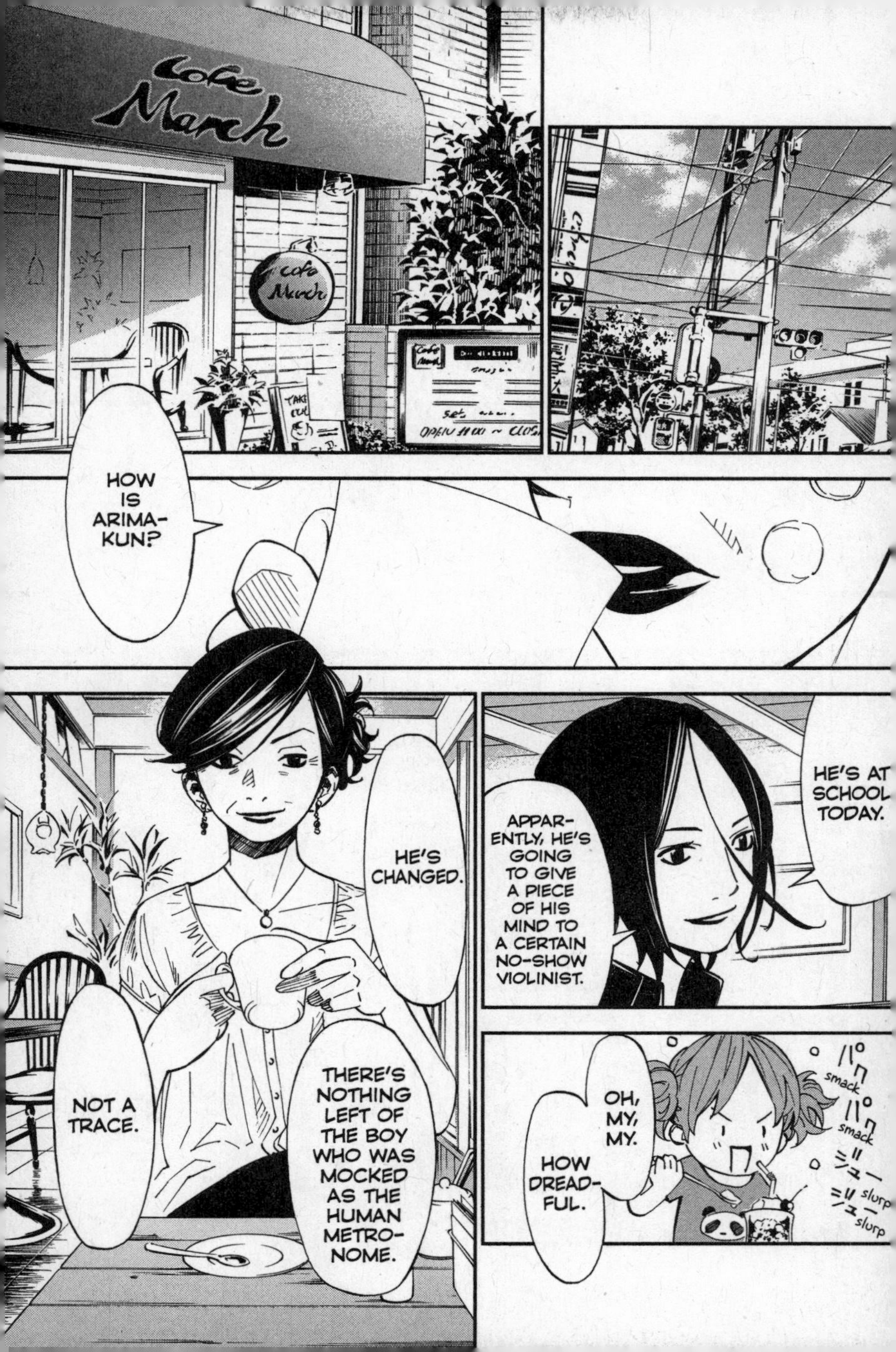

Cafe March
HOW IS ARIMA-KUN?
HE'S AT SCHOOL TODAY.
APPARENTLY, HE'S GOING TO GIVE A PIECE OF HIS MIND TO A CERTAIN NO-SHOW VIOLINIST.
OH, MY, MY.
HOW DREADFUL.
パク smack
パク smack
ジュー slurp
ジュー slurp
HE'S CHANGED.
THERE'S NOTHING LEFT OF THE BOY WHO WAS MOCKED AS THE HUMAN METRONOME.
NOT A TRACE.

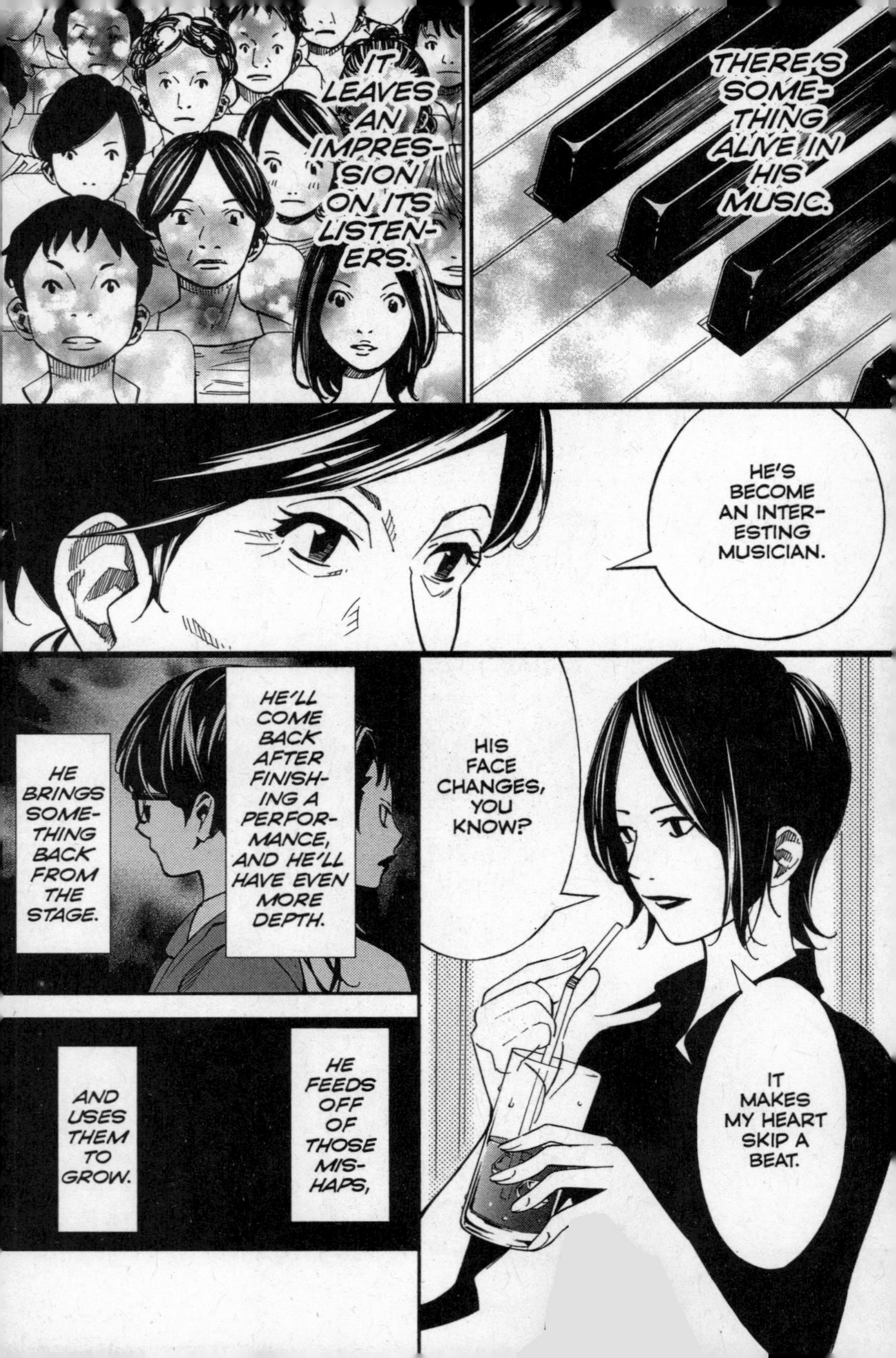
THERE'S SOMETHING ALIVE IN HIS MUSIC.
IT LEAVES AN IMPRESSION ON ITS LISTENERS.
HE'S BECOME AN INTERESTING MUSICIAN.
HIS FACE CHANGES, YOU KNOW?
IT MAKES MY HEART SKIP A BEAT.
HE'LL COME BACK AFTER FINISHING A PERFORMANCE, AND HE'LL HAVE EVEN MORE DEPTH.
HE BRINGS SOMETHING BACK FROM THE STAGE.
HE FEEDS OFF OF THOSE MISHAPS,
AND USES THEM TO GROW.

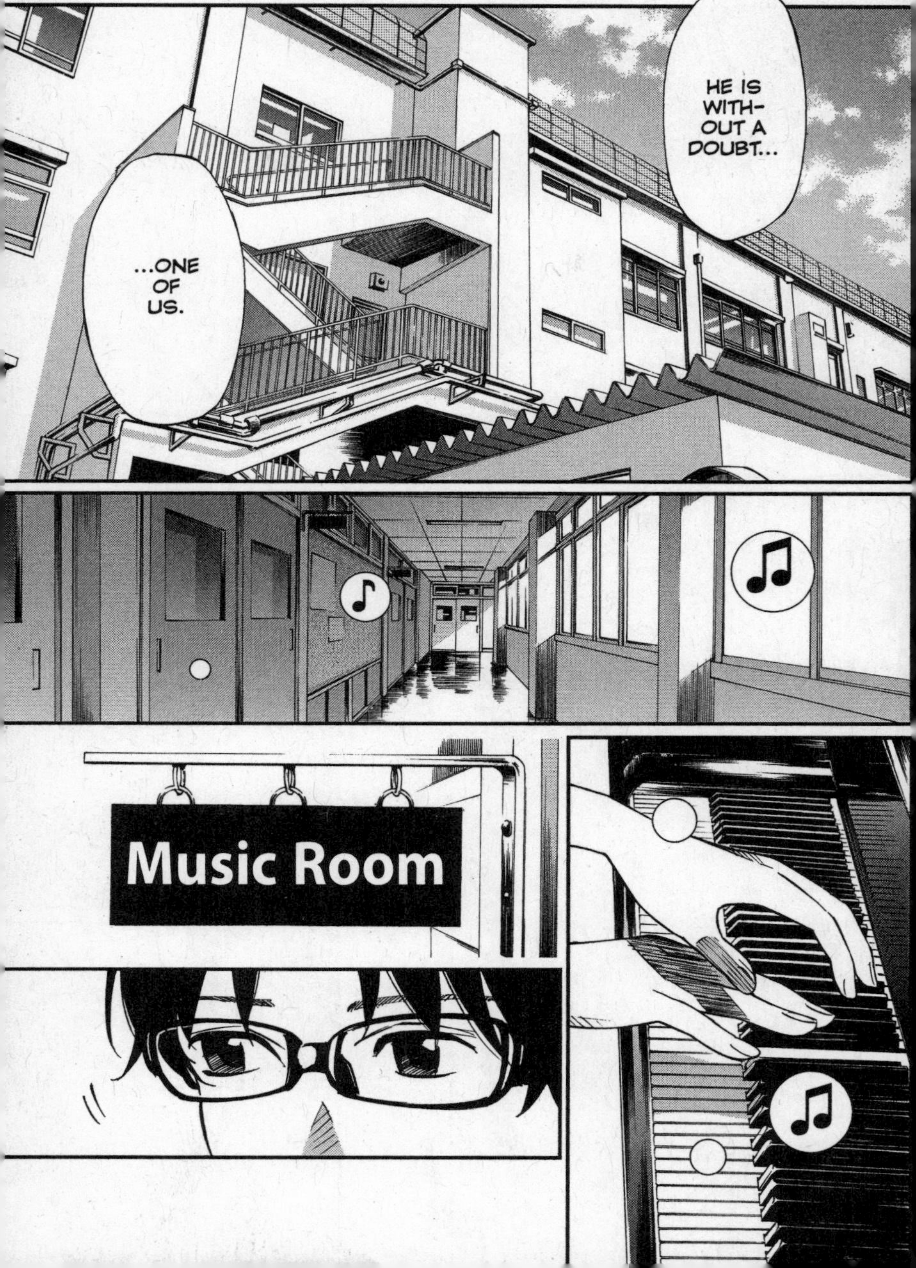
HE IS WITHOUT A DOUBT...
...ONE OF US.
Music Room

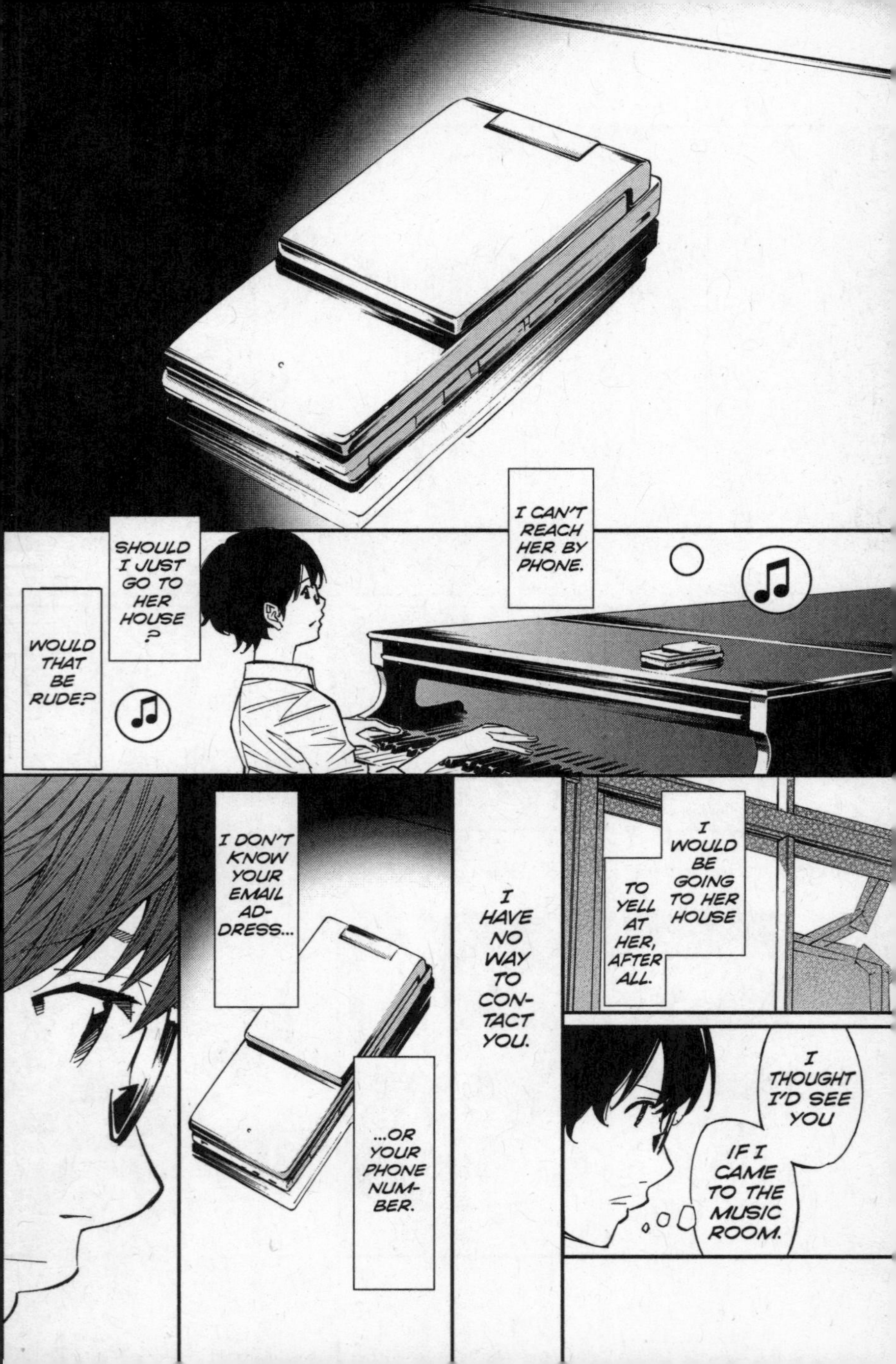
I CAN'T REACH HER BY PHONE.
SHOULD I JUST GO TO HER HOUSE ?
WOULD THAT BE RUDE?
I WOULD BE GOING TO HER HOUSE
TO YELL AT HER, AFTER ALL.
I THOUGHT I'D SEE YOU
IF I CAME TO THE MUSIC ROOM.
I HAVE NO WAY TO CONTACT YOU.
I DON'T KNOW YOUR EMAIL ADDRESS...
...OR YOUR PHONE NUMBER.

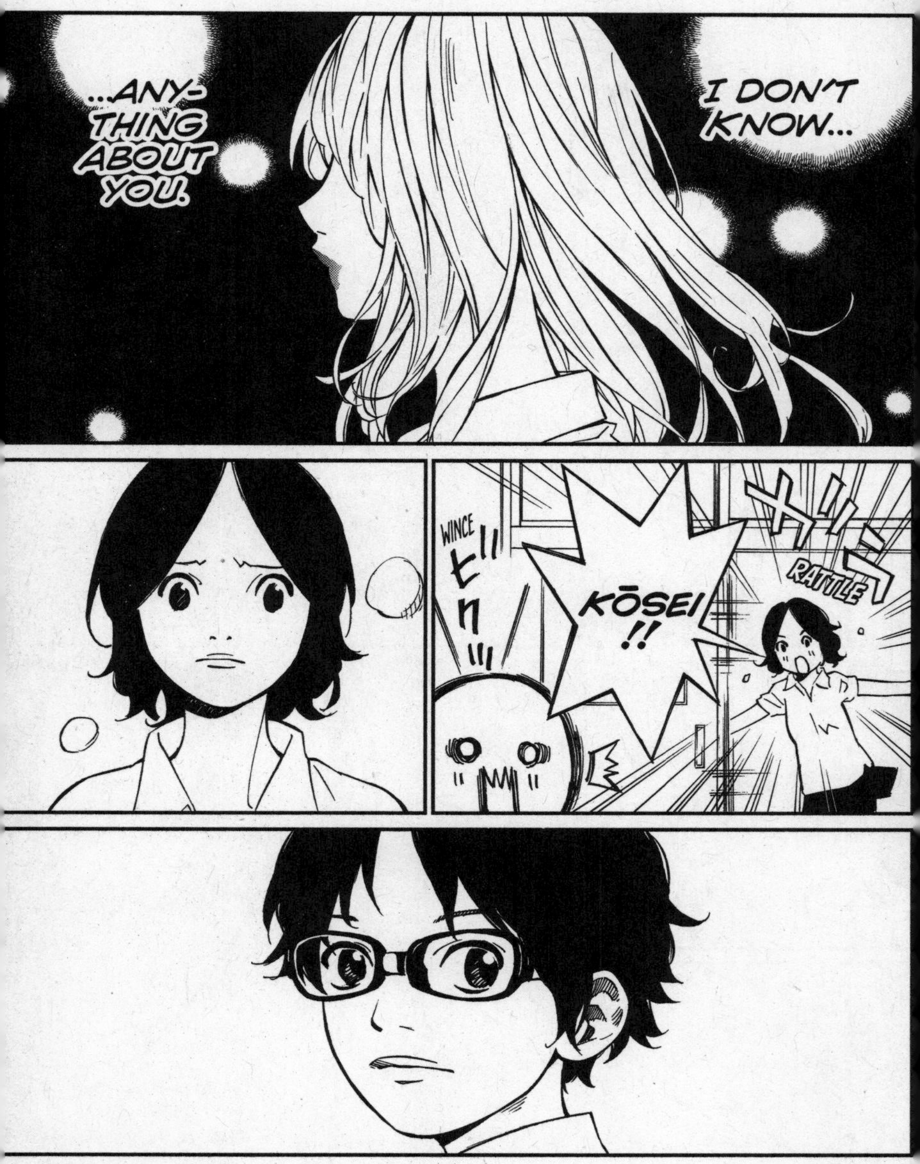
I DON'T KNOW...
...ANY-THING ABOUT YOU.
RATTLE
KŌSEI!!
WINCE

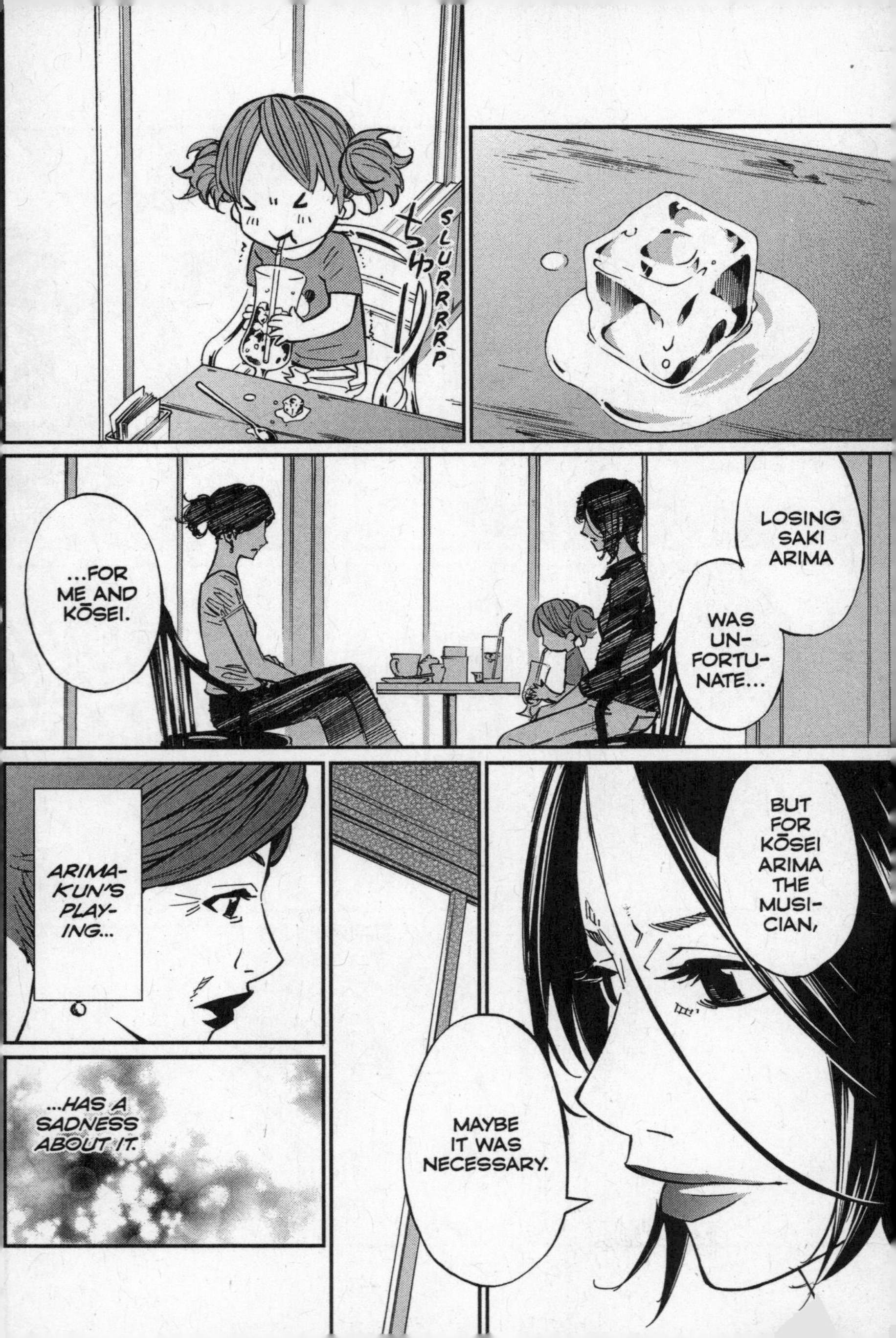
ちゅ
SLURRRRP
LOSING SAKI ARIMA
WAS UN-FORTU-NATE...
...FOR ME AND KŌSEI.
BUT FOR KŌSEI ARIMA THE MUSI-CIAN,
MAYBE IT WAS NECESSARY.
ARIMA-KUN'S PLAY-ING...
...HAS A SADNESS ABOUT IT.

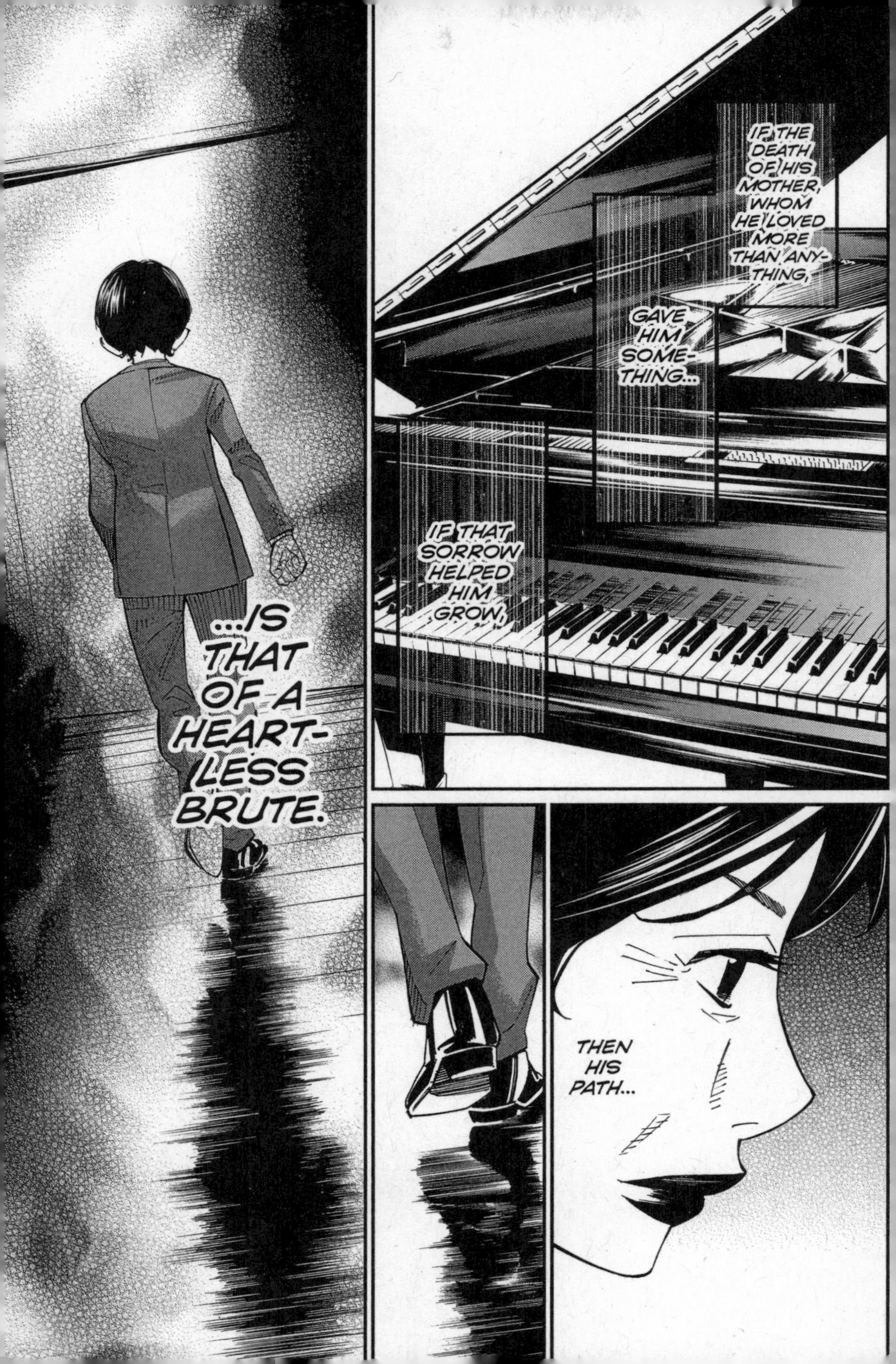
IF THE DEATH OF HIS MOTHER, WHOM HE LOVED MORE THAN ANY-THING,
GAVE HIM SOME-THING...
IF THAT SORROW HELPED HIM GROW,
THEN HIS PATH...
...IS THAT OF A HEART-LESS BRUTE.

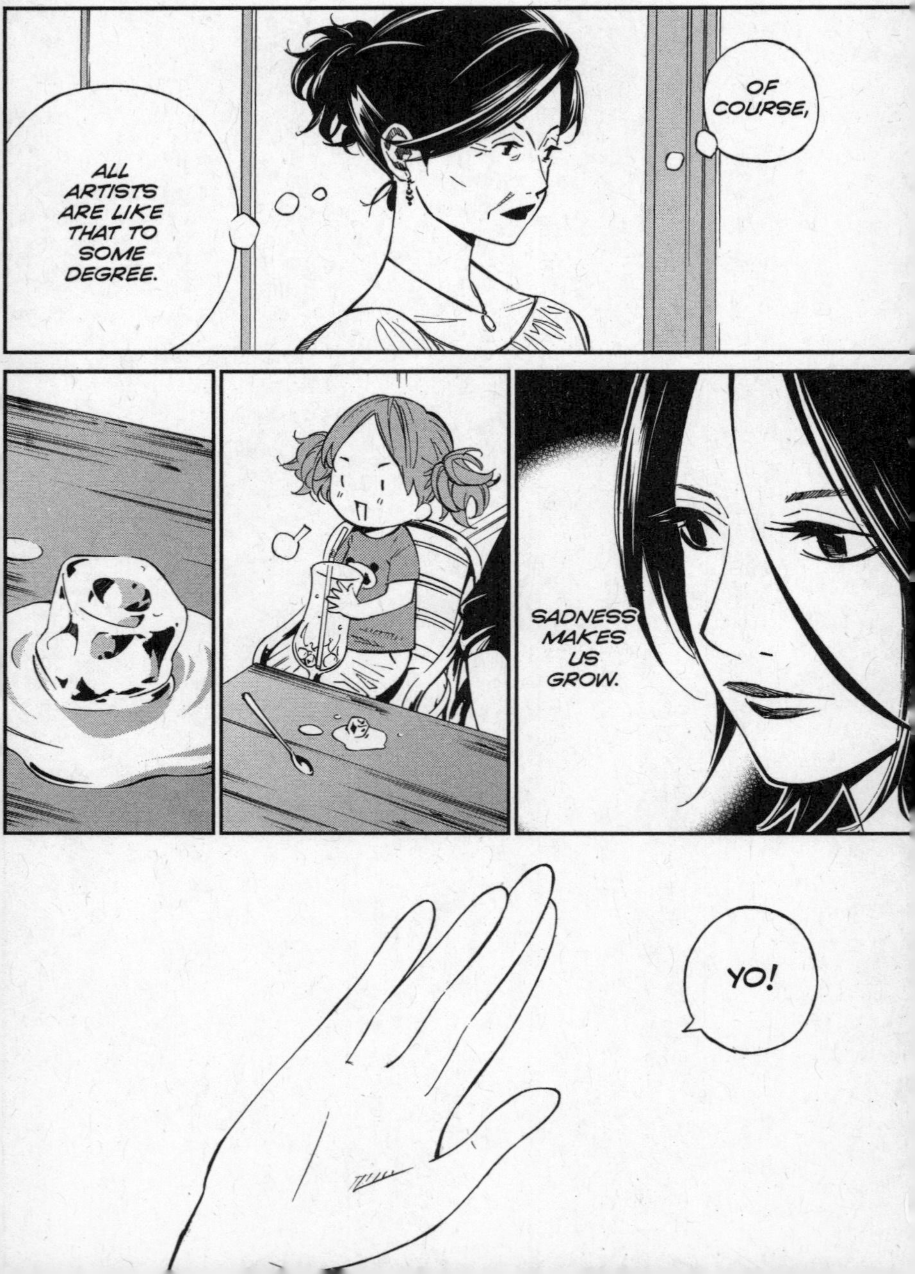
OF COURSE,
ALL ARTISTS ARE LIKE THAT TO SOME DEGREE.
SADNESS MAKES US GROW.
YO!

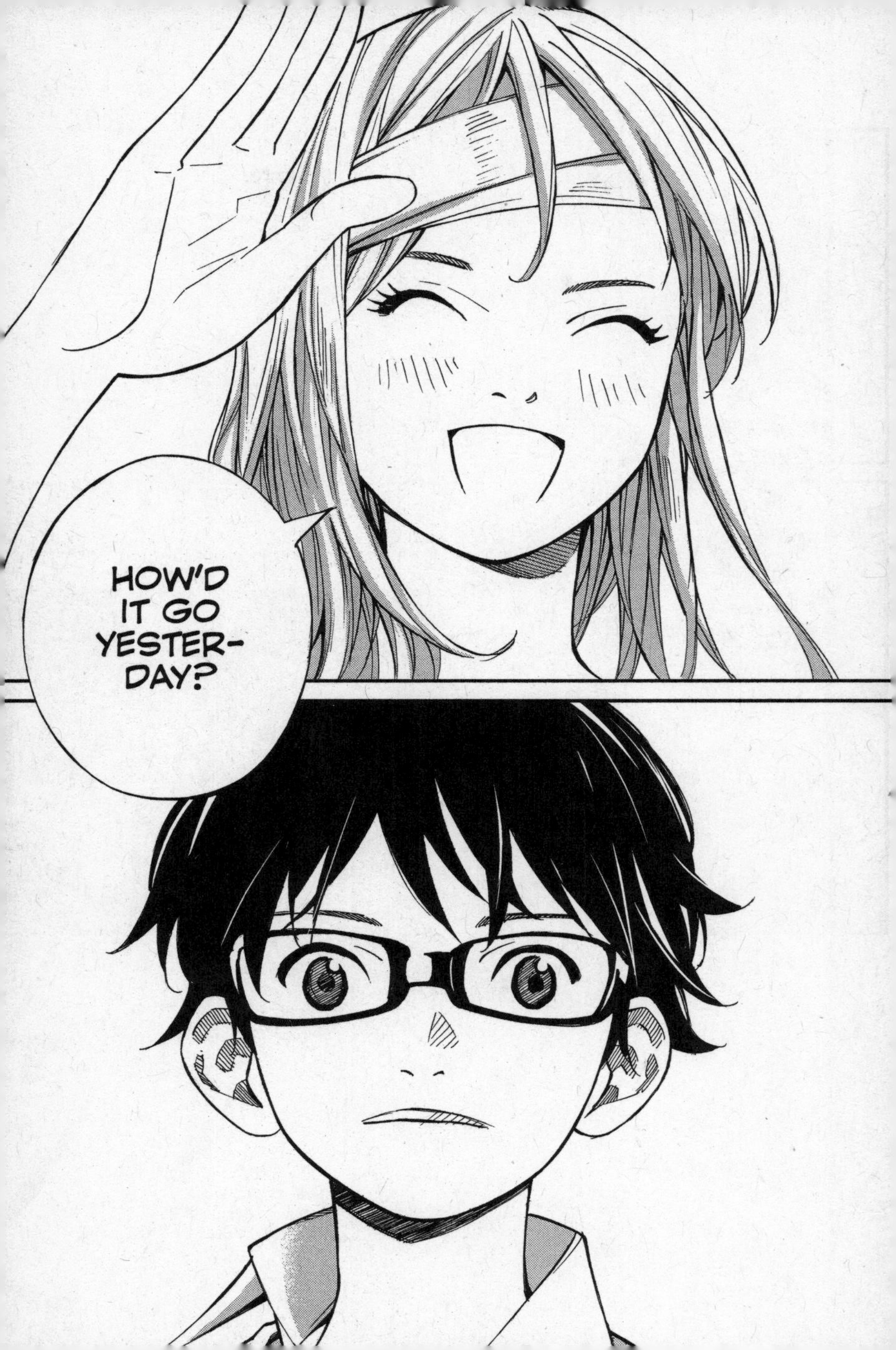
HOW'D IT GO YESTER-DAY?

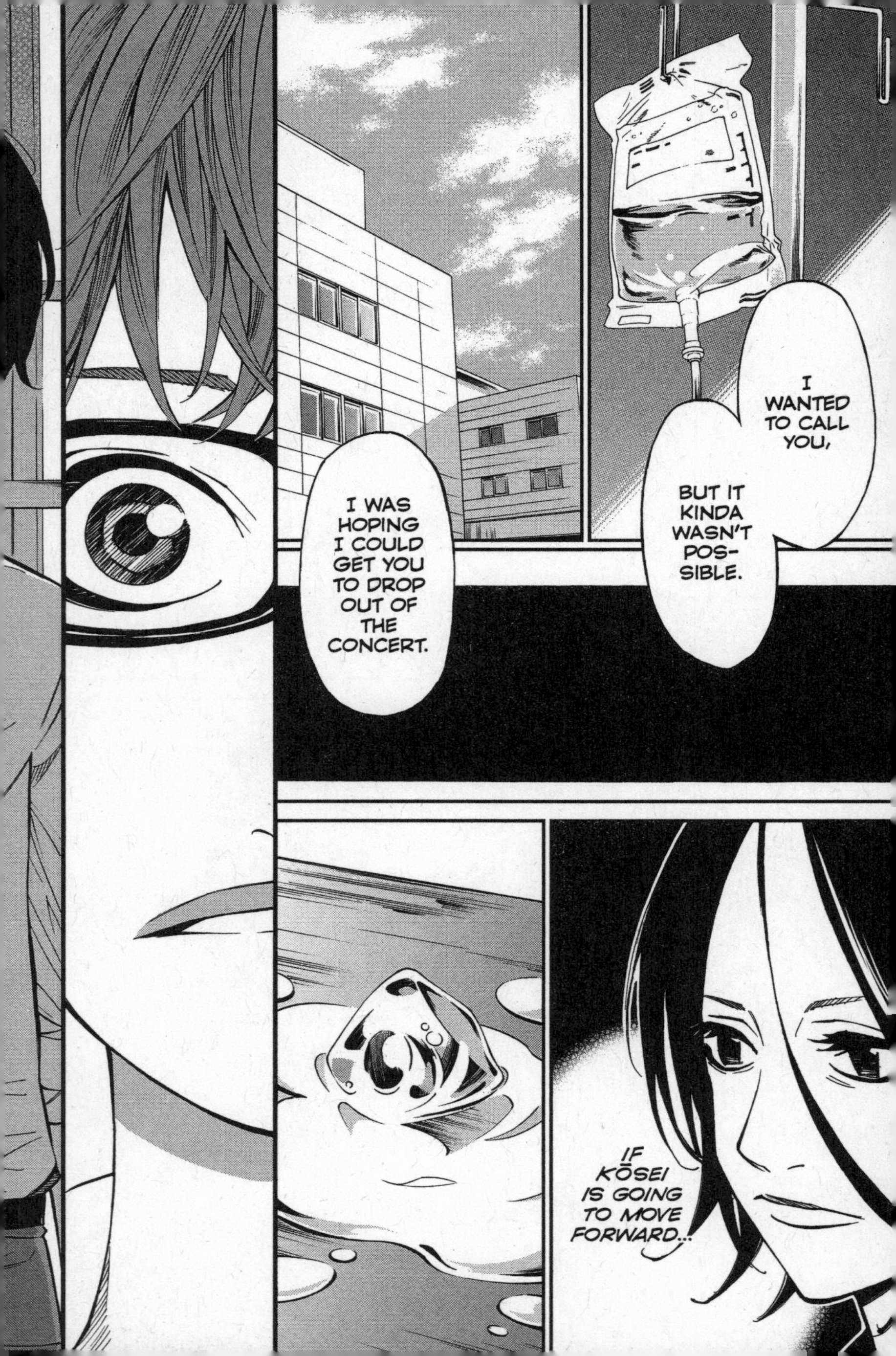
I WANTED TO CALL YOU,
BUT IT KINDA WASN'T POS-SIBLE.
I WAS HOPING I COULD GET YOU TO DROP OUT OF THE CONCERT.
IF KŌSEI IS GOING TO MOVE FORWARD...

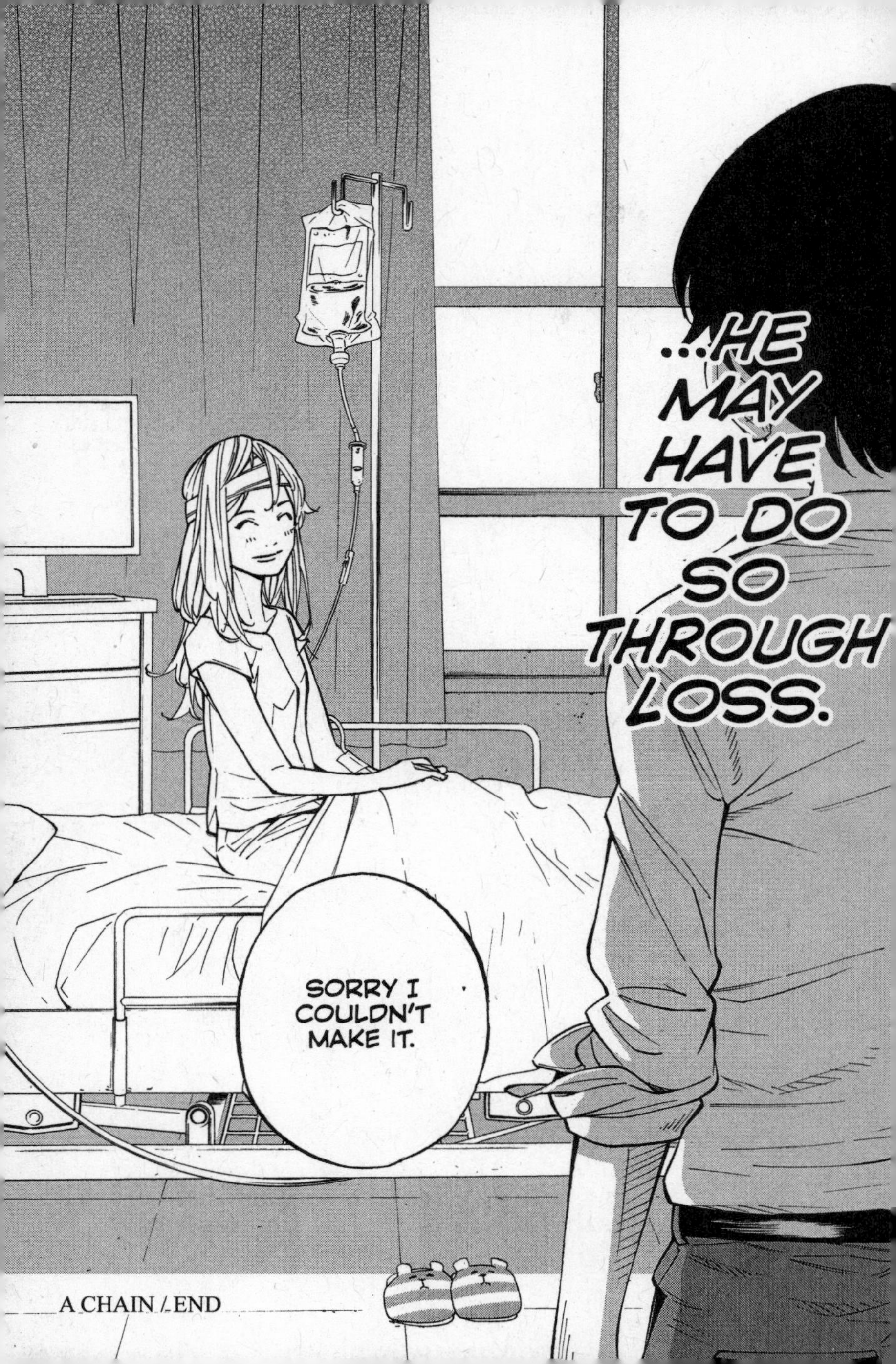
...HE MAY HAVE TO DO SO THROUGH LOSS.
SORRY I COULDN'T MAKE IT.
A CHAIN / END

I met the girl under full-bloomed cherry blossoms, and my fate has begun to change.

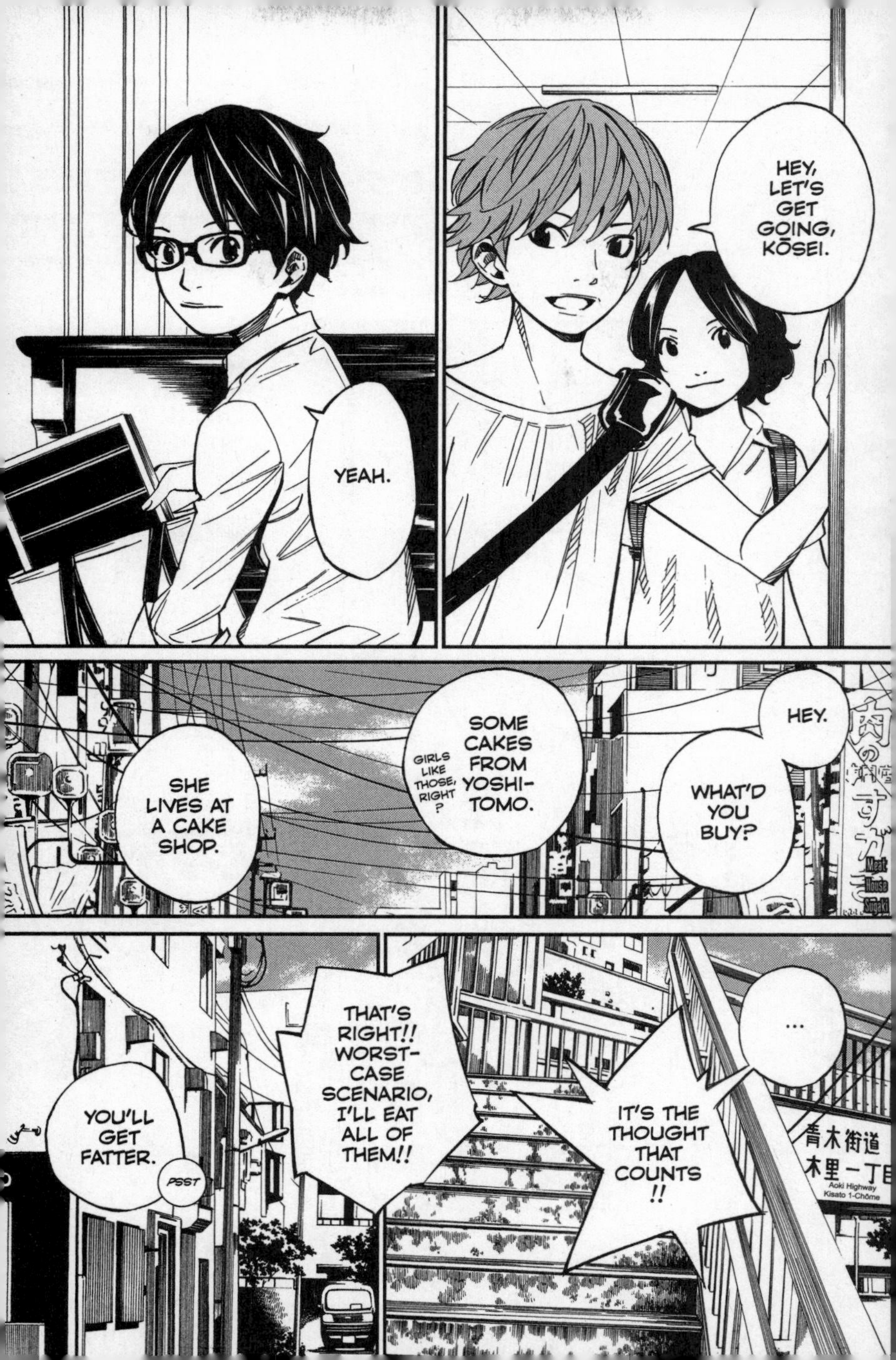
HEY, LET'S GET GOING, KŌSEI.
YEAH.
HEY.
WHAT'D YOU BUY?
SOME CAKES FROM YOSHI-TOMO.
GIRLS LIKE THOSE, RIGHT?
SHE LIVES AT A CAKE SHOP.
Meat House Sugaki
...
IT'S THE THOUGHT THAT COUNTS!!
青木街道
木里一丁目
Aoki Highway
Kisato 1-Chōme
THAT'S RIGHT!! WORST-CASE SCENARIO, I'LL EAT ALL OF THEM!!
YOU'LL GET FATTER.
PSST

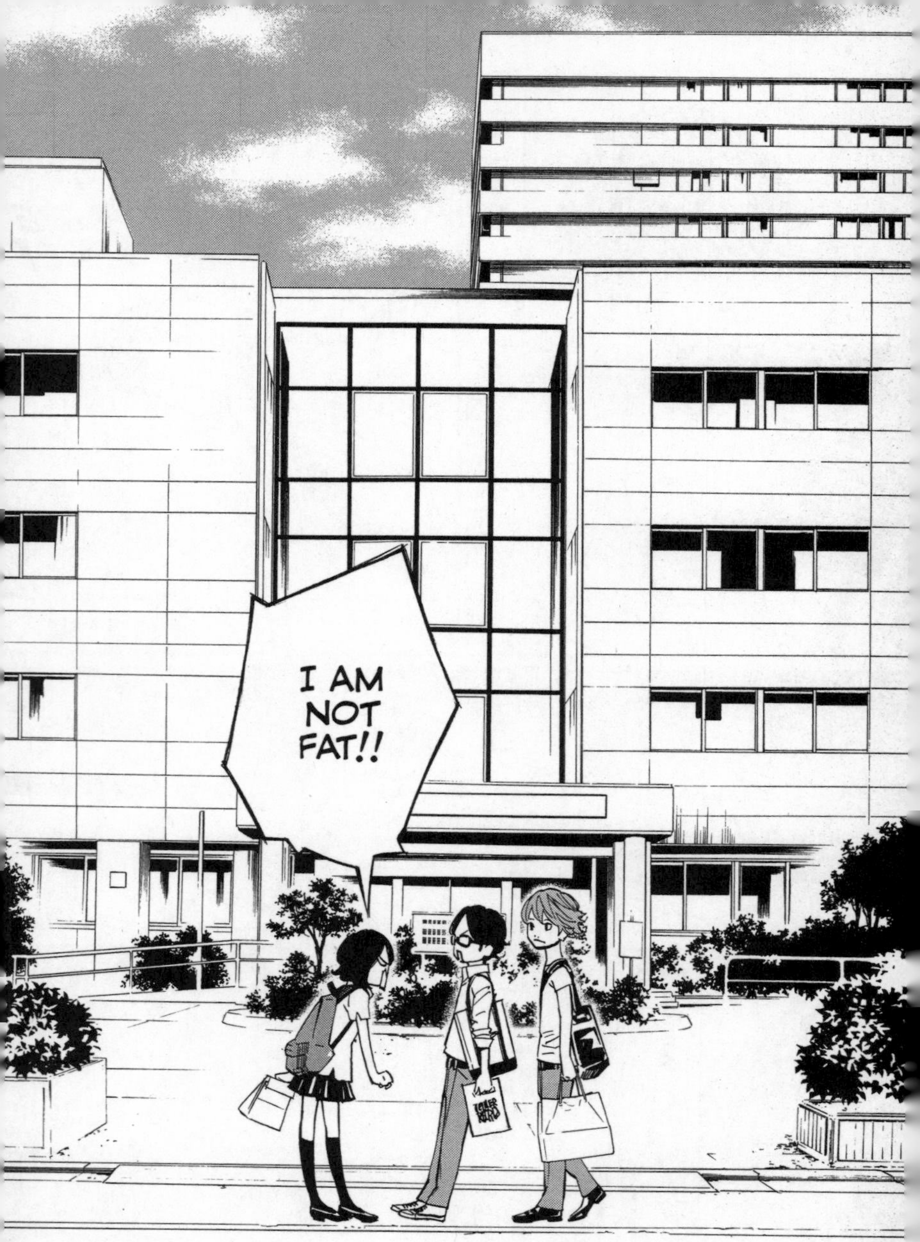
I AM NOT FAT!!

CHAPTER 27: SUPER-IMPOSED OUTLINES

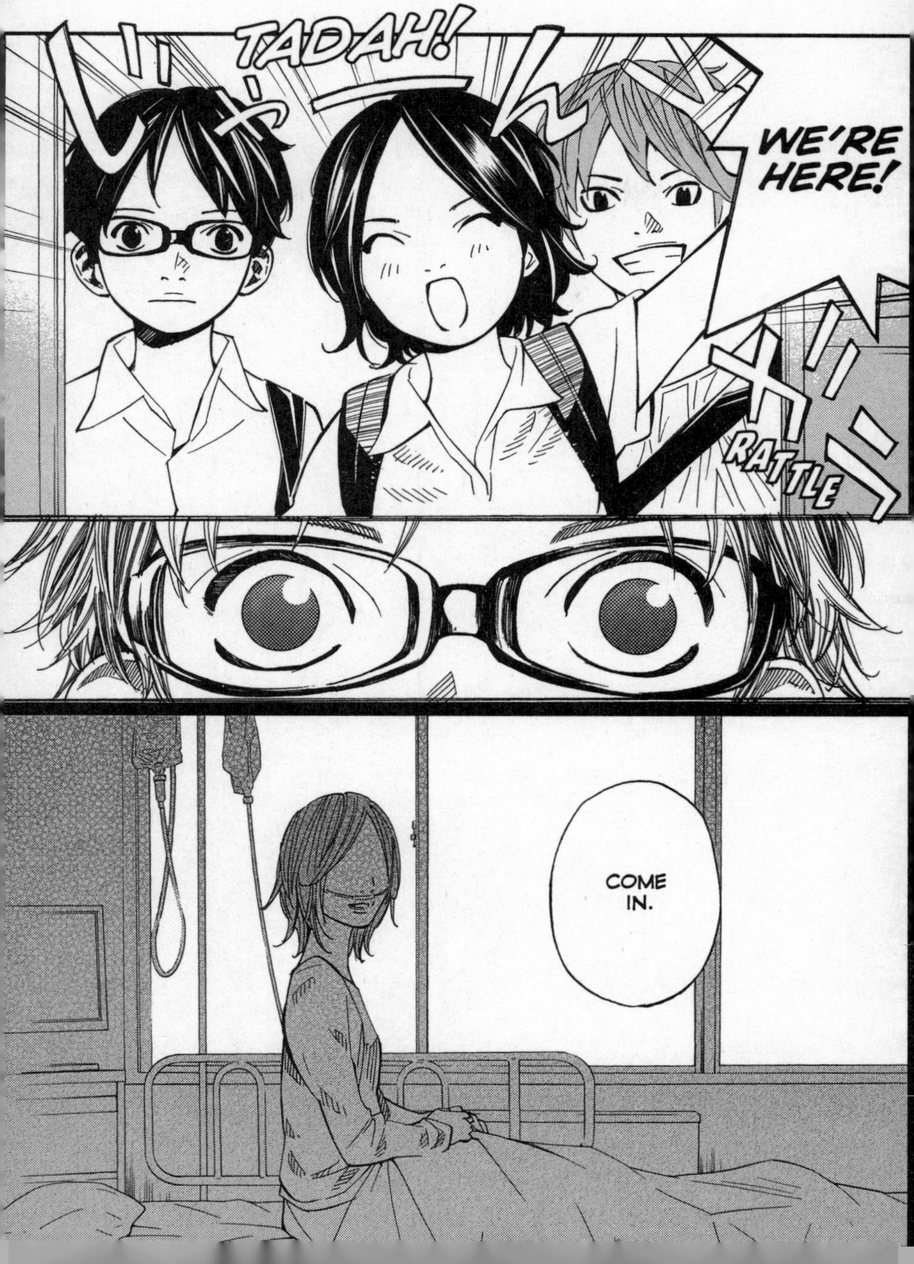
WE'RE HERE!
RATTLE
TADAH!
COME IN.

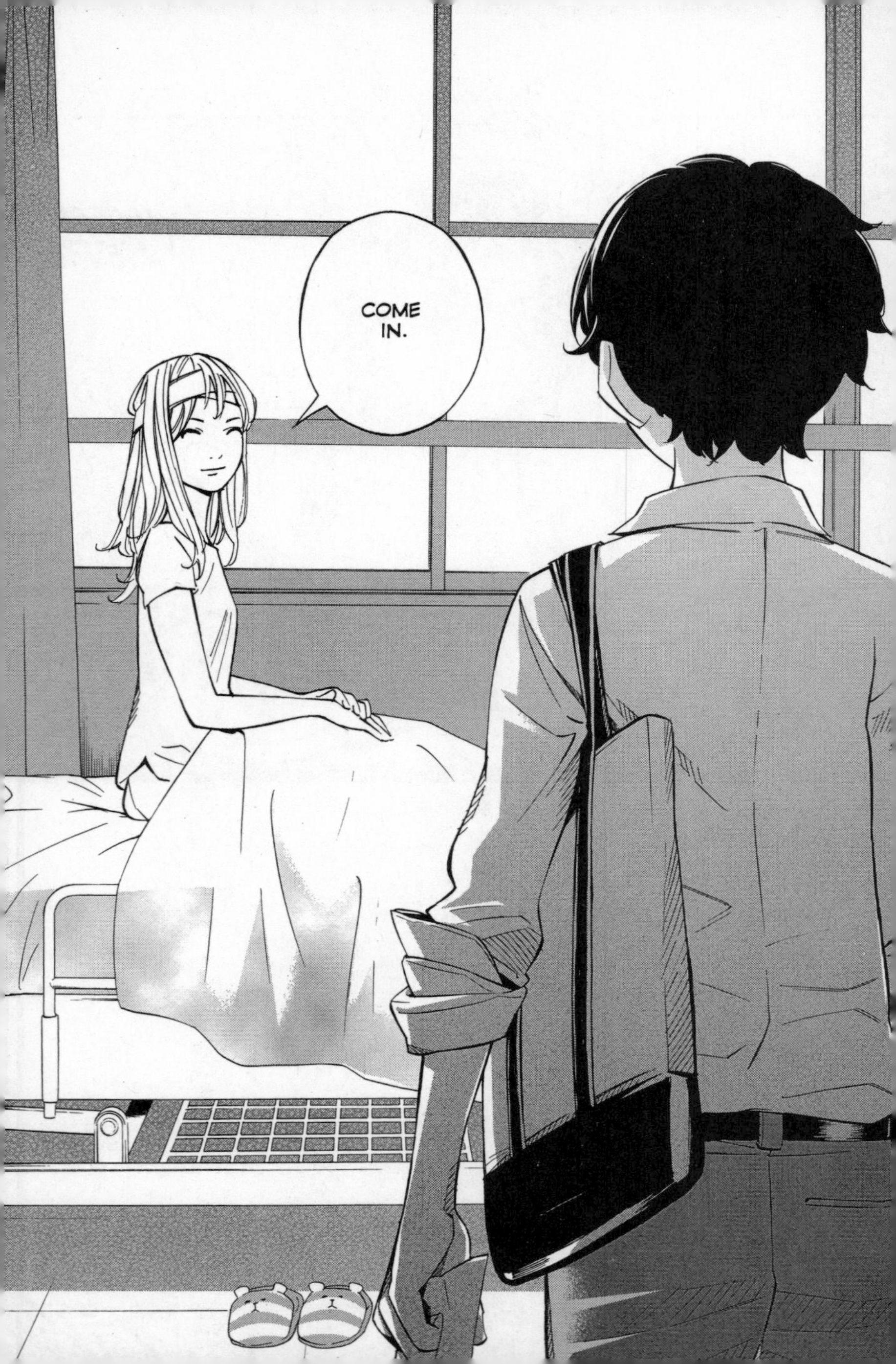
COME IN.

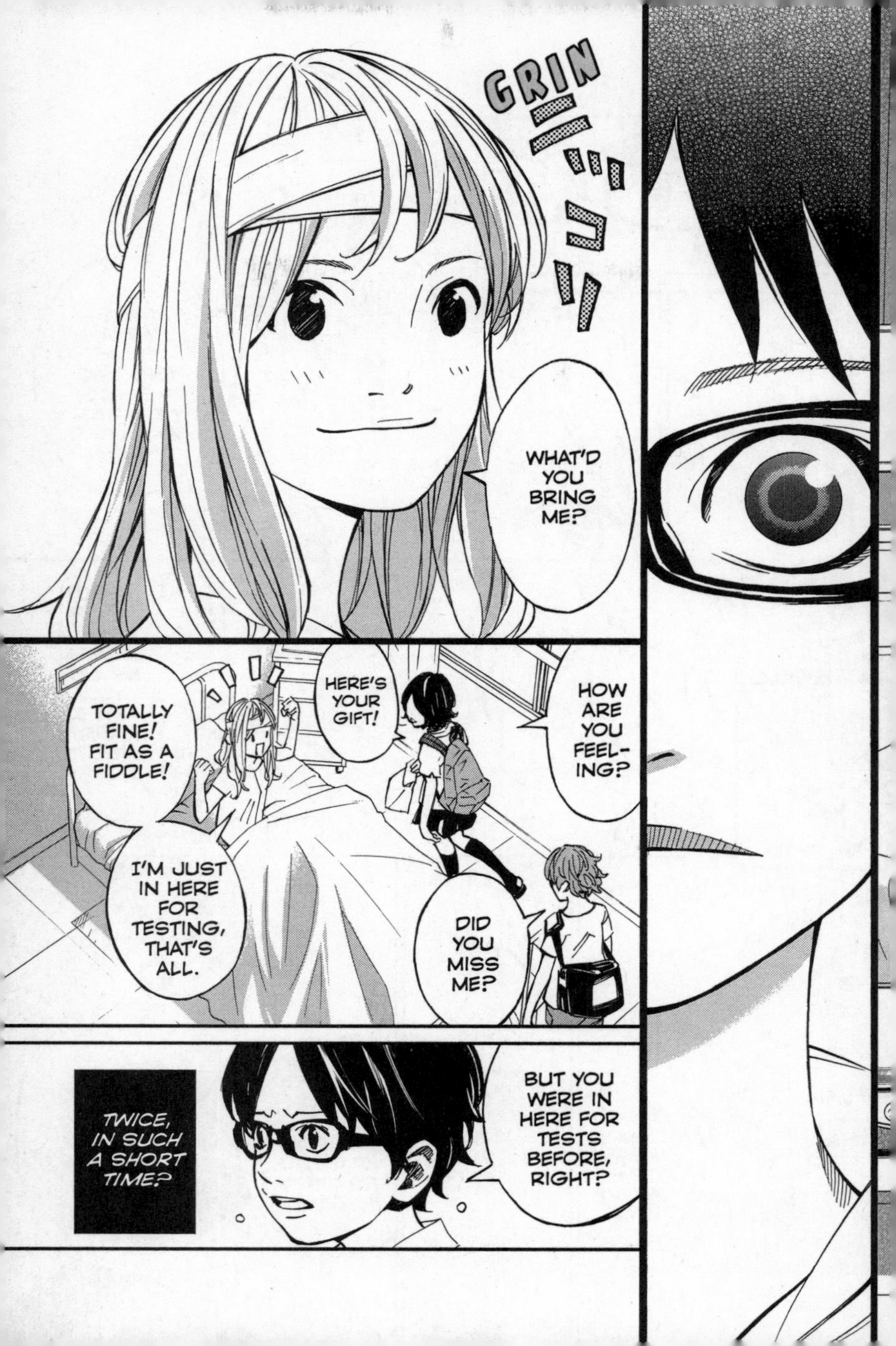
GRIN
WHAT'D YOU BRING ME?
HOW ARE YOU FEEL-ING?
HERE'S YOUR GIFT!
TOTALLY FINE! FIT AS A FIDDLE!
DID YOU MISS ME?
I'M JUST IN HERE FOR TESTING, THAT'S ALL.
BUT YOU WERE IN HERE FOR TESTS BEFORE, RIGHT?
TWICE, IN SUCH A SHORT TIME?

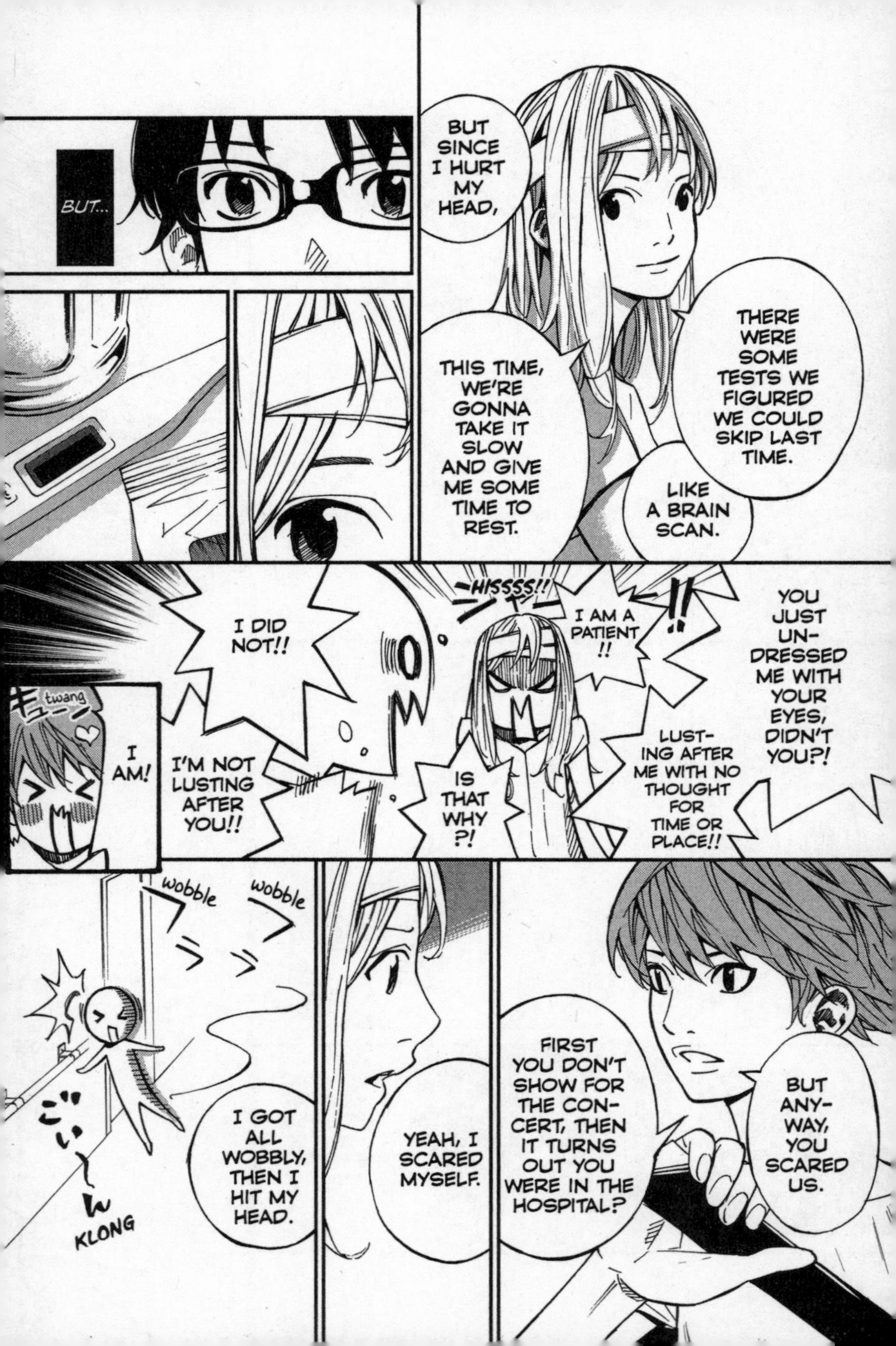
BUT SINCE I HURT MY HEAD,
THERE WERE SOME TESTS WE FIGURED WE COULD SKIP LAST TIME.
LIKE A BRAIN SCAN.
THIS TIME, WE'RE GONNA TAKE IT SLOW AND GIVE ME SOME TIME TO REST.
BUT...
YOU JUST UN-DRESSED ME WITH YOUR EYES, DIDN'T YOU?!
!!
I AM A PATIENT !!
—HISSSS!!
LUSTING AFTER ME WITH NO THOUGHT FOR TIME OR PLACE!!
IS THAT WHY ?!
I DID NOT!!
I'M NOT LUSTING AFTER YOU!!
twang
I AM!
BUT ANYWAY, YOU SCARED US.
FIRST YOU DON'T SHOW FOR THE CONCERT, THEN IT TURNS OUT YOU WERE IN THE HOSPITAL?
YEAH, I SCARED MYSELF.
I GOT ALL WOBBLY, THEN I HIT MY HEAD.
wobble
wobble
KLONG

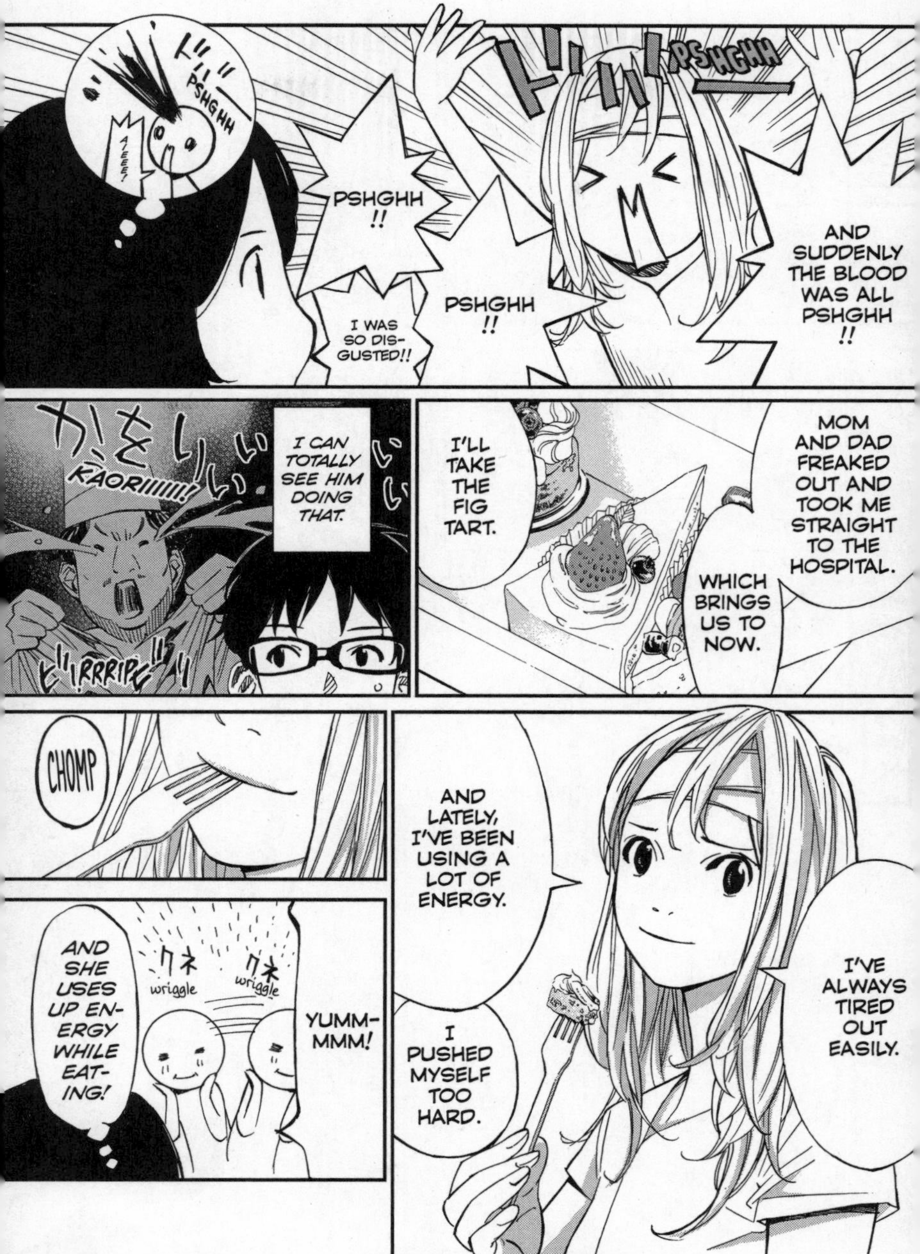
PSHGHH
AND SUDDENLY THE BLOOD WAS ALL PSHGHH!!
PSHGHH!!
PSHGHH!!
I WAS SO DIS-GUSTED!!
PSHGHH
AIEEE?
MOM AND DAD FREAKED OUT AND TOOK ME STRAIGHT TO THE HOSPITAL.
WHICH BRINGS US TO NOW.
I'LL TAKE THE FIG TART.
I CAN TOTALLY SEE HIM DOING THAT.
KAORI!!!!!!!!
RRRIP
I'VE ALWAYS TIRED OUT EASILY.
AND LATELY, I'VE BEEN USING A LOT OF ENERGY.
I PUSHED MYSELF TOO HARD.
CHOMP
YUMM-MMM!
wriggle
wriggle
AND SHE USES UP EN-ERGY WHILE EAT-ING!

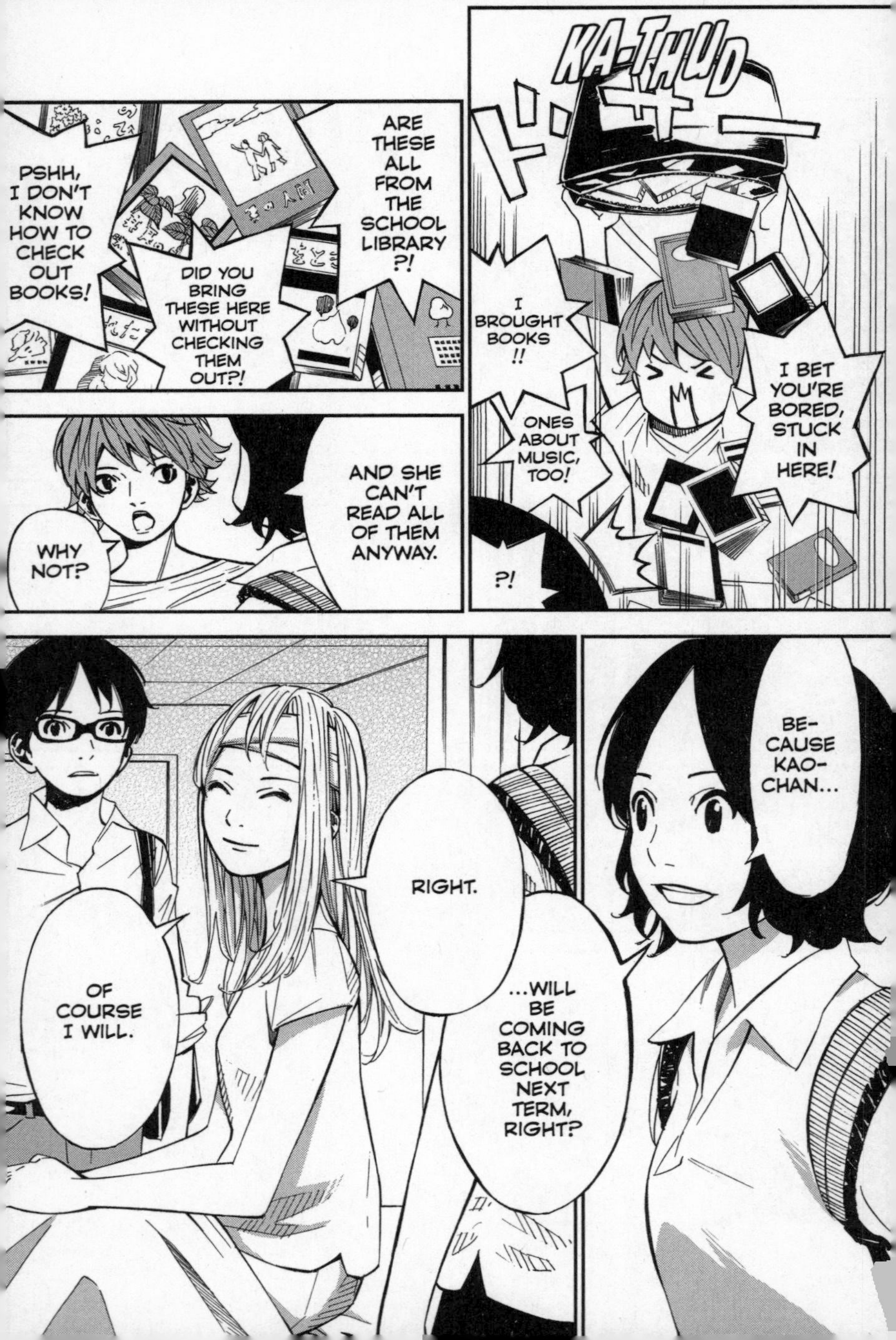
KA-THUD
I BROUGHT BOOKS!!
ONES ABOUT MUSIC, TOO!
I BET YOU'RE BORED, STUCK IN HERE!
?!
ARE THESE ALL FROM THE SCHOOL LIBRARY?!
DID YOU BRING THESE HERE WITHOUT CHECKING THEM OUT?!
PSHH, I DON'T KNOW HOW TO CHECK OUT BOOKS!
AND SHE CAN'T READ ALL OF THEM ANYWAY.
WHY NOT?
BE-CAUSE KAO-CHAN...
...WILL BE COMING BACK TO SCHOOL NEXT TERM, RIGHT?
RIGHT.
OF COURSE I WILL.

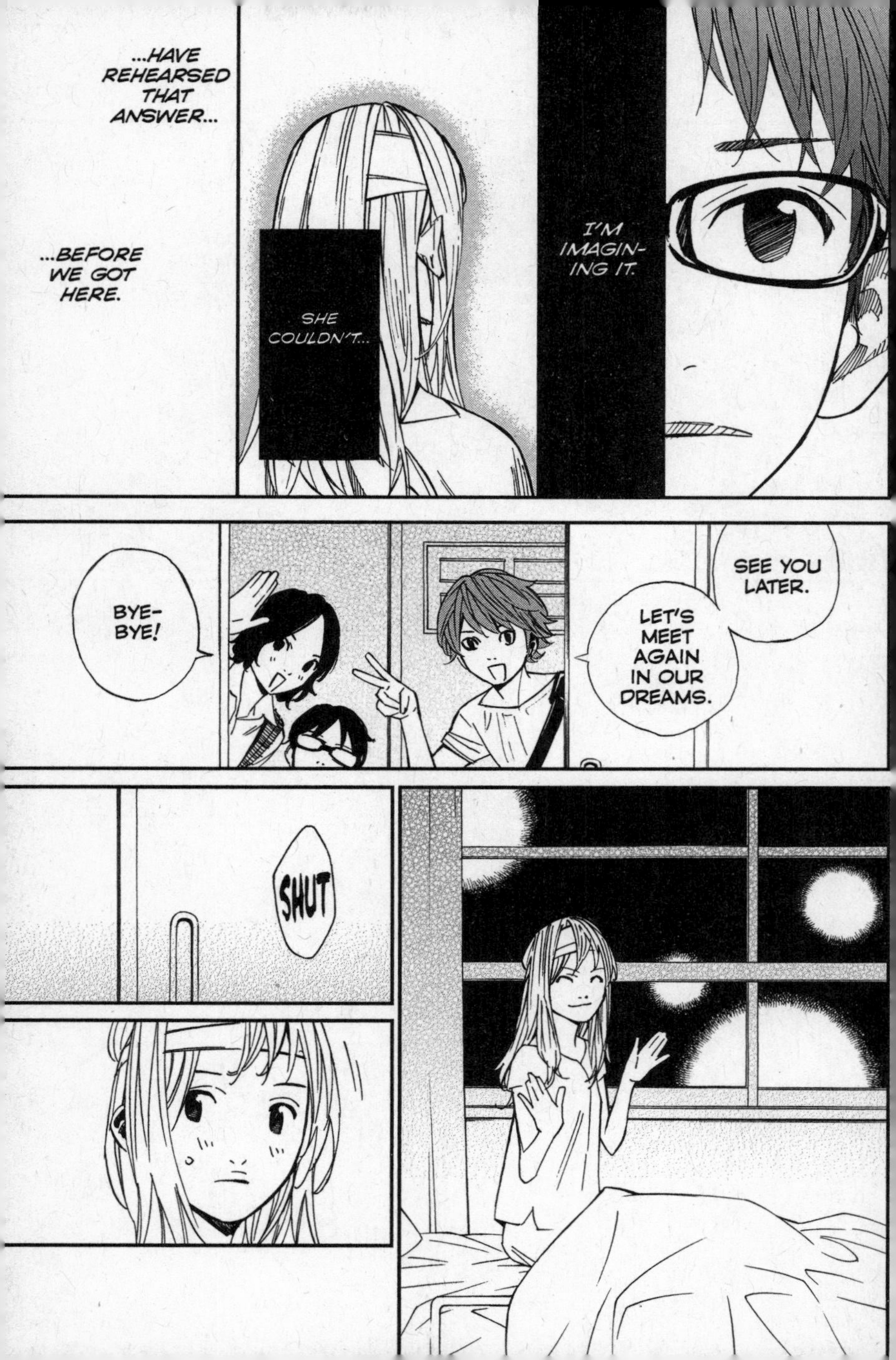
I'M IMAGINING IT.
SHE COULDN'T...
...HAVE REHEARSED THAT ANSWER...
...BEFORE WE GOT HERE.
SEE YOU LATER.
LET'S MEET AGAIN IN OUR DREAMS.
BYE-BYE!
SHUT

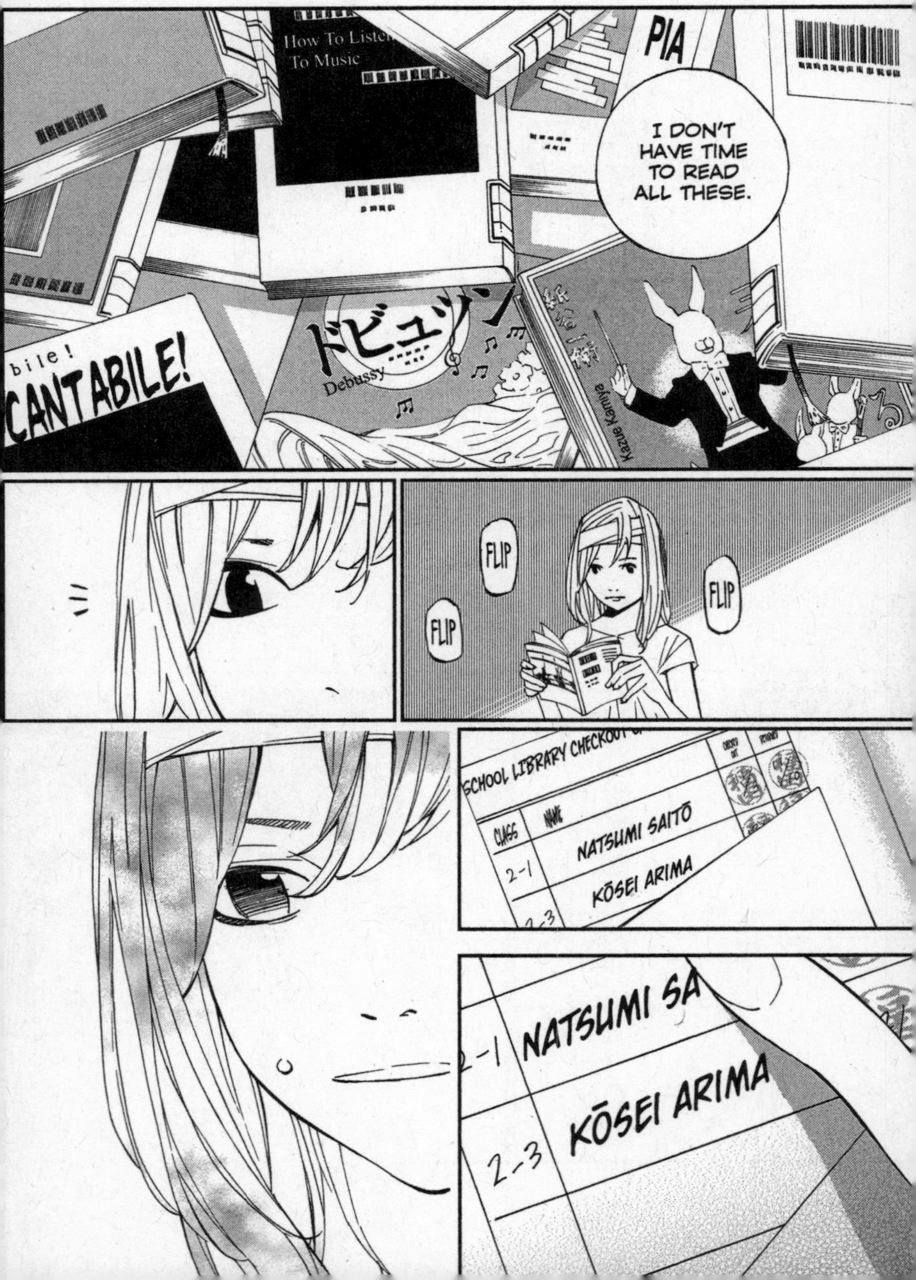
PIA
I DON'T HAVE TIME TO READ ALL THESE.
How To Listen To Music
Kazue Kamiya
Debussy
bile!
CANTABILE!
FLIP
FLIP
FLIP
SCHOOL LIBRARY CHECKOUT
CLASS
NAME
NATSUMI SAITŌ
2-1
KŌSEI ARIMA
2-3
NATSUMI SA
2-1
KŌSEI ARIMA
2-3

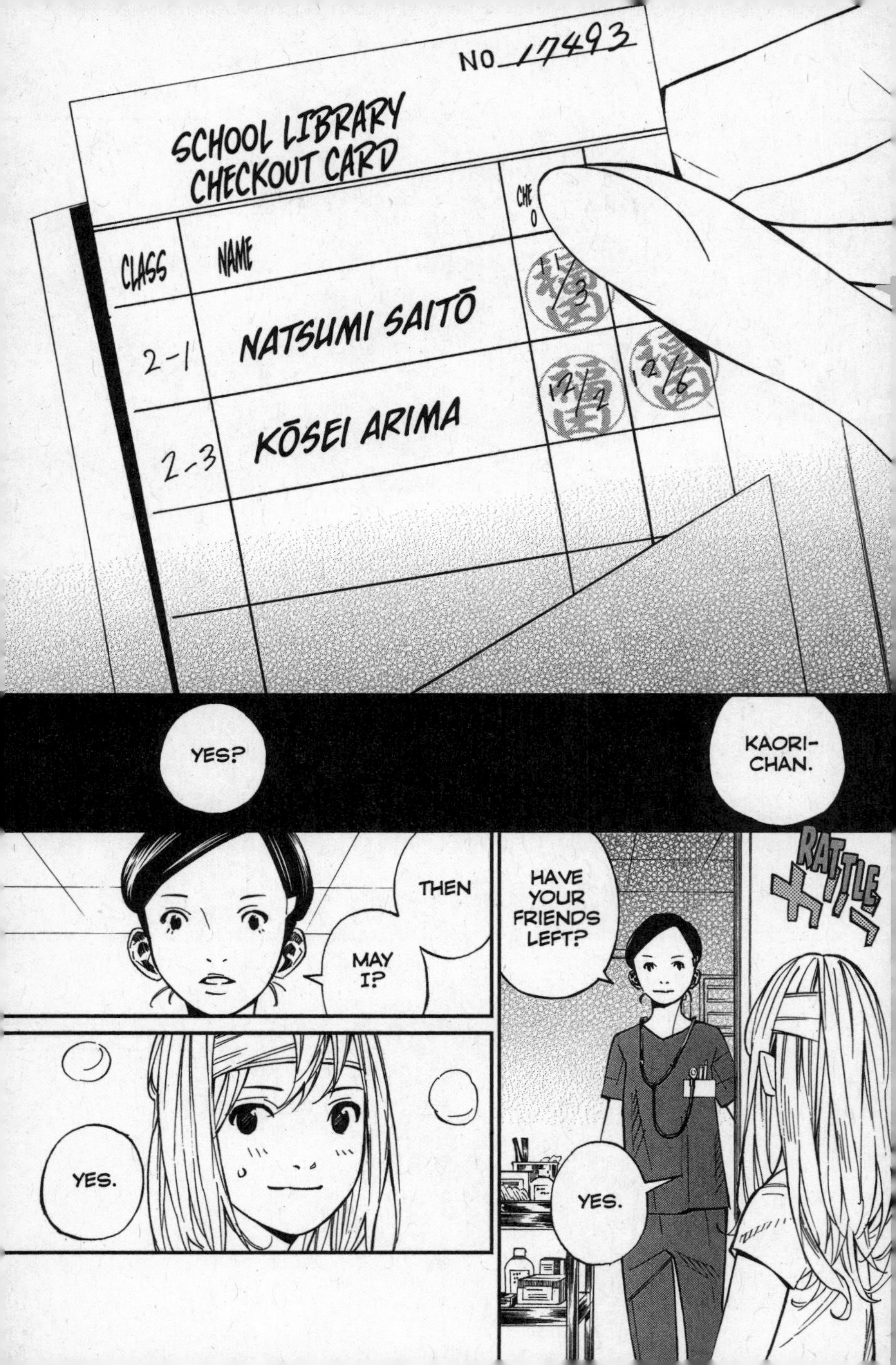
NO. 17493
SCHOOL LIBRARY CHECKOUT CARD
CLASS
NAME
2-1
NATSUMI SAITŌ
11/3
2-3
KŌSEI ARIMA
12/2
12/6
KAORI-CHAN.
YES?
RATTLE
HAVE YOUR FRIENDS LEFT?
YES.
THEN
MAY I?
YES.

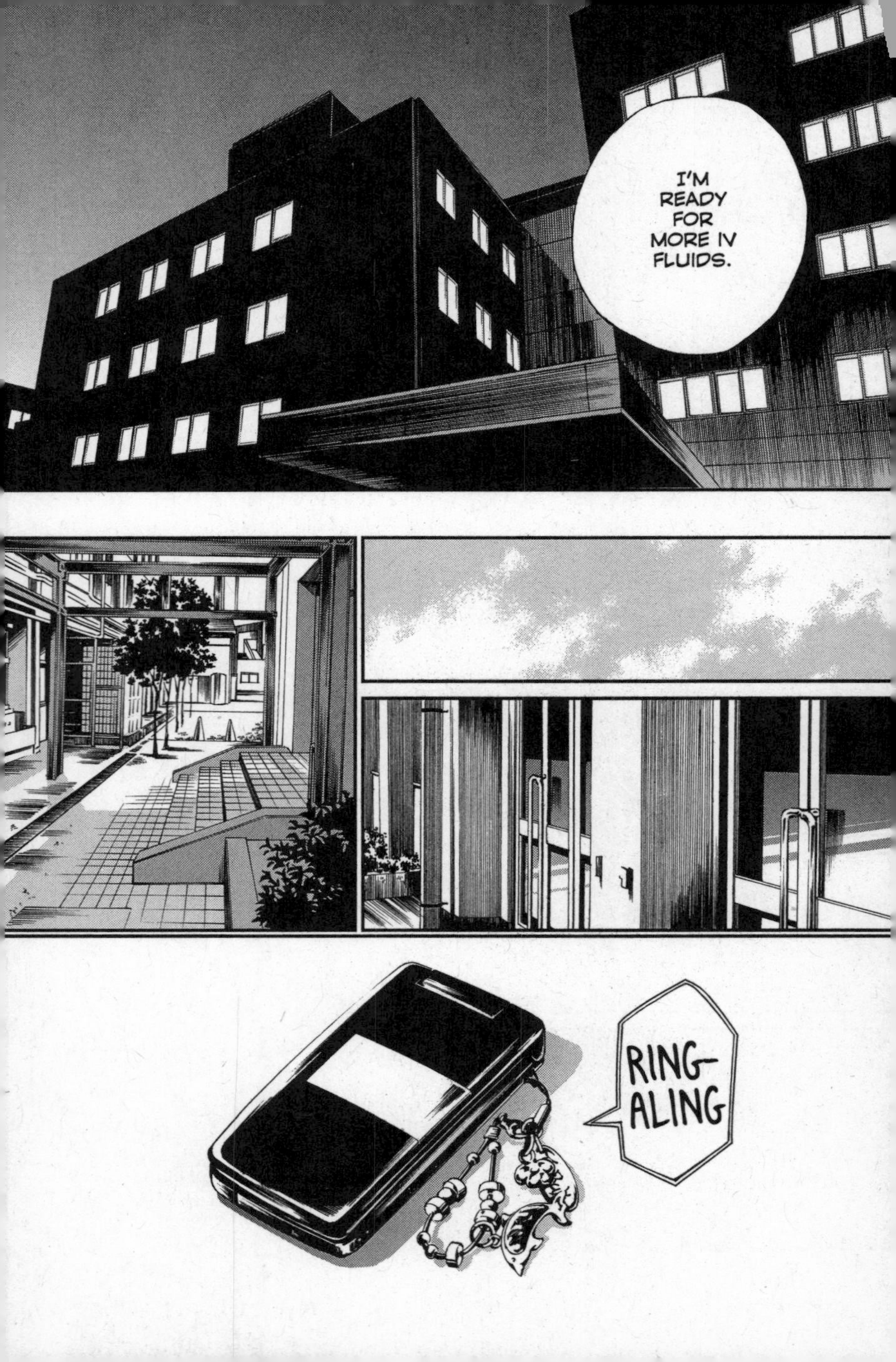
I'M READY FOR MORE IV FLUIDS.
RING-ALING

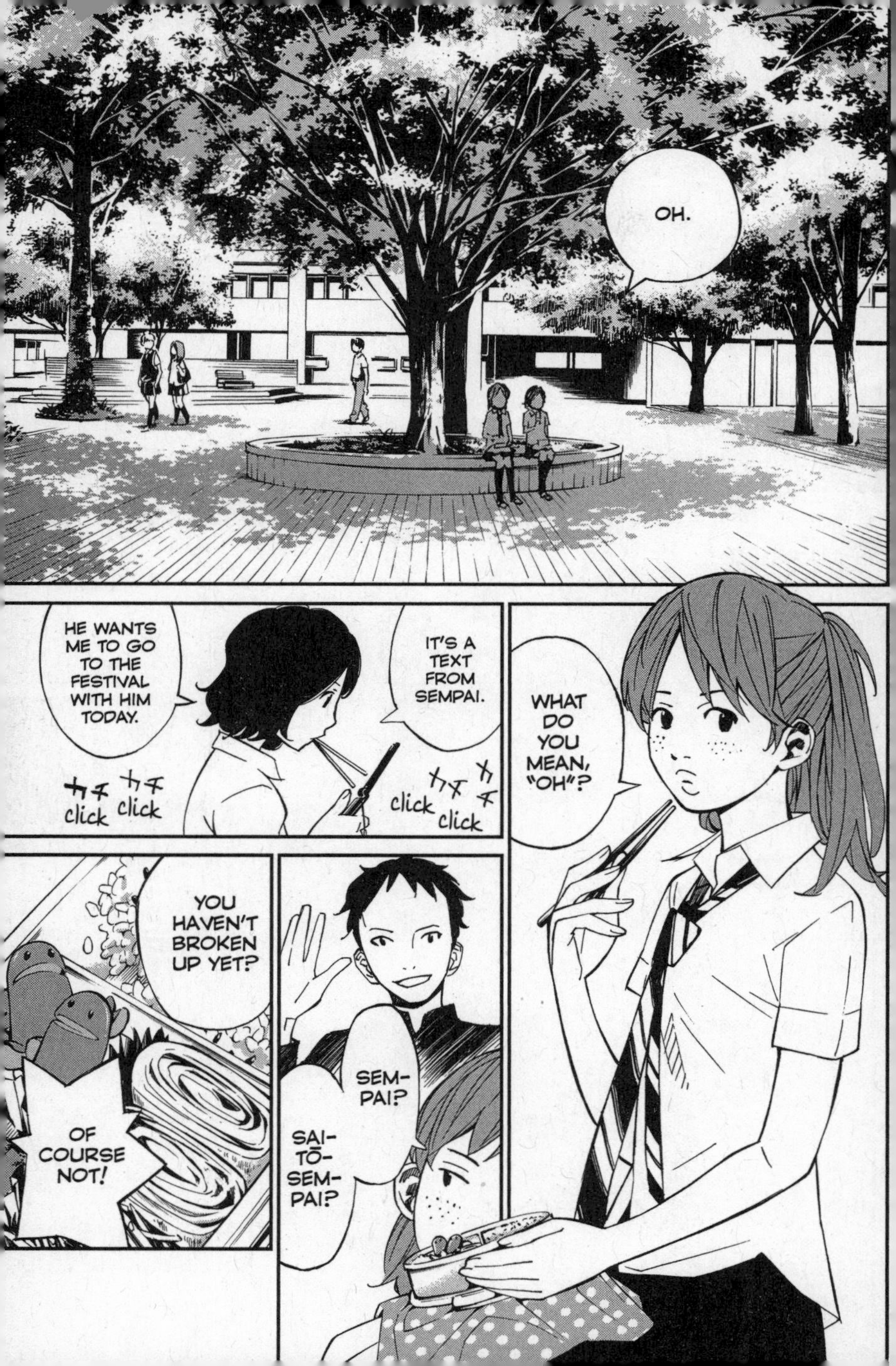
OH.
WHAT DO YOU MEAN, "OH"?
IT'S A TEXT FROM SEMPAI.
カチ click
カチ click
HE WANTS ME TO GO TO THE FESTIVAL WITH HIM TODAY.
カチ click
カチ click
SEMPAI?
SAI-TŌ-SEMPAI?
YOU HAVEN'T BROKEN UP YET?
OF COURSE NOT!

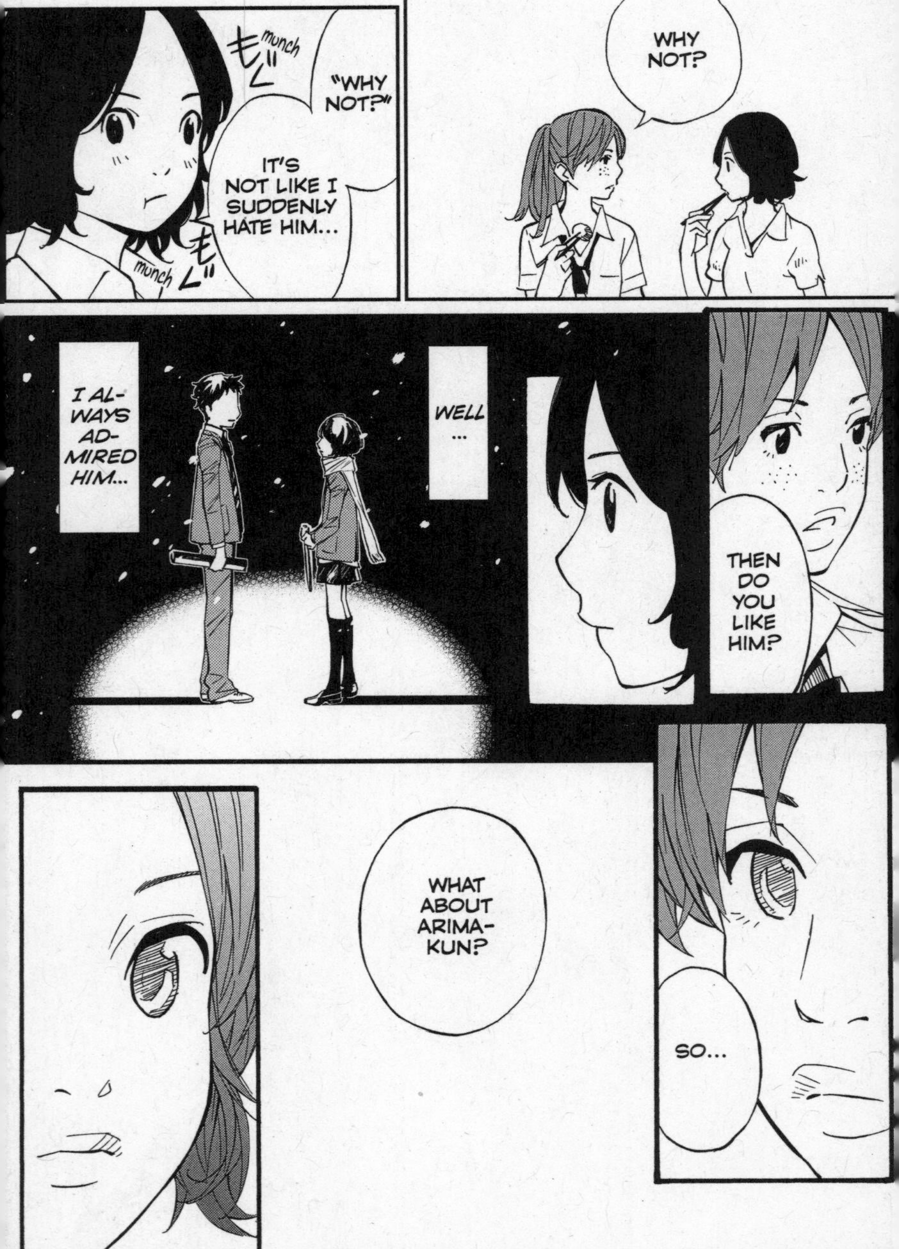
WHY NOT?
もぐ munch
"WHY NOT?"
IT'S NOT LIKE I SUDDENLY HATE HIM...
もぐ munch
THEN DO YOU LIKE HIM?
WELL ...
I ALWAYS ADMIRED HIM...
SO...
WHAT ABOUT ARIMA-KUN?

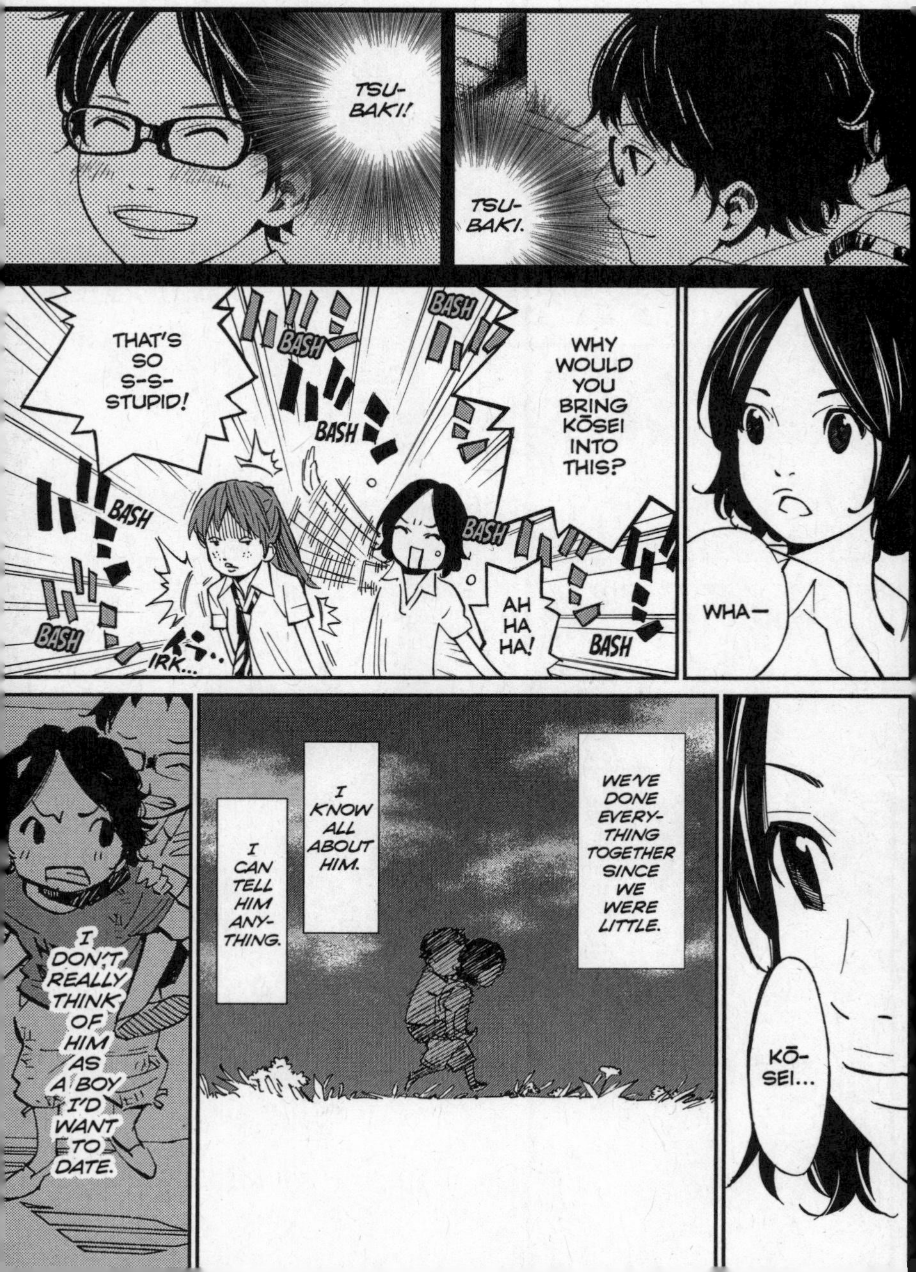

TSU-BAKI.
TSU-BAKI!
WHA—
WHY WOULD YOU BRING KŌSEI INTO THIS?
BASH
AH HA HA!
BASH
BASH
BASH
BASH
THAT'S SO S-S-STUPID!
BASH
BASH
IRK...
KŌ-SEI...
WE'VE DONE EVERY-THING TOGETHER SINCE WE WERE LITTLE.
I KNOW ALL ABOUT HIM.
I CAN TELL HIM ANY-THING.
I DON'T REALLY THINK OF HIM AS A BOY I'D WANT TO DATE.

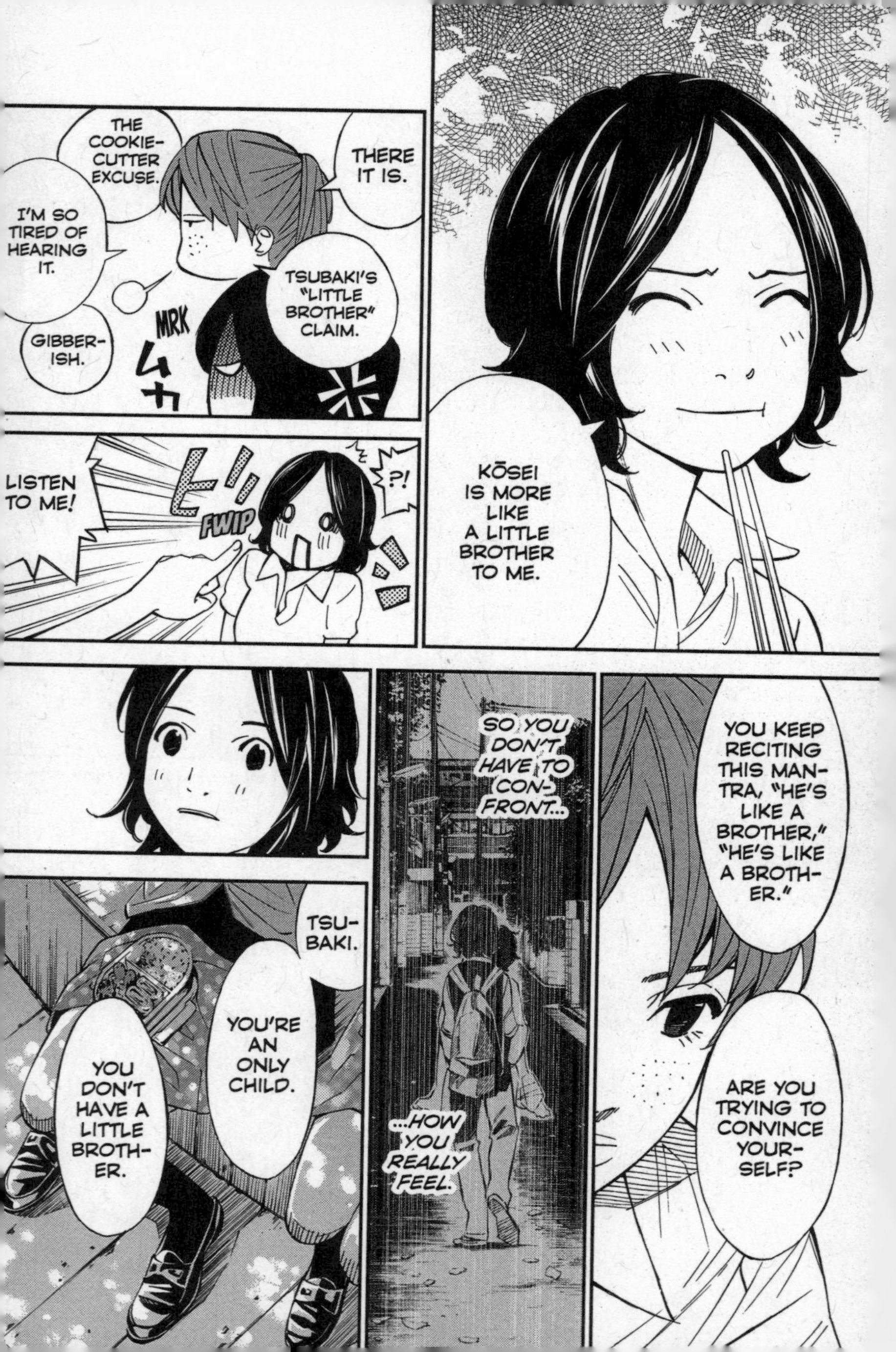
KŌSEI IS MORE LIKE A LITTLE BROTHER TO ME.
THERE IT IS.
THE COOKIE-CUTTER EXCUSE.
TSUBAKI'S "LITTLE BROTHER" CLAIM.
I'M SO TIRED OF HEARING IT.
GIBBERISH.
MRK
ムカ
?!
FWIP
LISTEN TO ME!
YOU KEEP RECITING THIS MANTRA, "HE'S LIKE A BROTHER," "HE'S LIKE A BROTHER."
ARE YOU TRYING TO CONVINCE YOURSELF?
SO YOU DON'T HAVE TO CONFRONT...
...HOW YOU REALLY FEEL.
TSUBAKI.
YOU'RE AN ONLY CHILD.
YOU DON'T HAVE A LITTLE BROTHER.

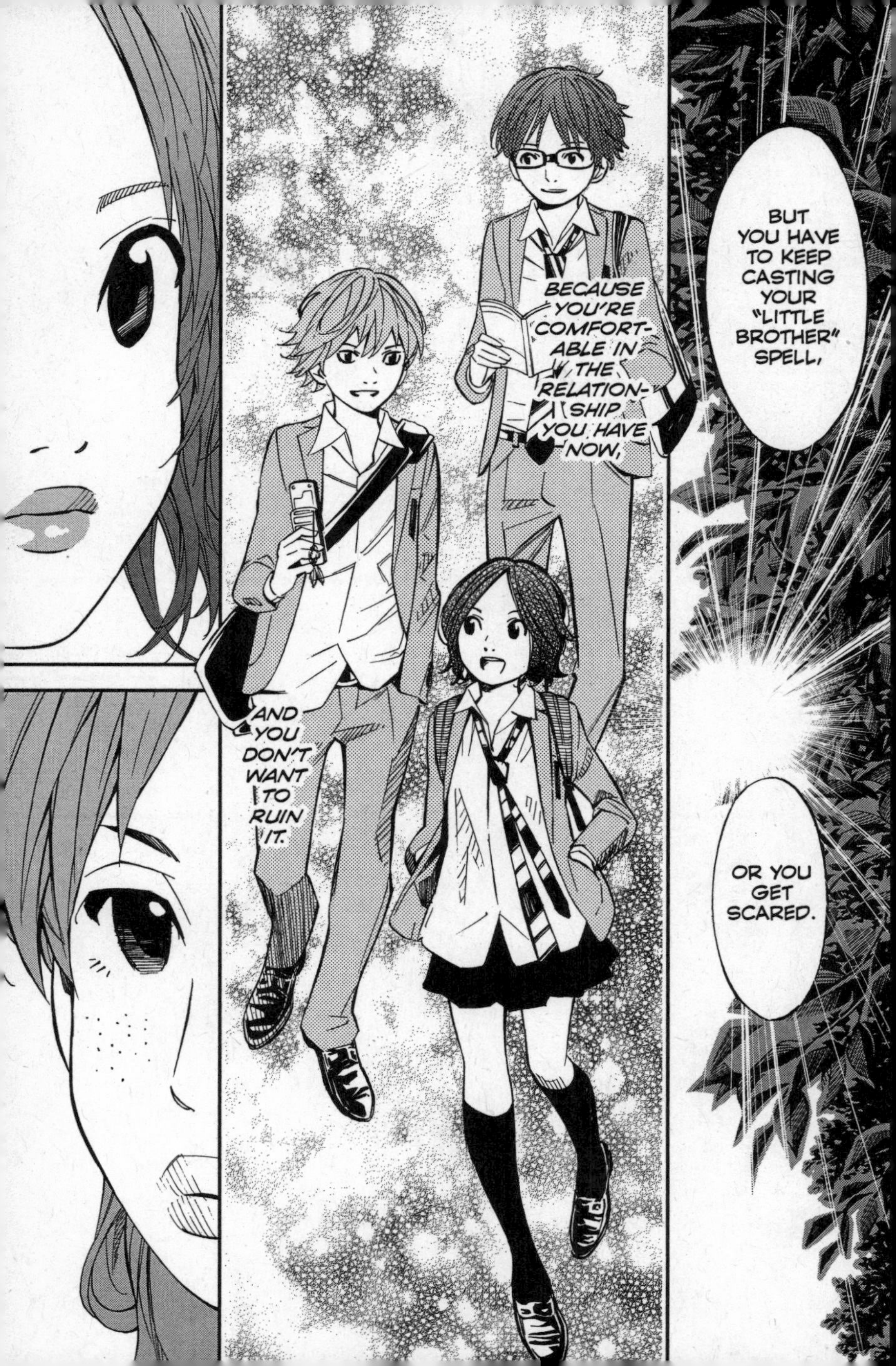
BUT YOU HAVE TO KEEP CASTING YOUR "LITTLE BROTHER" SPELL,
OR YOU GET SCARED.
BECAUSE YOU'RE COMFORTABLE IN THE RELATIONSHIP YOU HAVE NOW,
AND YOU DON'T WANT TO RUIN IT.

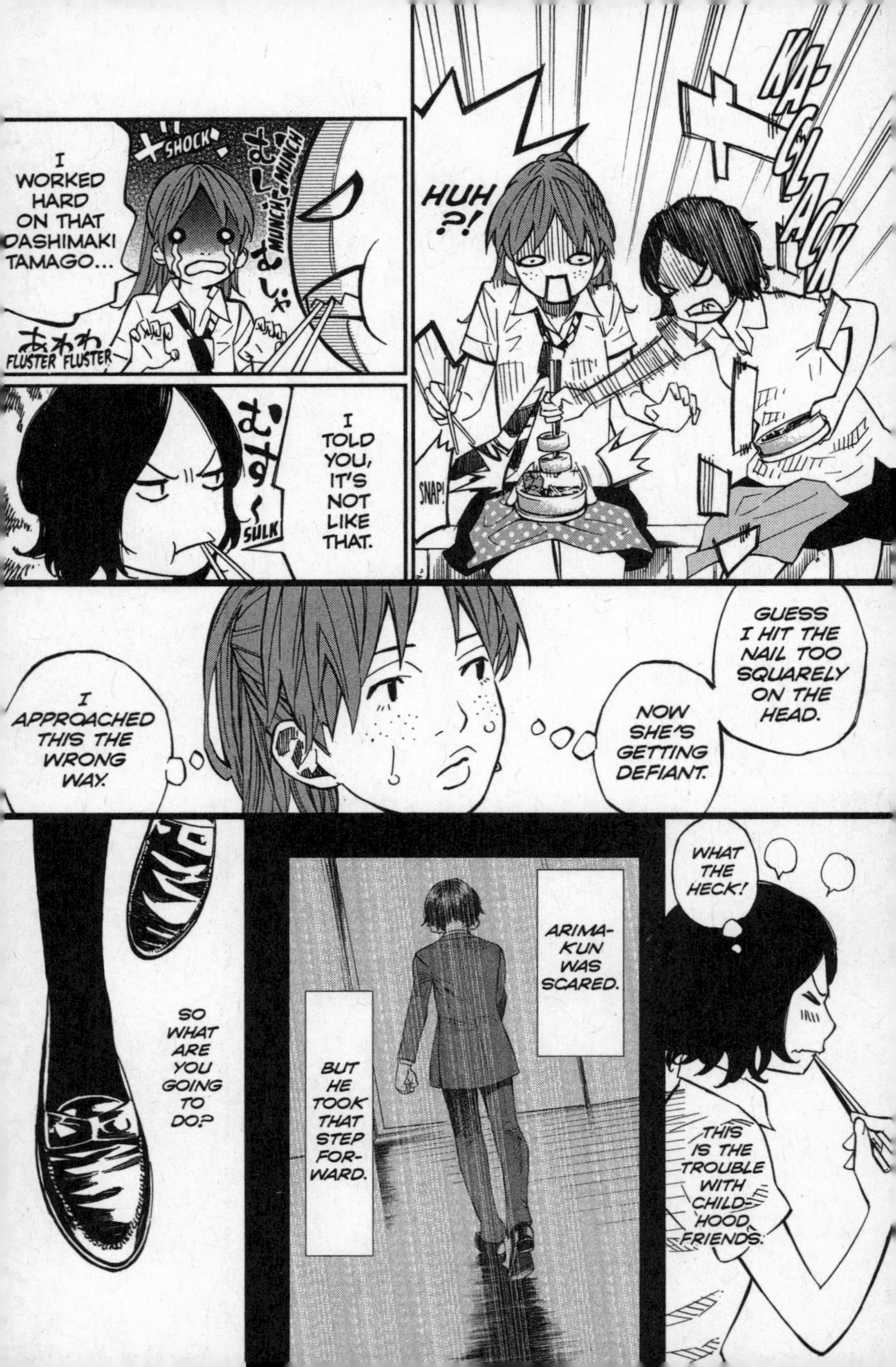
KACLACK
HUH?!
SNAP!
SHOCK
MUNCH MUNCH
I WORKED HARD ON THAT DASHIMAKI TAMAGO...
FLUSTER FLUSTER
SULK
I TOLD YOU, IT'S NOT LIKE THAT.
GUESS I HIT THE NAIL TOO SQUARELY ON THE HEAD.
NOW SHE'S GETTING DEFIANT.
I APPROACHED THIS THE WRONG WAY.
WHAT THE HECK!
THIS IS THE TROUBLE WITH CHILDHOOD FRIENDS.
ARIMA-KUN WAS SCARED.
BUT HE TOOK THAT STEP FORWARD.
SO WHAT ARE YOU GOING TO DO?

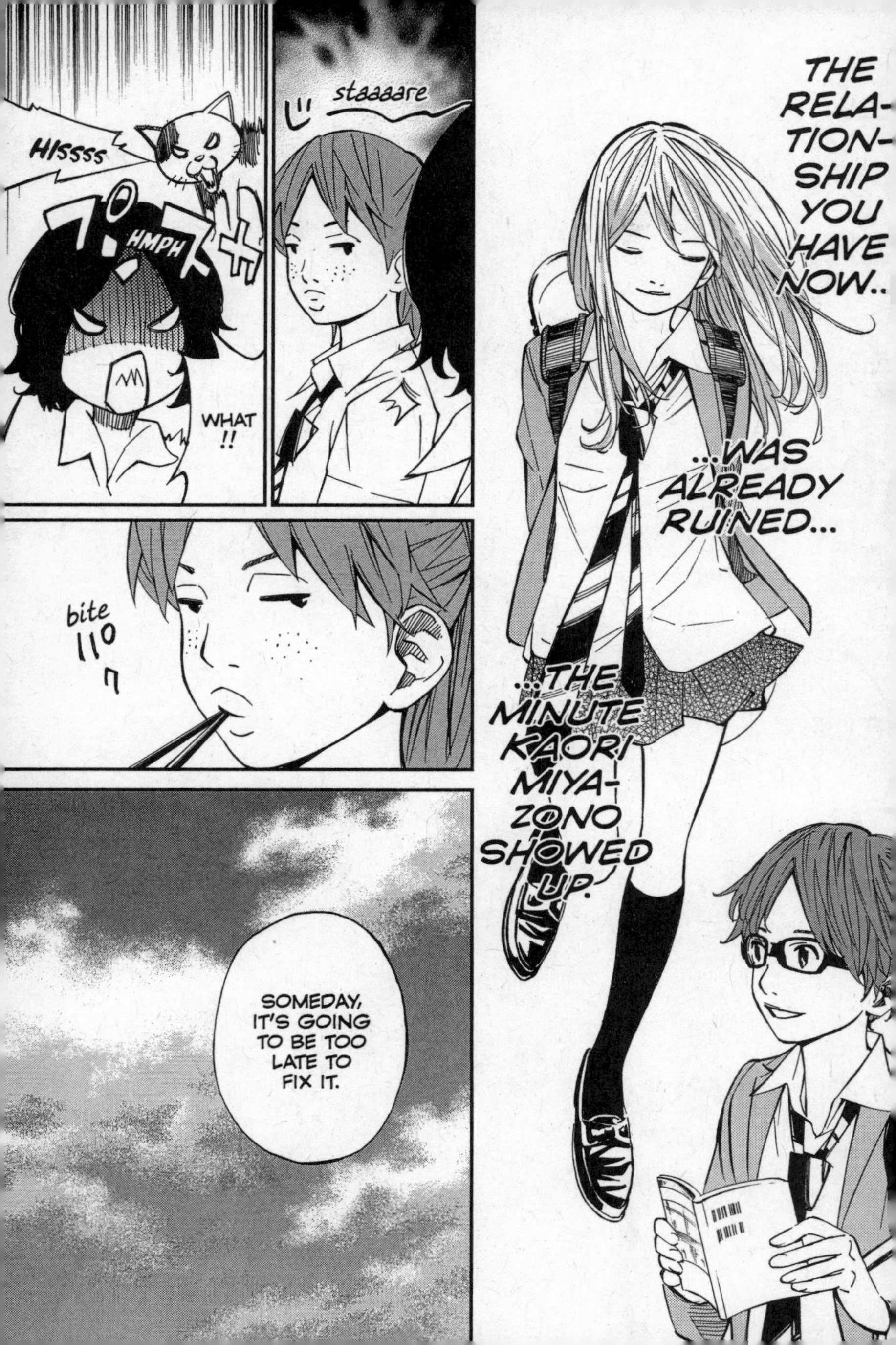
THE RELATIONSHIP YOU HAVE NOW...
...WAS ALREADY RUINED...
...THE MINUTE KAORI MIYAZONO SHOWED UP.
staaaare
HISSSS
HMPH
WHAT!!
bite
SOMEDAY, IT'S GOING TO BE TOO LATE TO FIX IT.

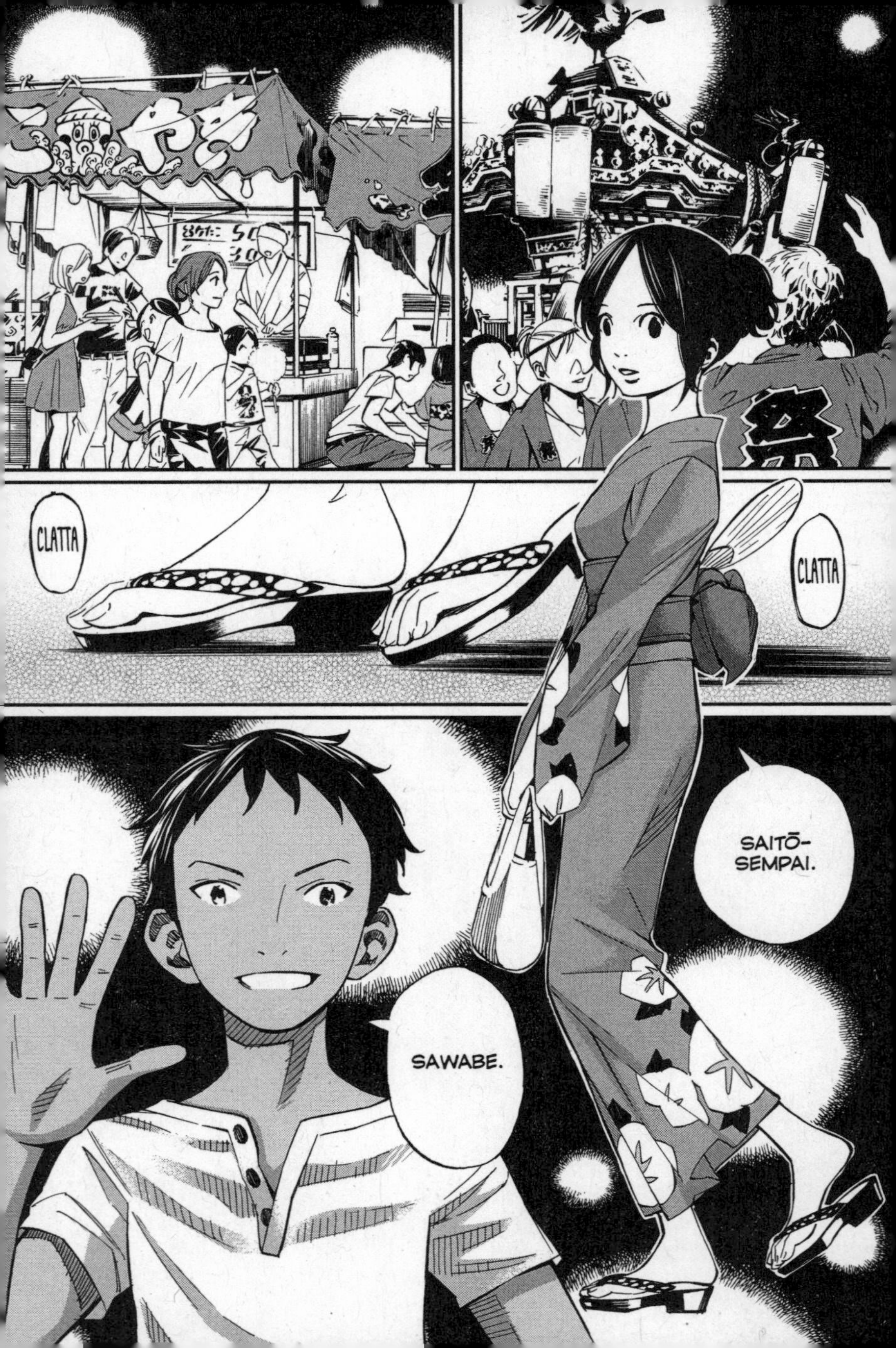
祭
CLATTA
CLATTA
SAITŌ-SEMPAI.
SAWABE.

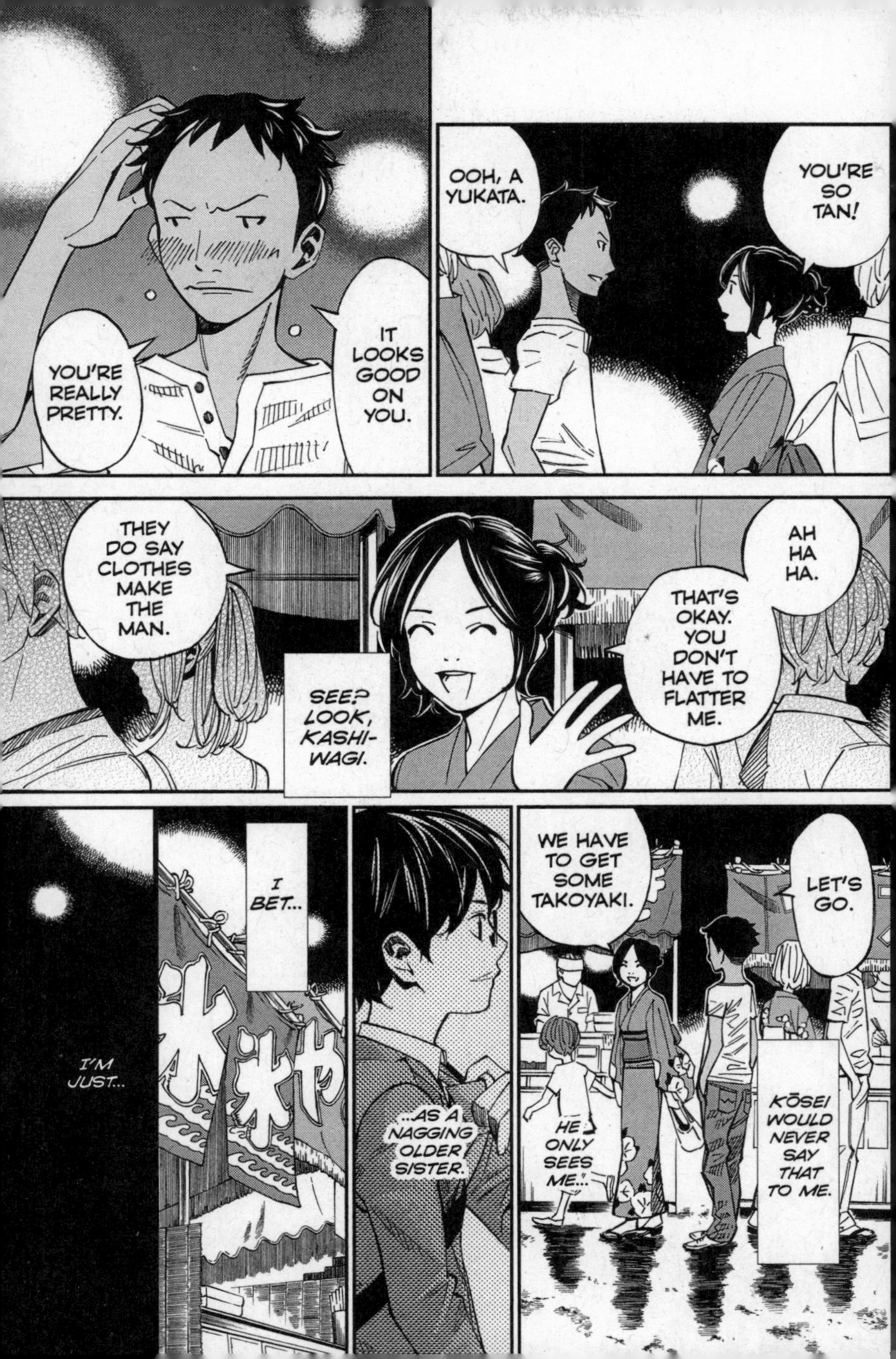
YOU'RE SO TAN!
OOH, A YUKATA.
IT LOOKS GOOD ON YOU.
YOU'RE REALLY PRETTY.
AH HA HA.
THAT'S OKAY. YOU DON'T HAVE TO FLATTER ME.
SEE? LOOK, KASHI-WAGI.
THEY DO SAY CLOTHES MAKE THE MAN.
LET'S GO.
WE HAVE TO GET SOME TAKOYAKI.
KŌSEI WOULD NEVER SAY THAT TO ME.
HE ONLY SEES ME...
...AS A NAGGING OLDER SISTER.
I BET...
I'M JUST...

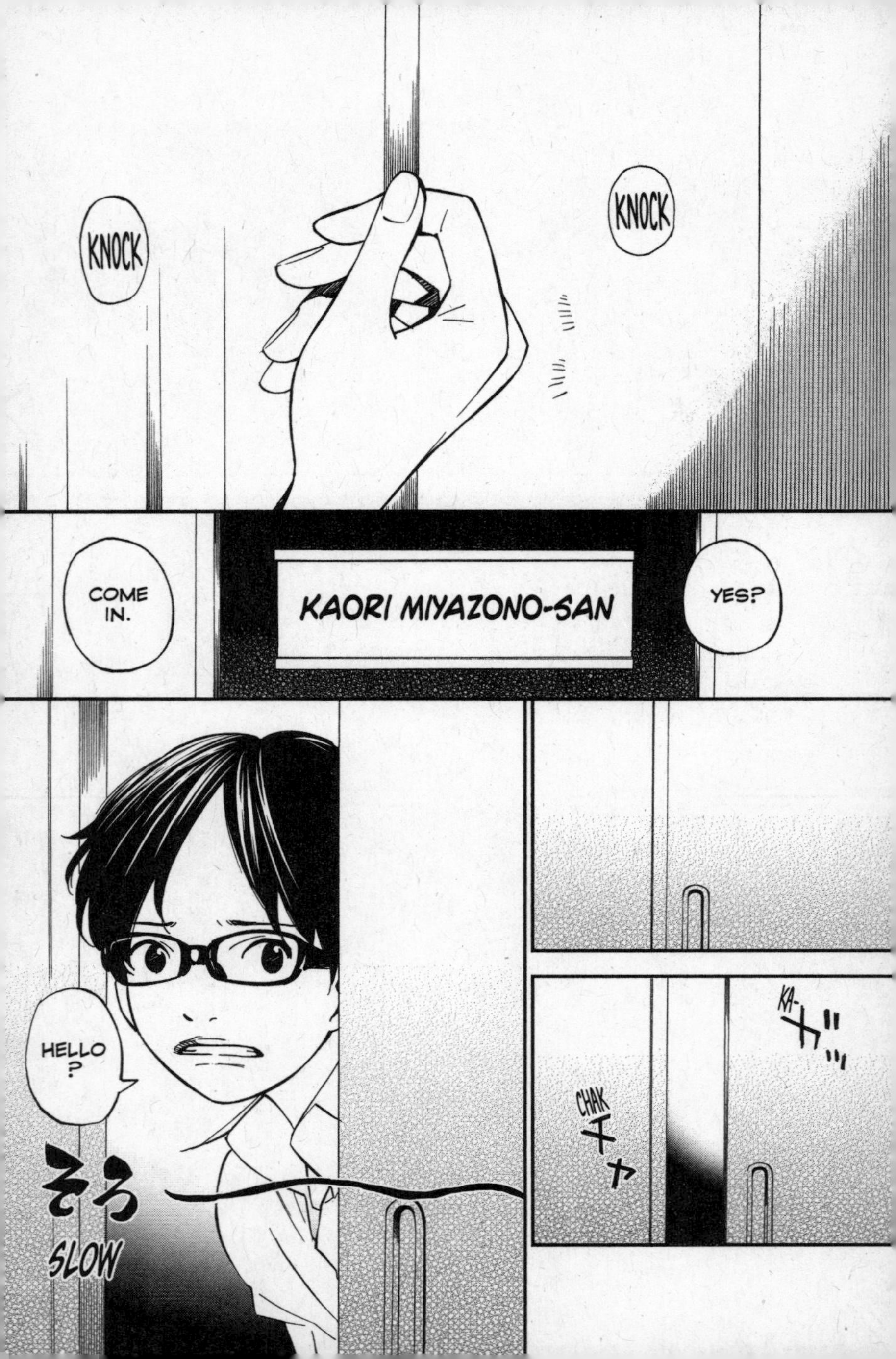

KNOCK
KNOCK
YES?
KAORI MIYAZONO-SAN
COME IN.
KA- ガッ
CHAK チャ
HELLO?
そろ SLOW

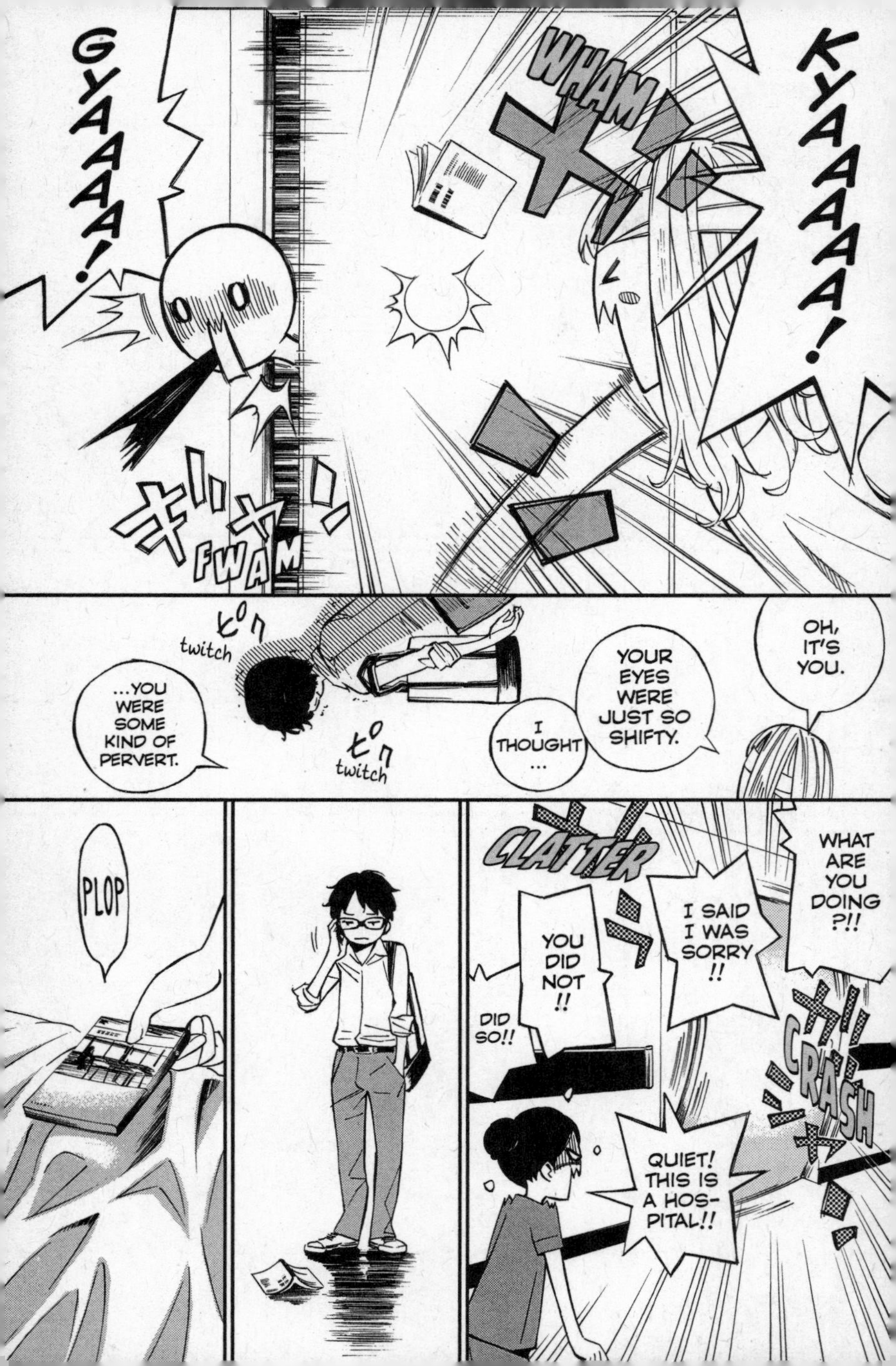
KYAAAAAA!
WHAM
GYAAAA!
FWAM
OH, IT'S YOU.
YOUR EYES WERE JUST SO SHIFTY.
I THOUGHT ...
twitch
...YOU WERE SOME KIND OF PERVERT.
twitch
WHAT ARE YOU DOING?!!
CLATTER
I SAID I WAS SORRY!!
YOU DID NOT!!
DID SO!!
CRASH
QUIET! THIS IS A HOS-PITAL!!
PLOP

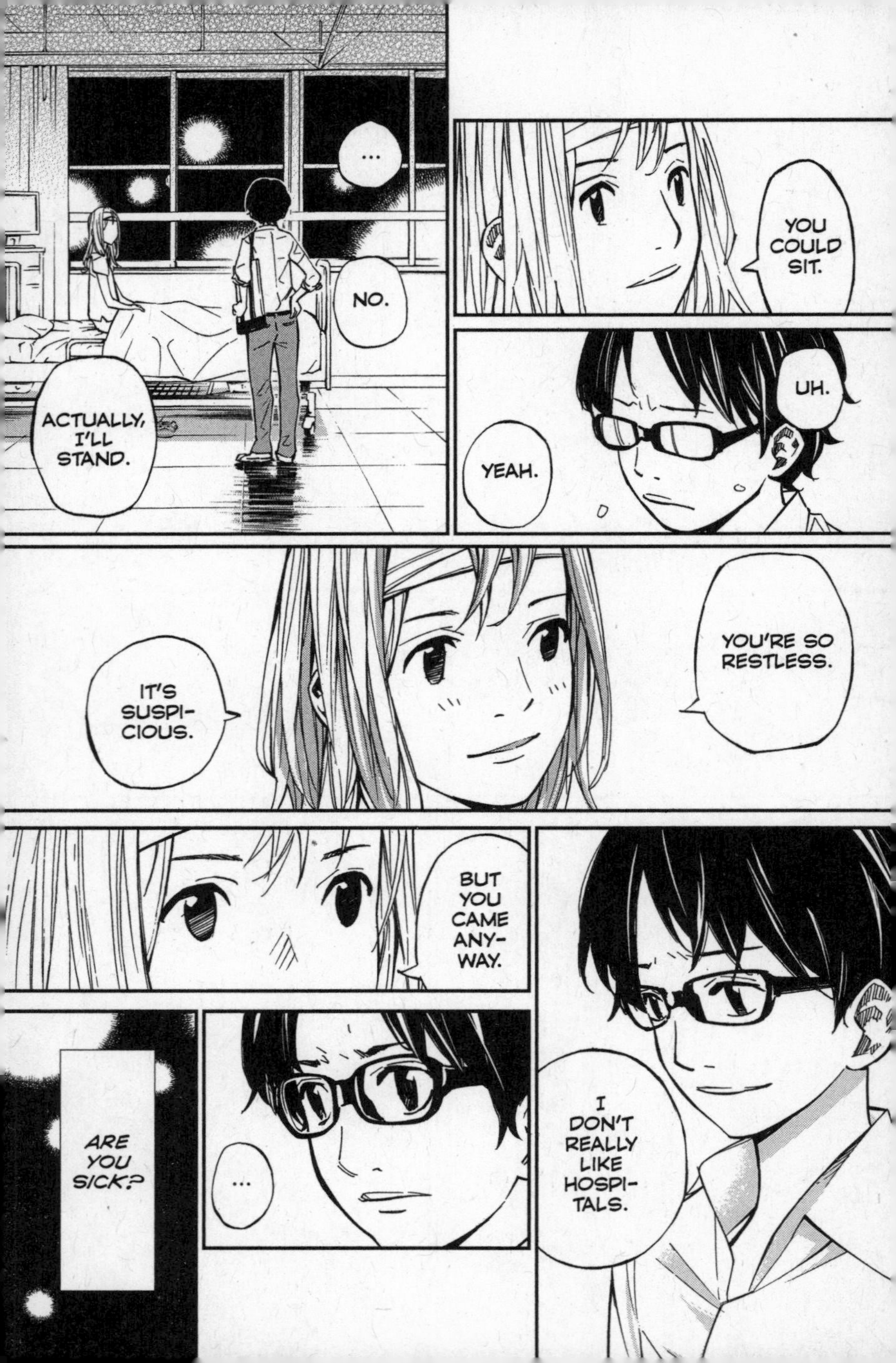
YOU COULD SIT.
UH.
YEAH.
...
NO.
ACTUALLY, I'LL STAND.
YOU'RE SO RESTLESS.
IT'S SUSPICIOUS.
I DON'T REALLY LIKE HOSPI-TALS.
BUT YOU CAME ANY-WAY.
...
ARE YOU SICK?

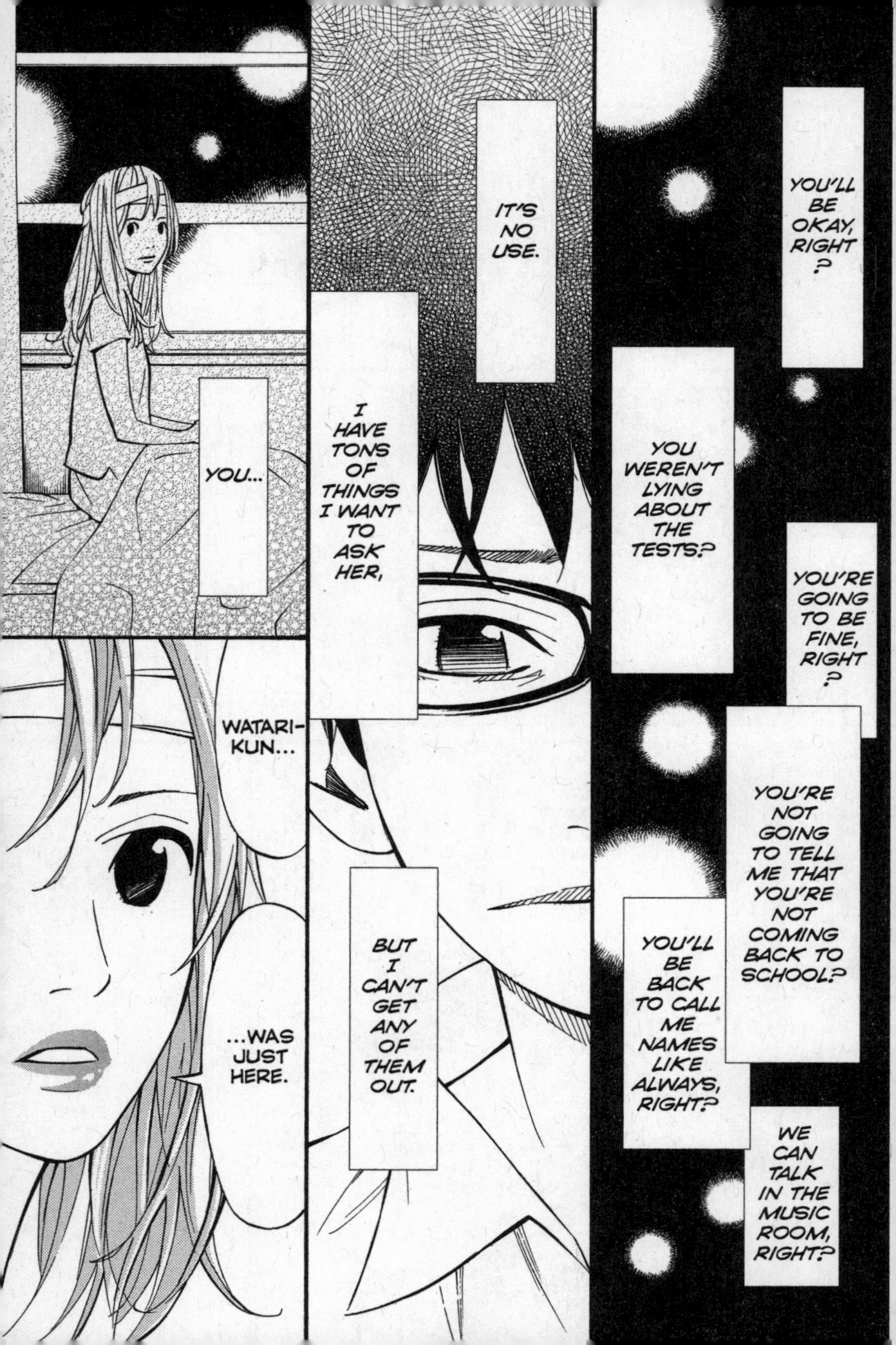
YOU'LL BE OKAY, RIGHT?
YOU WEREN'T LYING ABOUT THE TESTS?
YOU'RE GOING TO BE FINE, RIGHT?
YOU'RE NOT GOING TO TELL ME THAT YOU'RE NOT COMING BACK TO SCHOOL?
YOU'LL BE BACK TO CALL ME NAMES LIKE ALWAYS, RIGHT?
WE CAN TALK IN THE MUSIC ROOM, RIGHT?
IT'S NO USE.
I HAVE TONS OF THINGS I WANT TO ASK HER,
BUT I CAN'T GET ANY OF THEM OUT.
YOU...
WATARI-KUN...
...WAS JUST HERE.

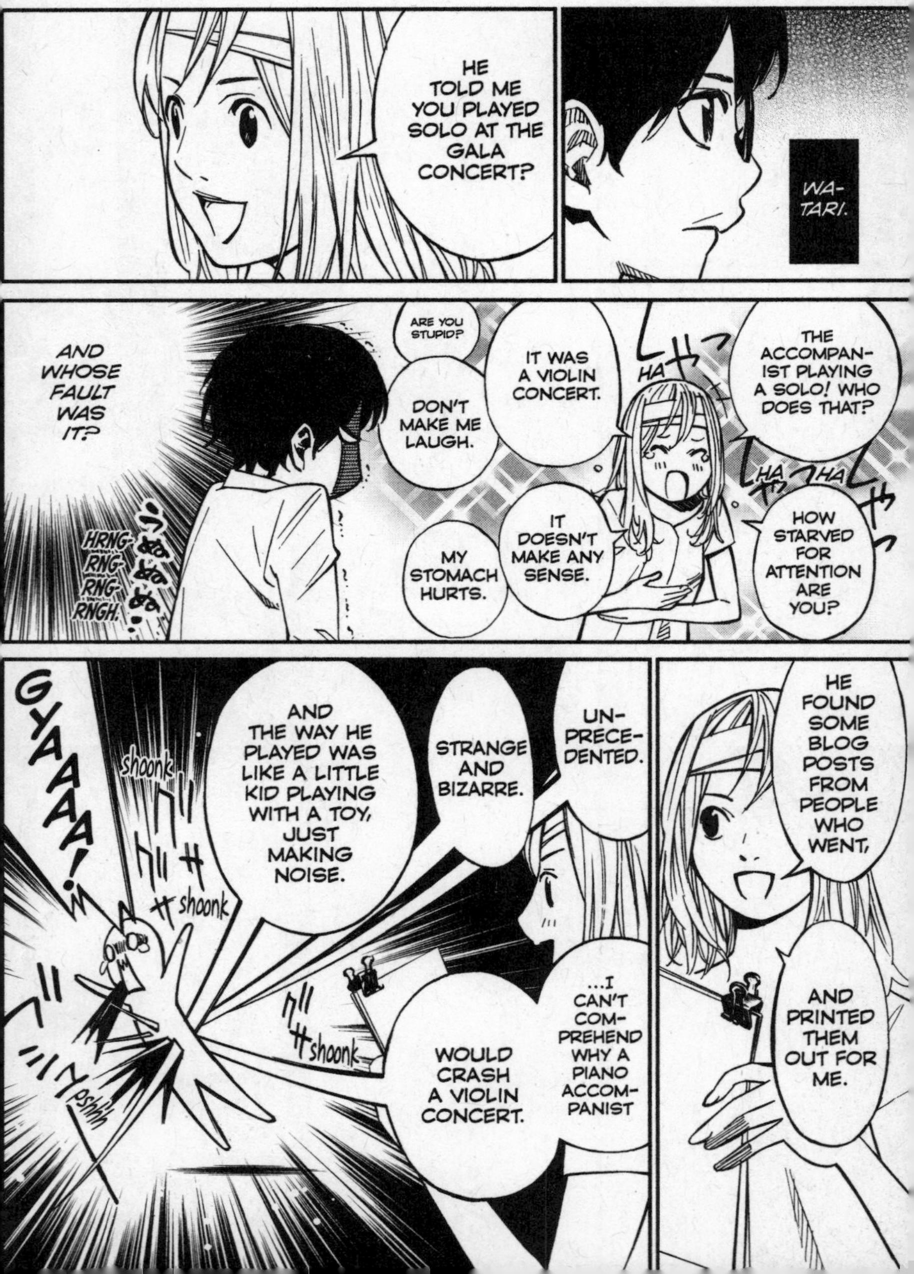
WA-
TARI.
HE TOLD ME YOU PLAYED SOLO AT THE GALA CONCERT?
THE ACCOMPAN-
IST PLAYING A SOLO! WHO DOES THAT?
HA
HA HA
HOW STARVED FOR ATTENTION ARE YOU?
IT WAS A VIOLIN CONCERT.
IT DOESN'T MAKE ANY SENSE.
ARE YOU STUPID?
DON'T MAKE ME LAUGH.
MY STOMACH HURTS.
HRNG-RNG-RNG-RNGH.
AND WHOSE FAULT WAS IT?
HE FOUND SOME BLOG POSTS FROM PEOPLE WHO WENT,
AND PRINTED THEM OUT FOR ME.
UN-
PRECE-
DENTED.
STRANGE AND BIZARRE.
AND THE WAY HE PLAYED WAS LIKE A LITTLE KID PLAYING WITH A TOY, JUST MAKING NOISE.
...I CAN'T COM-
PREHEND WHY A PIANO ACCOM-
PANIST
WOULD CRASH A VIOLIN CONCERT.
shoonk
shoonk
shoonk
GYAAAA!!
pshhh

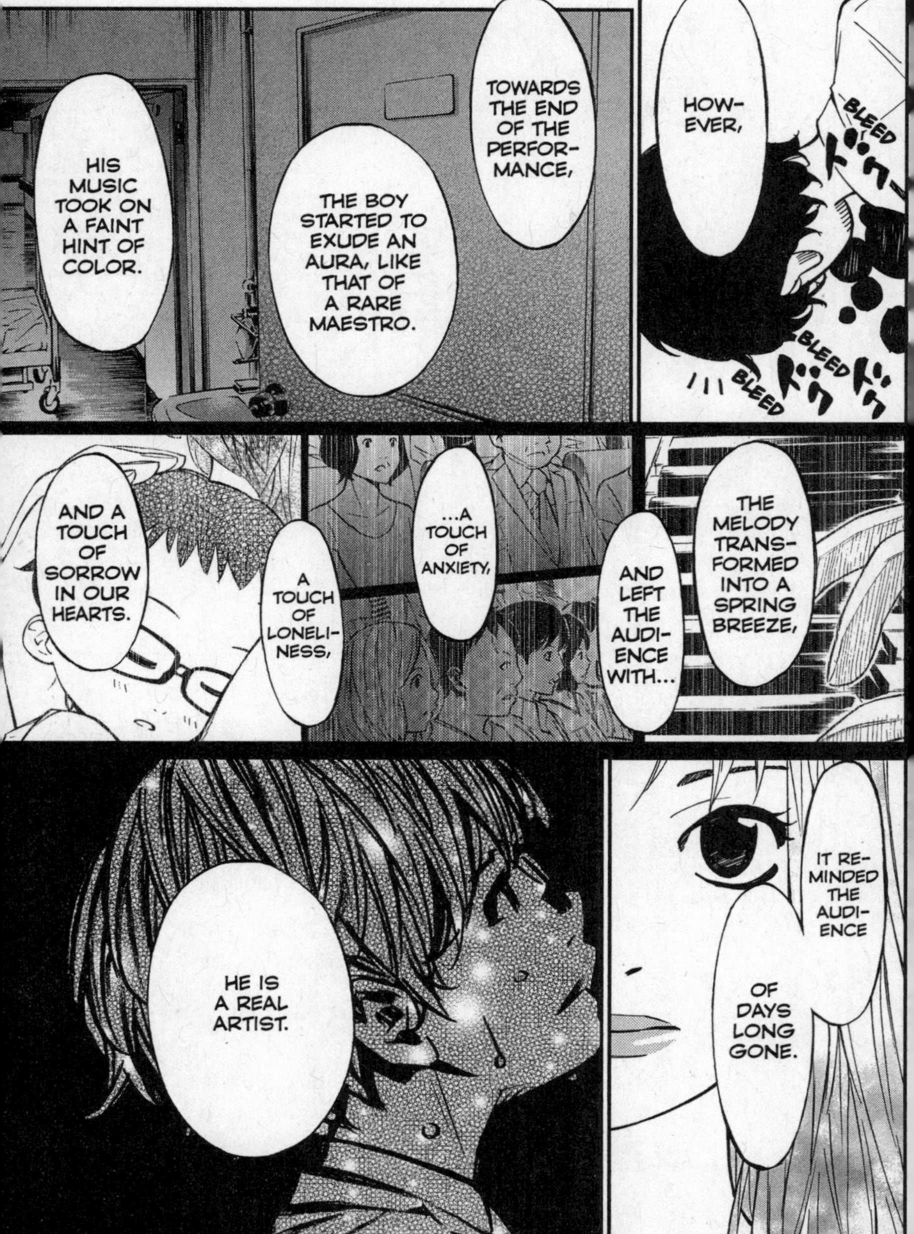
HOW-EVER,
BLEED
BLEED
BLEED
TOWARDS THE END OF THE PERFOR-MANCE,
THE BOY STARTED TO EXUDE AN AURA, LIKE THAT OF A RARE MAESTRO.
HIS MUSIC TOOK ON A FAINT HINT OF COLOR.
THE MELODY TRANS-FORMED INTO A SPRING BREEZE,
AND LEFT THE AUDI-ENCE WITH...
...A TOUCH OF ANXIETY,
A TOUCH OF LONELI-NESS,
AND A TOUCH OF SORROW IN OUR HEARTS.
IT RE-MINDED THE AUDI-ENCE
OF DAYS LONG GONE.
HE IS A REAL ARTIST.

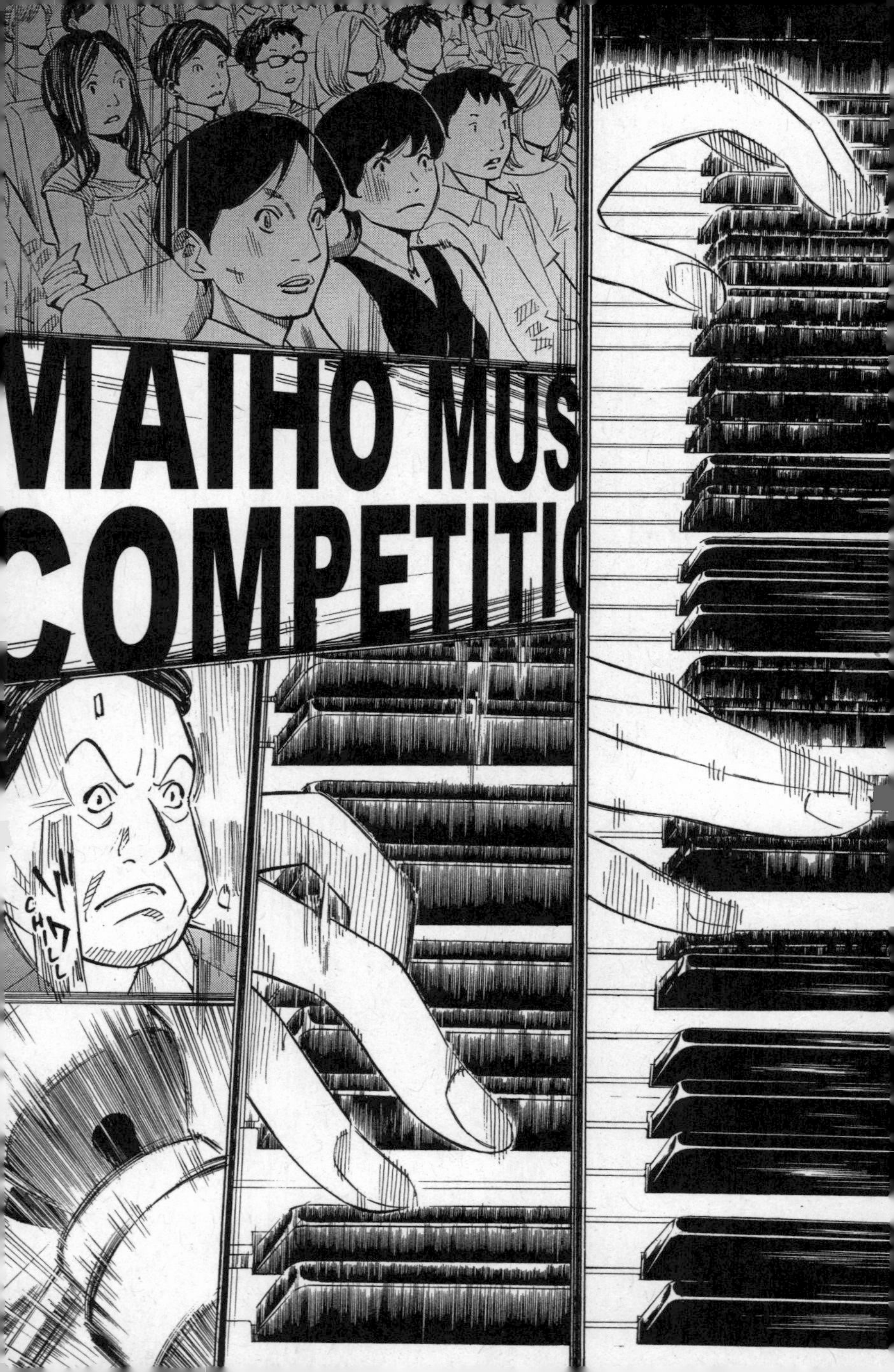
MAIHO MUS
COMPETITIO
CHILL

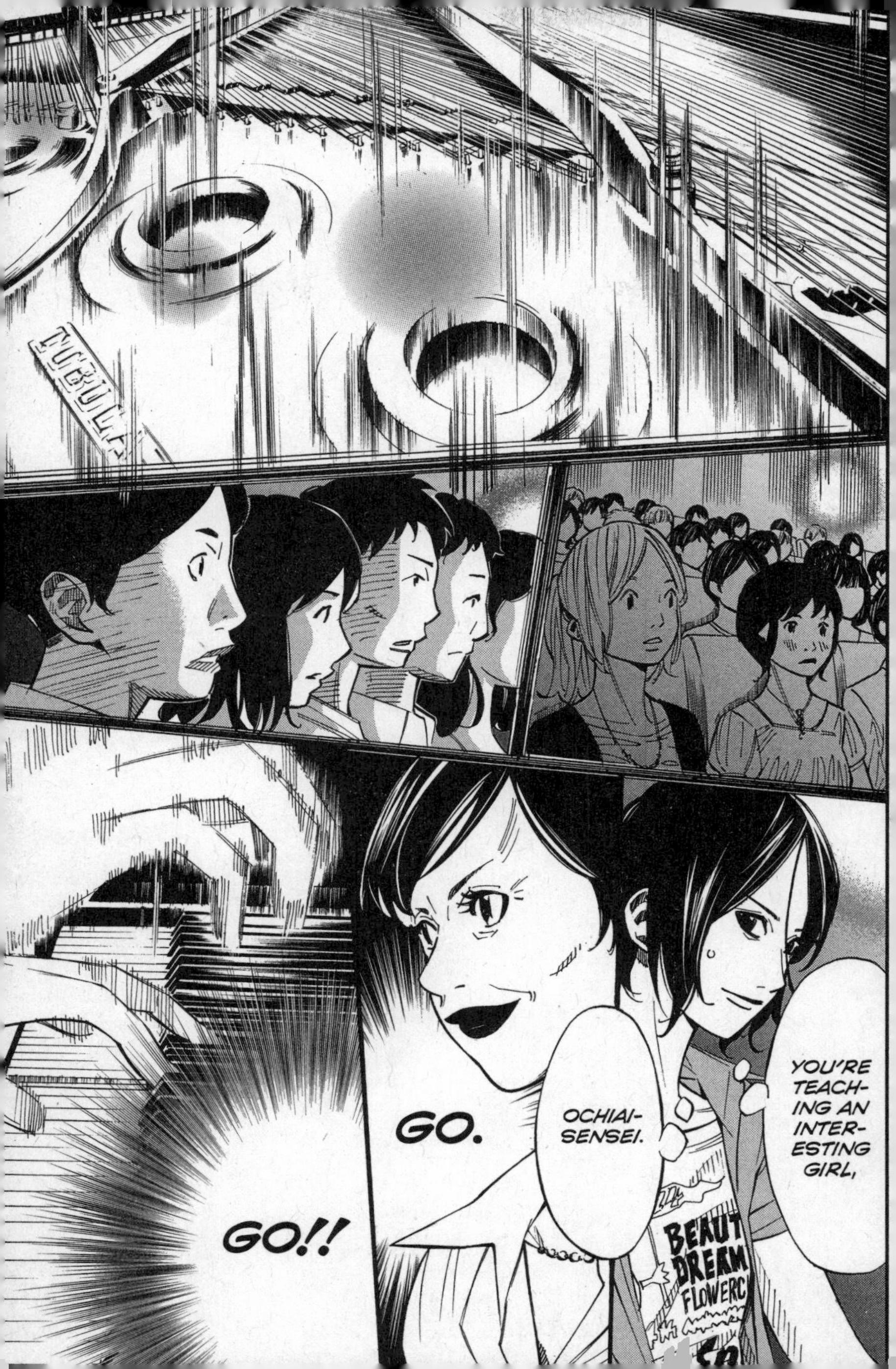
YOU'RE TEACHING AN INTERESTING GIRL,
OCHIAI-SENSEI.
GO.
GO!!

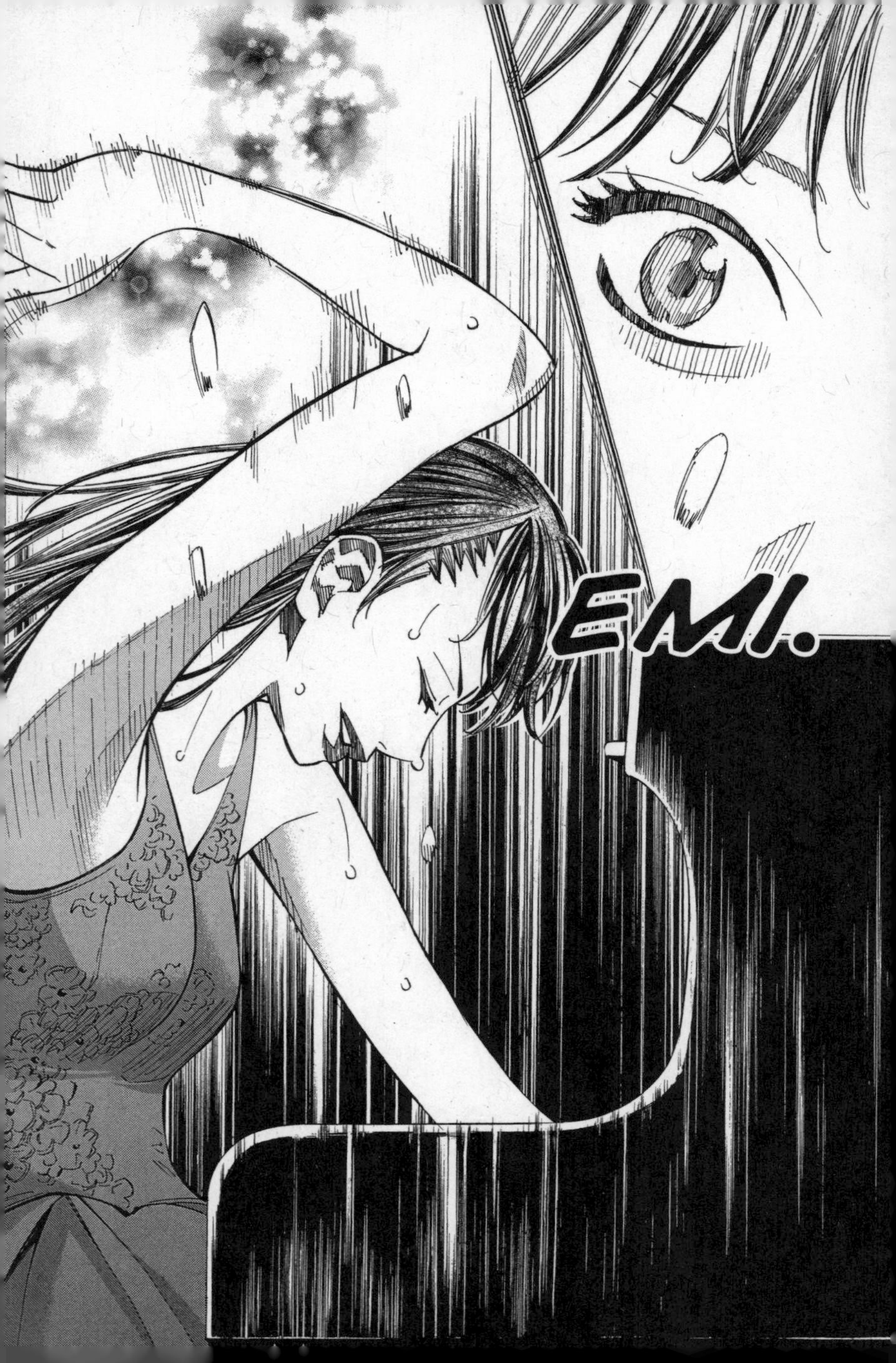
EMI.

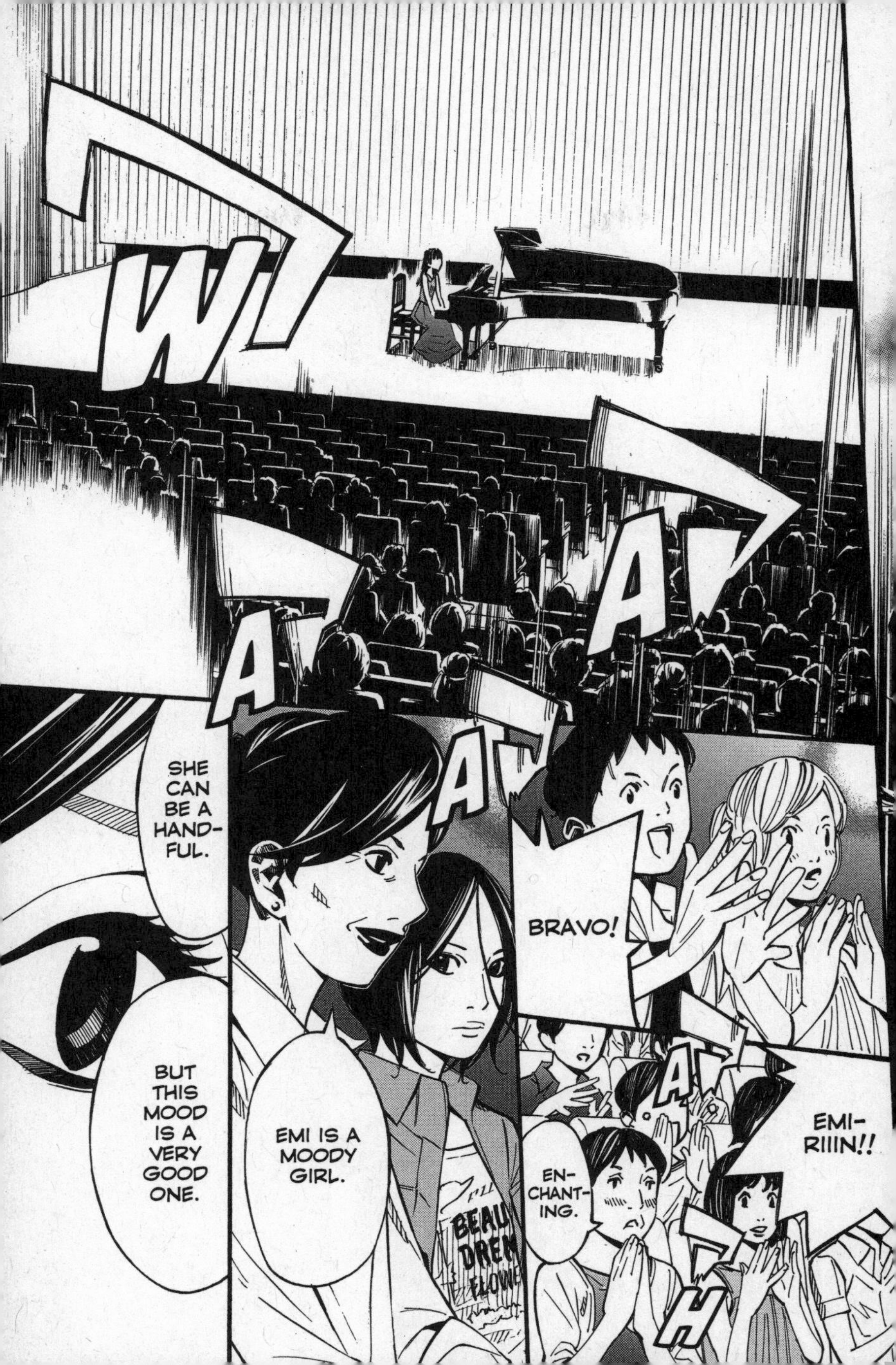
WAAAAH
EMI-RIIIN!!
BRAVO!
EN-CHANT-ING.
EMI IS A MOODY GIRL.
SHE CAN BE A HAND-FUL.
BUT THIS MOOD IS A VERY GOOD ONE.

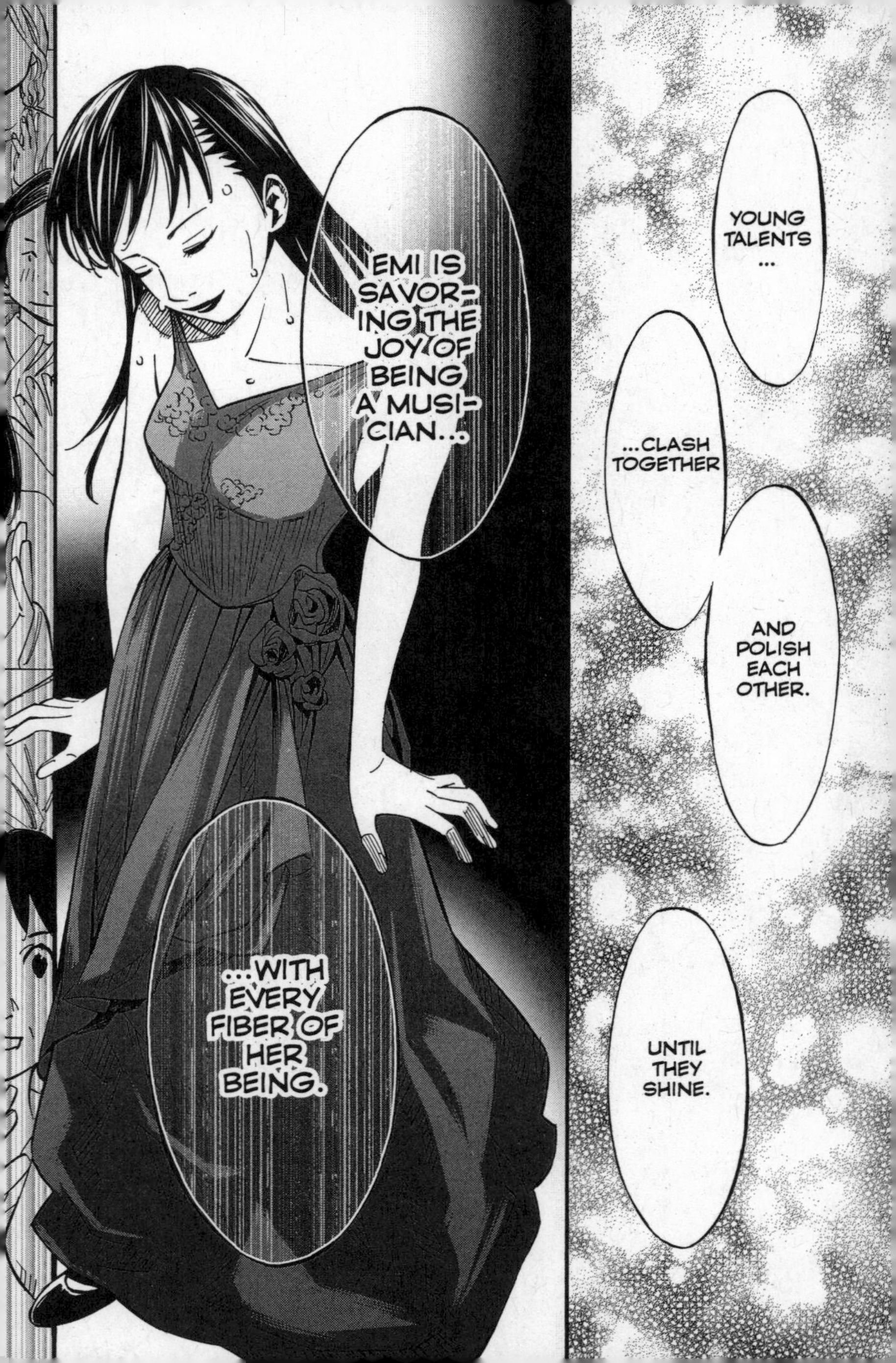
YOUNG TALENTS ...
...CLASH TOGETHER
AND POLISH EACH OTHER.
UNTIL THEY SHINE.
EMI IS SAVOR-ING THE JOY OF BEING A MUSI-CIAN...
...WITH EVERY FIBER OF HER BEING.

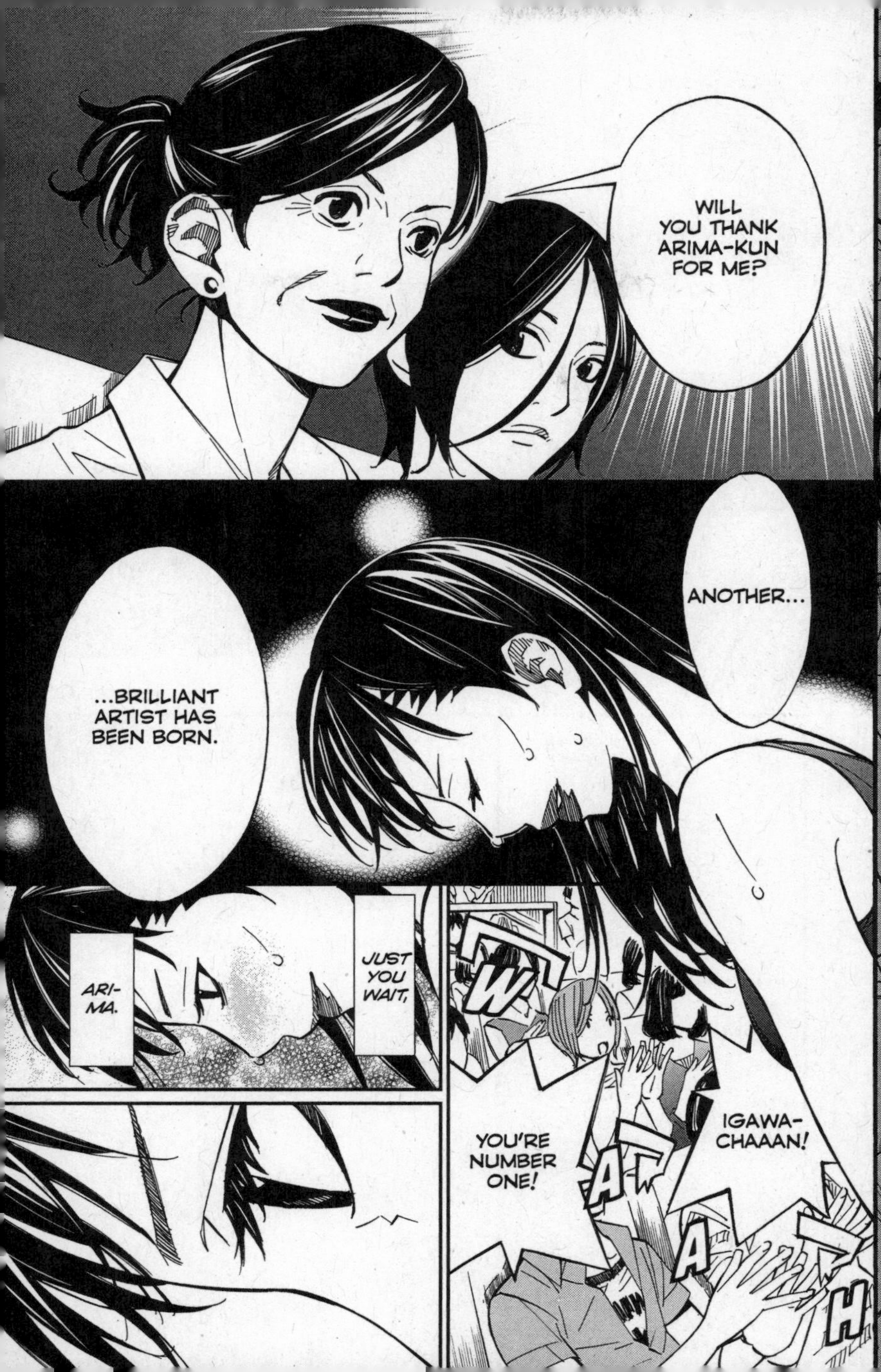
WILL YOU THANK ARIMA-KUN FOR ME?
ANOTHER...
...BRILLIANT ARTIST HAS BEEN BORN.
WAAAH
IGAWA-CHAAAN!
YOU'RE NUMBER ONE!
JUST YOU WAIT,
ARI-MA.

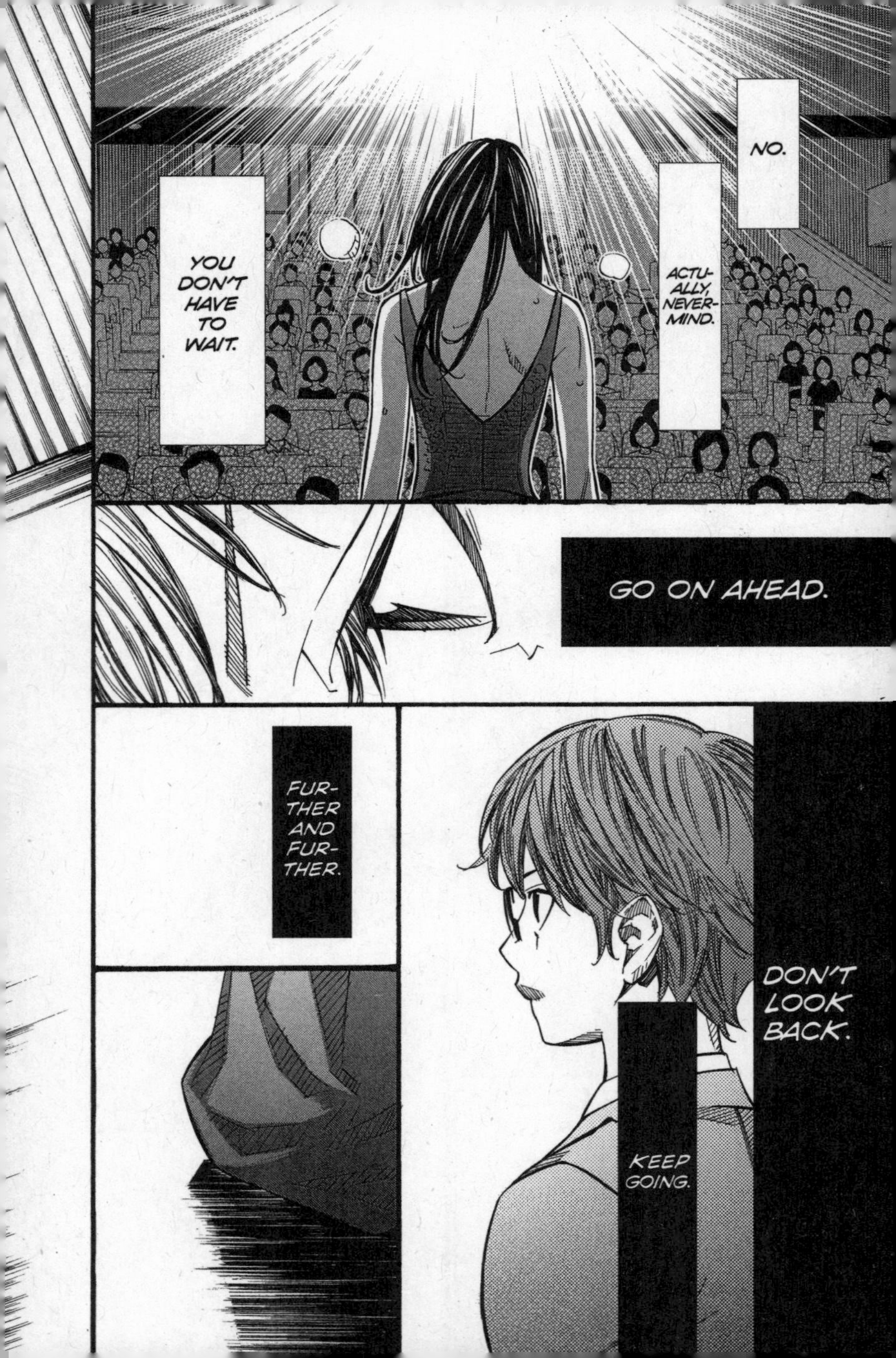
NO.
ACTU-ALLY, NEVER-MIND.
YOU DON'T HAVE TO WAIT.
GO ON AHEAD.
DON'T LOOK BACK.
KEEP GOING.
FUR-THER AND FUR-THER.

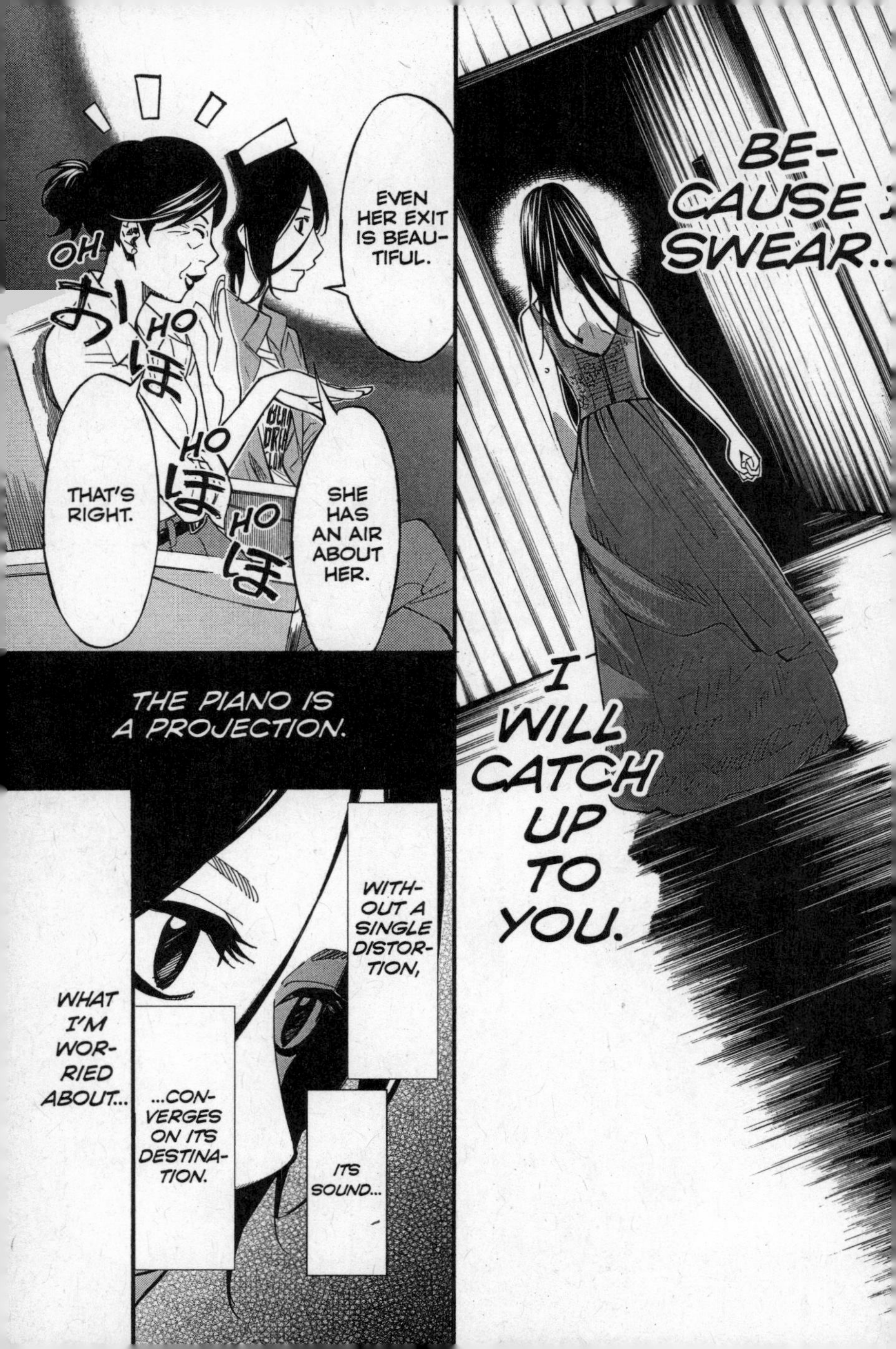
BECAUSE I SWEAR...
I WILL CATCH UP TO YOU.
EVEN HER EXIT IS BEAUTIFUL.
SHE HAS AN AIR ABOUT HER.
THAT'S RIGHT.
OH HO HO HO
おほほほ
THE PIANO IS A PROJECTION.
WITHOUT A SINGLE DISTORTION,
ITS SOUND...
...CONVERGES ON ITS DESTINATION.
WHAT I'M WORRIED ABOUT...

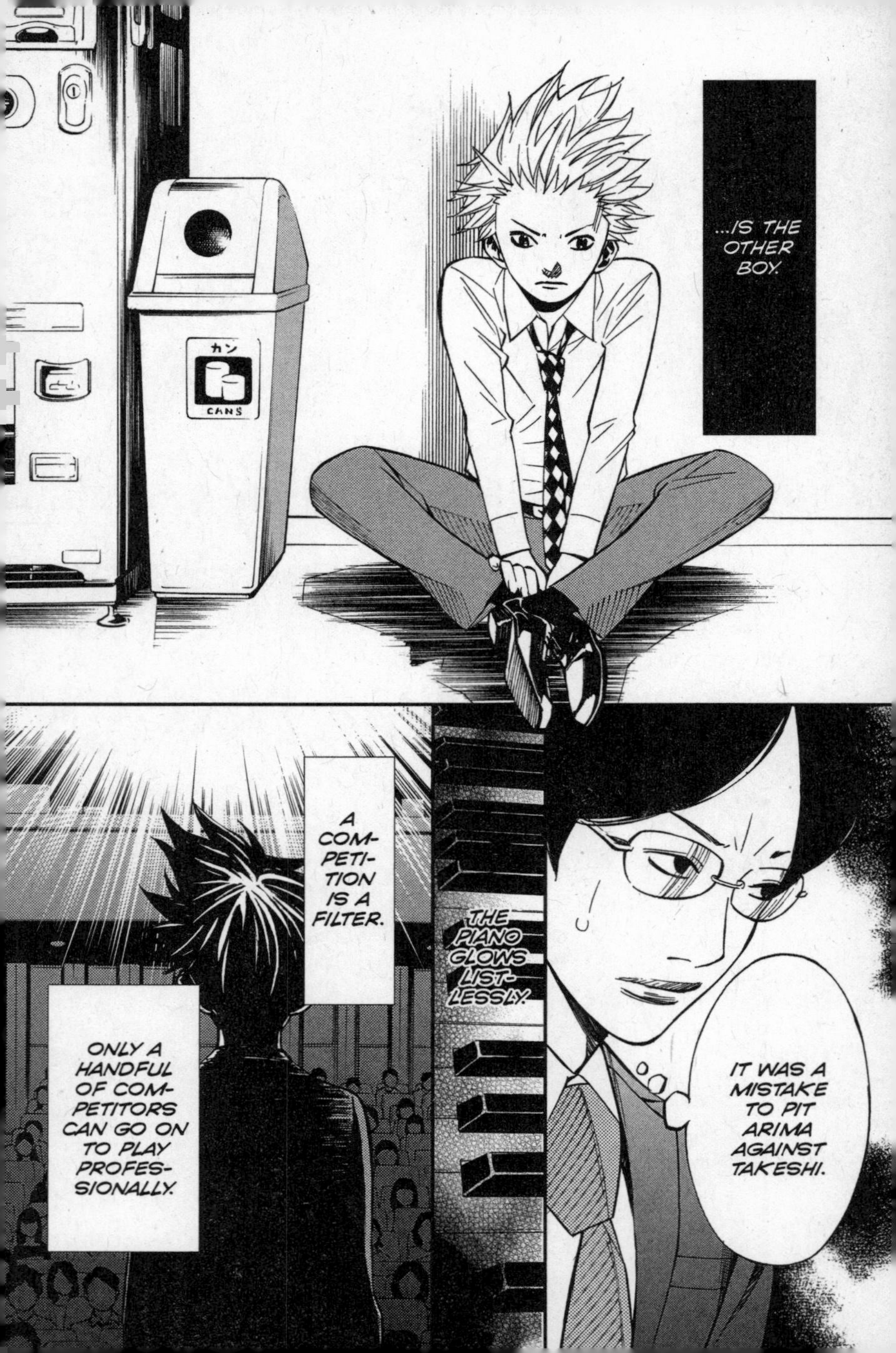
...IS THE OTHER BOY.
カン
CANS
IT WAS A MISTAKE TO PIT ARIMA AGAINST TAKESHI.
THE PIANO GLOWS LIST-LESSLY.
A COM-PETI-TION IS A FILTER.
ONLY A HANDFUL OF COM-PETITORS CAN GO ON TO PLAY PROFES-SIONALLY.

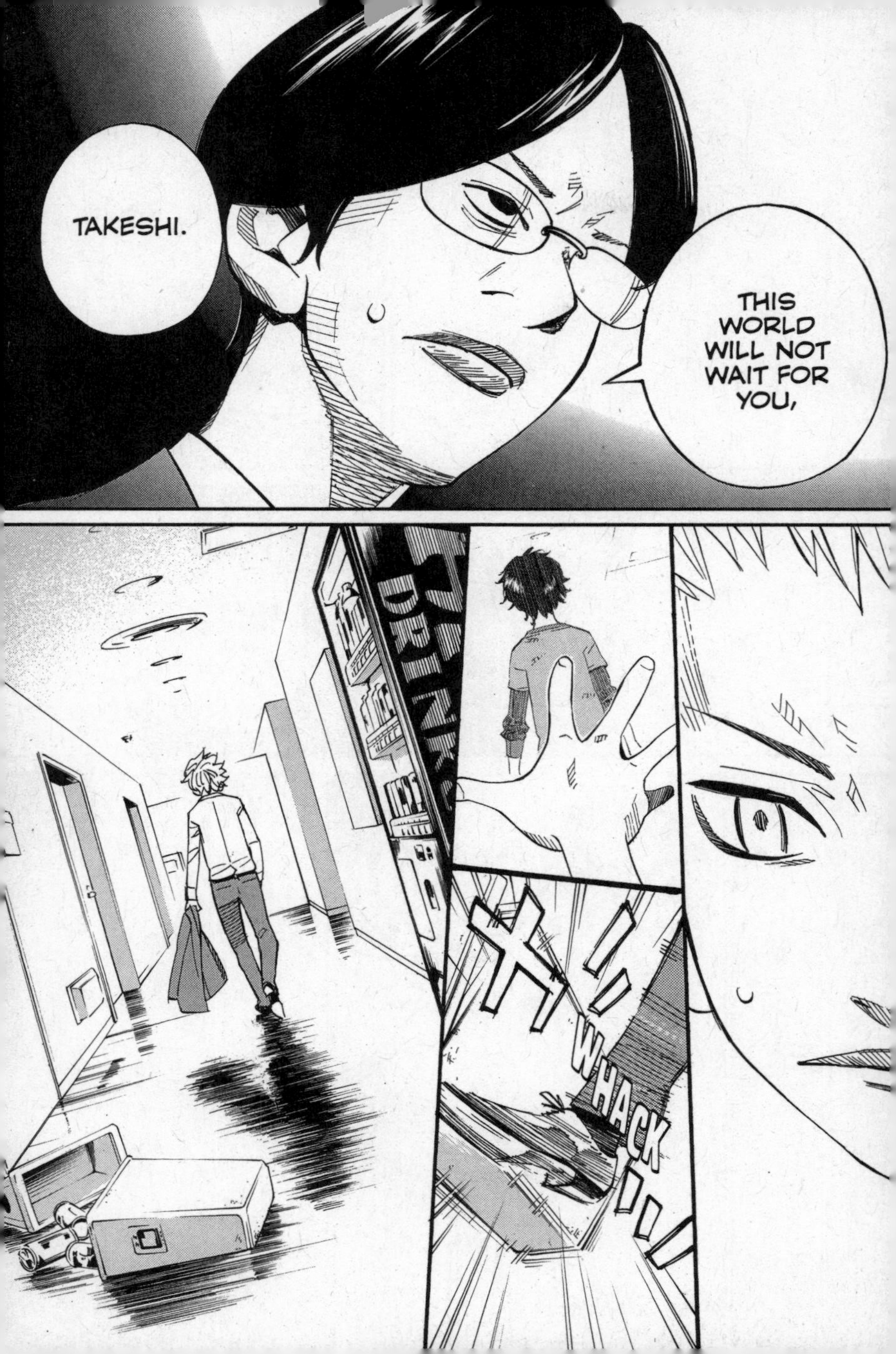
THIS WORLD WILL NOT WAIT FOR YOU,
TAKESHI.
WHACK
DRINK

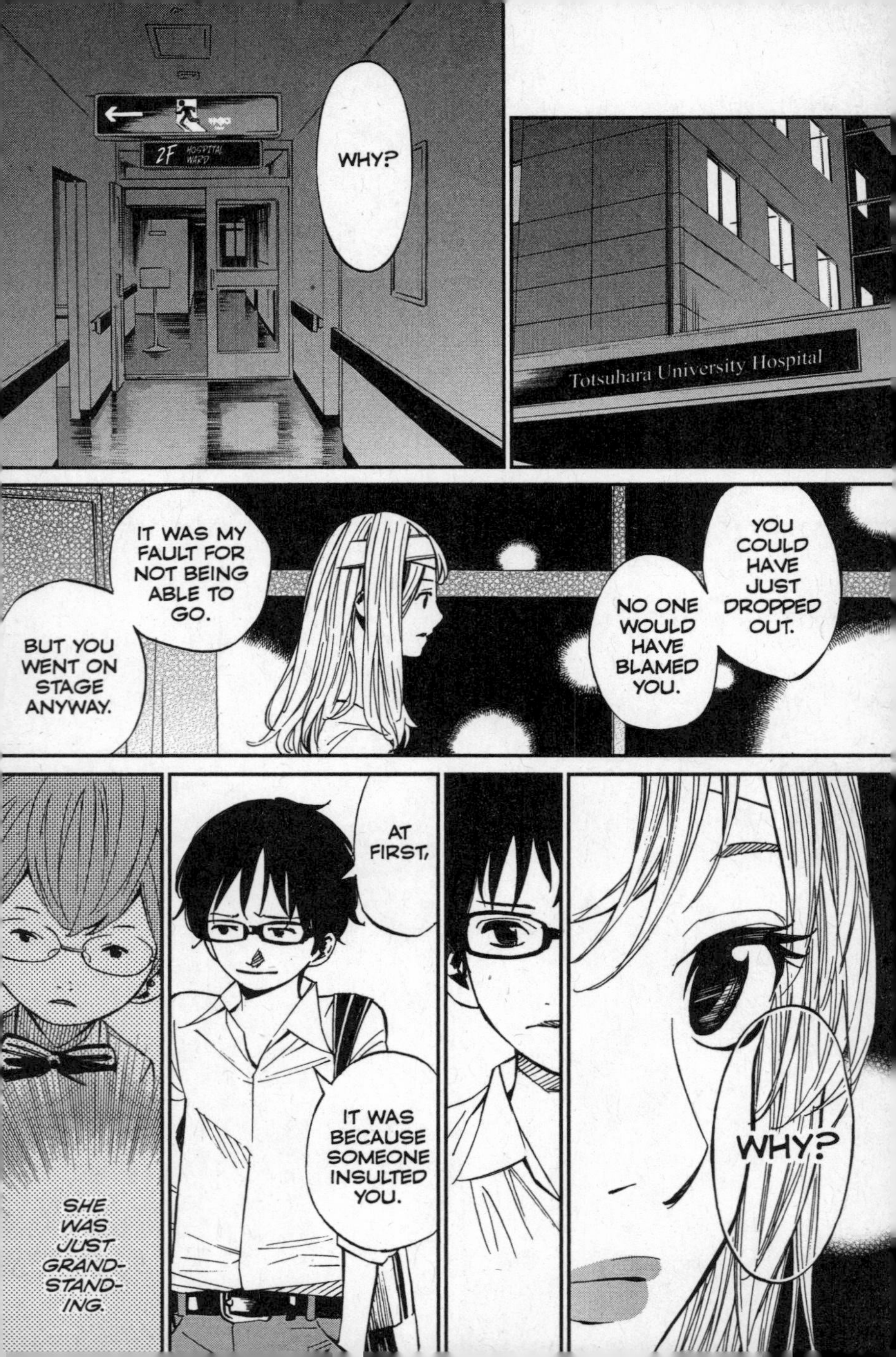
Totsuhara University Hospital
2F HOSPITAL WARD
WHY?
YOU COULD HAVE JUST DROPPED OUT.
NO ONE WOULD HAVE BLAMED YOU.
IT WAS MY FAULT FOR NOT BEING ABLE TO GO.
BUT YOU WENT ON STAGE ANYWAY.
WHY?
AT FIRST,
IT WAS BECAUSE SOMEONE INSULTED YOU.
SHE WAS JUST GRAND-STANDING.

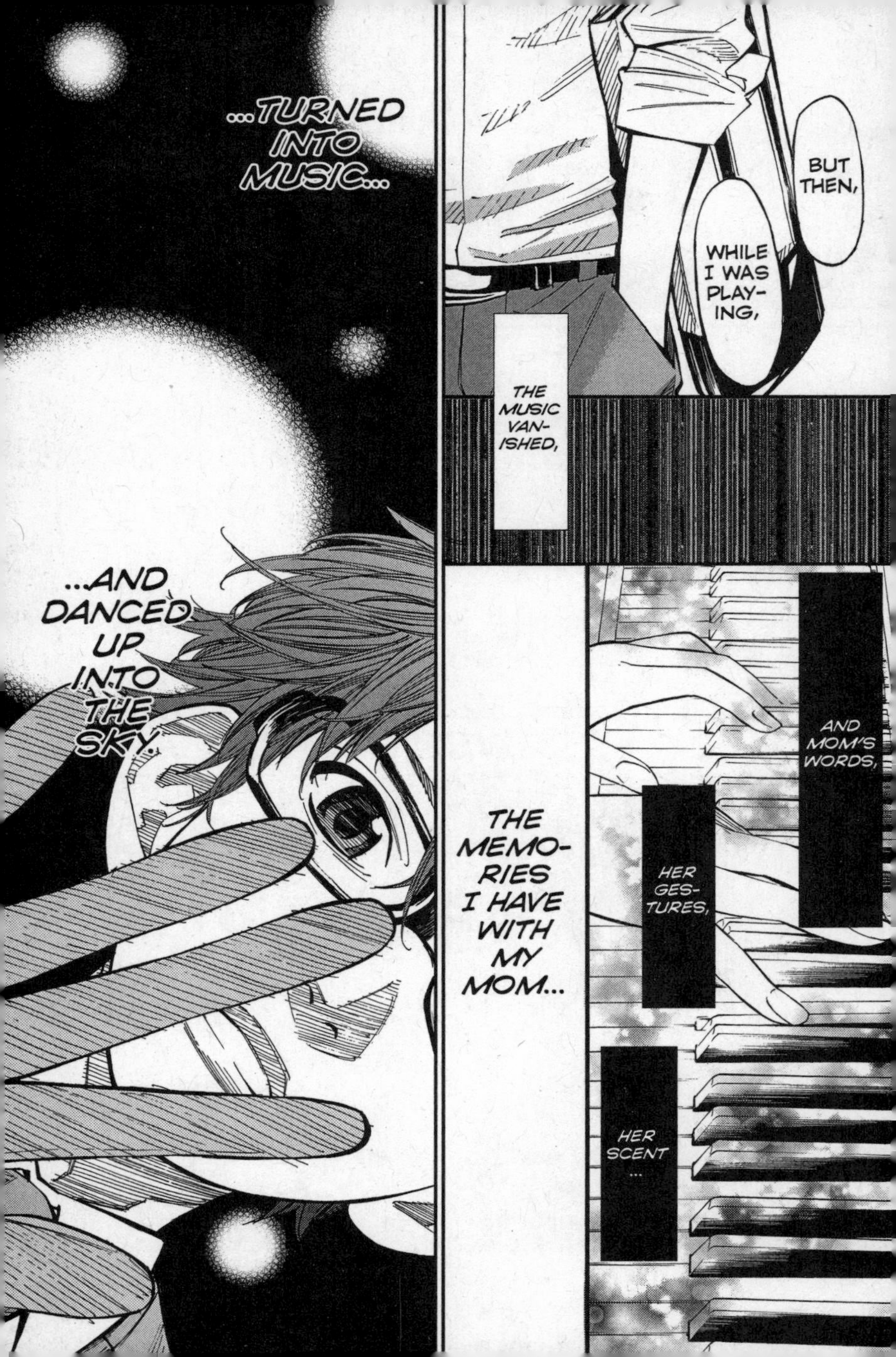
BUT THEN,
WHILE I WAS PLAY-ING,
THE MUSIC VAN-ISHED,
AND MOM'S WORDS,
HER GES-TURES,
HER SCENT...
THE MEMO-RIES I HAVE WITH MY MOM...
...TURNED INTO MUSIC...
...AND DANCED UP INTO THE SKY.

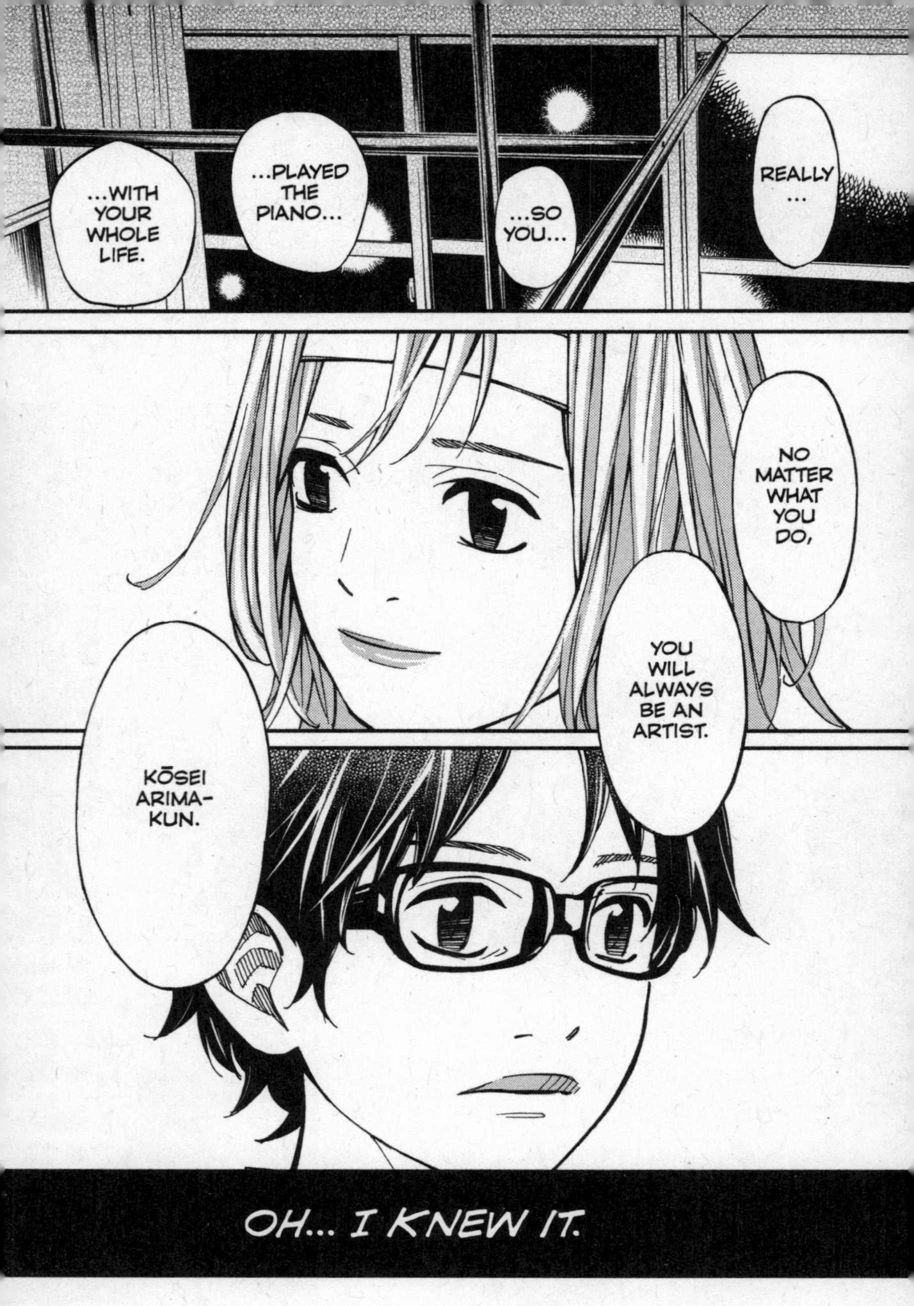
REALLY...
...SO YOU...
...PLAYED THE PIANO...
...WITH YOUR WHOLE LIFE.
NO MATTER WHAT YOU DO,
YOU WILL ALWAYS BE AN ARTIST.
KŌSEI ARIMA-KUN.
OH... I KNEW IT.

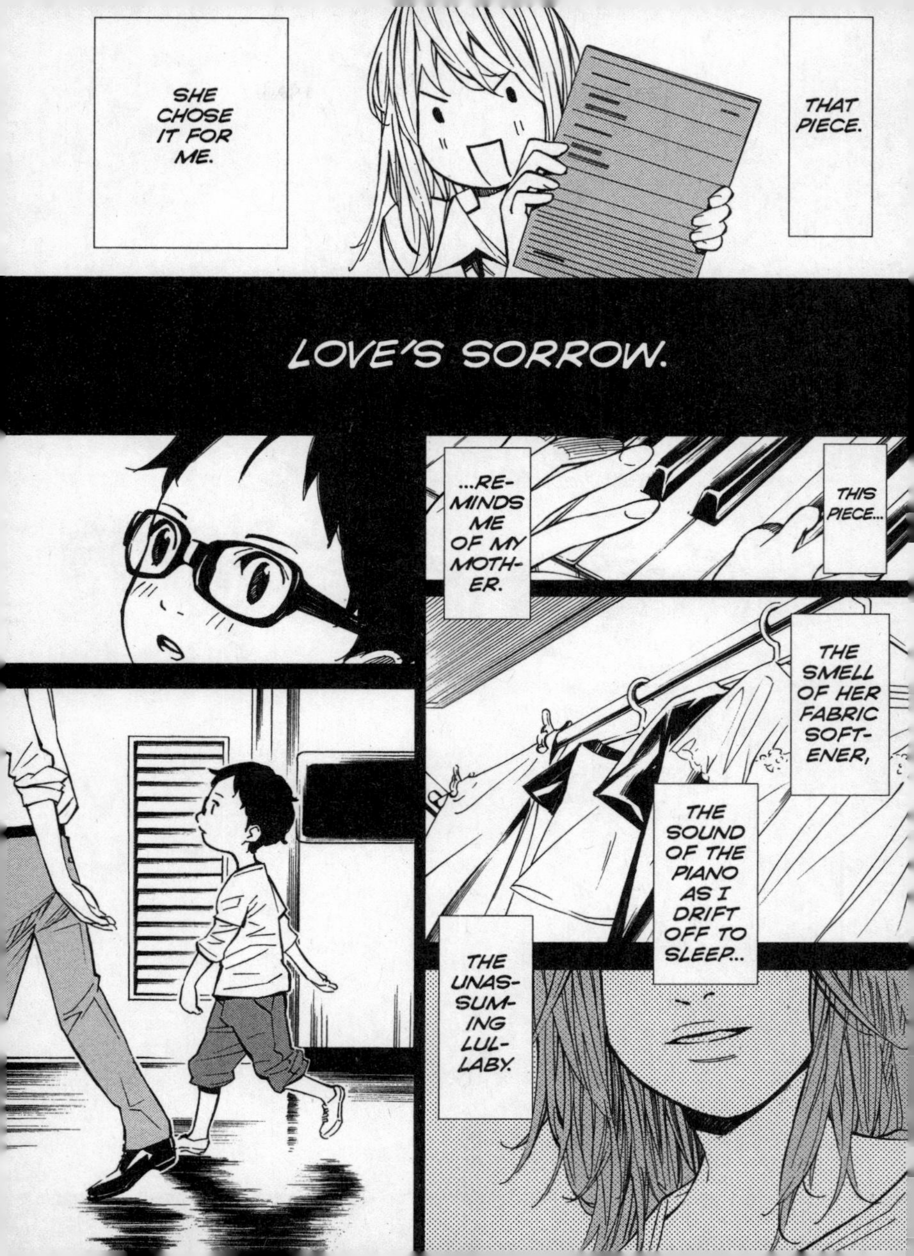
THAT PIECE.
SHE CHOSE IT FOR ME.
LOVE'S SORROW.
THIS PIECE...
...REMINDS ME OF MY MOTHER.
THE SMELL OF HER FABRIC SOFTENER,
THE SOUND OF THE PIANO AS I DRIFT OFF TO SLEEP...
THE UNASSUMING LULLABY.

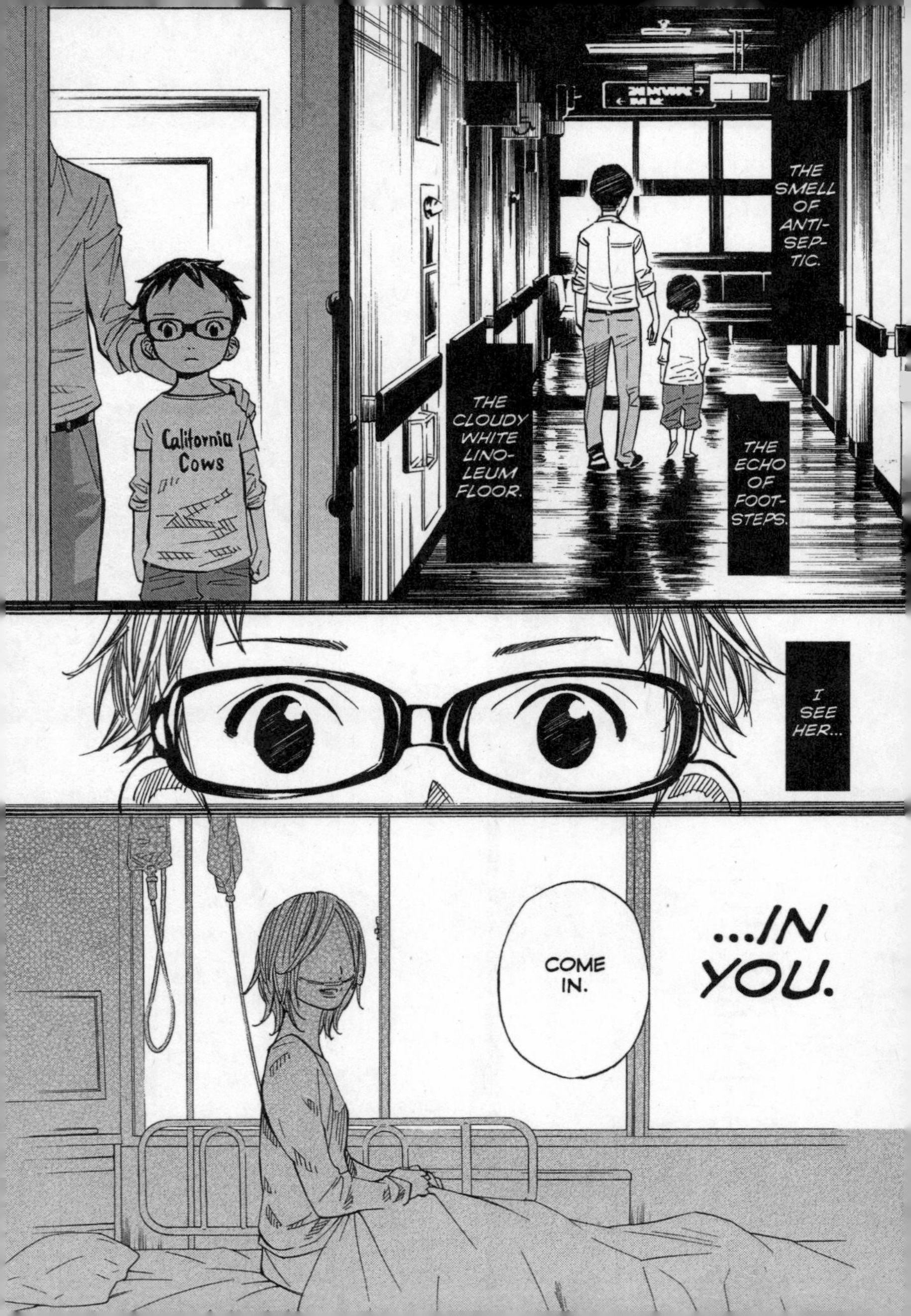
THE SMELL OF ANTISEPTIC.
THE ECHO OF FOOTSTEPS.
THE CLOUDY WHITE LINOLEUM FLOOR.
California Cows
I SEE HER...
...IN YOU.
COME IN.

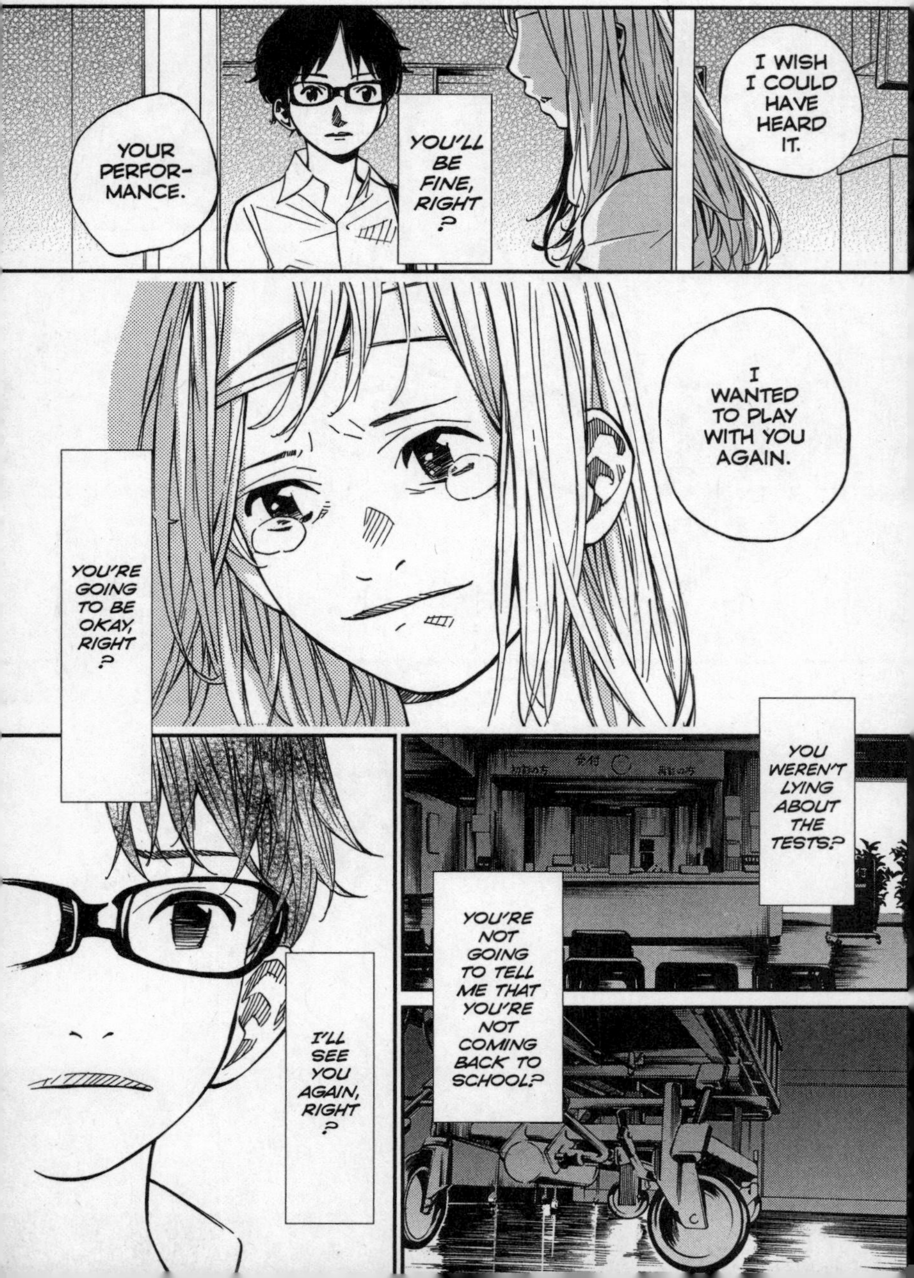
I WISH I COULD HAVE HEARD IT.
YOU'LL BE FINE, RIGHT?
YOUR PERFOR-MANCE.
I WANTED TO PLAY WITH YOU AGAIN.
YOU'RE GOING TO BE OKAY, RIGHT?
YOU WEREN'T LYING ABOUT THE TESTS?
YOU'RE NOT GOING TO TELL ME THAT YOU'RE NOT COMING BACK TO SCHOOL?
I'LL SEE YOU AGAIN, RIGHT?

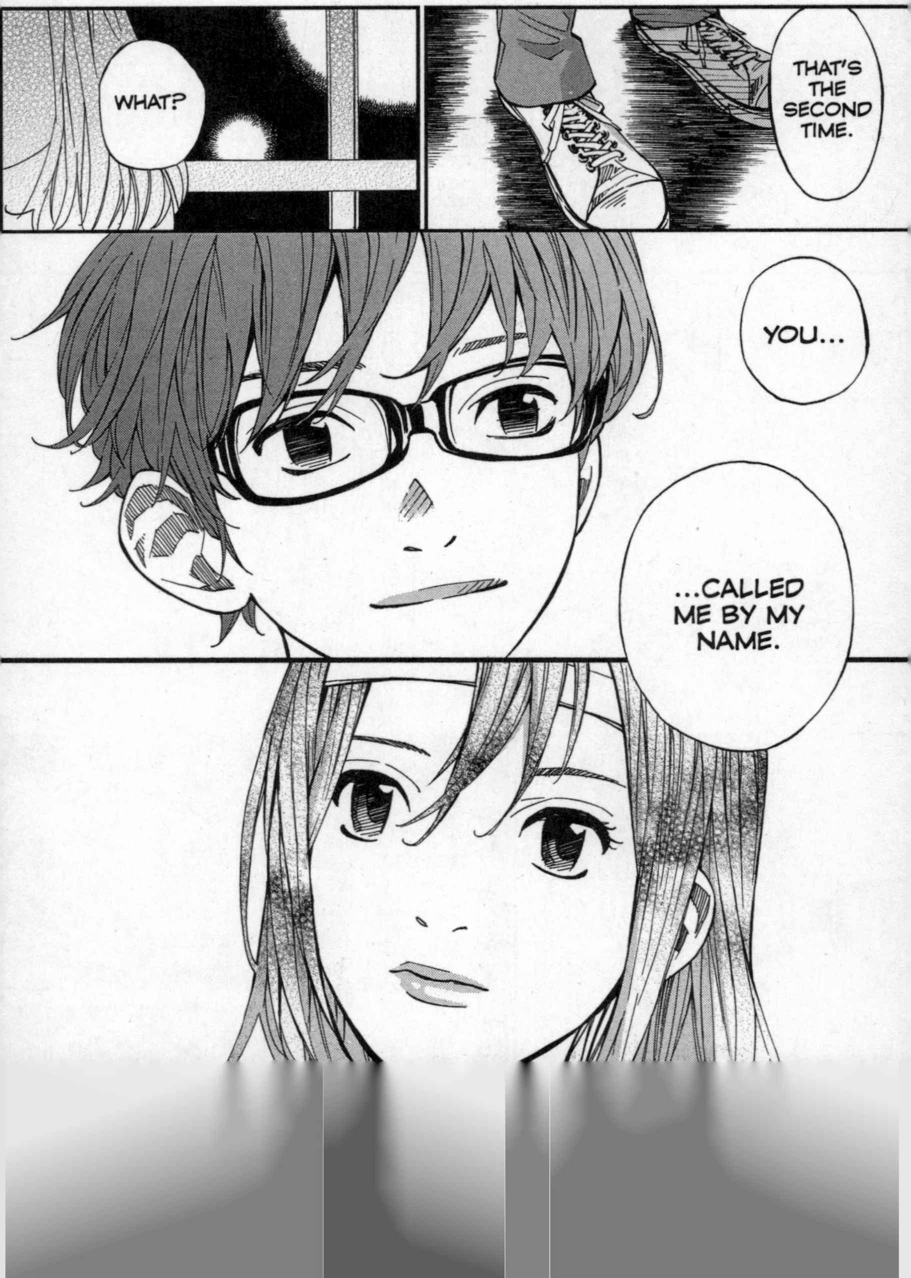
THAT'S THE SECOND TIME.
WHAT?
YOU...
...CALLED ME BY MY NAME.

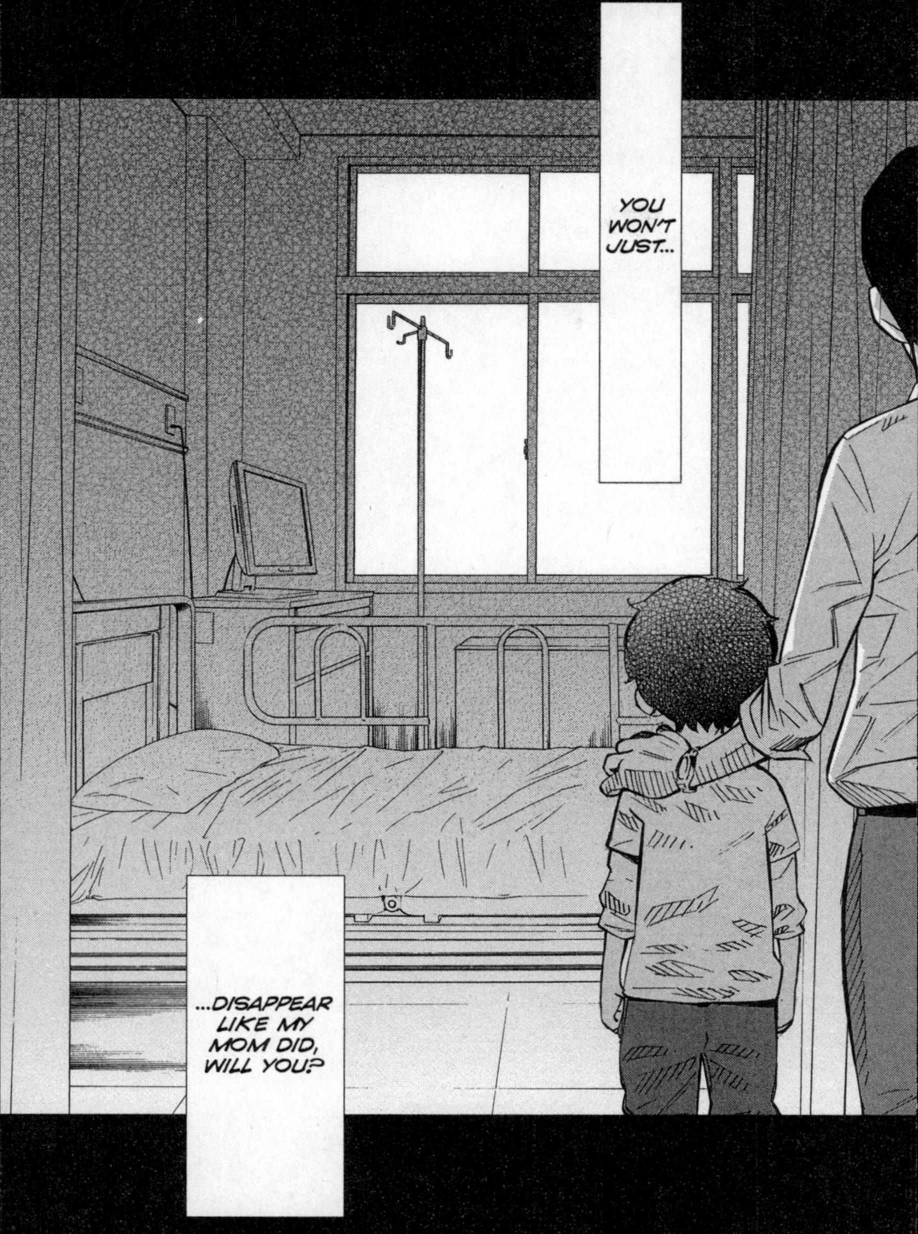
YOU WON'T JUST...
...DISAPPEAR LIKE MY MOM DID, WILL YOU?

SUPERIMPOSED OUTLINES / END

Your Lie in April

I met the girl under full-bloomed cherry blossoms, and my fate has begun to change.

Chapter 28: Footprints

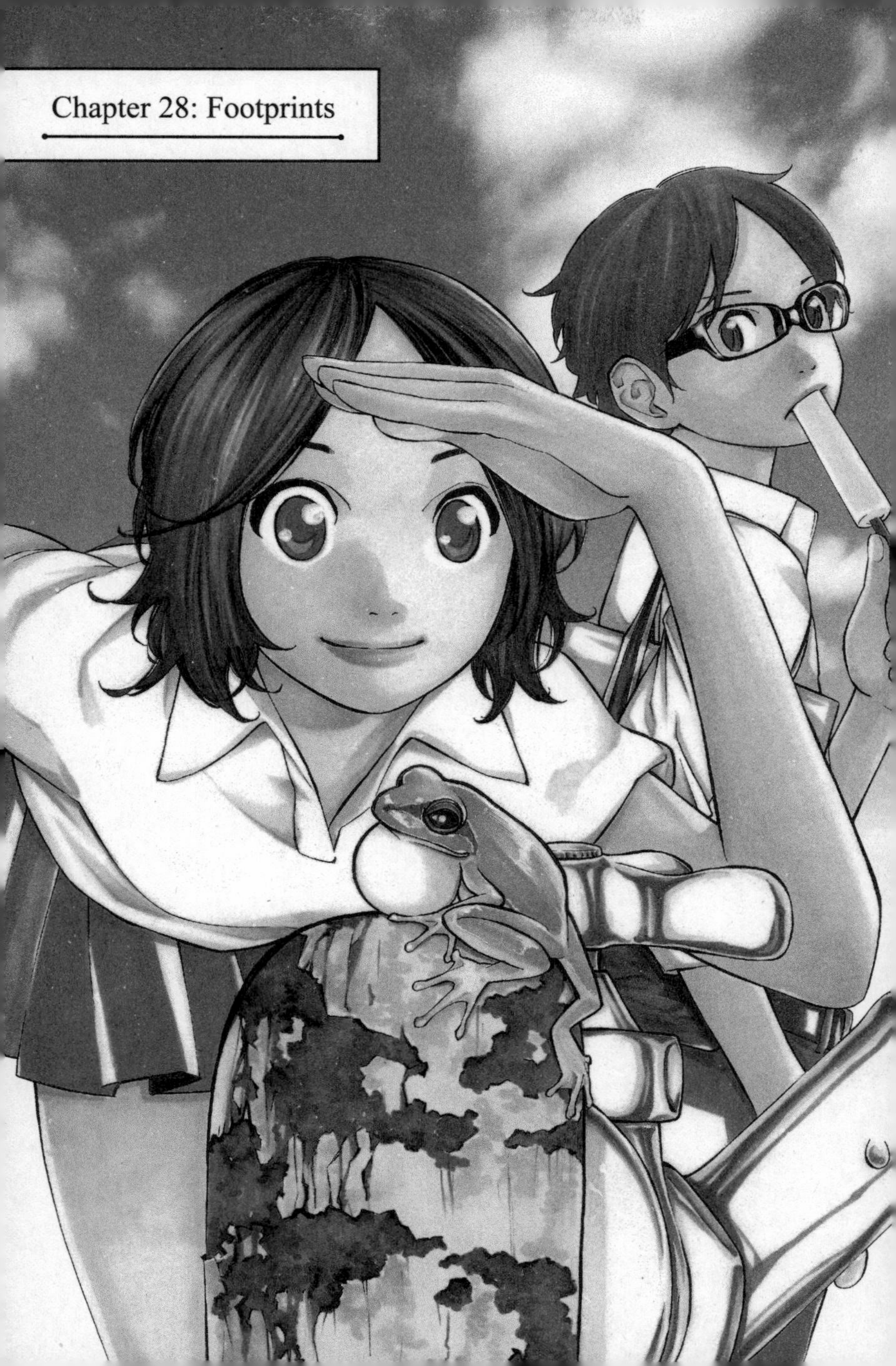

Your Lie in April

I met the girl under full-bloomed cherry blossoms, and my fate has begun to change.

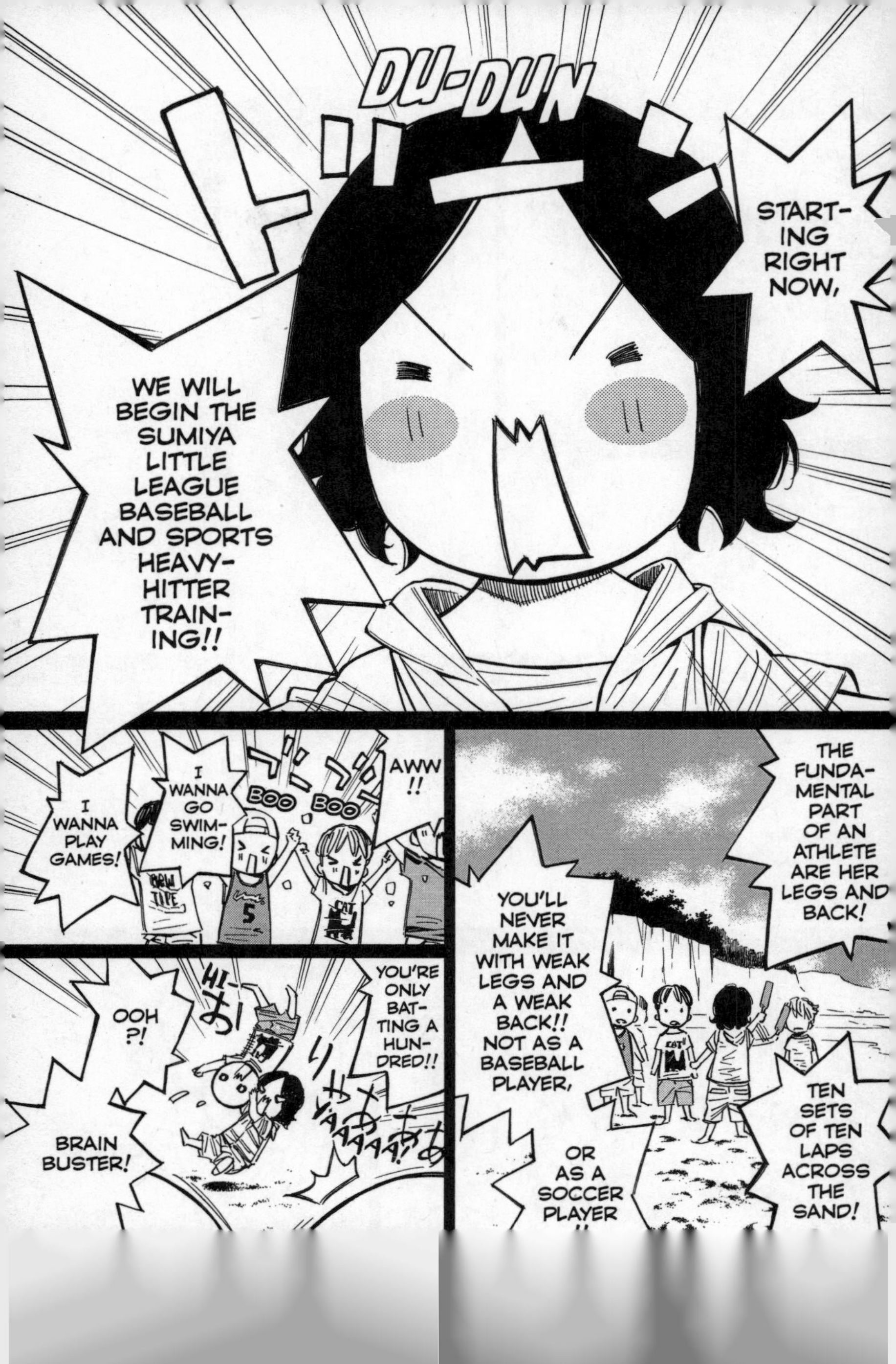

DU-DUN
STARTING RIGHT NOW,
WE WILL BEGIN THE SUMIYA LITTLE LEAGUE BASEBALL AND SPORTS HEAVY-HITTER TRAINING!!
THE FUNDAMENTAL PART OF AN ATHLETE ARE HER LEGS AND BACK!
YOU'LL NEVER MAKE IT WITH WEAK LEGS AND A WEAK BACK!! NOT AS A BASEBALL PLAYER,
OR AS A SOCCER PLAYER
TEN SETS OF TEN LAPS ACROSS THE SAND!
AWW!!
BOO BOO
I WANNA GO SWIMMING!
I WANNA PLAY GAMES!
YOU'RE ONLY BATTING A HUNDRED!!
HI-
YAAAAAA!
OOH?!
BRAIN BUSTER!

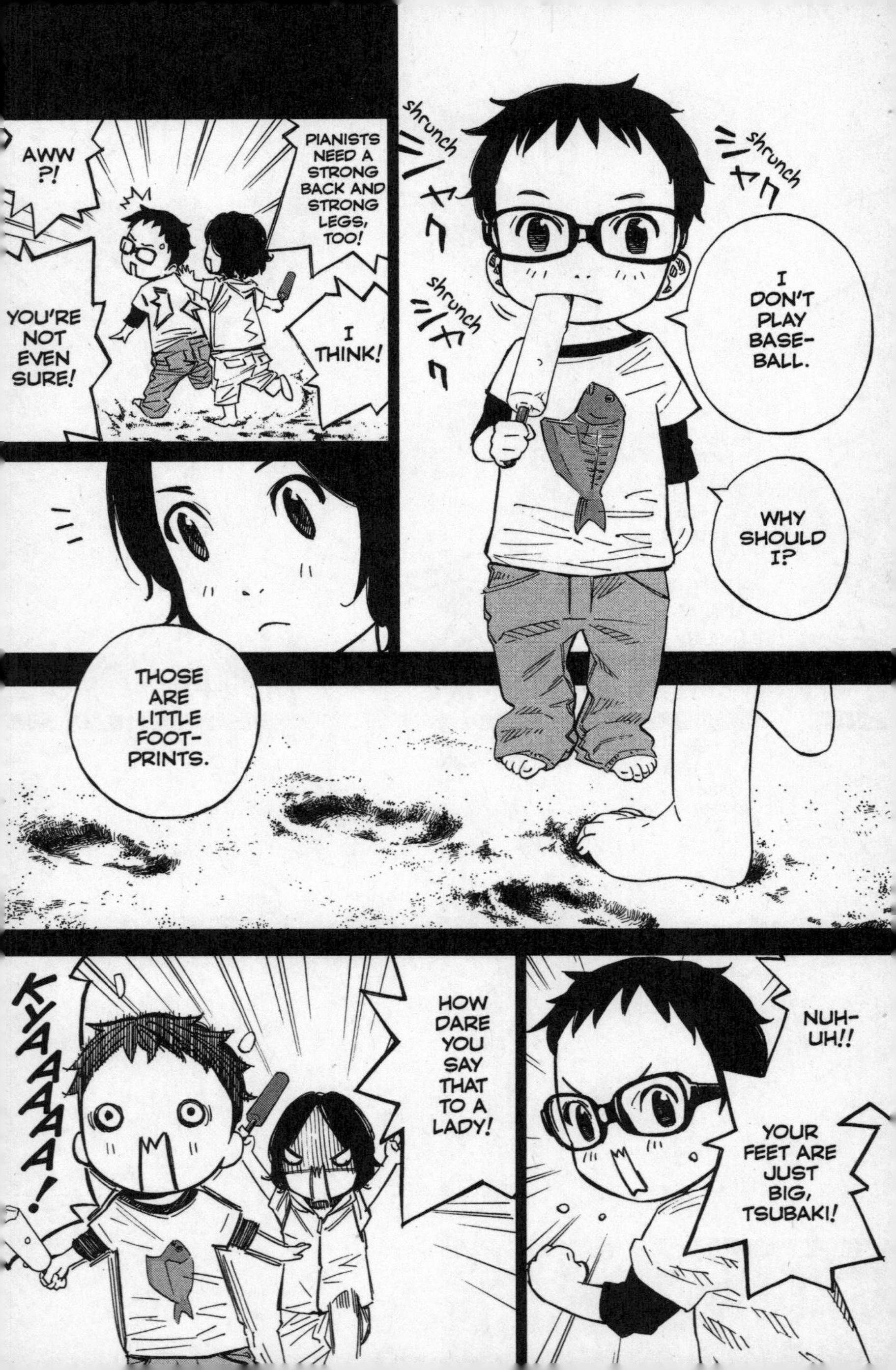
shrunch
shrunch
shrunch
I DON'T PLAY BASE-BALL.
WHY SHOULD I?
PIANISTS NEED A STRONG BACK AND STRONG LEGS, TOO!
AWW ?!
I THINK!
YOU'RE NOT EVEN SURE!
THOSE ARE LITTLE FOOT-PRINTS.
NUH-UH!!
YOUR FEET ARE JUST BIG, TSUBAKI!
HOW DARE YOU SAY THAT TO A LADY!
KYAAAAA!

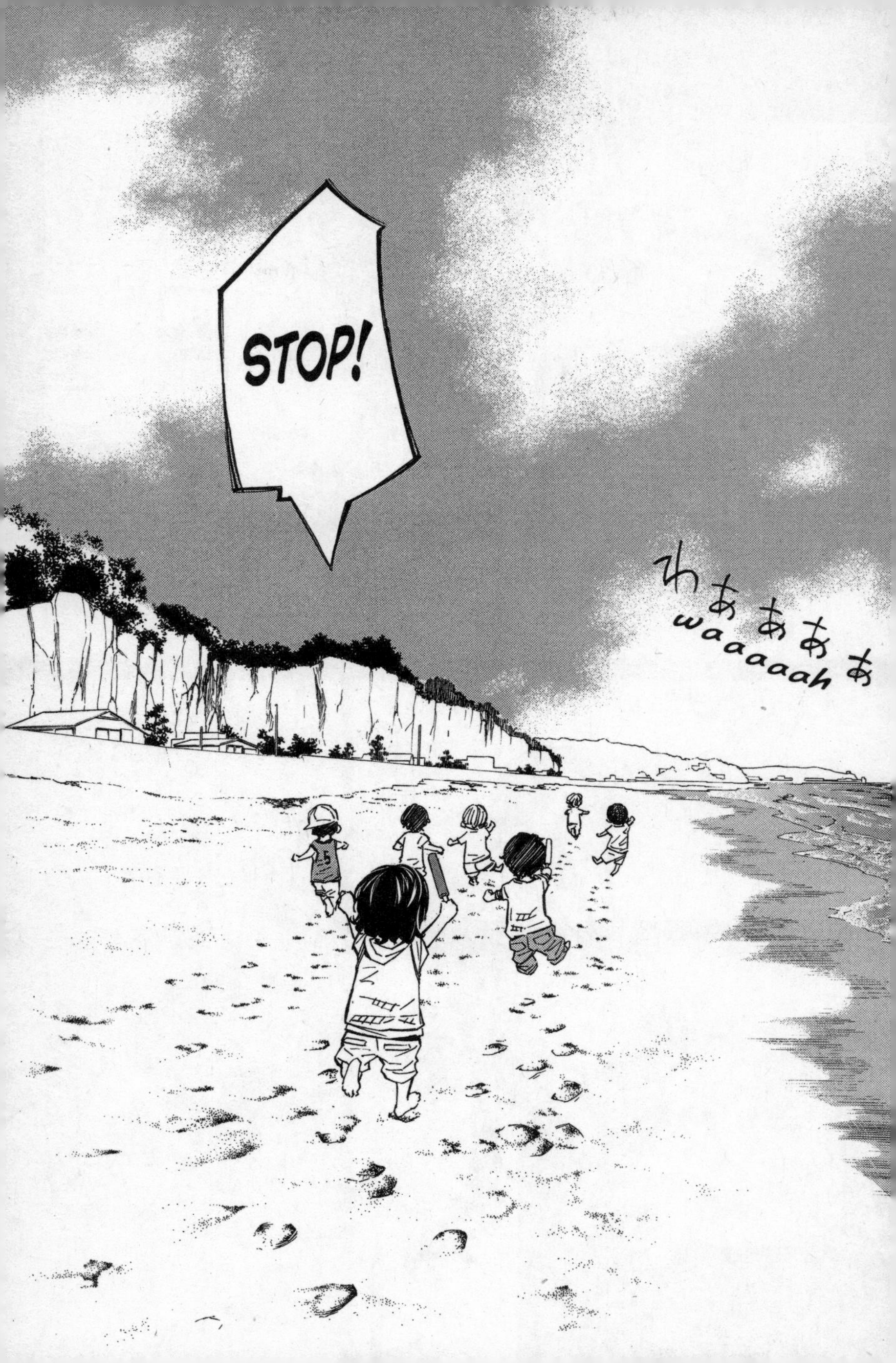
STOP!
わあああぁ
waaaaaah

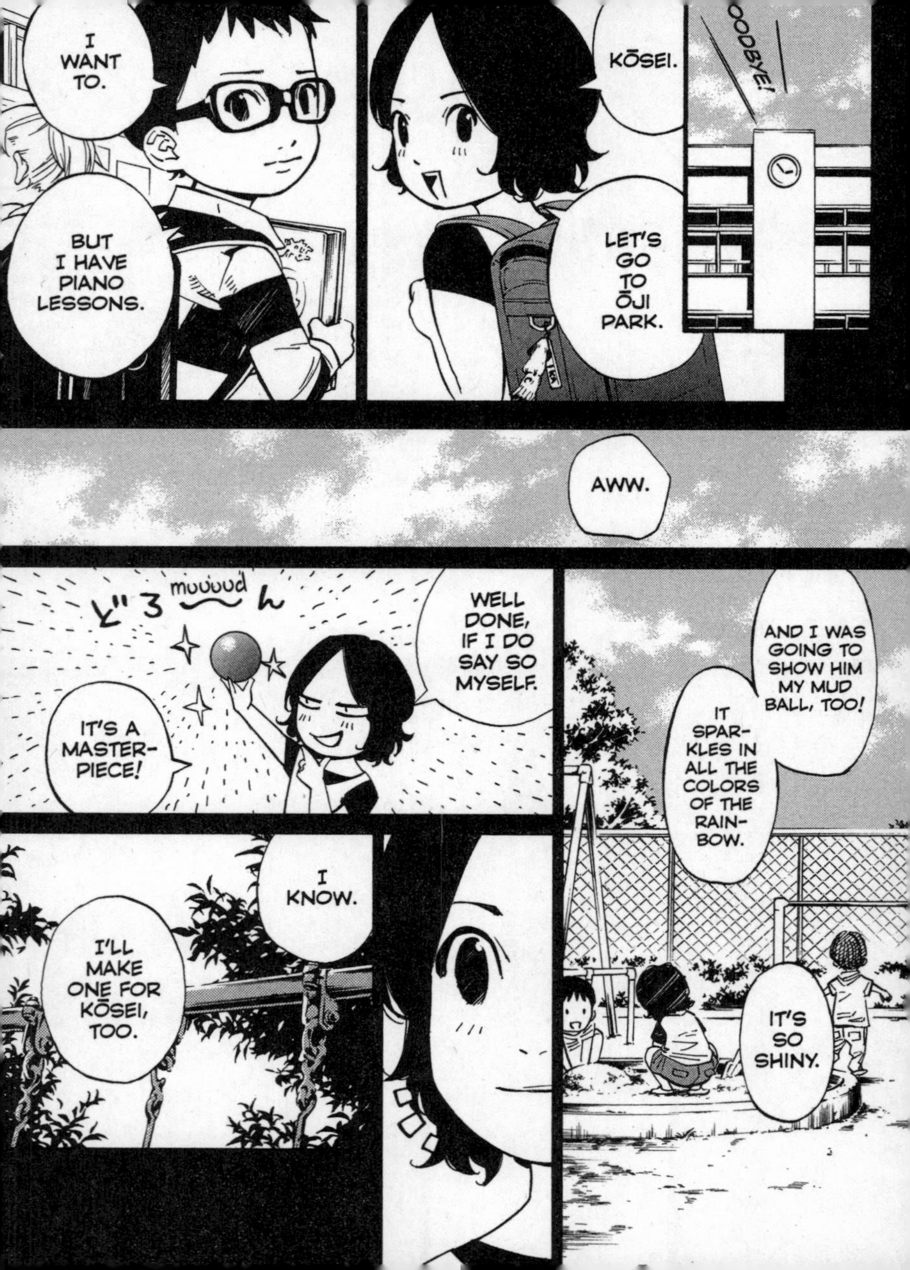
OODBYE!
KŌSEI.
LET'S GO TO ŌJI PARK.
I WANT TO.
BUT I HAVE PIANO LESSONS.
AWW.
AND I WAS GOING TO SHOW HIM MY MUD BALL, TOO!
IT SPARKLES IN ALL THE COLORS OF THE RAINBOW.
IT'S SO SHINY.
WELL DONE, IF I DO SAY SO MYSELF.
どろ〜ん
muuuud
IT'S A MASTERPIECE!
I KNOW.
I'LL MAKE ONE FOR KŌSEI, TOO.

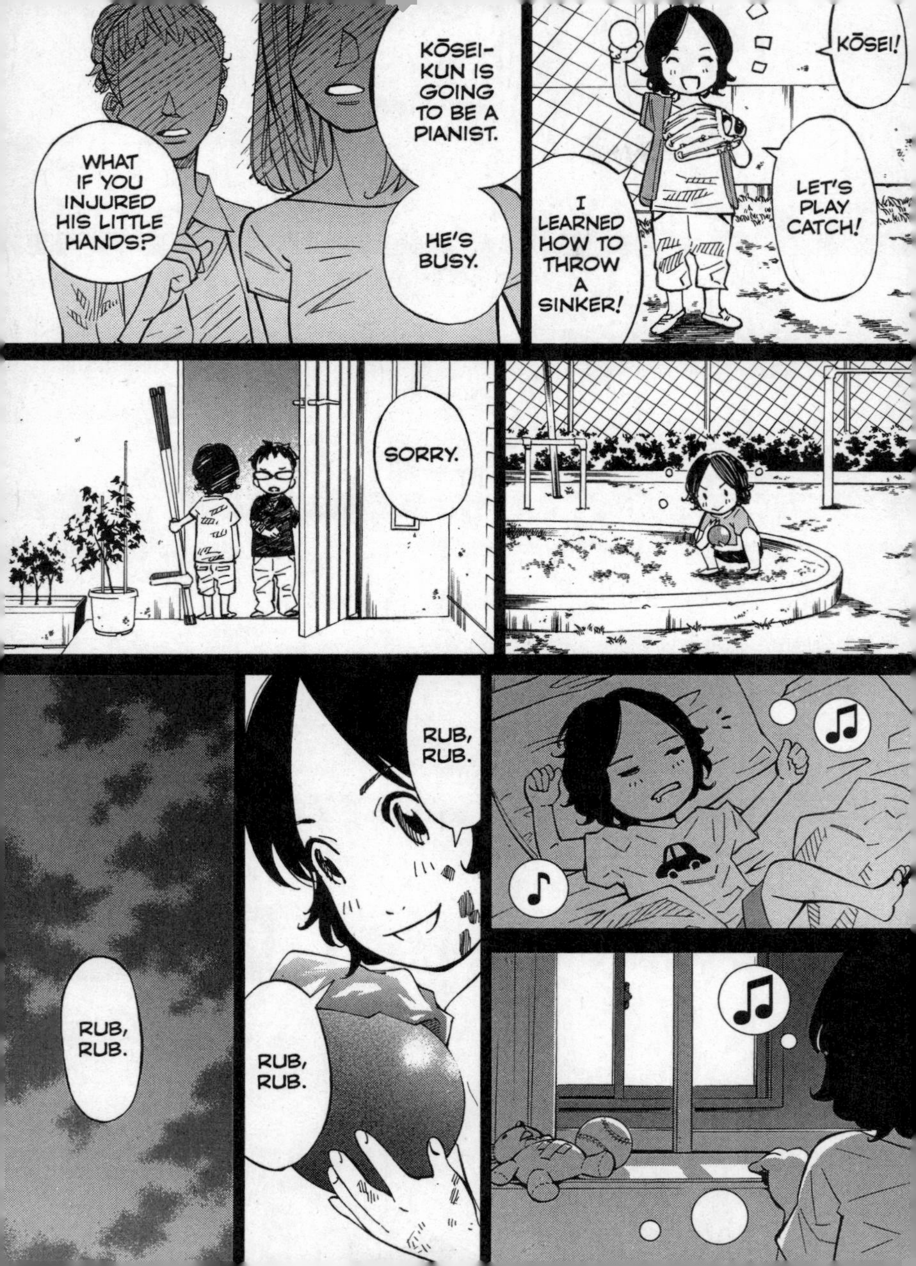
KŌSEI!
LET'S PLAY CATCH!
I LEARNED HOW TO THROW A SINKER!
KŌSEI-KUN IS GOING TO BE A PIANIST.
HE'S BUSY.
WHAT IF YOU INJURED HIS LITTLE HANDS?
SORRY.
RUB, RUB.
RUB, RUB.
RUB, RUB.

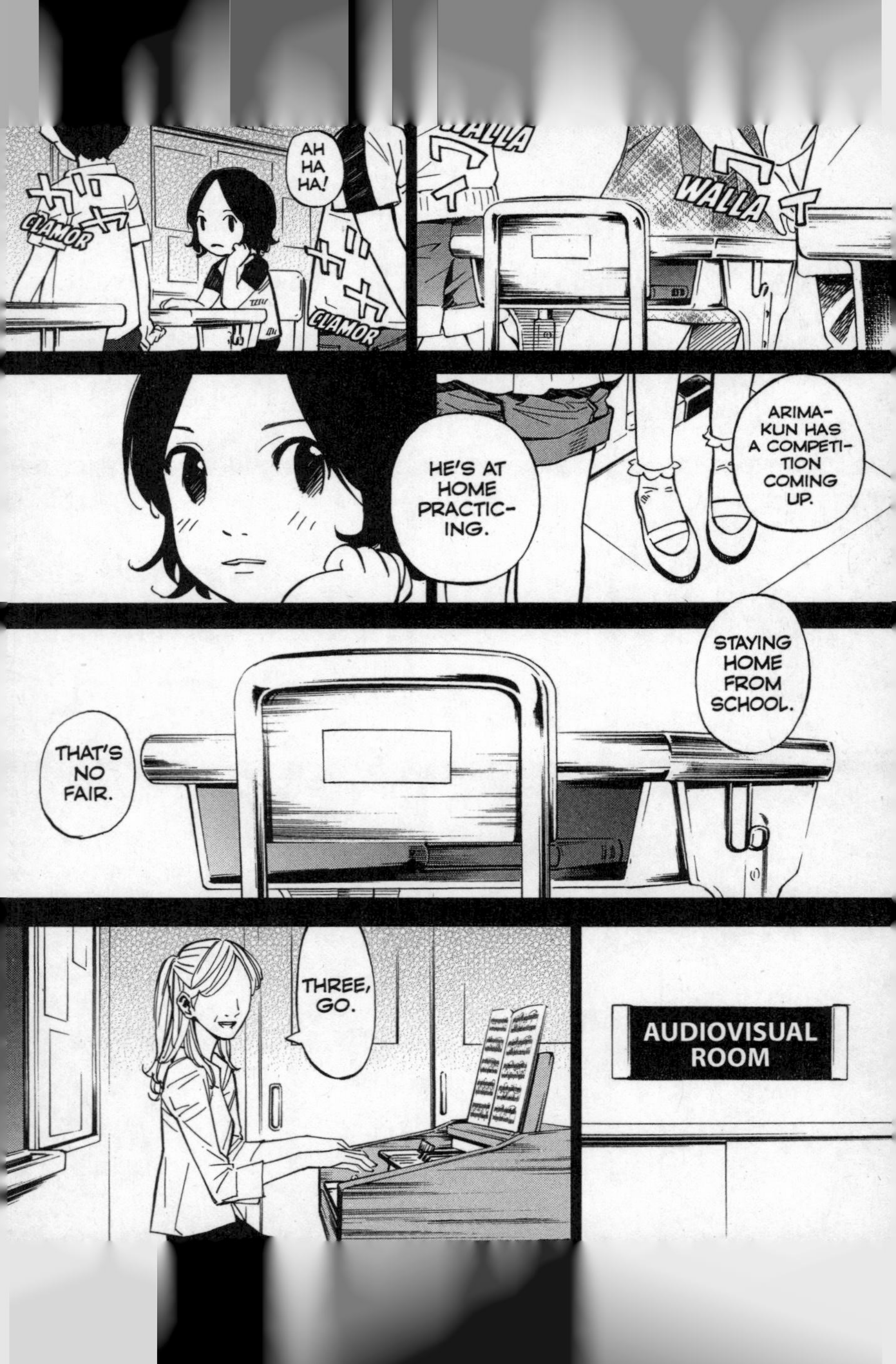
WALLA
WALLA
AH HA HA!
CLAMOR
CLAMOR
ARIMA-KUN HAS A COMPETITION COMING UP.
HE'S AT HOME PRACTICING.
STAYING HOME FROM SCHOOL.
THAT'S NO FAIR.
AUDIOVISUAL ROOM
THREE, GO.

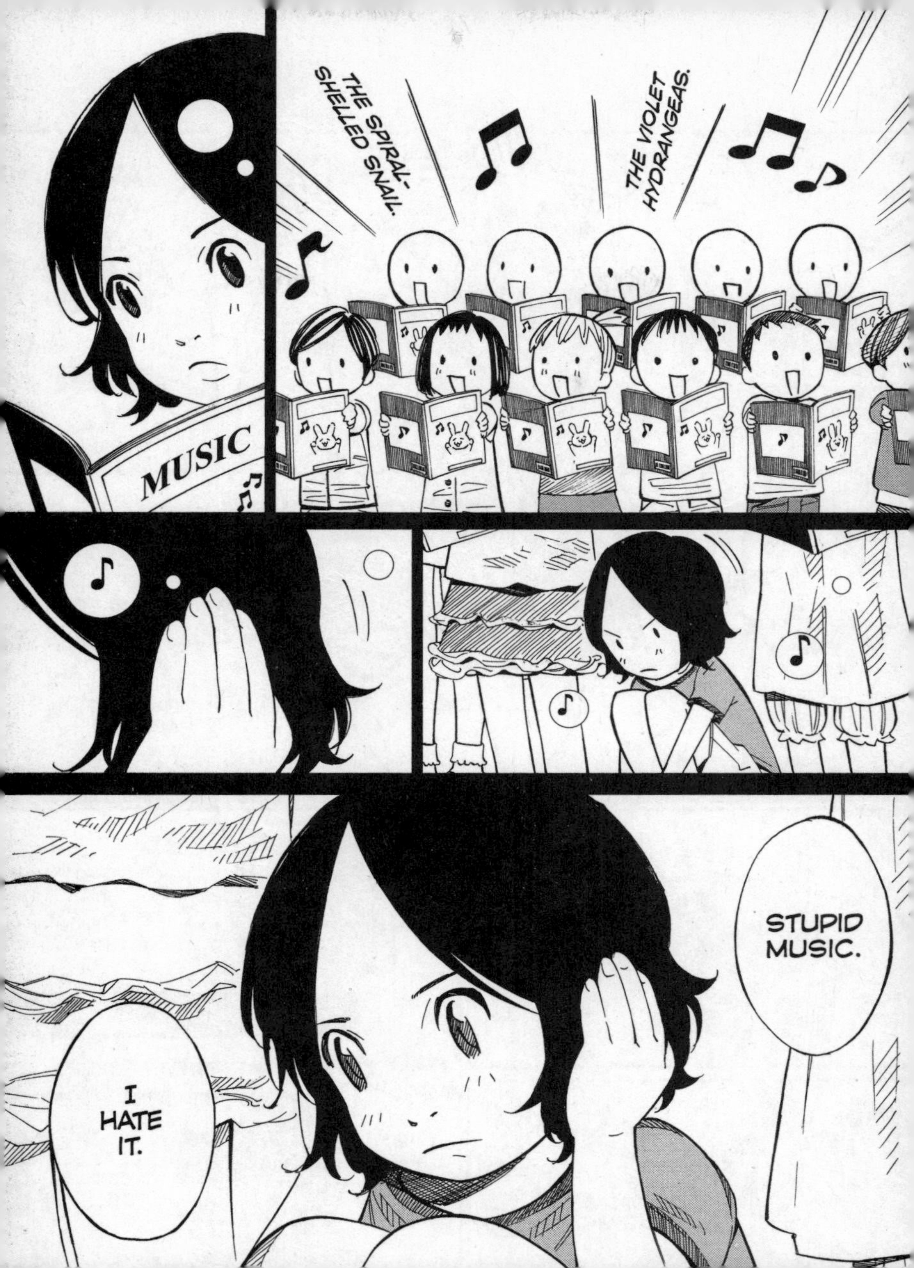
THE VIOLET HYDRANGEAS.
THE SPIRAL-SHELLED SNAIL.
MUSIC
STUPID MUSIC.
I HATE IT.

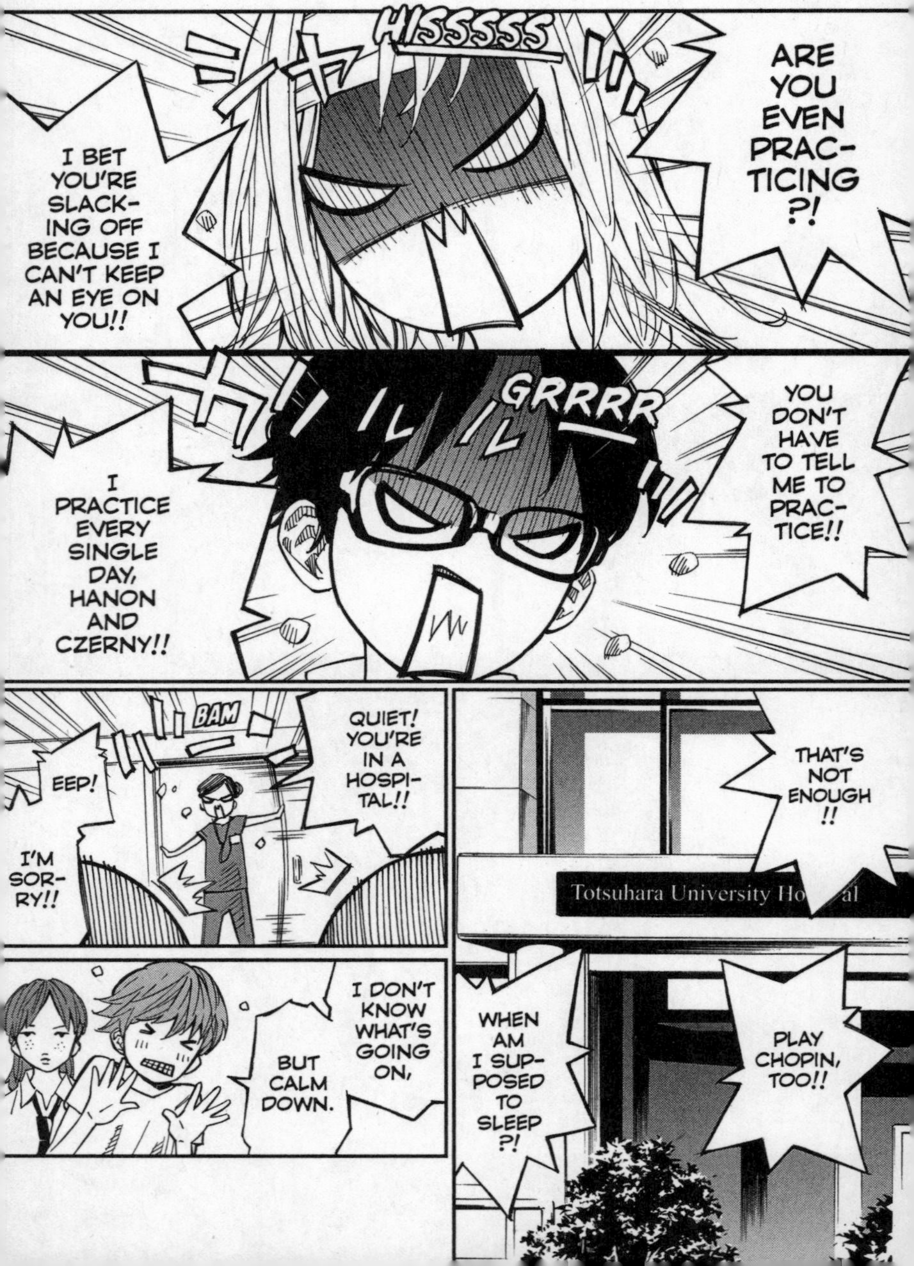
HISSSSS
ARE YOU EVEN PRAC-TICING?!
I BET YOU'RE SLACK-ING OFF BECAUSE I CAN'T KEEP AN EYE ON YOU!!
GRRRR
YOU DON'T HAVE TO TELL ME TO PRAC-TICE!!
I PRACTICE EVERY SINGLE DAY, HANON AND CZERNY!!
THAT'S NOT ENOUGH!!
Totsuhara University Ho al
PLAY CHOPIN, TOO!!
WHEN AM I SUP-POSED TO SLEEP?!
BAM
QUIET! YOU'RE IN A HOSPI-TAL!!
EEP!
I'M SOR-RY!!
I DON'T KNOW WHAT'S GOING ON,
BUT CALM DOWN.

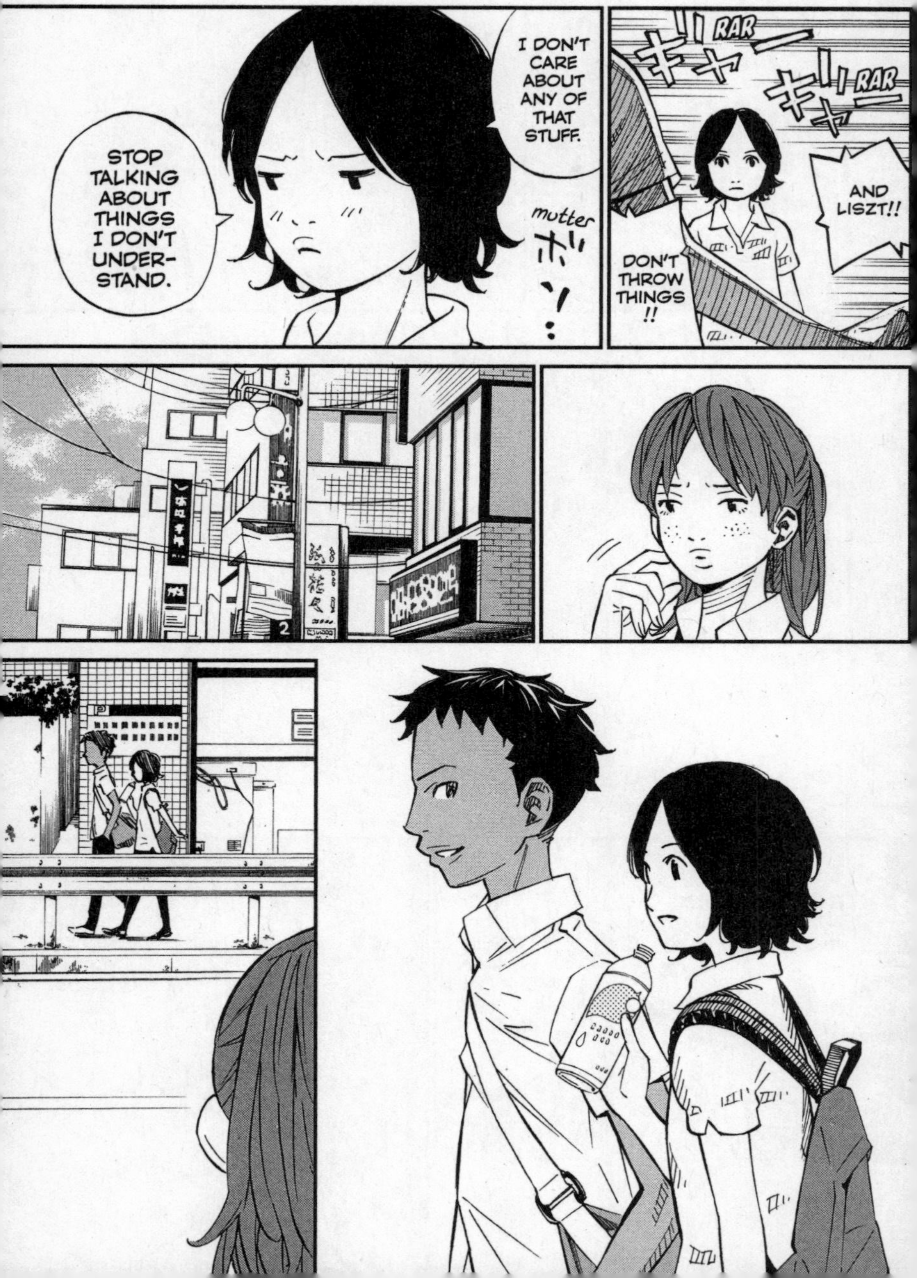
RAR
RAR
AND LISZT!!
DON'T THROW THINGS!!
I DON'T CARE ABOUT ANY OF THAT STUFF.
STOP TALKING ABOUT THINGS I DON'T UNDER-STAND.
mutter

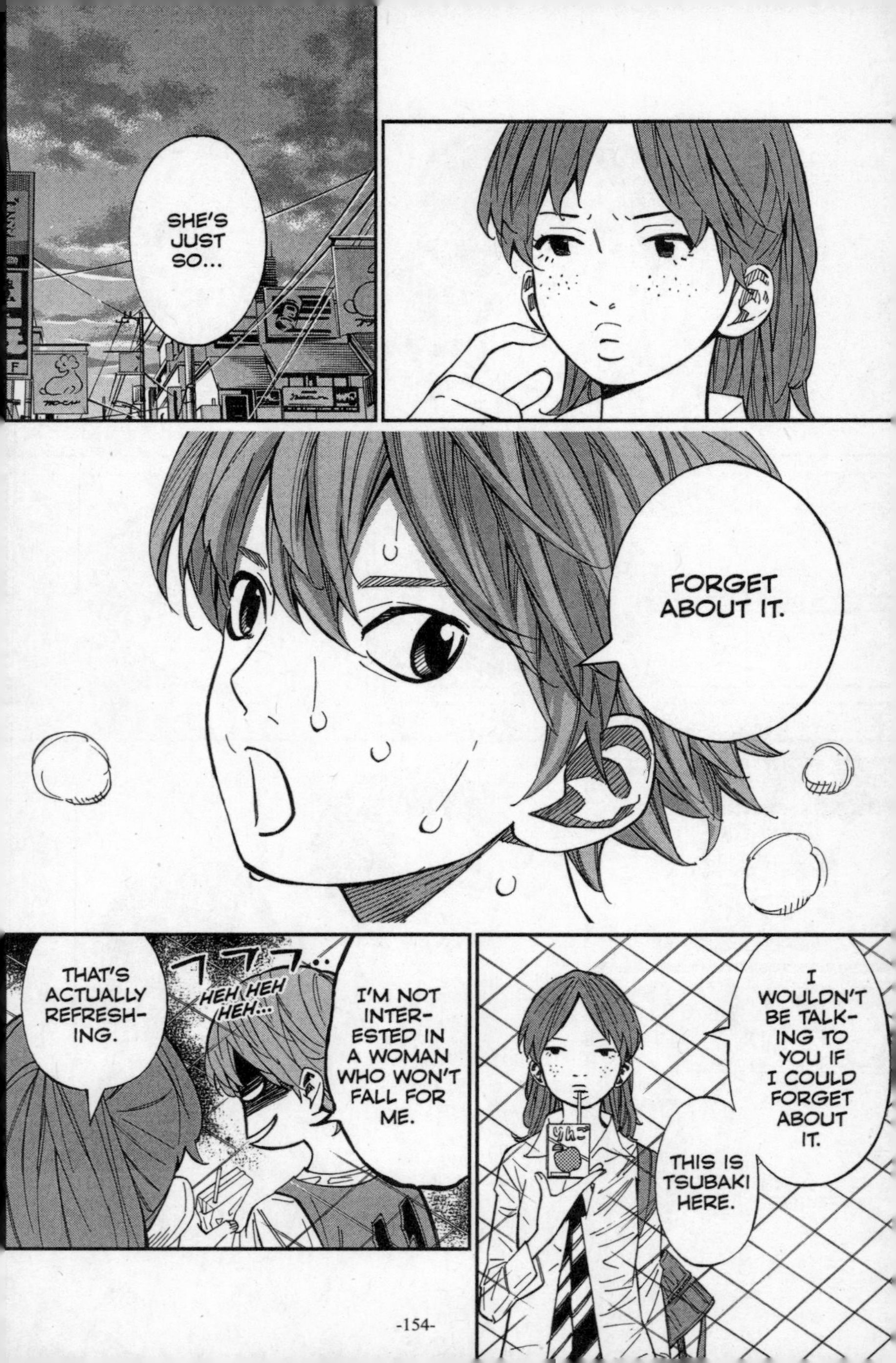
SHE'S JUST SO...
FORGET ABOUT IT.
I WOULDN'T BE TALKING TO YOU IF I COULD FORGET ABOUT IT.
THIS IS TSUBAKI HERE.
I'M NOT INTERESTED IN A WOMAN WHO WON'T FALL FOR ME.
HEH HEH HEH...
THAT'S ACTUALLY REFRESHING.

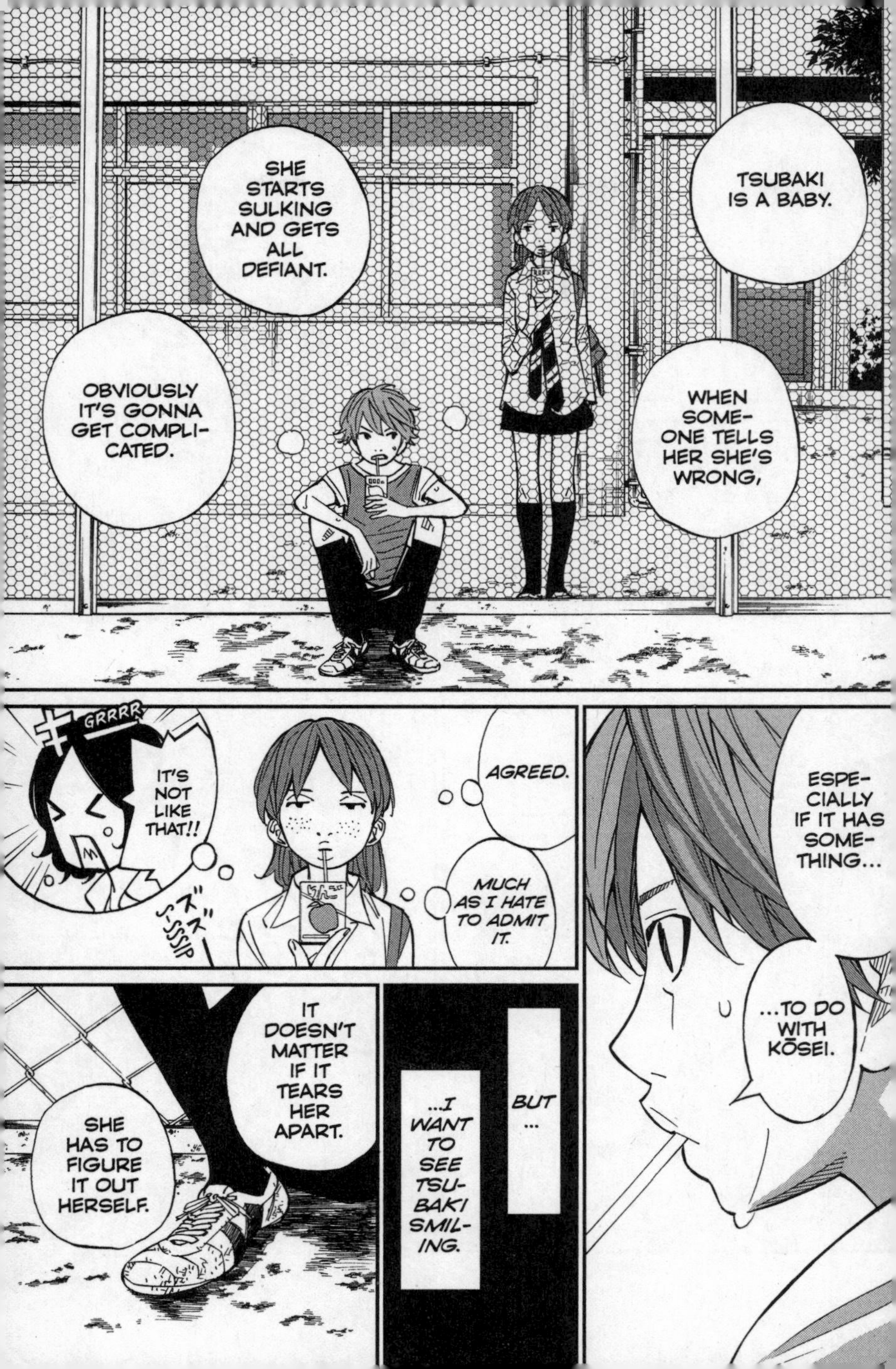
TSUBAKI IS A BABY.
WHEN SOMEONE TELLS HER SHE'S WRONG,
SHE STARTS SULKING AND GETS ALL DEFIANT.
OBVIOUSLY IT'S GONNA GET COMPLICATED.
ESPECIALLY IF IT HAS SOMETHING...
...TO DO WITH KŌSEI.
AGREED.
MUCH AS I HATE TO ADMIT IT.
GRRRR
IT'S NOT LIKE THAT!!
ズズ S-SSSIP
BUT...
...I WANT TO SEE TSUBAKI SMILING.
IT DOESN'T MATTER IF IT TEARS HER APART.
SHE HAS TO FIGURE IT OUT HERSELF.

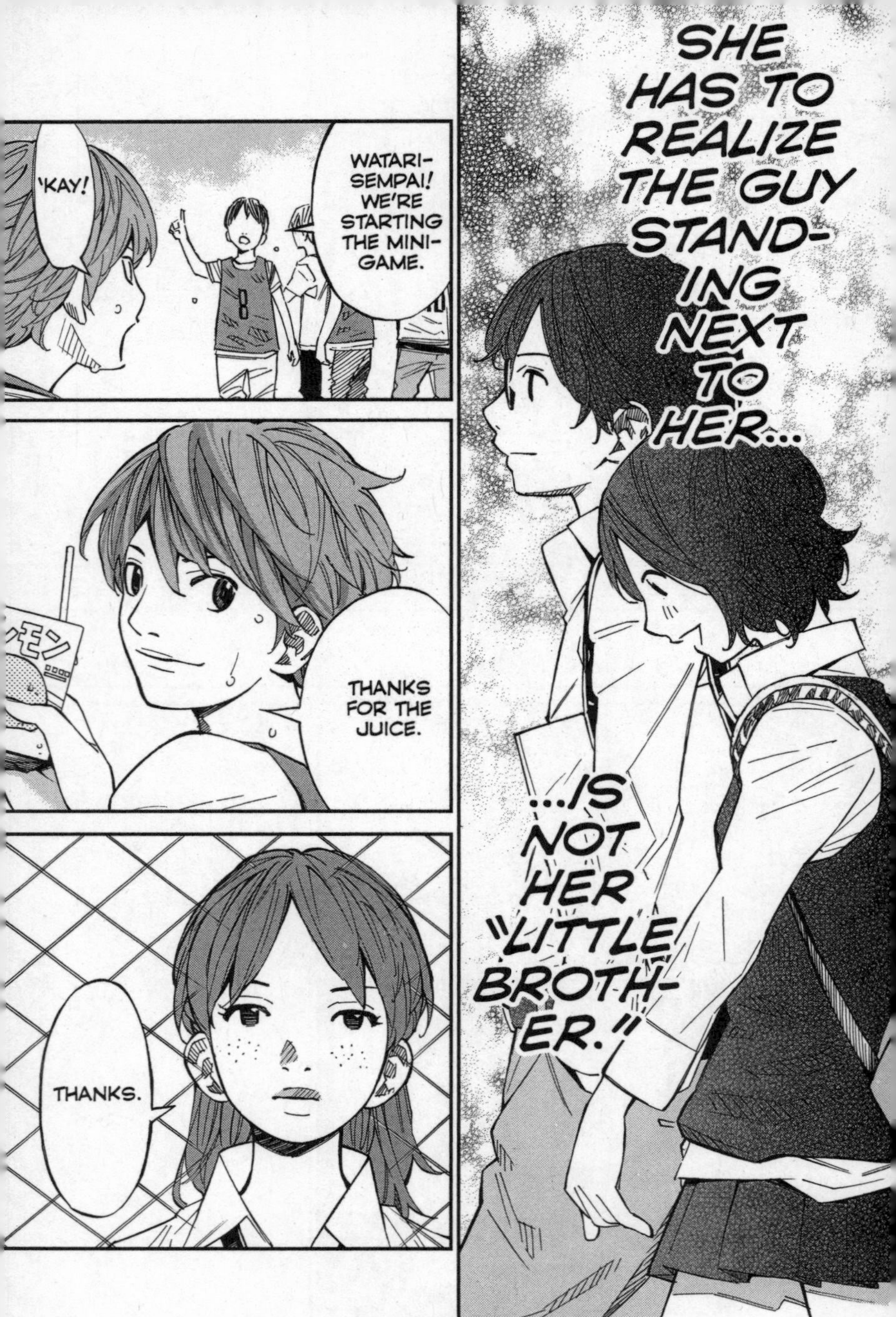
SHE HAS TO REALIZE THE GUY STANDING NEXT TO HER...
...IS NOT HER "LITTLE BROTHER."
WATARI-SEMPAI! WE'RE STARTING THE MINI-GAME.
'KAY!
THANKS FOR THE JUICE.
THANKS.

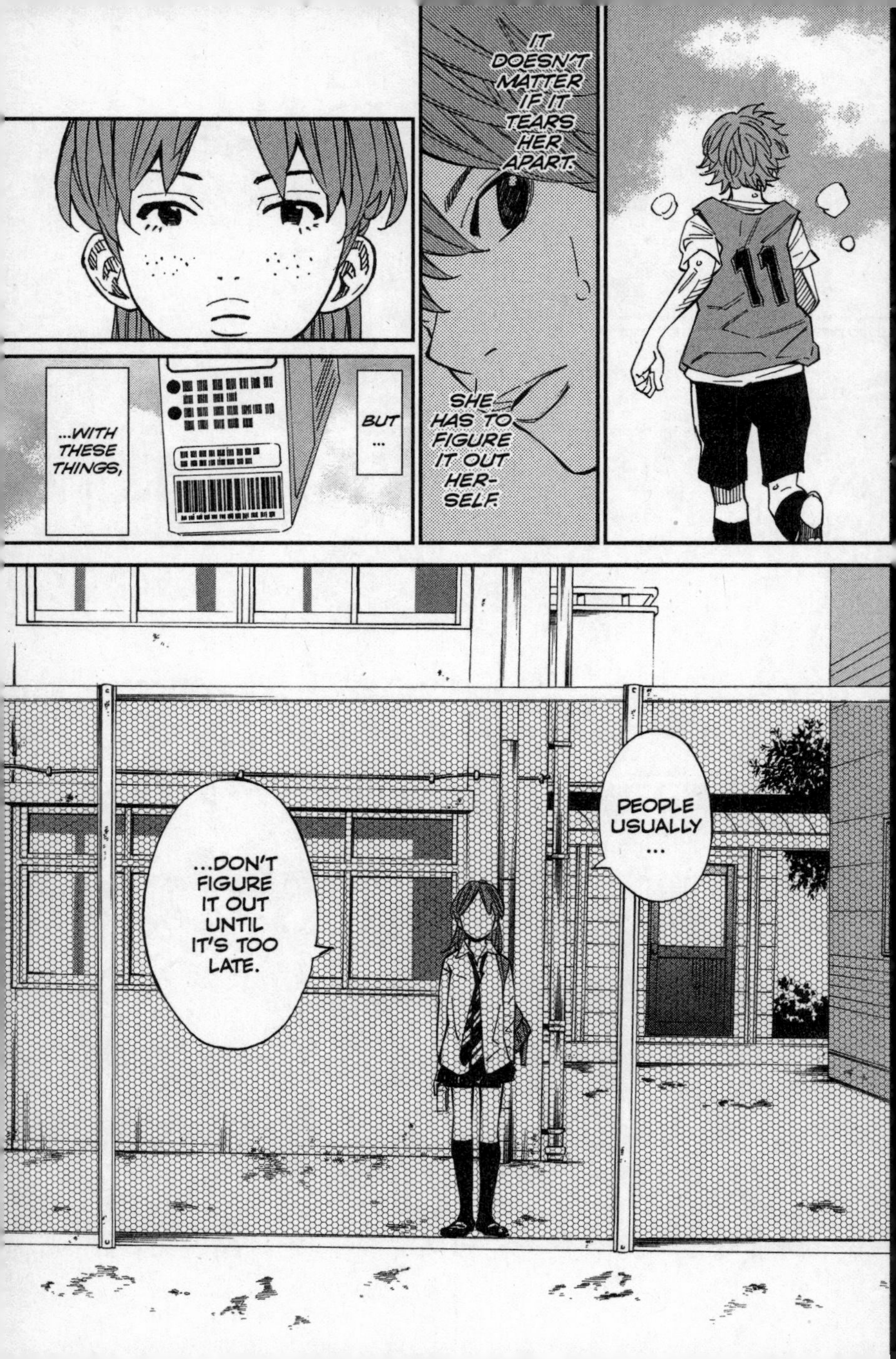
IT DOESN'T MATTER IF IT TEARS HER APART.
SHE HAS TO FIGURE IT OUT HER-SELF.
BUT ...
...WITH THESE THINGS,
PEOPLE USUALLY ...
...DON'T FIGURE IT OUT UNTIL IT'S TOO LATE.

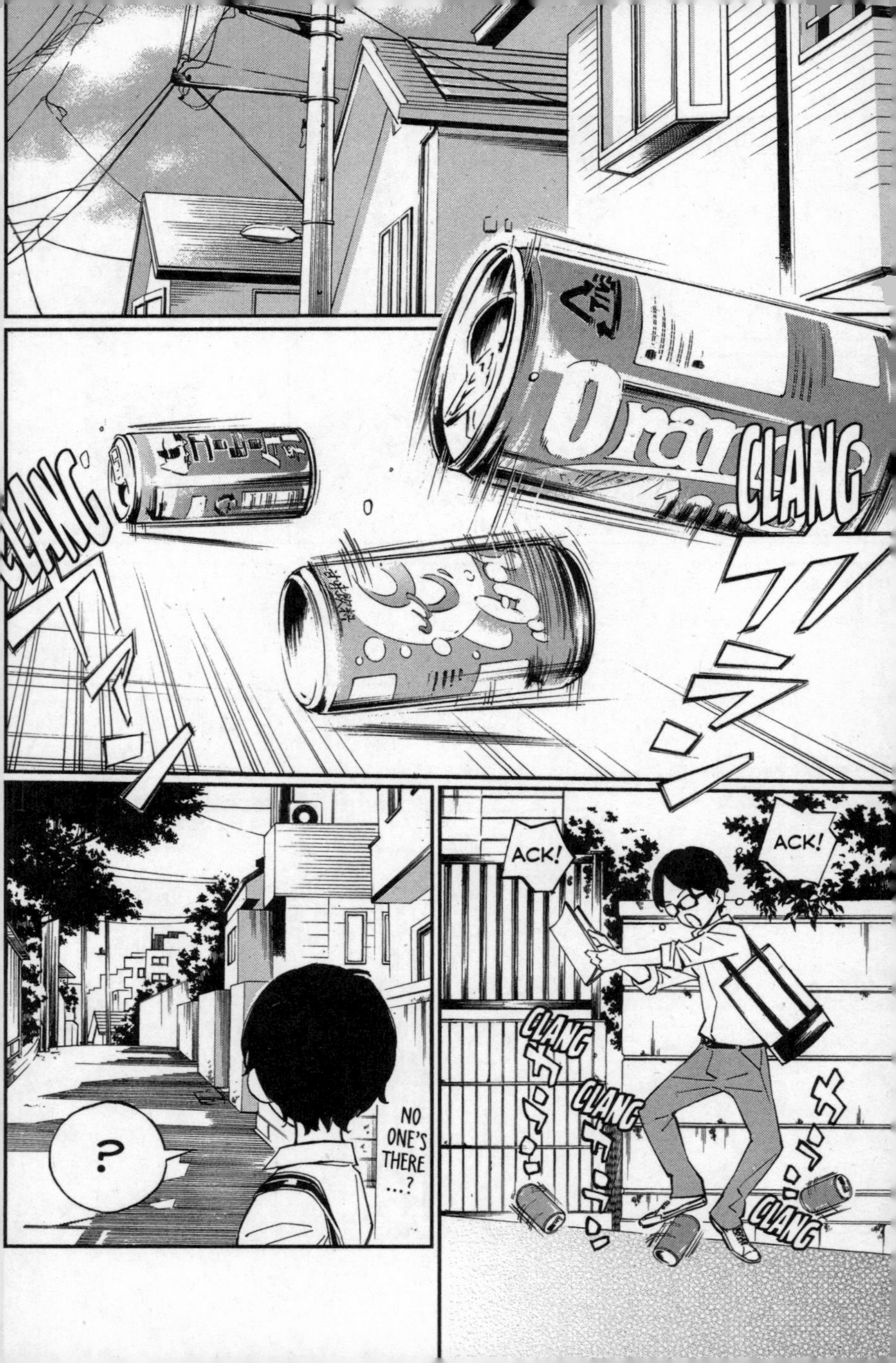
CLANG
CLANG
ACK!
ACK!
CLANG
CLANG
CLANG
NO ONE'S THERE ...?
?

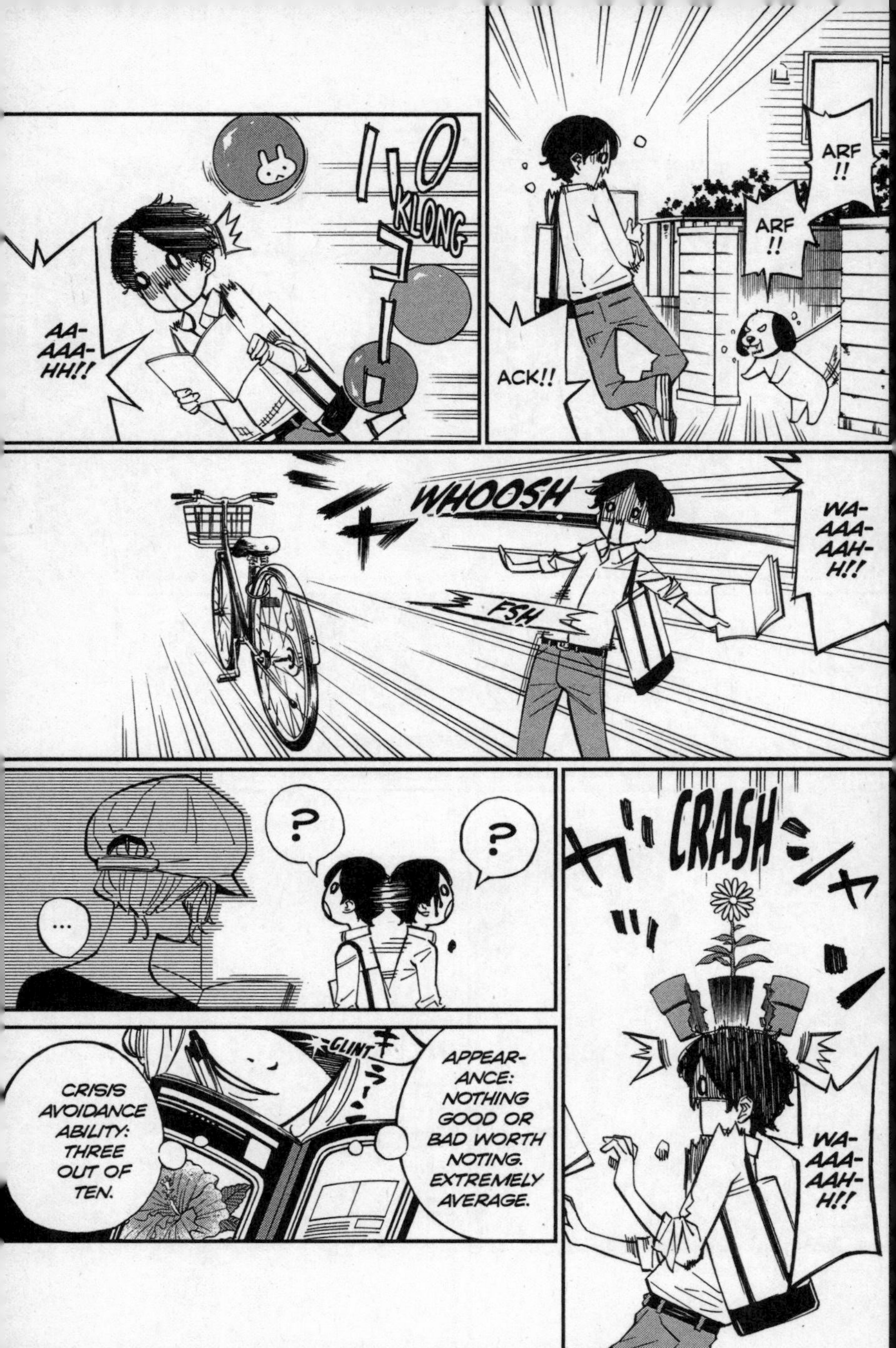
ARF!!
ARF!!
ACK!!
KLONG
AA-AAA-HH!!
WA-AAA-AAH-H!!
WHOOSH
FSH
CRASH
WA-AAA-AAH-H!!
?
?
...
APPEAR-ANCE: NOTHING GOOD OR BAD WORTH NOTING. EXTREMELY AVERAGE.
GLINT
CRISIS AVOIDANCE ABILITY: THREE OUT OF TEN.

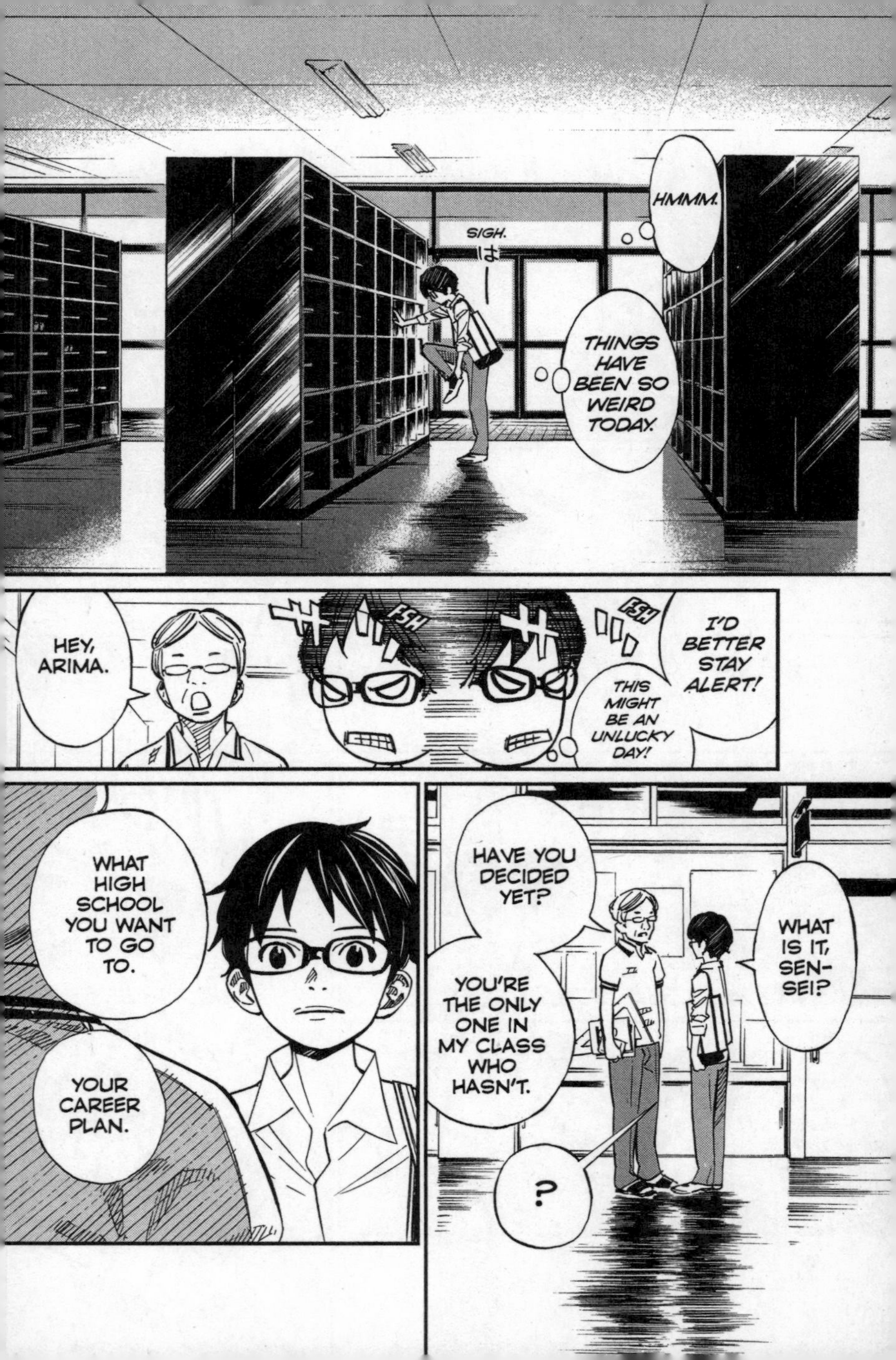
HMMM.
THINGS HAVE BEEN SO WEIRD TODAY.
SIGH.
はー
I'D BETTER STAY ALERT!
THIS MIGHT BE AN UNLUCKY DAY!
FSH
FSH
HEY, ARIMA.
WHAT IS IT, SEN-SEI?
HAVE YOU DECIDED YET?
YOU'RE THE ONLY ONE IN MY CLASS WHO HASN'T.
?
WHAT HIGH SCHOOL YOU WANT TO GO TO.
YOUR CAREER PLAN.

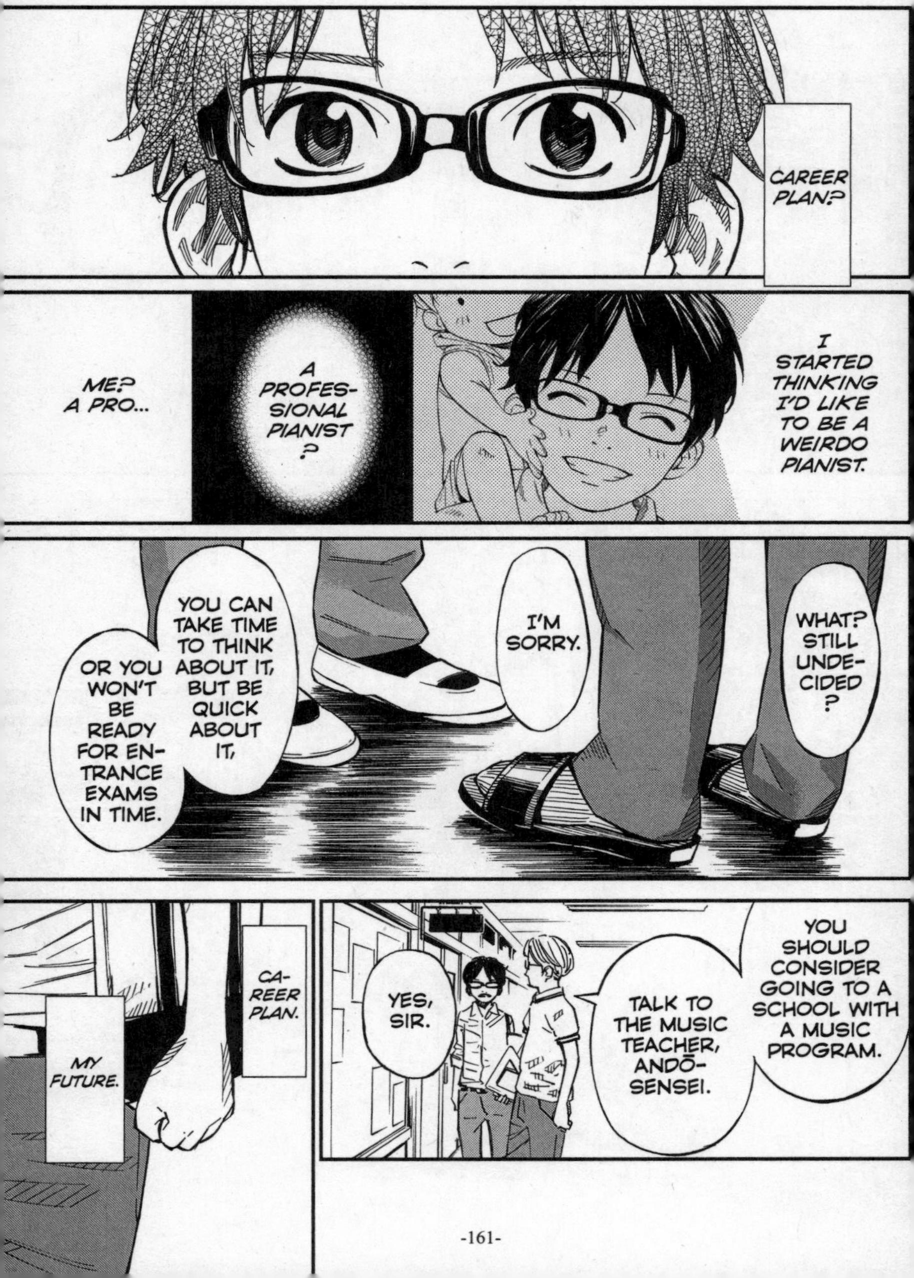
CAREER PLAN?
I STARTED THINKING I'D LIKE TO BE A WEIRDO PIANIST.
A PROFES-SIONAL PIANIST?
ME? A PRO...
WHAT? STILL UNDE-CIDED?
I'M SORRY.
YOU CAN TAKE TIME TO THINK ABOUT IT, BUT BE QUICK ABOUT IT,
OR YOU WON'T BE READY FOR EN-TRANCE EXAMS IN TIME.
YOU SHOULD CONSIDER GOING TO A SCHOOL WITH A MUSIC PROGRAM.
TALK TO THE MUSIC TEACHER, ANDŌ-SENSEI.
YES, SIR.
CA-REER PLAN.
MY FUTURE.

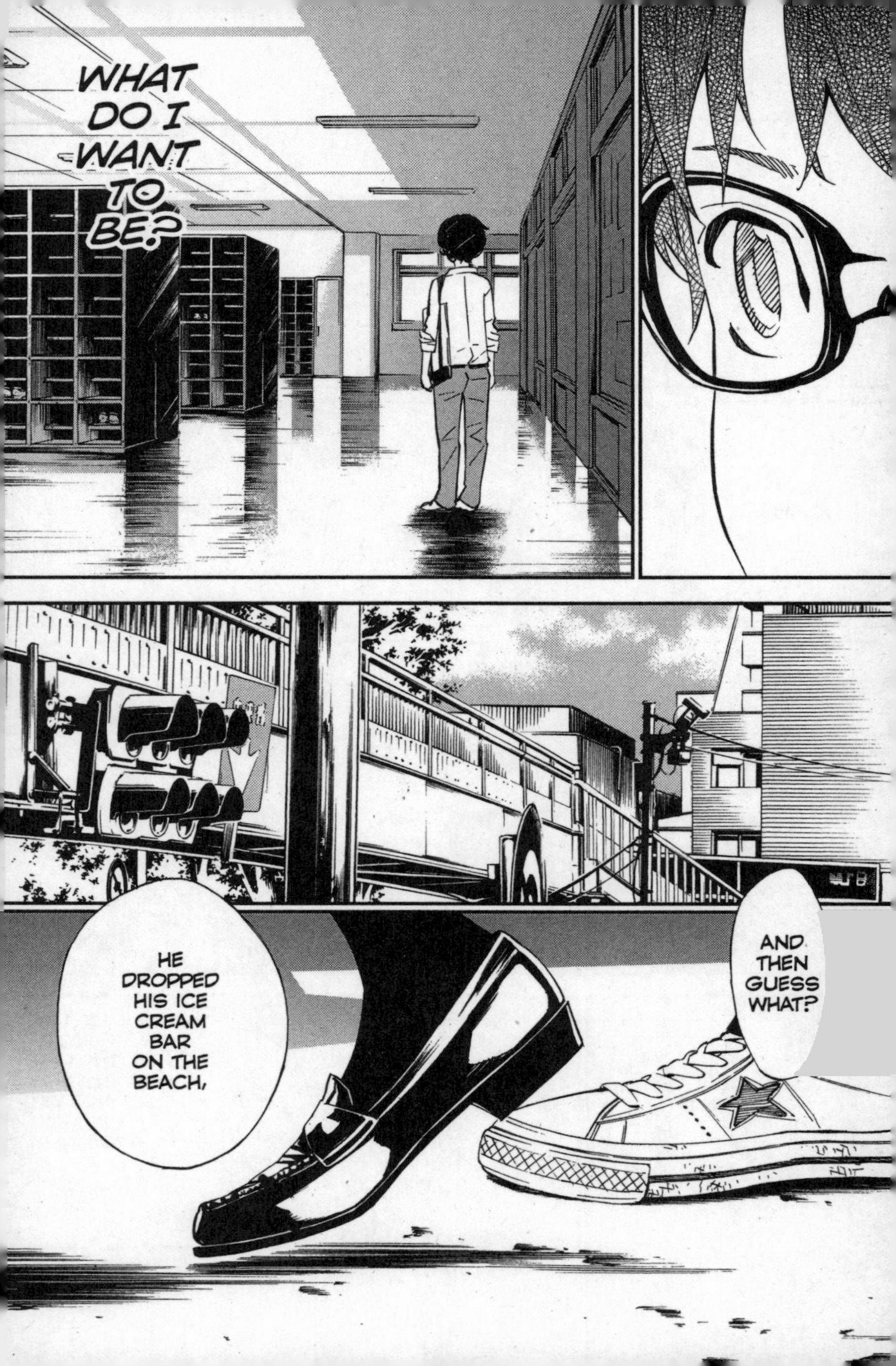
WHAT DO I WANT TO BE?
HE DROPPED HIS ICE CREAM BAR ON THE BEACH,
AND THEN GUESS WHAT?

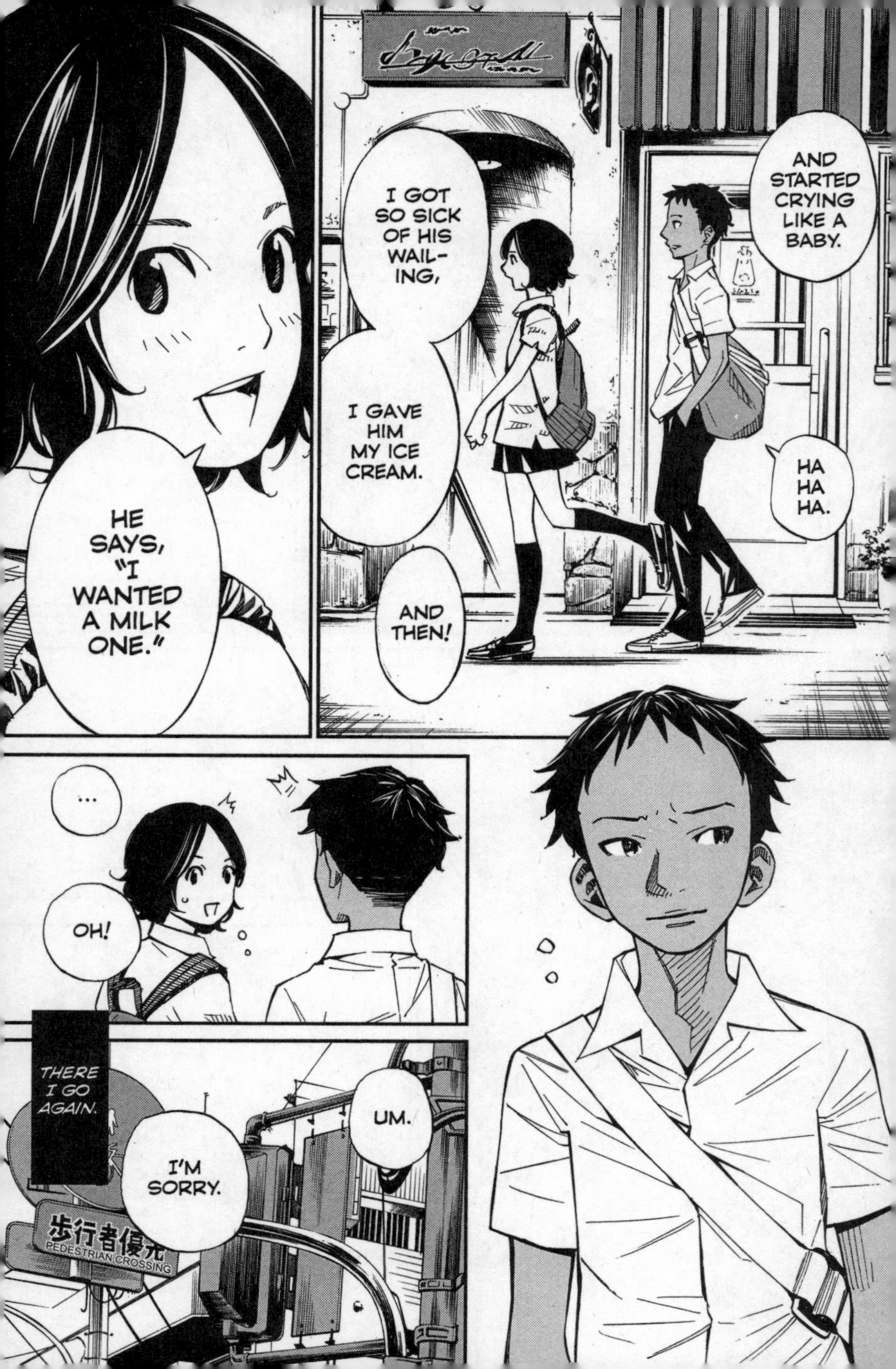

AND STARTED CRYING LIKE A BABY.
I GOT SO SICK OF HIS WAIL-ING,
I GAVE HIM MY ICE CREAM.
HA HA HA.
AND THEN!
HE SAYS, "I WANTED A MILK ONE."
...
OH!
UM.
I'M SORRY.
THERE I GO AGAIN.
歩行者優先
PEDESTRIAN CROSSING

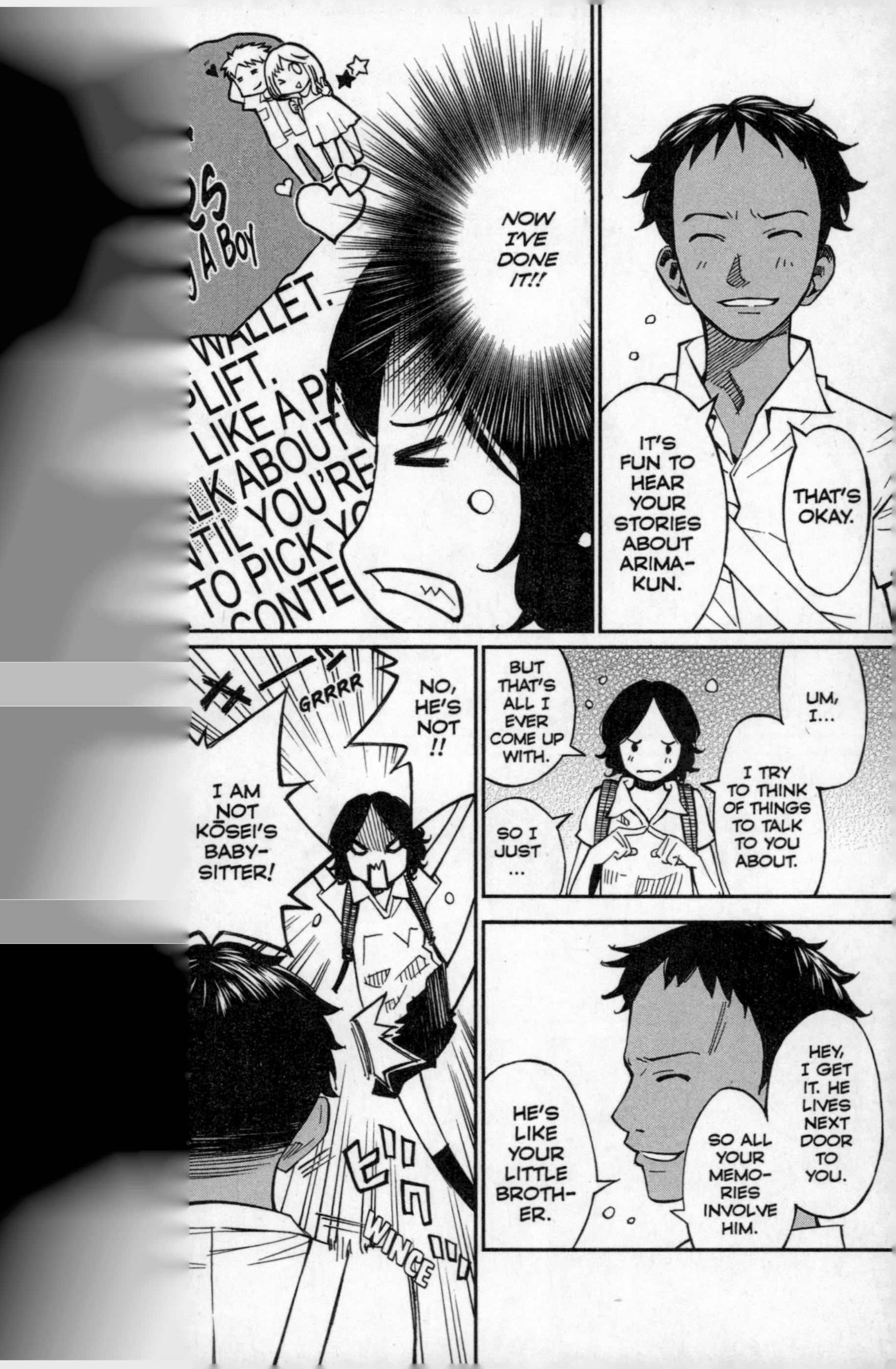

THAT'S OKAY.
IT'S FUN TO HEAR YOUR STORIES ABOUT ARIMA-KUN.
NOW I'VE DONE IT!!
UM, I...
I TRY TO THINK OF THINGS TO TALK TO YOU ABOUT.
BUT THAT'S ALL I EVER COME UP WITH.
SO I JUST ...
HEY, I GET IT. HE LIVES NEXT DOOR TO YOU.
SO ALL YOUR MEMORIES INVOLVE HIM.
HE'S LIKE YOUR LITTLE BROTHER.
NO, HE'S NOT!!
GRRRR
I AM NOT KŌSEI'S BABY-SITTER!
WINCE

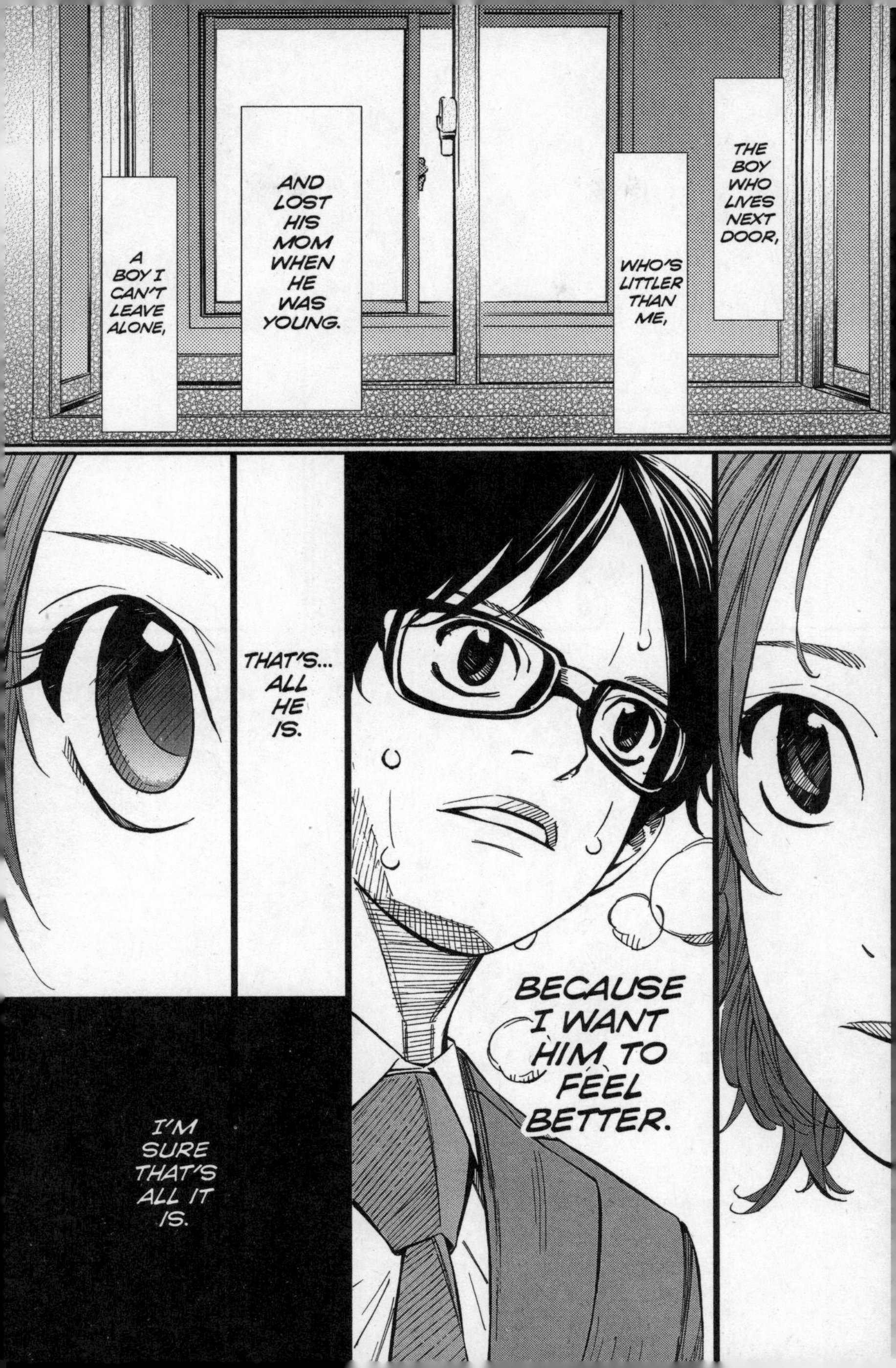
THE BOY WHO LIVES NEXT DOOR,
WHO'S LITTLER THAN ME,
AND LOST HIS MOM WHEN HE WAS YOUNG.
A BOY I CAN'T LEAVE ALONE,
BECAUSE I WANT HIM TO FEEL BETTER.
THAT'S... ALL HE IS.
I'M SURE THAT'S ALL IT IS.

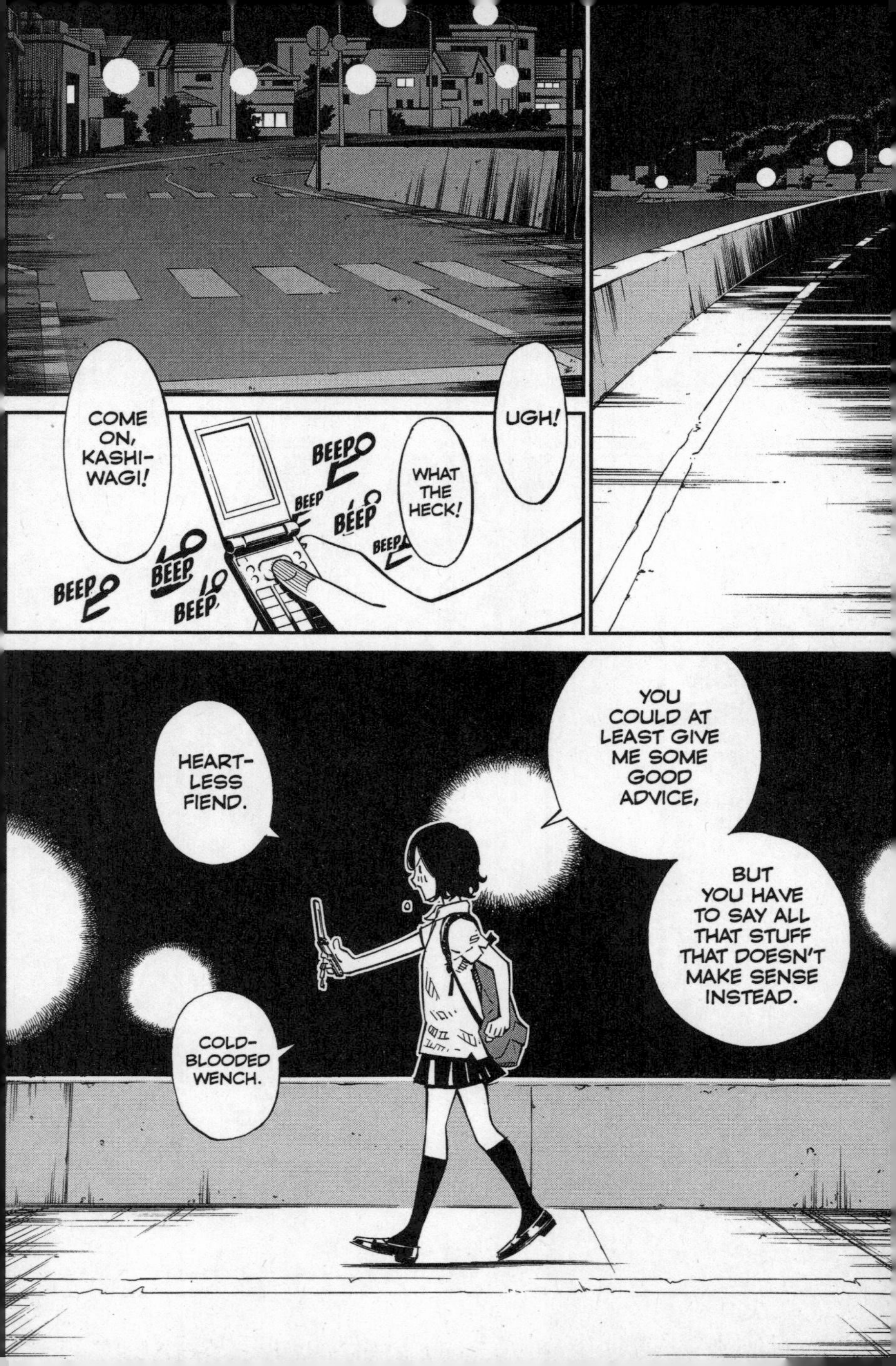
UGH!
WHAT THE HECK!
BEEP
BEEP
BEEP
BEEP
COME ON, KASHI-WAGI!
BEEP
BEEP
BEEP
YOU COULD AT LEAST GIVE ME SOME GOOD ADVICE,
BUT YOU HAVE TO SAY ALL THAT STUFF THAT DOESN'T MAKE SENSE INSTEAD.
HEART-LESS FIEND.
COLD-BLOODED WENCH.

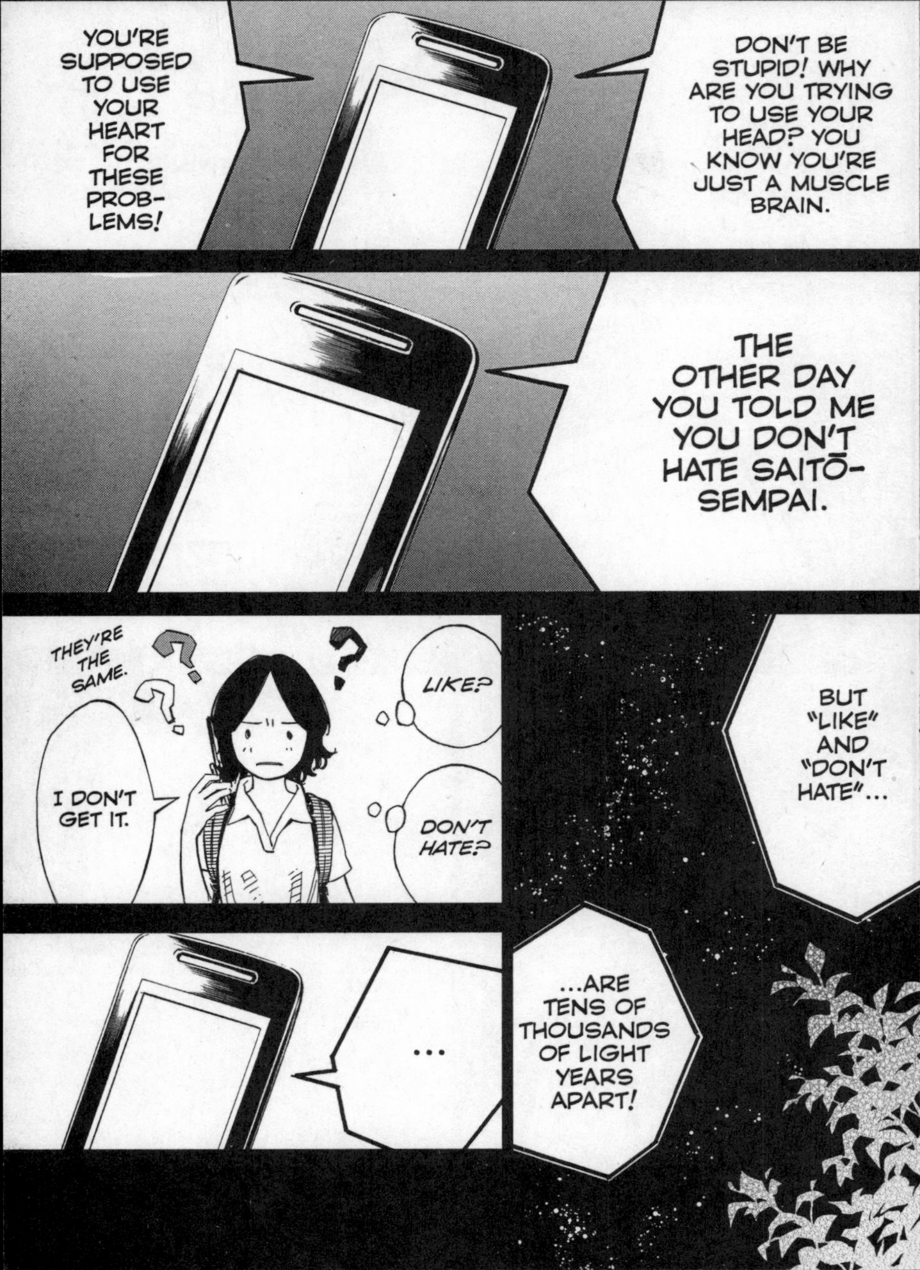
DON'T BE STUPID! WHY ARE YOU TRYING TO USE YOUR HEAD? YOU KNOW YOU'RE JUST A MUSCLE BRAIN.
YOU'RE SUPPOSED TO USE YOUR HEART FOR THESE PROB-LEMS!
THE OTHER DAY YOU TOLD ME YOU DON'T HATE SAITŌ-SEMPAI.
BUT "LIKE" AND "DON'T HATE"...
...ARE TENS OF THOUSANDS OF LIGHT YEARS APART!
LIKE?
THEY'RE THE SAME.
DON'T HATE?
I DON'T GET IT.
...

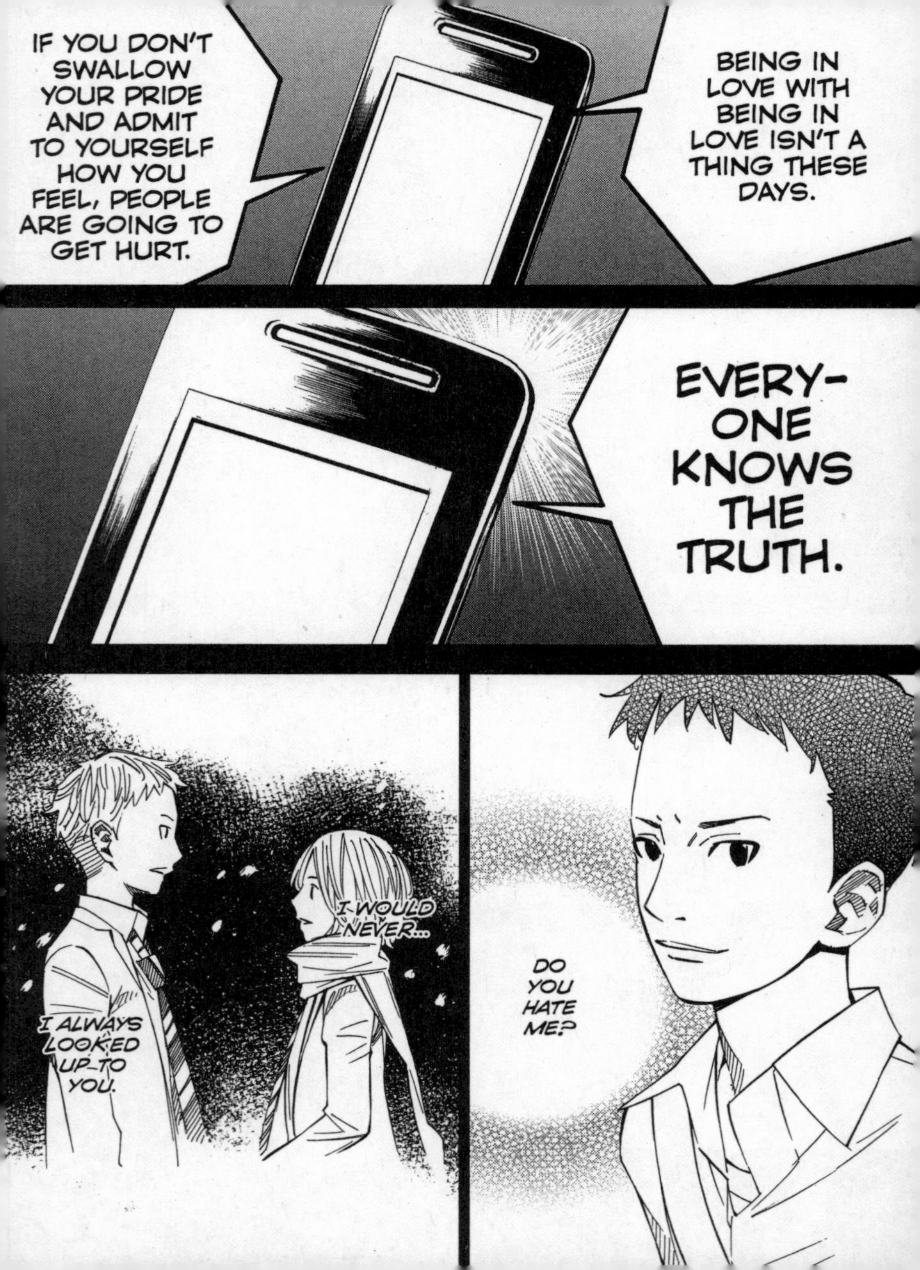
BEING IN LOVE WITH BEING IN LOVE ISN'T A THING THESE DAYS.
IF YOU DON'T SWALLOW YOUR PRIDE AND ADMIT TO YOURSELF HOW YOU FEEL, PEOPLE ARE GOING TO GET HURT.
EVERY-ONE KNOWS THE TRUTH.
DO YOU HATE ME?
I WOULD NEVER...
I ALWAYS LOOKED UP TO YOU.

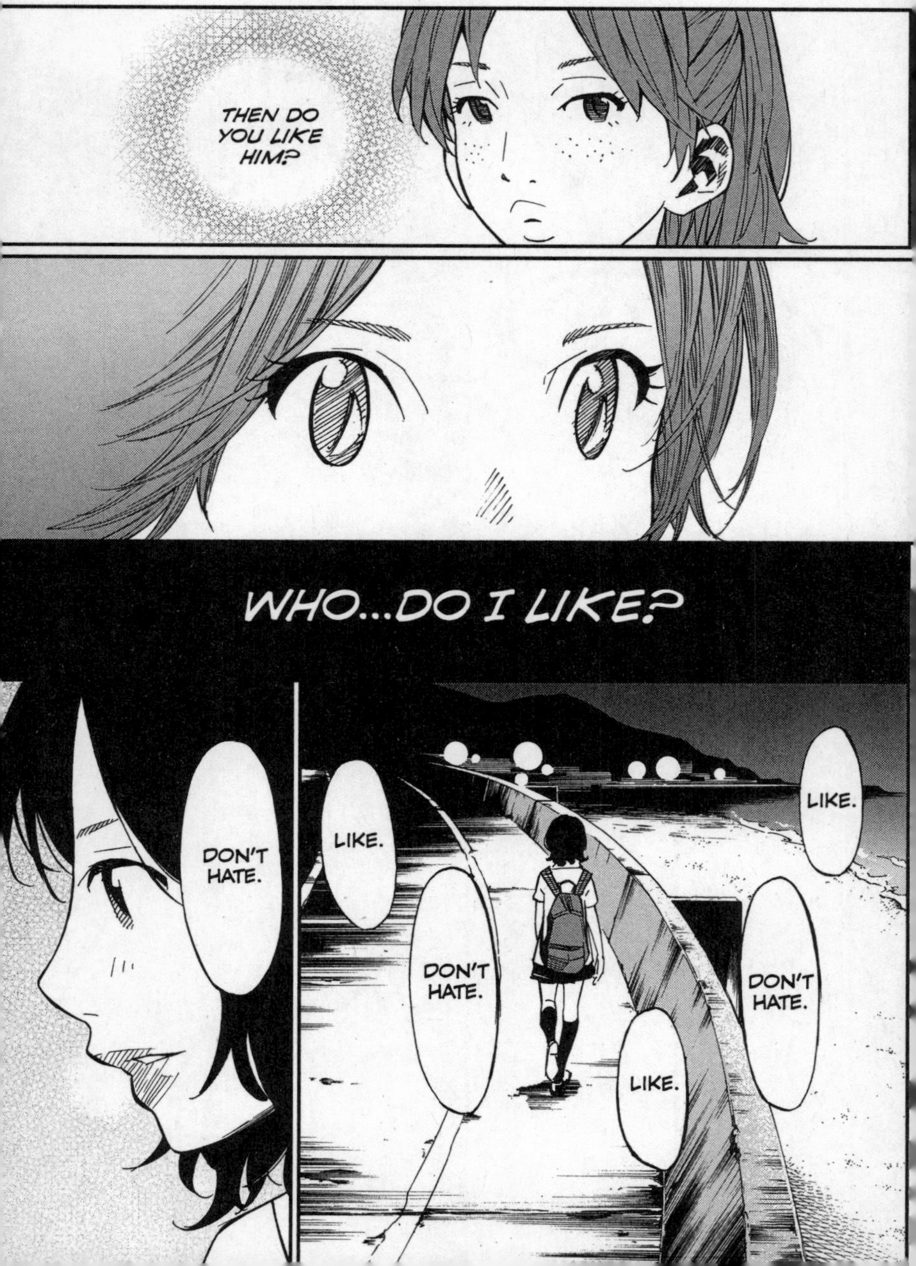
THEN DO YOU LIKE HIM?
WHO...DO I LIKE?
LIKE.
DON'T HATE.
LIKE.
LIKE.
DON'T HATE.
DON'T HATE.

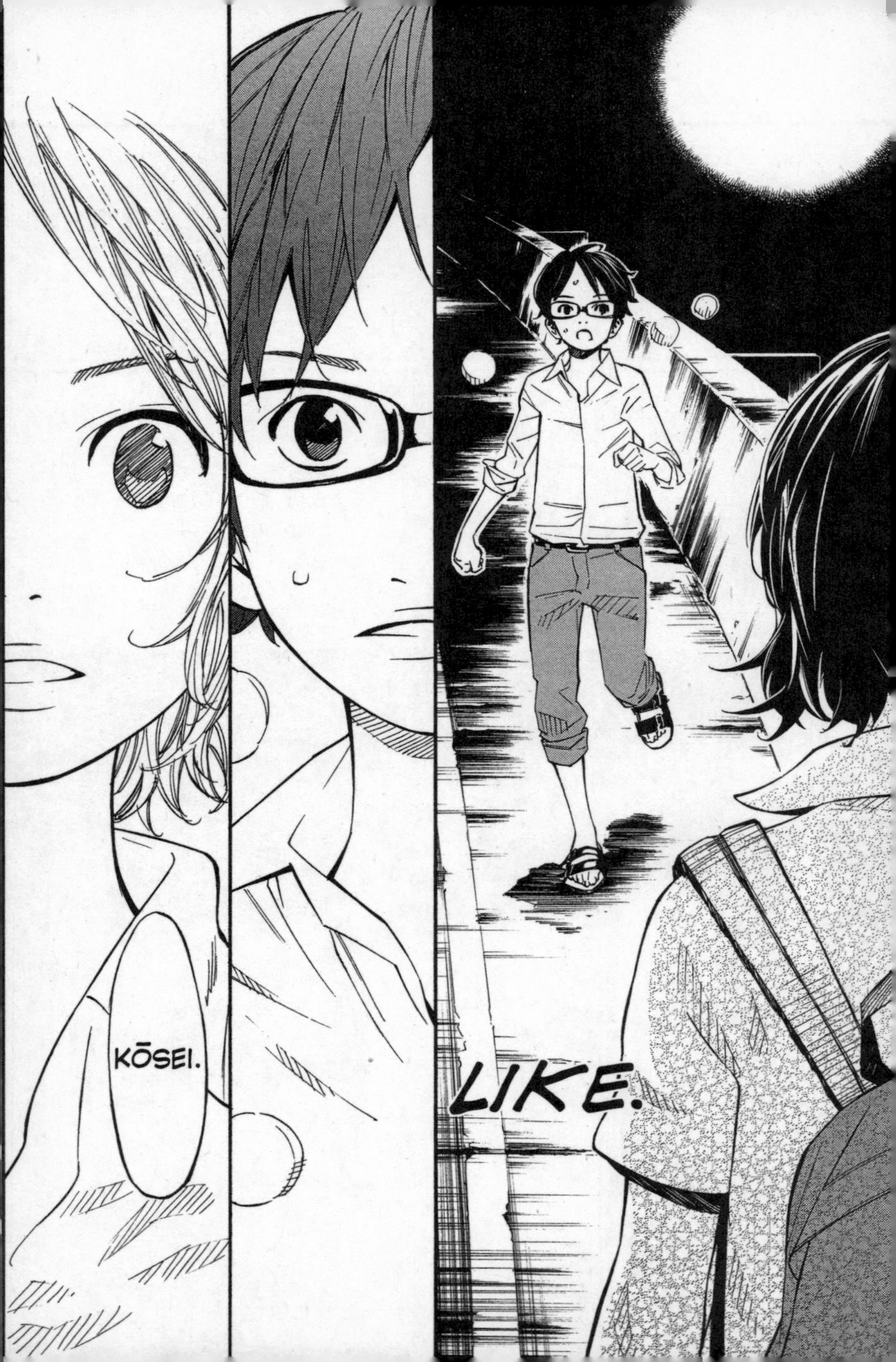
LIKE.
KŌSEI.

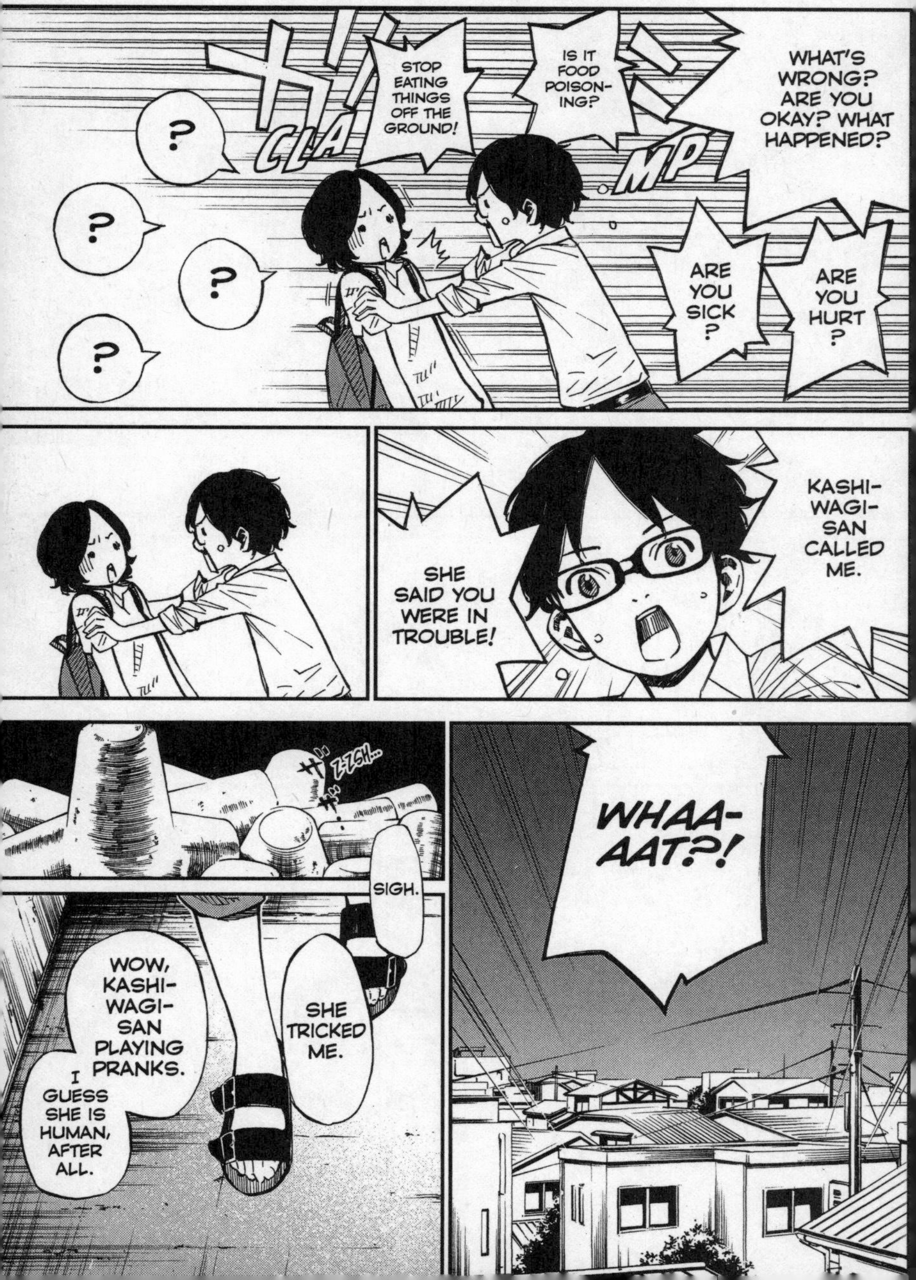
WHAT'S WRONG? ARE YOU OKAY? WHAT HAPPENED?
ARE YOU HURT?
ARE YOU SICK?
CLA
MP
IS IT FOOD POISONING?
STOP EATING THINGS OFF THE GROUND!
?
?
?
?
KASHIWAGI-SAN CALLED ME.
SHE SAID YOU WERE IN TROUBLE!
WHAAA-AAT?!
Z-ZSH...
SIGH.
SHE TRICKED ME.
WOW, KASHIWAGI-SAN PLAYING PRANKS.
I GUESS SHE IS HUMAN, AFTER ALL.

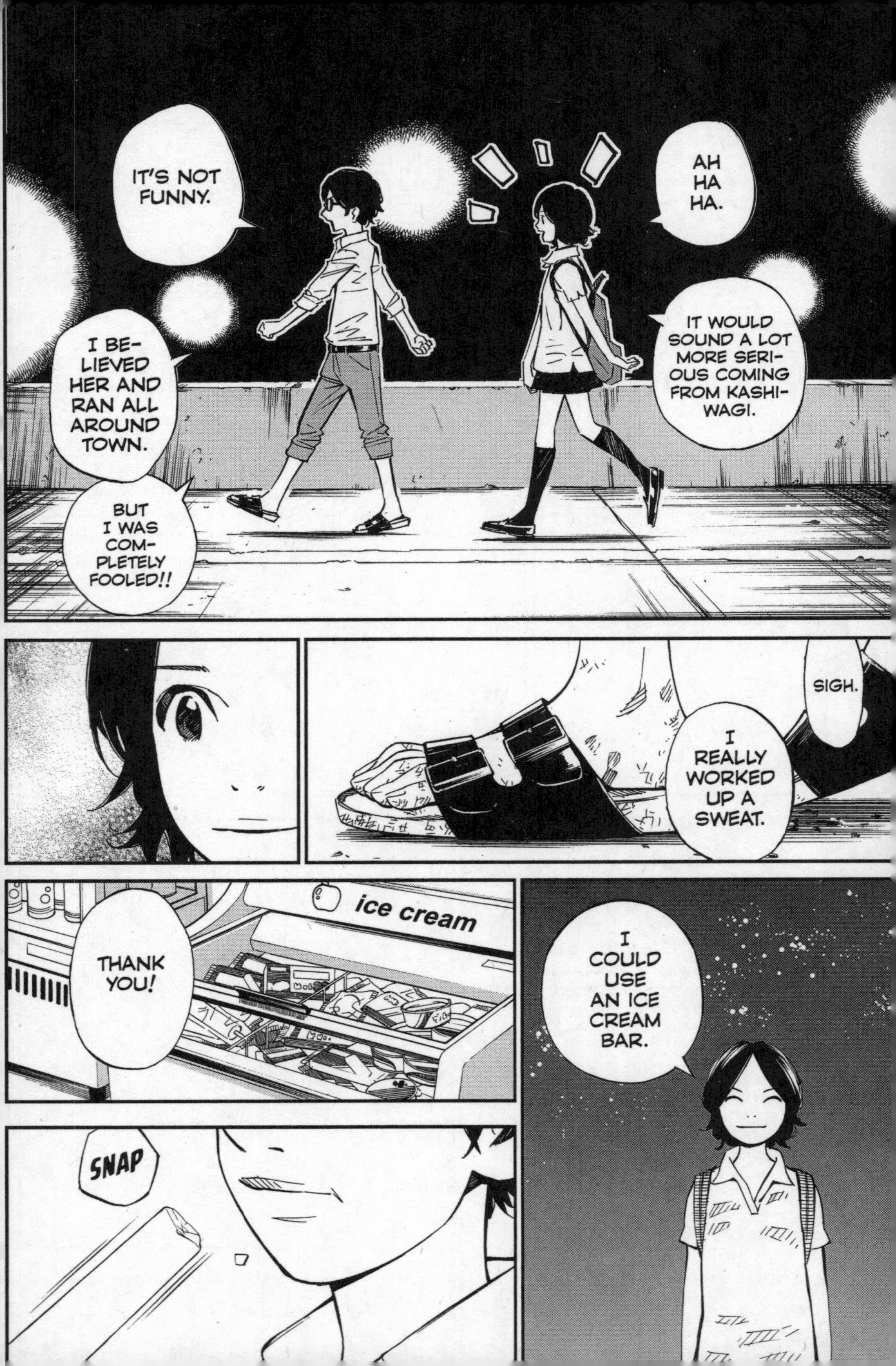

AH HA HA.
IT'S NOT FUNNY.
IT WOULD SOUND A LOT MORE SERIOUS COMING FROM KASHIWAGI.
I BELIEVED HER AND RAN ALL AROUND TOWN.
BUT I WAS COMPLETELY FOOLED!!
SIGH.
I REALLY WORKED UP A SWEAT.
I COULD USE AN ICE CREAM BAR.
ice cream
THANK YOU!
SNAP

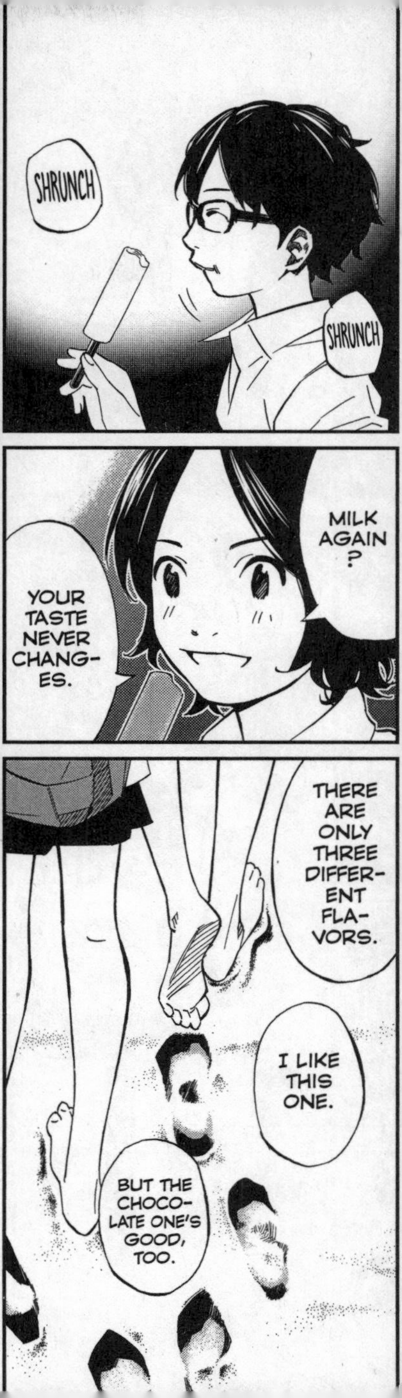
SHRUNCH
SHRUNCH
MILK AGAIN?
YOUR TASTE NEVER CHANGES.
THERE ARE ONLY THREE DIFFERENT FLAVORS.
I LIKE THIS ONE.
BUT THE CHOCOLATE ONE'S GOOD, TOO.
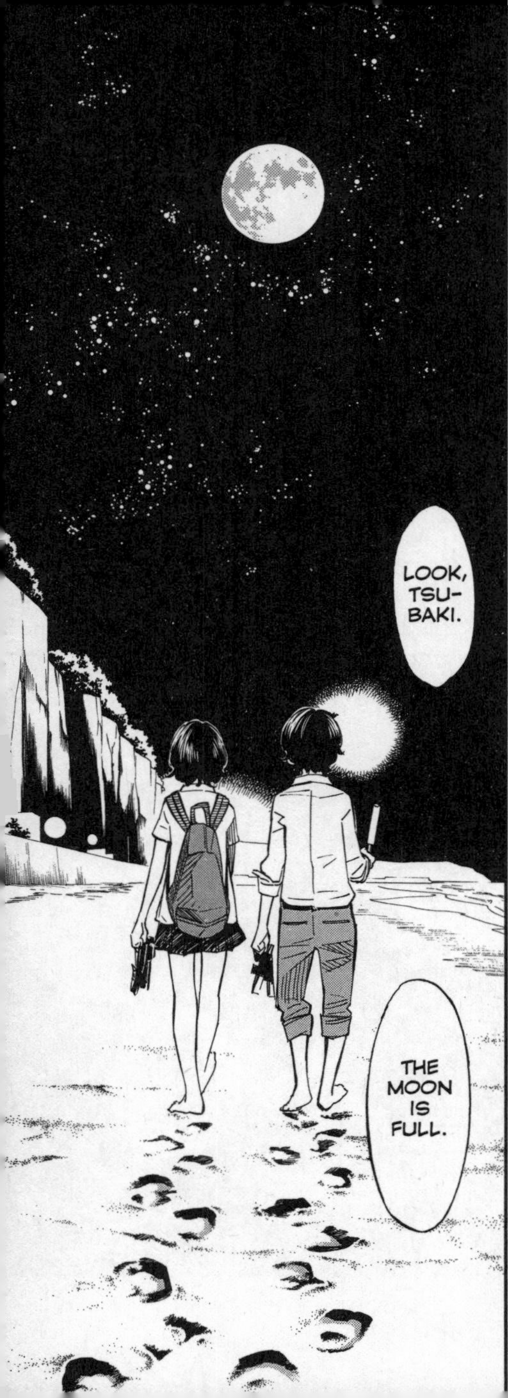
LOOK, TSUBAKI.
THE MOON IS FULL.

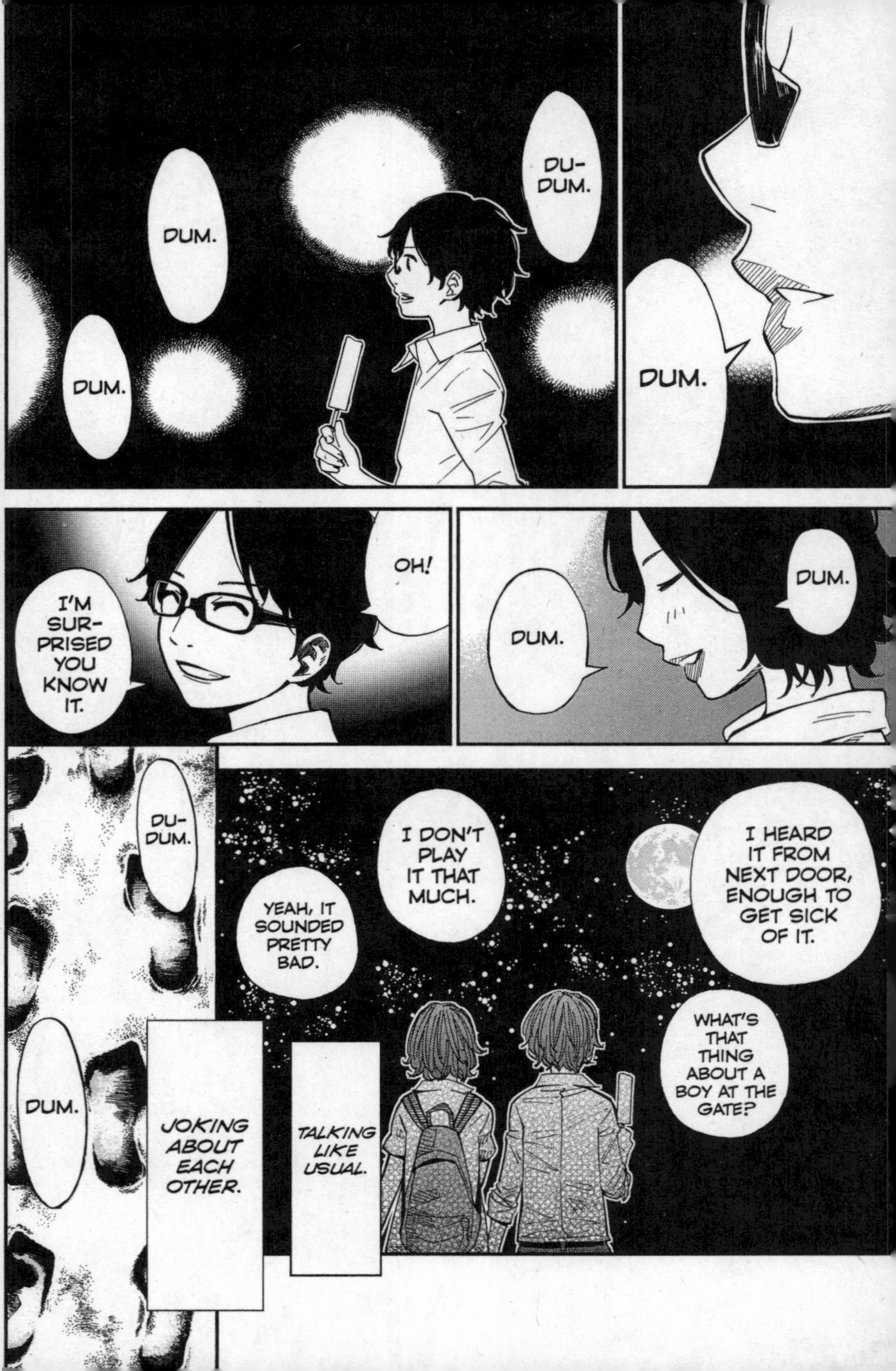
DUM.
DU-DUM.
DUM.
DUM.
DUM.
DUM.
OH!
I'M SURPRISED YOU KNOW IT.
I HEARD IT FROM NEXT DOOR, ENOUGH TO GET SICK OF IT.
I DON'T PLAY IT THAT MUCH.
YEAH, IT SOUNDED PRETTY BAD.
WHAT'S THAT THING ABOUT A BOY AT THE GATE?
TALKING LIKE USUAL.
JOKING ABOUT EACH OTHER.
DU-DUM.
DUM.

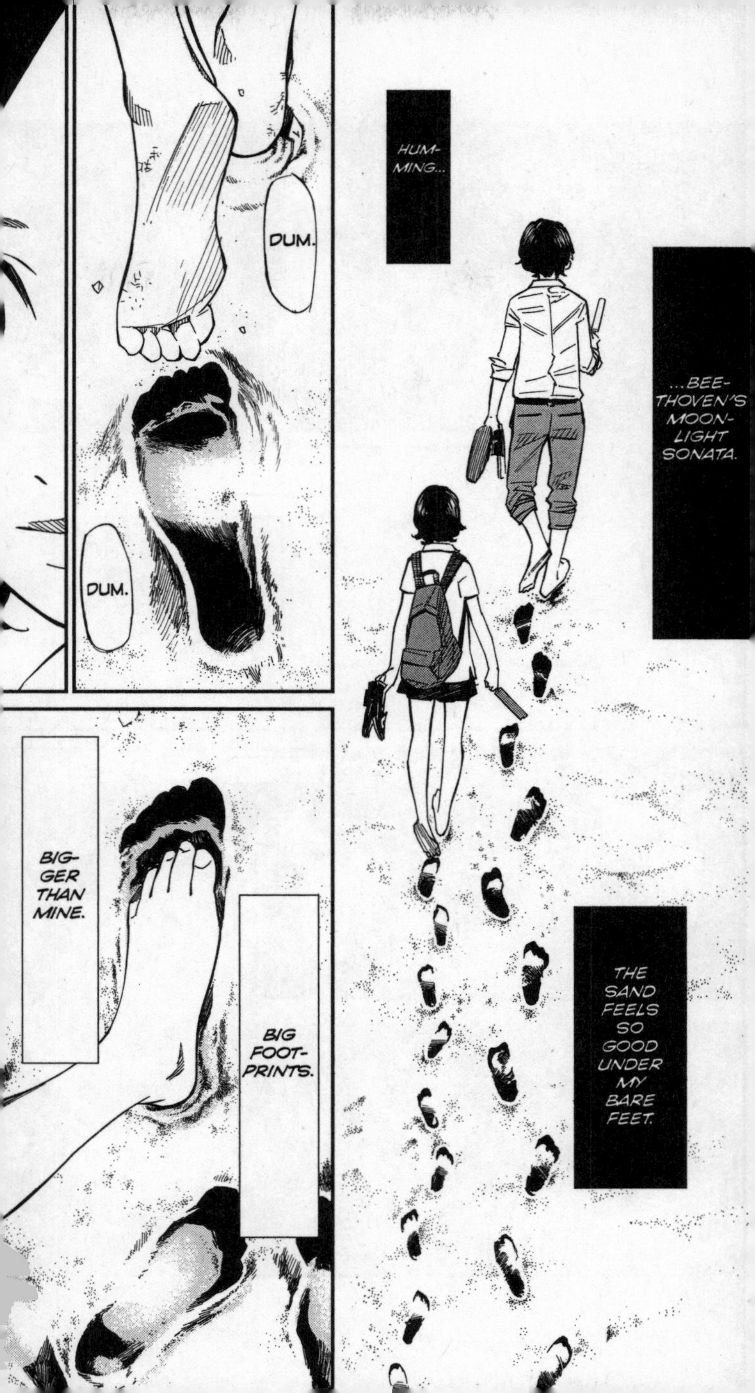
HUM-MING...
...BEE-THOVEN'S MOON-LIGHT SONATA.
THE SAND FEELS SO GOOD UNDER MY BARE FEET.
DUM.
DUM.
BIG FOOT-PRINTS.
BIG-GER THAN MINE.

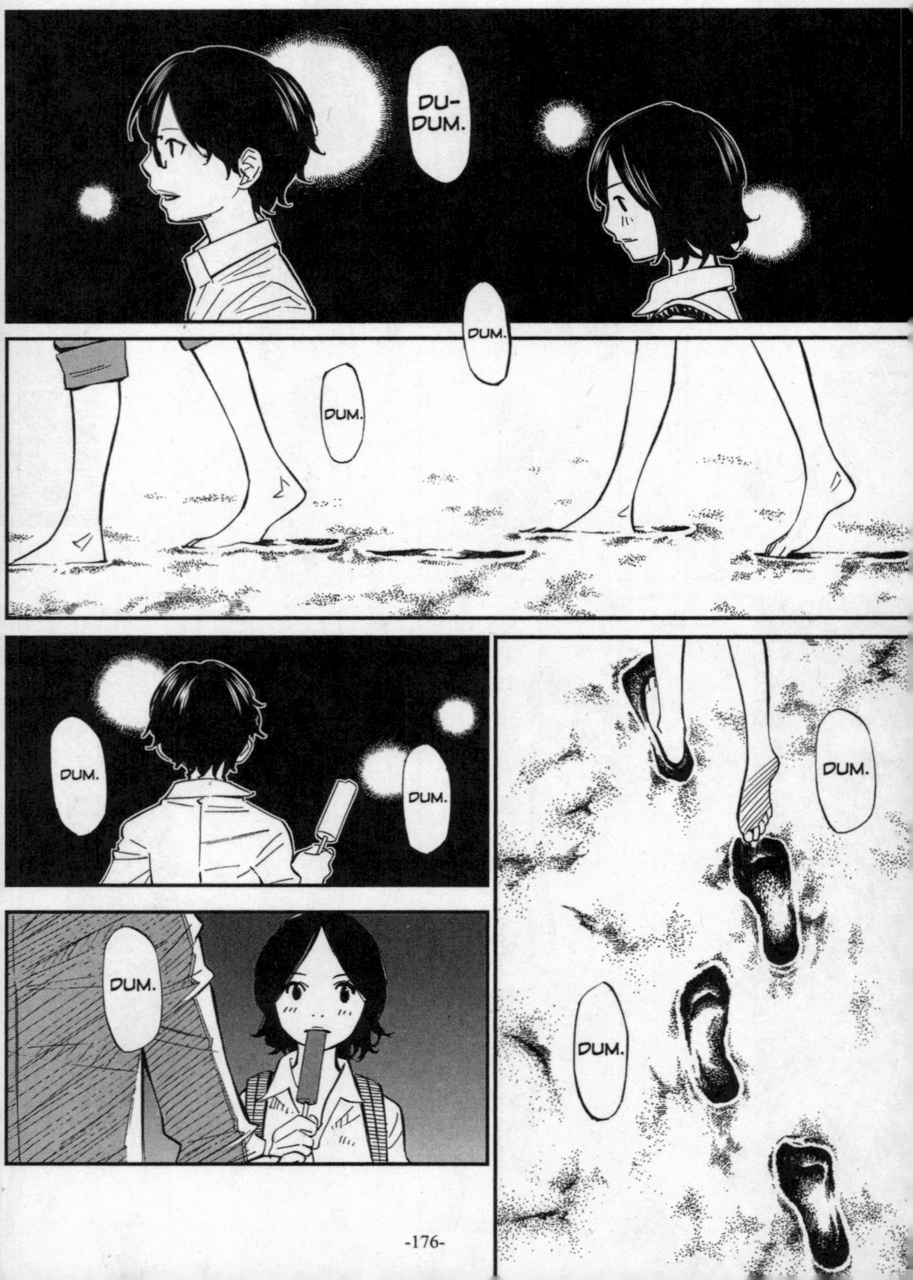

DU-
DUM.
DUM.
DUM.
DUM.
DUM.
DUM.
DUM.
DUM.

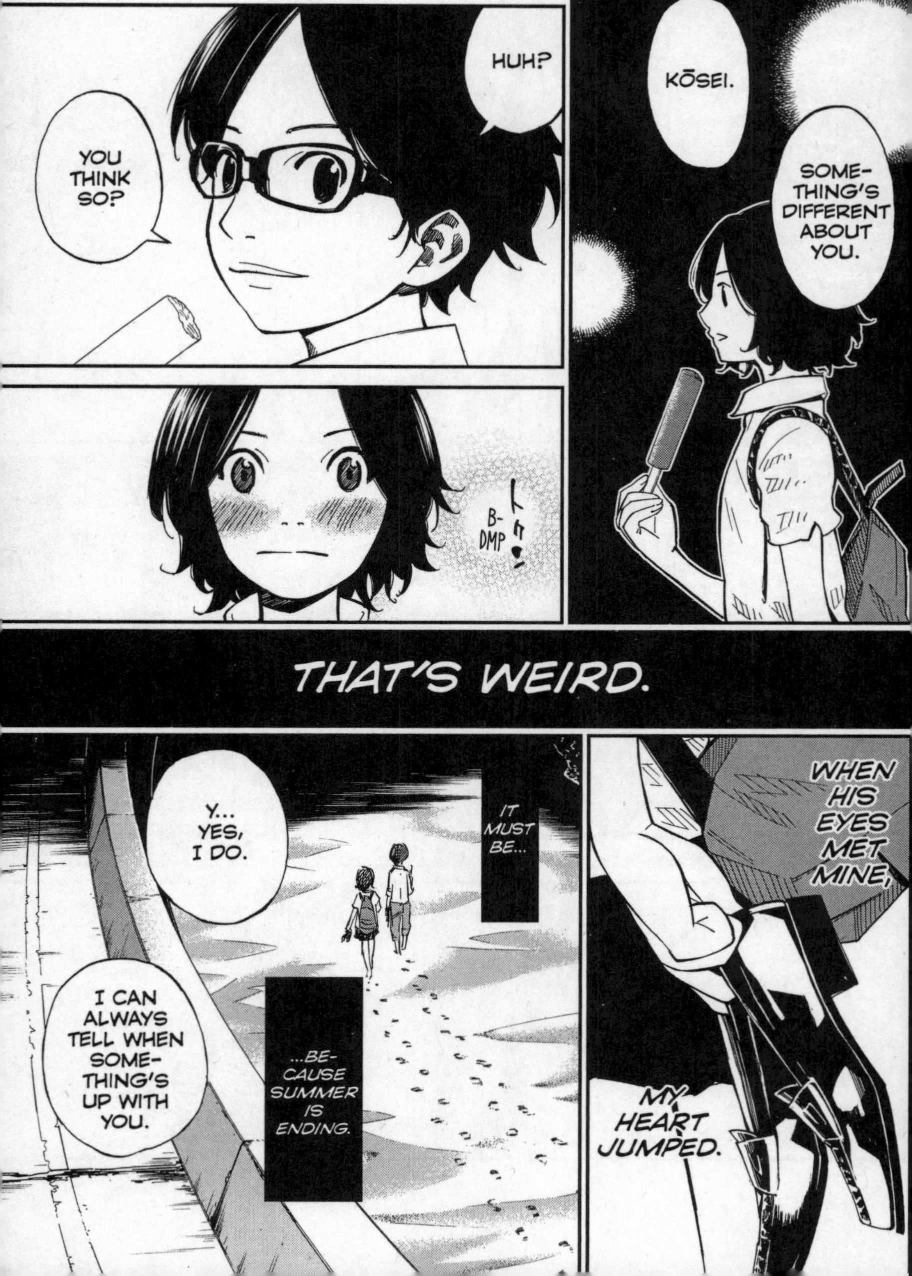
KŌSEI.
SOME-THING'S DIFFERENT ABOUT YOU.
HUH?
YOU THINK SO?
B-DMP
THAT'S WEIRD.
WHEN HIS EYES MET MINE,
MY HEART JUMPED.
IT MUST BE...
Y... YES, I DO.
...BE-CAUSE SUMMER IS ENDING.
I CAN ALWAYS TELL WHEN SOME-THING'S UP WITH YOU.

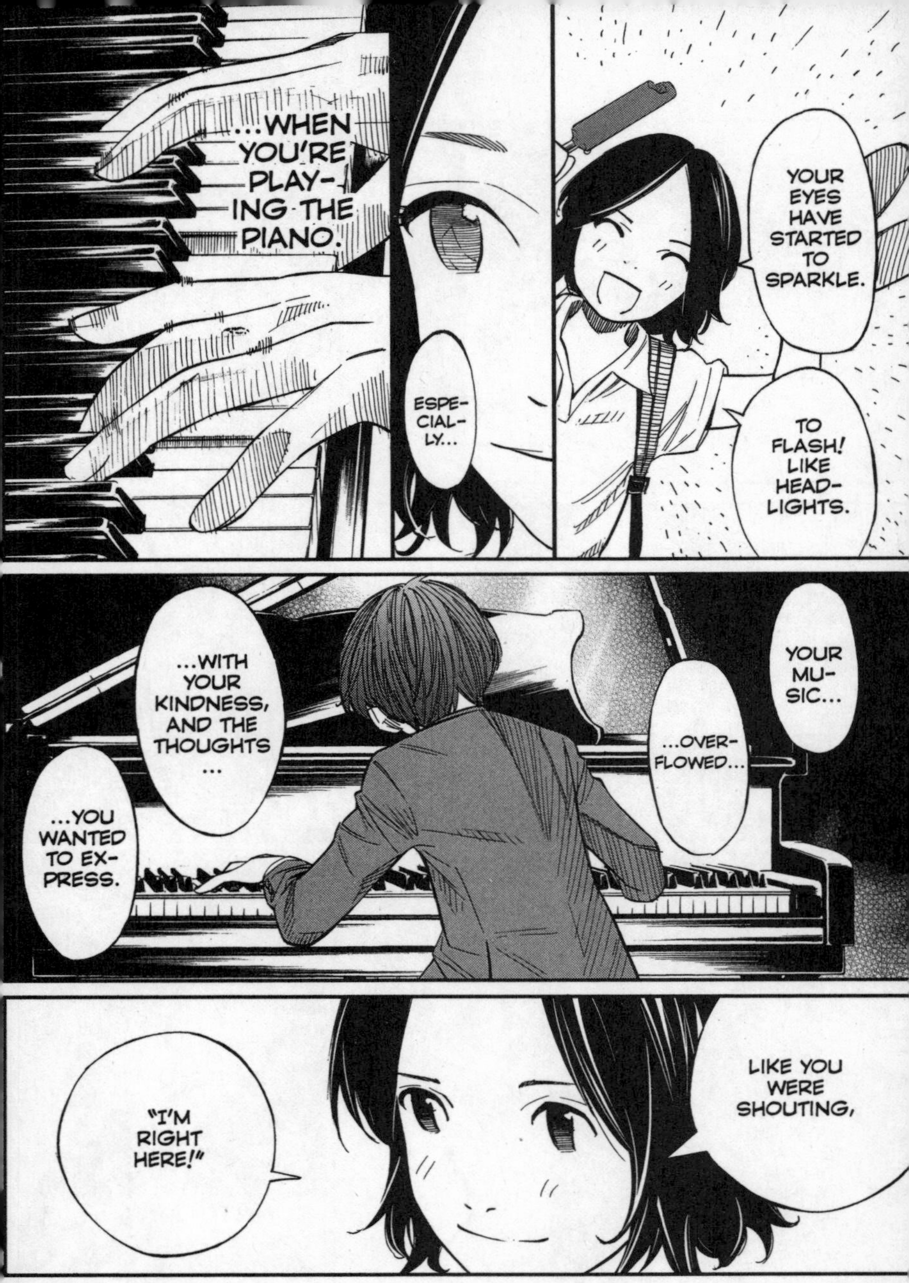
YOUR EYES HAVE STARTED TO SPARKLE.
TO FLASH! LIKE HEADLIGHTS.
ESPECIALLY...
...WHEN YOU'RE PLAYING THE PIANO.
YOUR MUSIC...
...OVERFLOWED...
...WITH YOUR KINDNESS, AND THE THOUGHTS...
...YOU WANTED TO EXPRESS.
LIKE YOU WERE SHOUTING,
"I'M RIGHT HERE!"

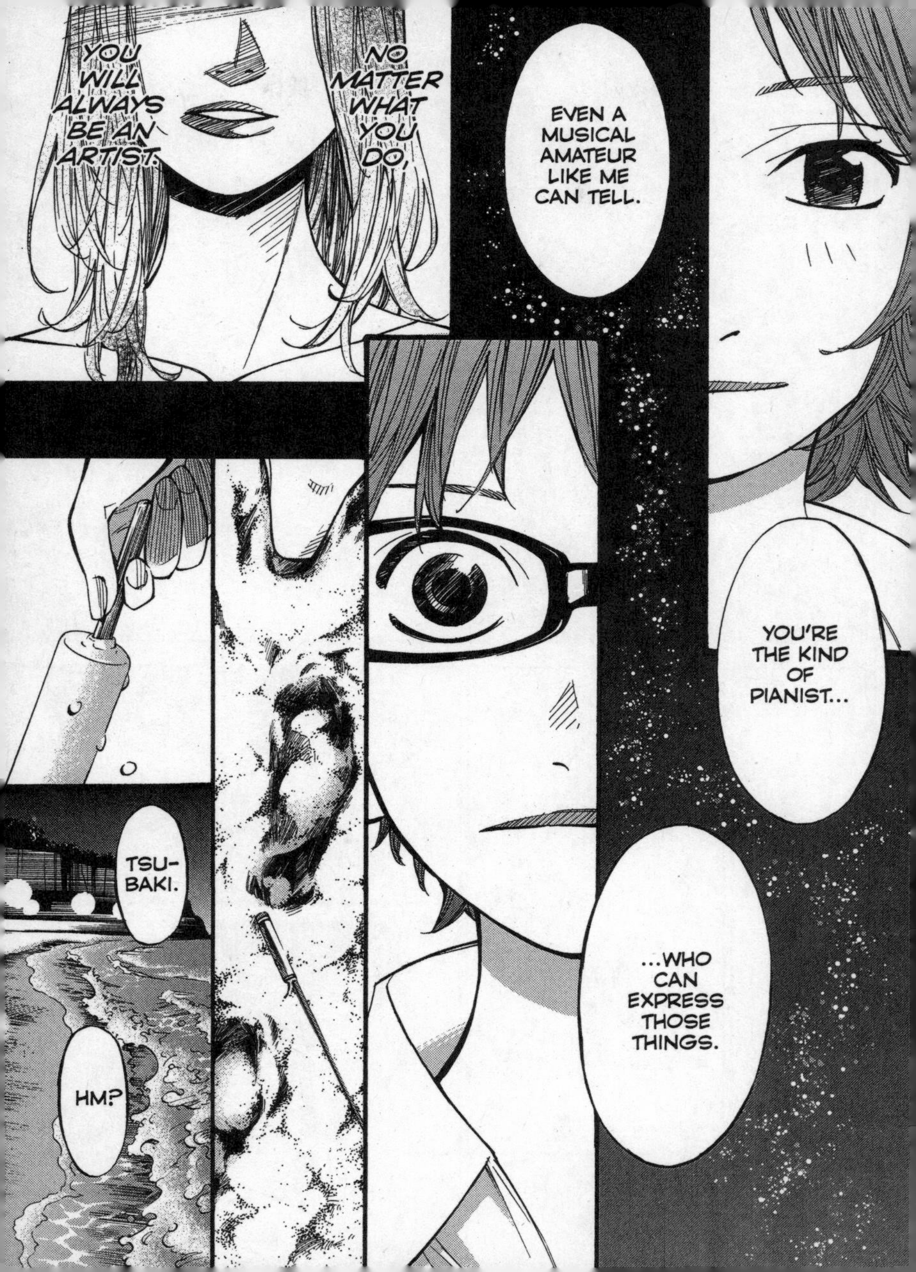
EVEN A MUSICAL AMATEUR LIKE ME CAN TELL.
YOU'RE THE KIND OF PIANIST...
...WHO CAN EXPRESS THOSE THINGS.
NO MATTER WHAT YOU DO,
YOU WILL ALWAYS BE AN ARTIST.
TSU-BAKI.
HM?

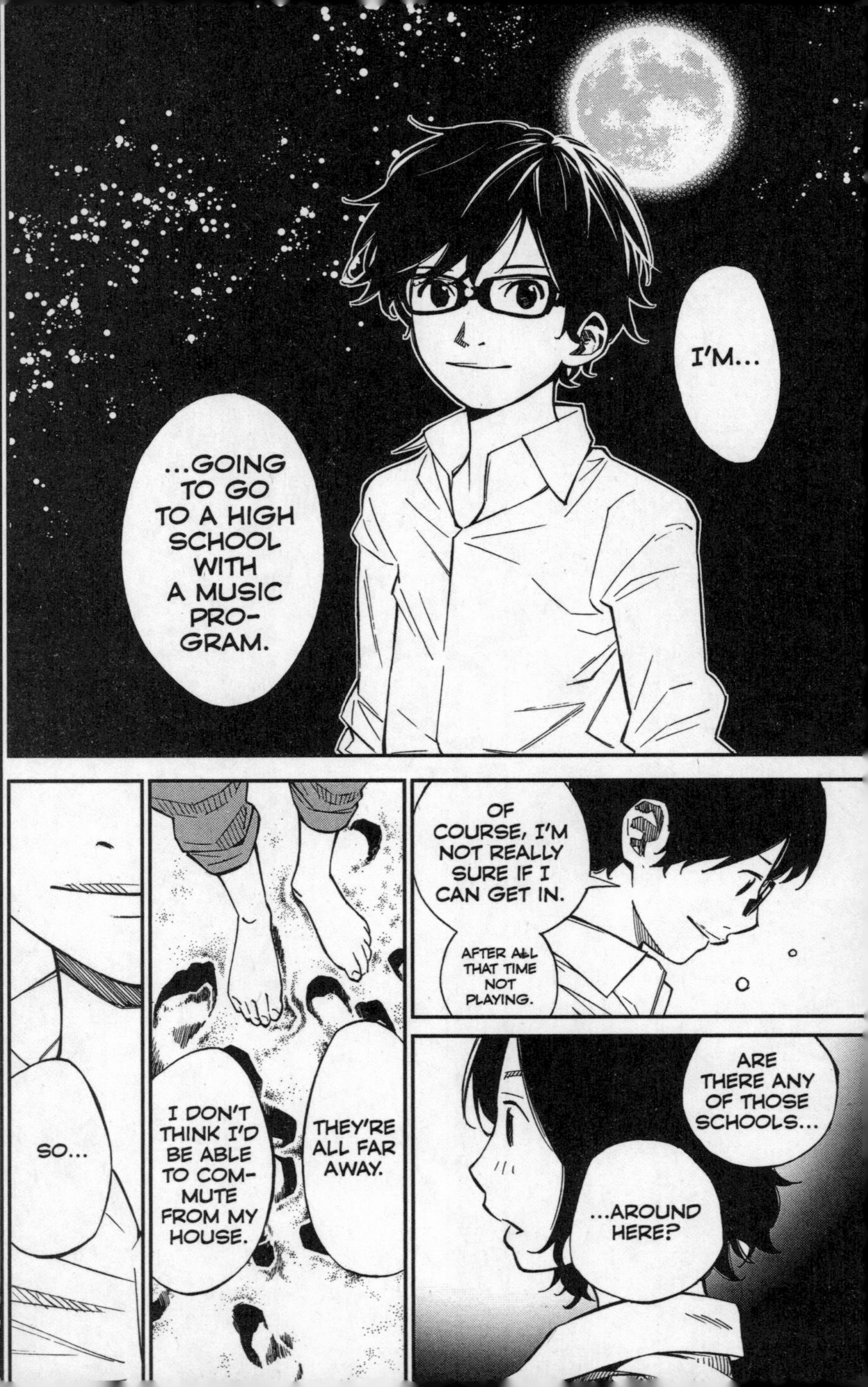
I'M...
...GOING TO GO TO A HIGH SCHOOL WITH A MUSIC PRO-GRAM.
OF COURSE, I'M NOT REALLY SURE IF I CAN GET IN.
AFTER ALL THAT TIME NOT PLAYING.
ARE THERE ANY OF THOSE SCHOOLS...
...AROUND HERE?
THEY'RE ALL FAR AWAY.
I DON'T THINK I'D BE ABLE TO COM-MUTE FROM MY HOUSE.
SO...

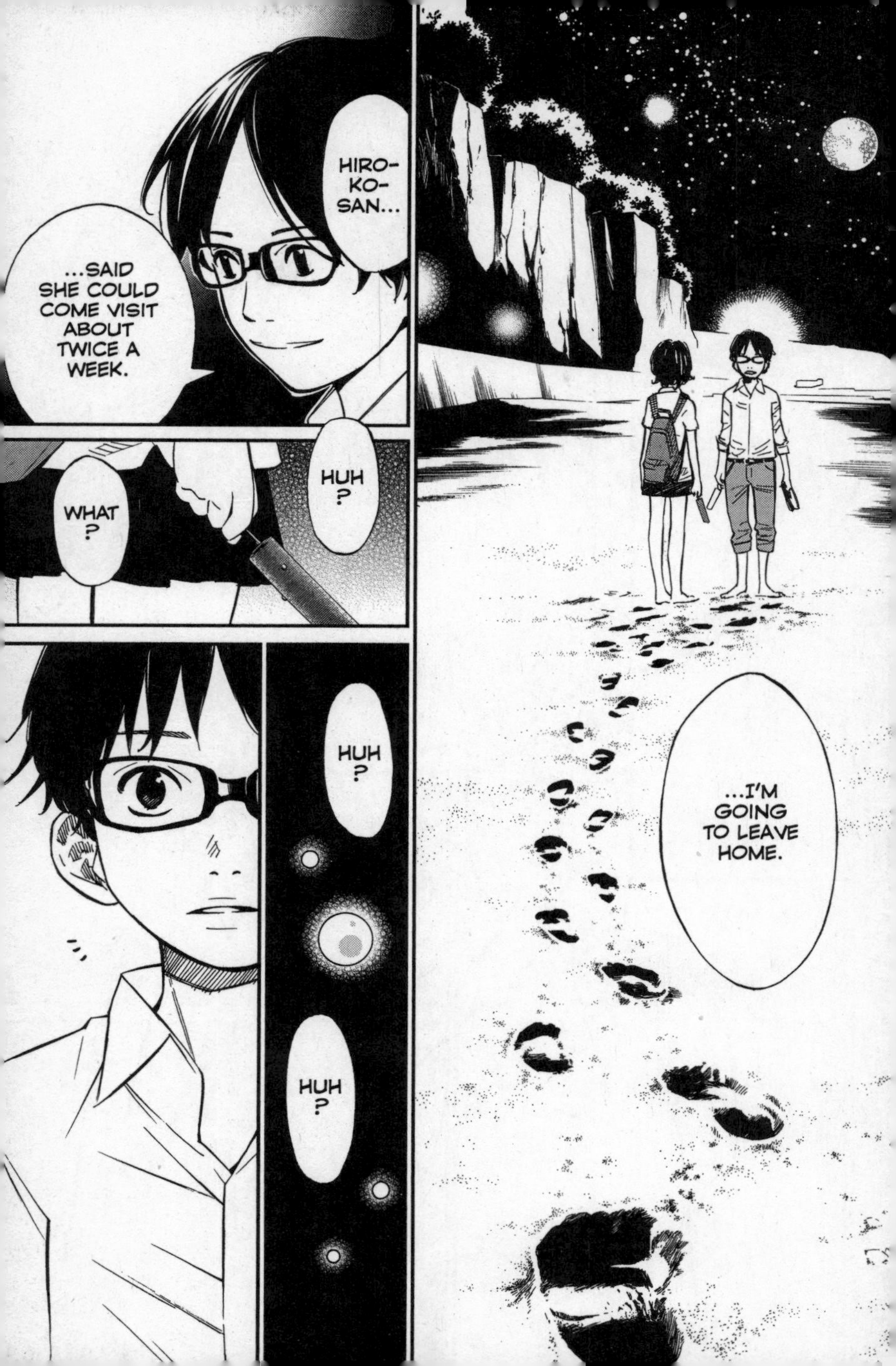
...I'M GOING TO LEAVE HOME.
HIRO-KO-SAN...
...SAID SHE COULD COME VISIT ABOUT TWICE A WEEK.
HUH?
WHAT?
HUH?
HUH?

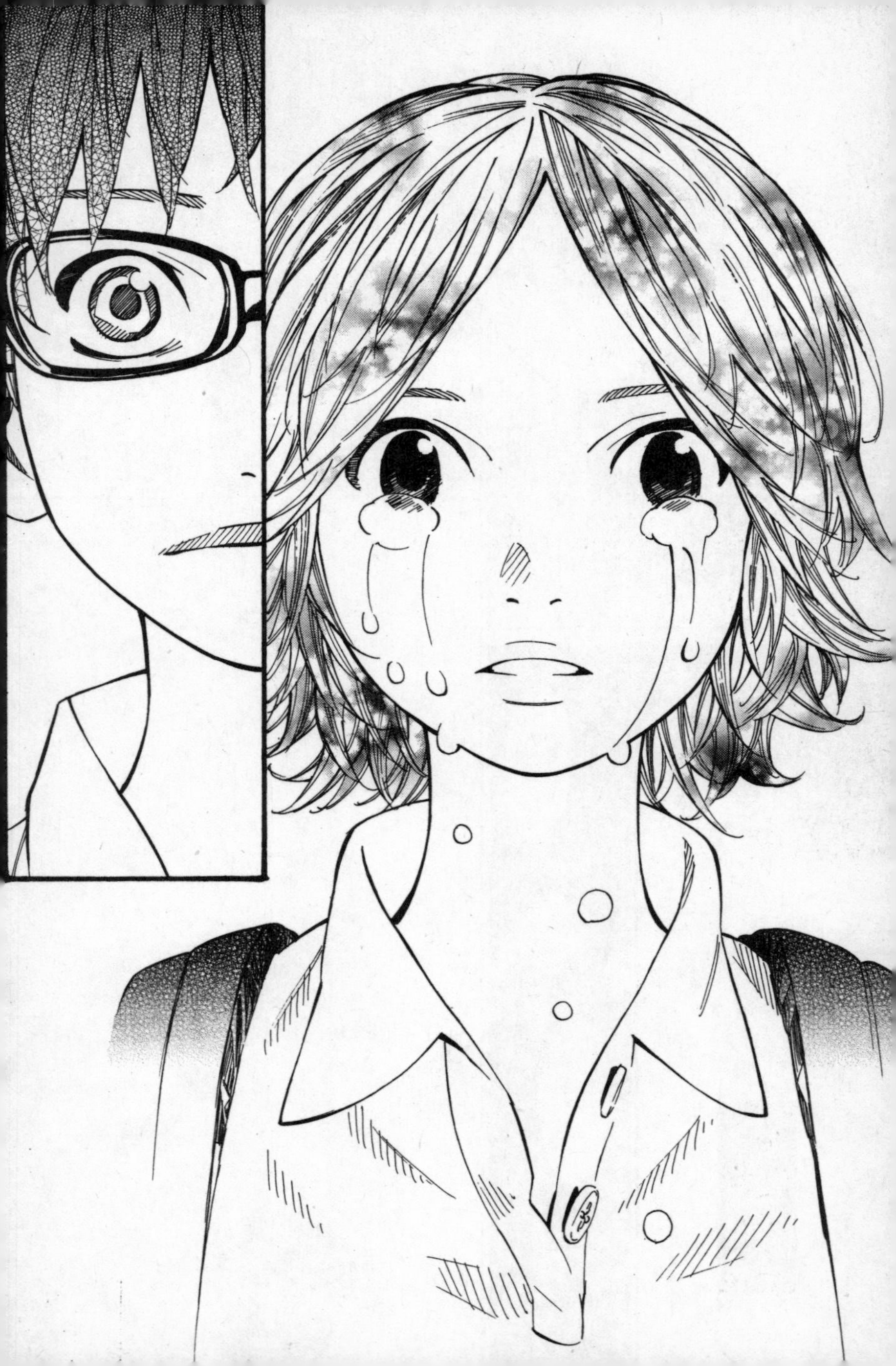

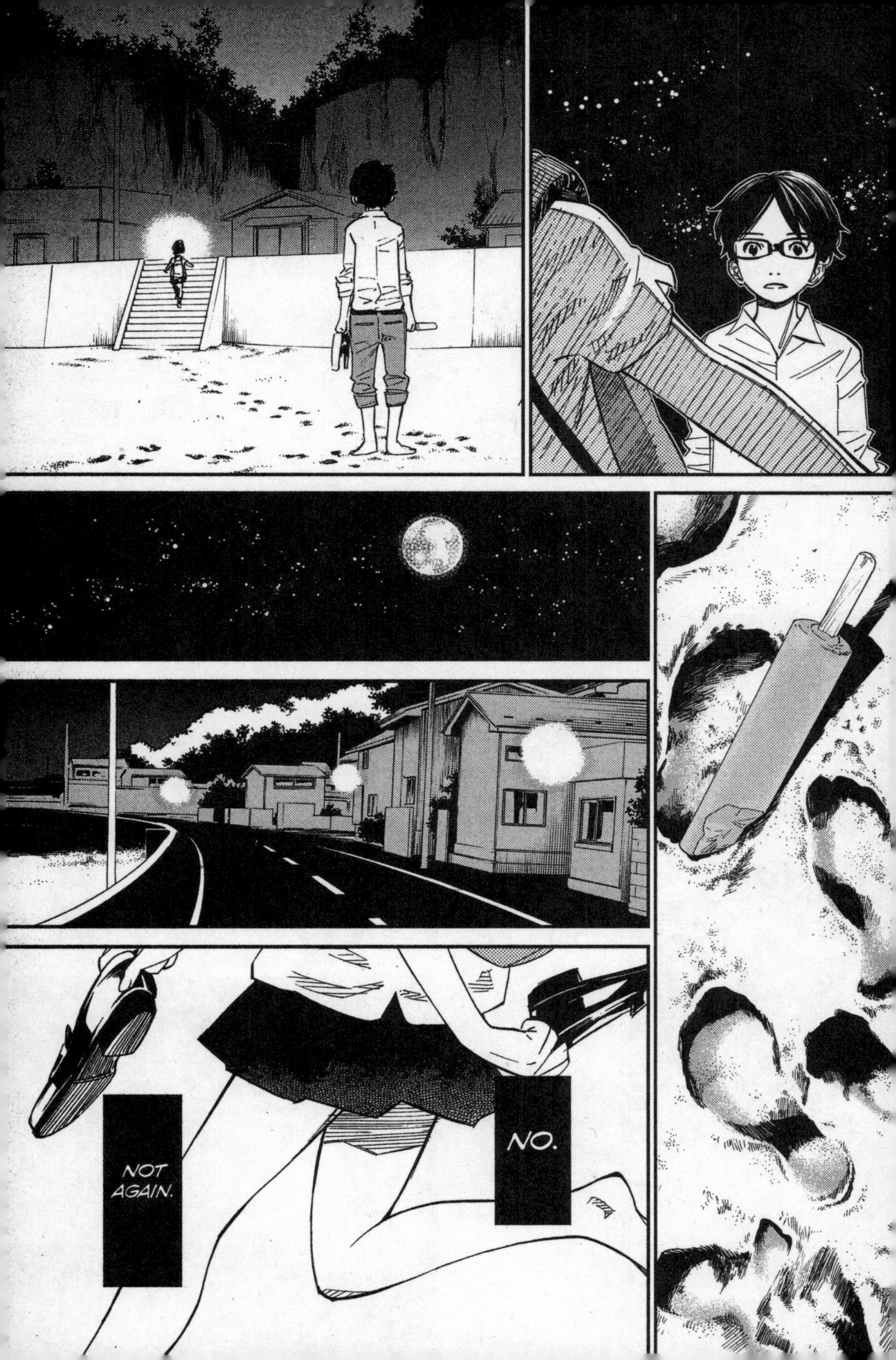
NO.
NOT AGAIN.

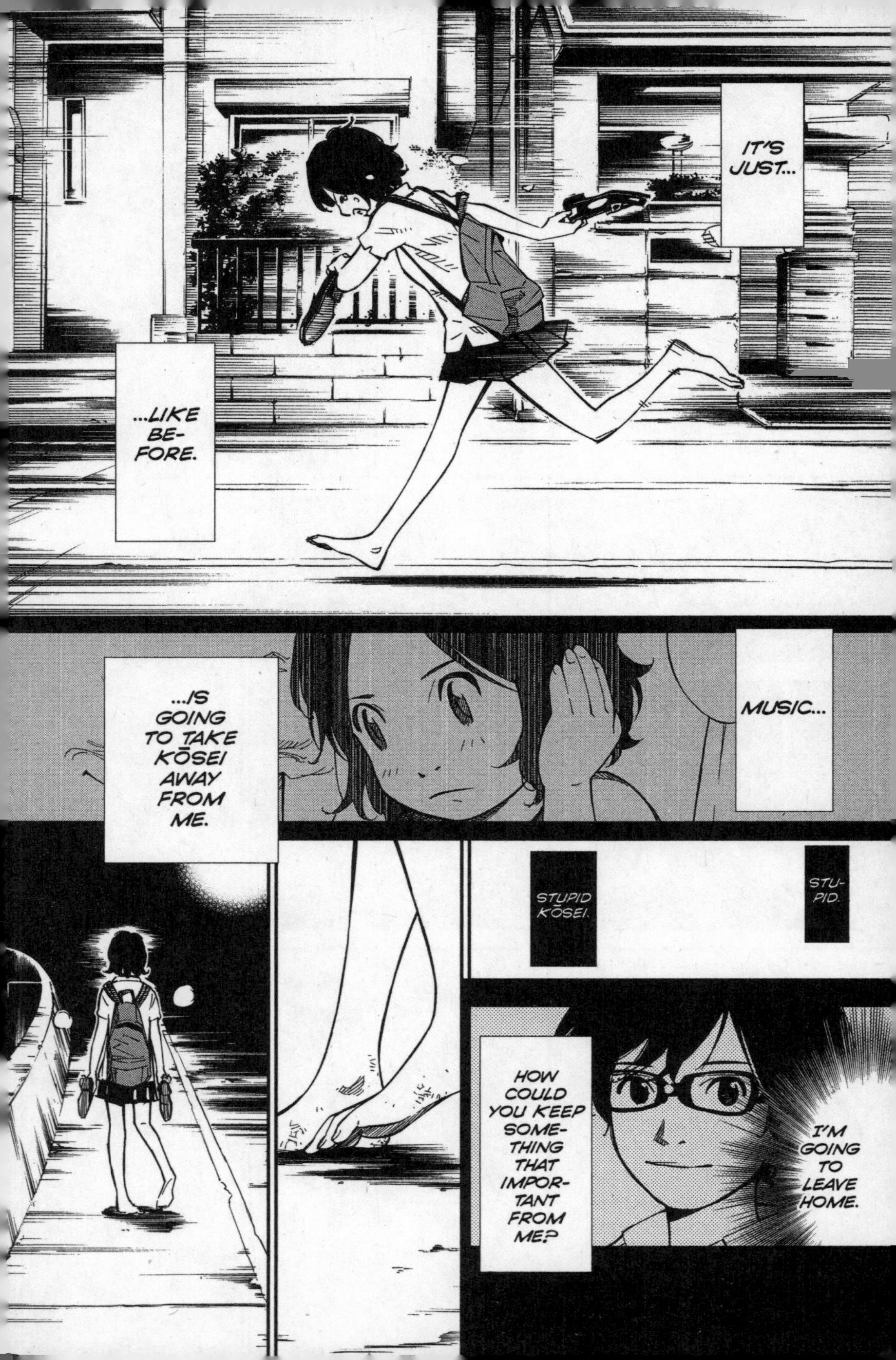
IT'S JUST...
...LIKE BEFORE.
MUSIC...
...IS GOING TO TAKE KŌSEI AWAY FROM ME.
STUPID.
STUPID KŌSEI.
I'M GOING TO LEAVE HOME.
HOW COULD YOU KEEP SOMETHING THAT IMPORTANT FROM ME?

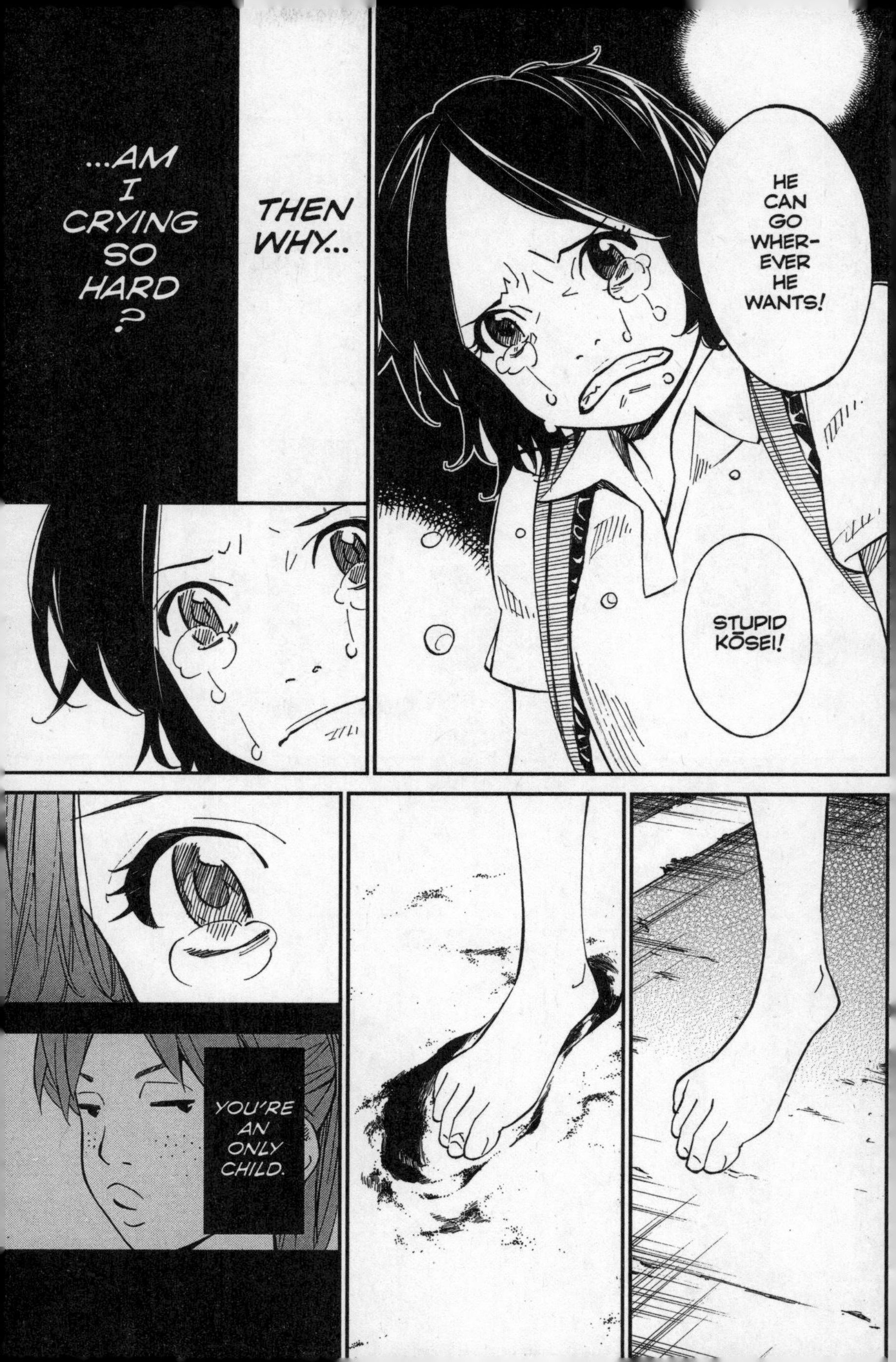
HE CAN GO WHER-EVER HE WANTS!
STUPID KŌSEI!
THEN WHY...
...AM I CRYING SO HARD?
YOU'RE AN ONLY CHILD.

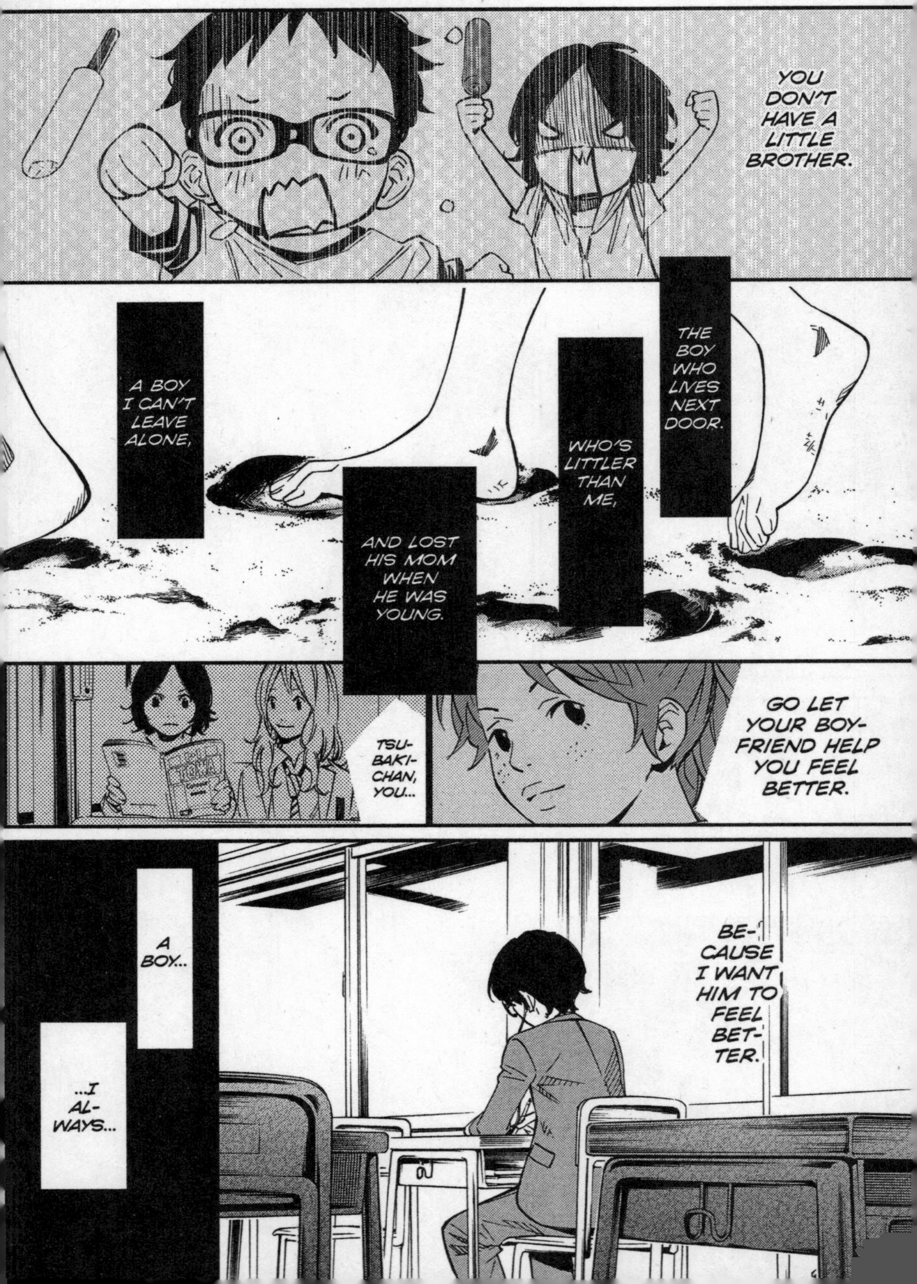
YOU DON'T HAVE A LITTLE BROTHER.
THE BOY WHO LIVES NEXT DOOR.
WHO'S LITTLER THAN ME,
AND LOST HIS MOM WHEN HE WAS YOUNG.
A BOY I CAN'T LEAVE ALONE,
GO LET YOUR BOY-FRIEND HELP YOU FEEL BETTER.
TSU-BAKI-CHAN, YOU...
BE-CAUSE I WANT HIM TO FEEL BET-TER.
A BOY...
...I AL-WAYS...

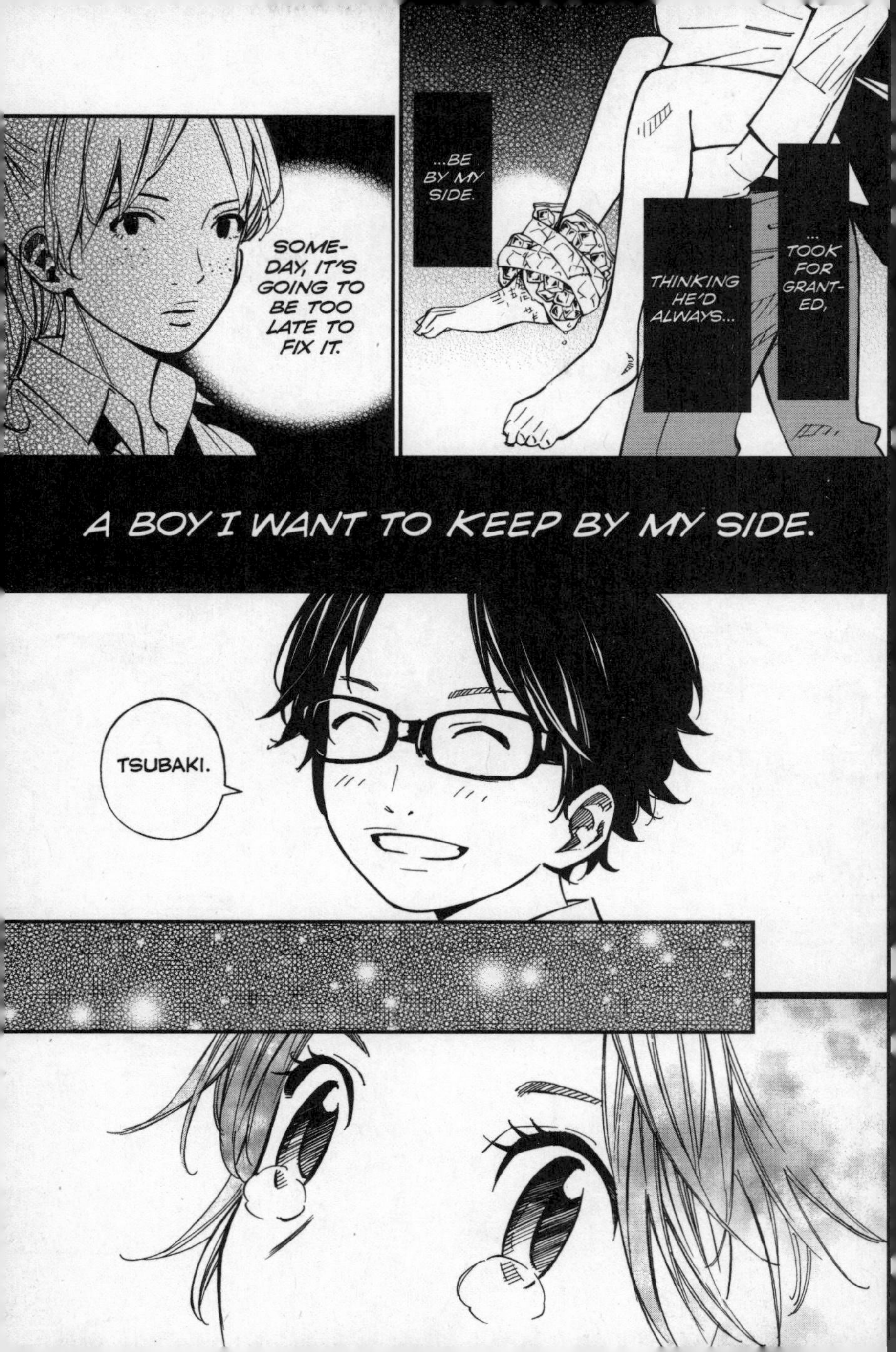
...TOOK FOR GRANT-ED,
THINKING HE'D ALWAYS...
...BE BY MY SIDE.
SOME-DAY, IT'S GOING TO BE TOO LATE TO FIX IT.
A BOY I WANT TO KEEP BY MY SIDE.
TSUBAKI.

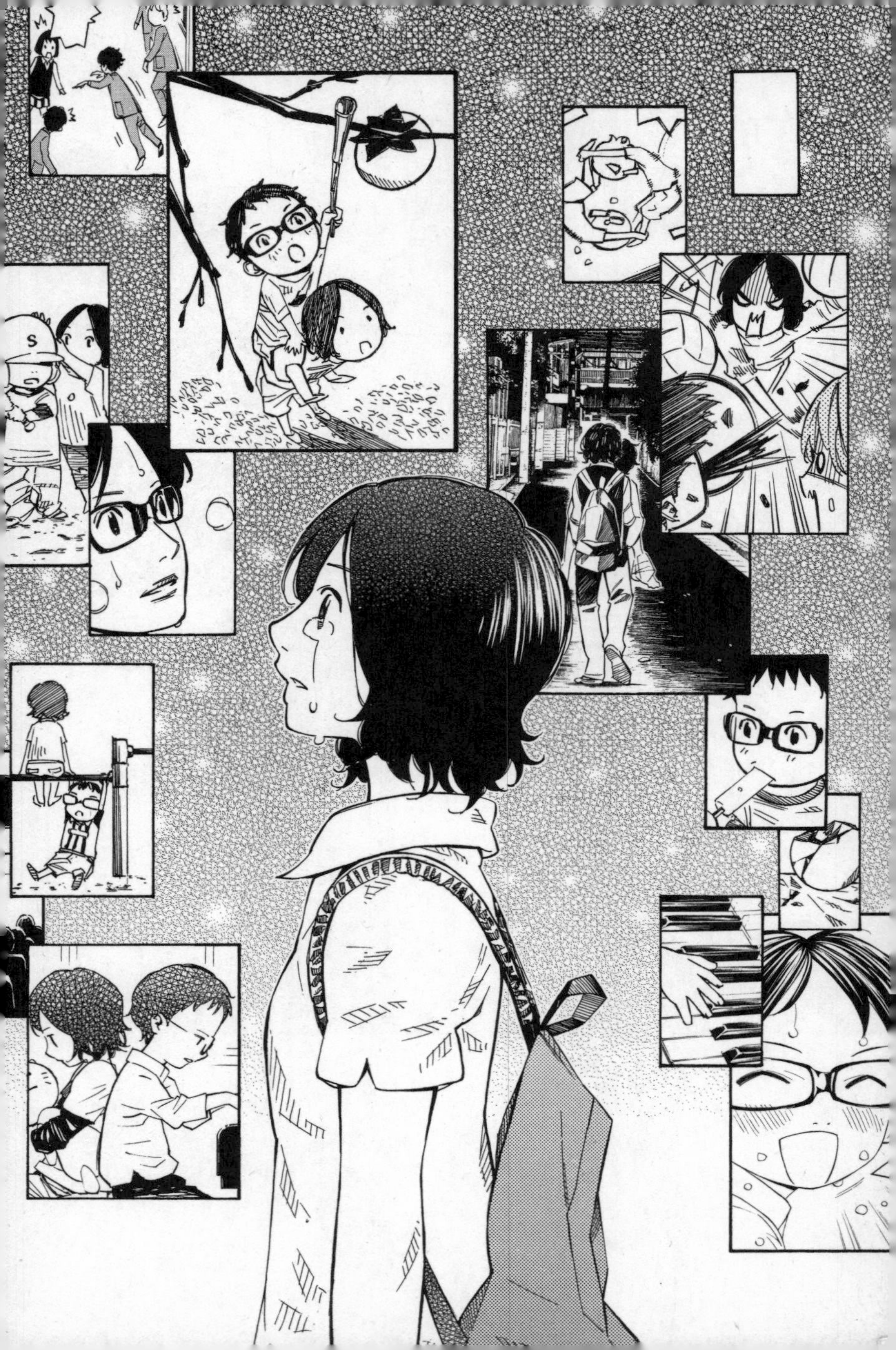

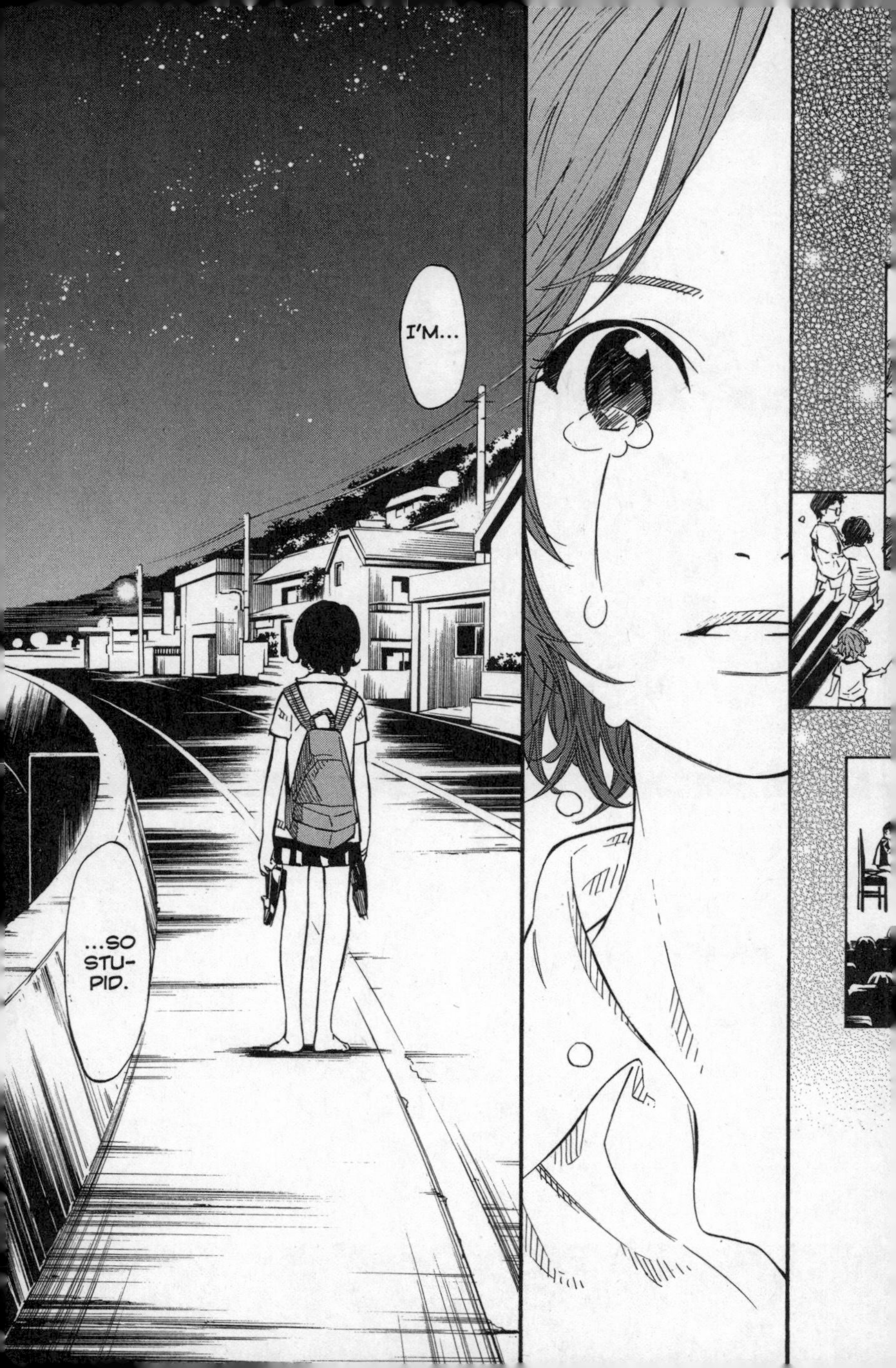
I'M...
...SO STU-PID.

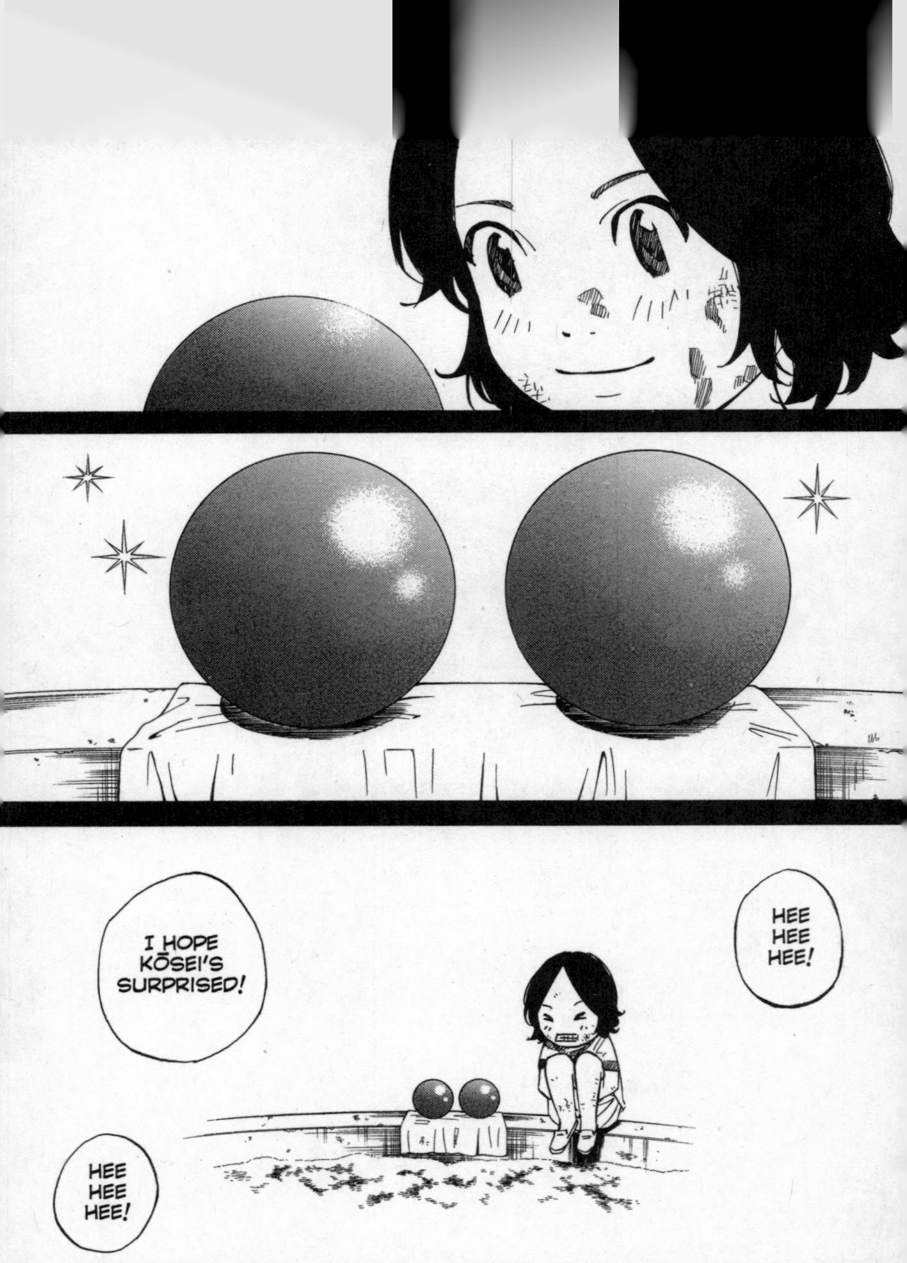
HEE HEE HEE!
I HOPE KŌSEI'S SURPRISED!
HEE HEE HEE!

Special Thanks:

AKINORI ŌSAWA

MASANORI SUGANO

RIEKO IKEDA

KAORI YAMAZAKI

Translation Notes

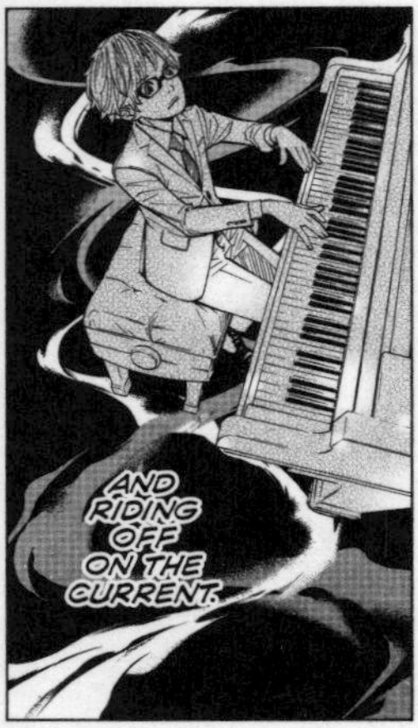
AND RIDING OFF ON THE CURRENT.

Riding off on the current,
page 11

To be more accurate, Kōsei says that the music does a *kaiyū,* which can refer to taking a circular tour, but is more often used to talk about wandering the seas, or more specifically, fish migration. In other words, everything about Kōsei turns into music and begins to migrate through his dark ocean.

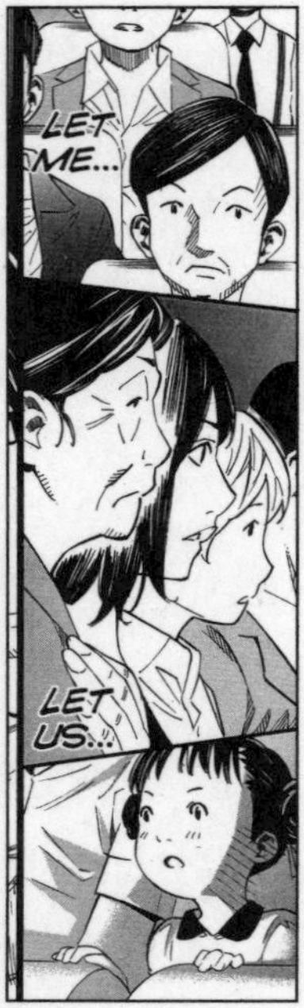
LET ME...
LET US...

Let me... Let us...
page 31

Here, the whole audience is begging to hear more of this music. To demonstrate that every individual in the audience shares this sentiment, the author used two different first-person pronouns, *boku* and *watashi*. Both of them mean "me," but the former is used more typically by men, while women are more likely to use the latter. The point is, everyone in the audience, male and female, is touched by Kōsei's performance.

Artists,
page 92

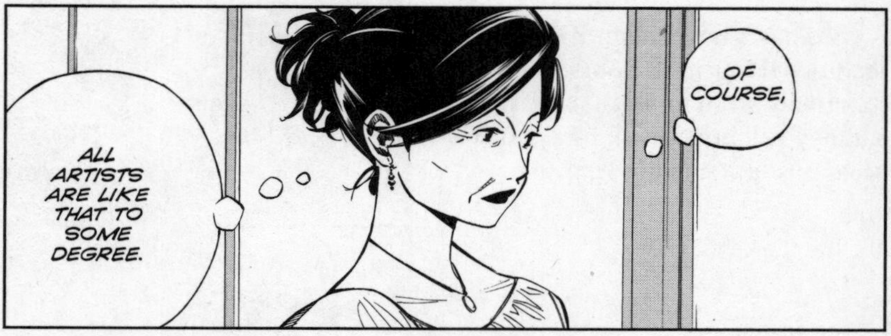
OF COURSE,
ALL ARTISTS ARE LIKE THAT TO SOME DEGREE.

The word here translated as "artist" is *hyōgensha*, which literally means "one who expresses." Unfortunately, "expressionism" refers to specific styles of art, so translating the term literally would give it an entirely different meaning. In this case, the word is used to refer to someone whose main occupation is to express things, feelings, etc. in words, pictures, or music.

Dashimaki tamago,
page 114

Literally meaning "egg wrapped with *dashi,*" a *dashimaki tamago* is a type of Japanese omelet. As the name implies, it is made of egg mixed with *dashi*, which is a kind of soup stock made from seaweed and fish.

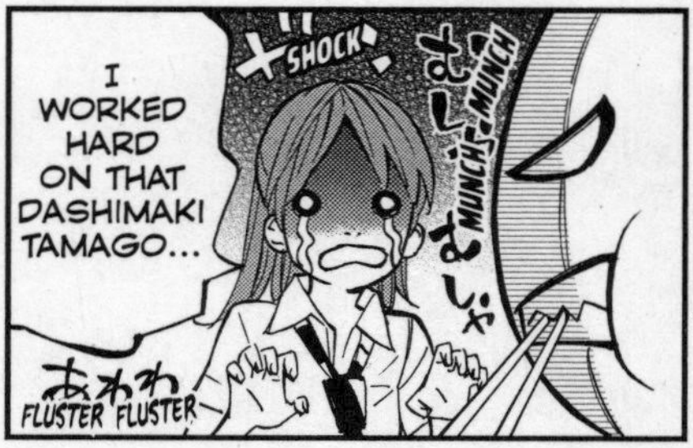
MUNCH MUNCH
SHOCK
I WORKED HARD ON THAT DASHIMAKI TAMAGO...
FLUSTER FLUSTER

Yukata,
page 117

A *yukata* is a light summer kimono. Traditional Japanese clothing isn't as commonly worn in Japan these days, but they still bring it out for special occasions like summer festivals.

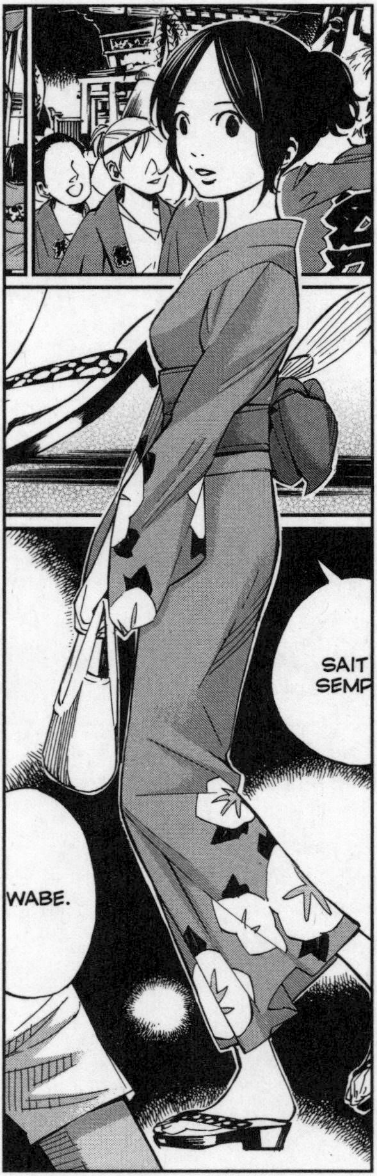
SAIT
SEMP
WABE.

What's that thing about a boy at the gate?, page 174

The thing about a boy at the gate is the proverb, "a boy at a temple gate recites sutras untaught." In other words, spend enough time listening to something, and eventually you'll pick up on it whether you want to or not. An equivalent saying in English (though not common enough to help the readers recognize it any better) is "a saint's maid quotes Latin."

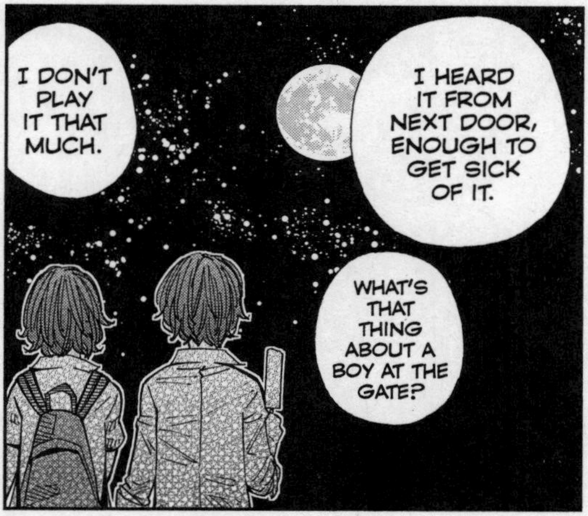
I HEARD IT FROM NEXT DOOR, ENOUGH TO GET SICK OF IT.
I DON'T PLAY IT THAT MUCH.
WHAT'S THAT THING ABOUT A BOY AT THE GATE?

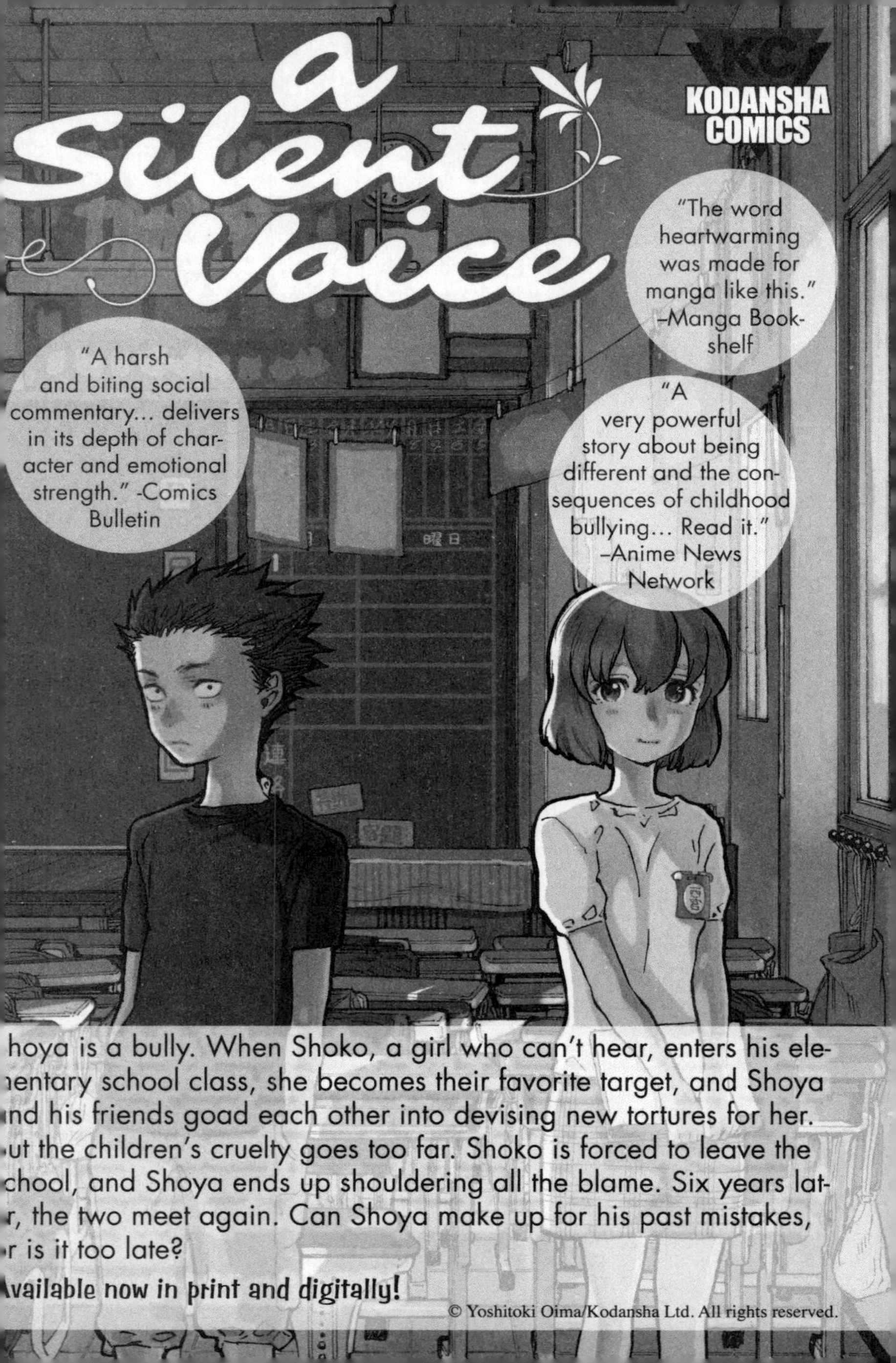
a Silent Voice
KODANSHA COMICS
"The word heartwarming was made for manga like this." –Manga Bookshelf
"A harsh and biting social commentary... delivers in its depth of character and emotional strength." -Comics Bulletin
"A very powerful story about being different and the consequences of childhood bullying... Read it." –Anime News Network
hoya is a bully. When Shoko, a girl who can't hear, enters his ele-
ientary school class, she becomes their favorite target, and Shoya
nd his friends goad each other into devising new tortures for her.
ut the children's cruelty goes too far. Shoko is forced to leave the
chool, and Shoya ends up shouldering all the blame. Six years lat-
r, the two meet again. Can Shoya make up for his past mistakes,
r is it too late?
vailable now in print and digitally!
© Yoshitoki Oima/Kodansha Ltd. All rights reserved.

My Little Monster

OPPOSITES ATTRACT...MAYBE?

Haru Yoshida is feared as an unstable and violent "monster." Mizutani Shizuku is a grade-obsessed student with no friends. Fate brings these two together to form the most unlikely pair. Haru firmly believes he's in love with Mizutani and she firmly believes

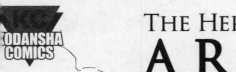

A Kodansha Comics Trade Paperback Original
Your Lie in April volume 7 copyright © 2013 Naoshi Arakawa
English translation copyright © 2016 Naoshi Arakawa

Published in the United States by Kodansha Comics, an imprint of Kodansha USA Publishing, LLC, New York.

Publication rights for this English edition arranged through Kodansha Ltd, Tokyo.

ISBN 978-1-63236-177-6

Special thanks:
Akinori Osawa, Rieko Ikeda, and Kaori Yamazaki

Printed in the United States of America.

www.kodanshacomics.com

9 8 7 6 5 4 3 2 1
Translation: Alethea and Athena Nibley
Lettering: Scott Brown
Editing: David Yoo
Kodansha Comics edition cover design by Phil Balsman

TOMARE! STOP

You're going the wrong way!

Manga is a completely different type of reading experience.

To start at the beginning, Go to the end!

at's right! Authentic manga is read the traditional Japanese way—om right to left, exactly the opposite of how American books are ad. It's easy to follow: Just go to the other end of the book and read ch page—and each panel—from right side to left side, starting at e top right. Now you're experiencing manga as it was meant to be!